DISSENT AND THE STATE

Edited by C.E.S. Franks

Y0-BDW-642

Toronto
OXFORD UNIVERSITY PRESS
1989

Oxford University Press, 70 Wynford Drive, Don Mills, Ontario, M3C 1J9

Toronto   Oxford   New York   Delhi   Bombay   Calcutta   Madras   Karachi
Petaling Jaya   Singapore   Hong Kong   Tokyo   Nairobi   Dar es Salaam   Cape Town
Melbourne   Auckland

and associated companies in
Berlin   Ibadan

CANADIAN CATALOGUING IN PUBLICATION DATA

Main entry under title:

Dissent and the state

Bibliography: p.
Includes index.
ISBN 0-19-540742-3

1. Dissenters.   2. Government, Resistance to.
3. Civil rights.   4. Political crimes and offenses.
I. Franks, C.E.S.

JC328.3.D58 1989   323.44   C89-094133-5

Contents

Contributors

G. GRANT AMYOT
Department of Political Studies
Queen's University

STANLEY BARRETT
Department of Sociology and
   Anthropology
University of Guelph

CHRISTIAN BAY
Department of Political Science
University of Toronto

AUREL BRAUN
Department of Political Science
University of Toronto

PHILIPPE FAUCHER
Département de Science Politique
Université de Montréal

KEVIN FITZGIBBONS
Département de Science Politique
Université de Montréal

ELIZABETH GRACE
Development Studies
University of Sussex

JANINE KRIEBER
Département de Science Politique
Université Laval

COLIN LEYS
Department of Political Studies
Queen's University

ALLAN MACDONALD
Osgoode Hall Law School
York University

ATHAN G. THEOHARIS
Department of History
Marquette University

REG WHITAKER
Department of Political Science
York University

JOHN D. WHYTE
Faculty of Law
Queen's University

Acknowledgements

This book has been produced with the help of many people. I am especially grateful to those who either commented on the papers at various stages of presentation at the conference on Advocacy, Protest and Dissent at the Donald Gordon Centre at Queen's University in February 1988, or later as the papers were in the process of preparation for publication. These include Peter Russell, Philip Resnick, Mildred A. Schwarz, and Jock Gunn, each of whom offered comments on all papers to the respective authors. Additional commentators and chairmen of sessions at the conference were Murray Rankin, Will Kymlicka, Doug Williams, Alistair MacLeod, Stephen Page, Jorge Nef, Deena White, John Meisel, and Geoffrey Smith. Each provided a valuable contribution towards this exploration of dissent in its modern context.

There were other participants at the conference, to whom appreciation is also owed. These include the Hon. James F. Kelleher, the then Solicitor General of Canada, the Hon. Ronald G. Atkey, chairman of the Security Intelligence Review Committee, and Reid Morden, Director of the Canadian Security Intelligence Service. Dr Richard Gosse, then Inspector General of the Security Service, and Maurice Archdeacon, the Executive Secretary of the Security Intelligence Review Committee, have encouraged and supported the project from inception to completion. The Security Intelligence Review Committee, and the Office of the Inspector General of the Security Service, jointly sponsored the project.

A further debt of gratitude is owed to all the participants in the conference. It turned out to be a rare and useful opportunity for the academics and others who are on the outside, and are often critical of security activities, to meet those involved in security work and for the two groups to exchange views on the problems of dissent and the state. Though on many issues their opinions were far from unanimous, discussion was stimulating, and each side both presented its views and heard those of the other in a serious and constructive manner.

I would also like to express my appreciation to Sally Livingston and Richard Teleky of Oxford University Press, and to Shirley Fraser, who did the typing.

C.E.S. FRANKS
QUEEN'S UNIVERSITY

Introduction

C . E . S . F R A N K S

This book explores one of the most difficult challenges any government can face: the problem of when to treat dissent, whether expressed in opinion or in action, as legitimate political behaviour that should be accommodated within normal political processes, and when to treat it as illegitimate and a threat to individuals and society. The book has its origins in the efforts of successive Canadian governments to come to terms with this problem. Canada, the peaceable kingdom, has not been immune to violent and destructive dissent—nor to extreme responses by government. It was the rebellions of 1837 in Upper and Lower Canada that led to Lord Durham's famous report and the beginnings of representative and responsible government. The prairie provinces were settled only in the late nineteenth century, after two rebellions under the Métis leader Louis Riel had been crushed. The Winnipeg General Strike of 1919 was treated by government as a form of rebellion. Canadian labour history contains many ugly confrontations between police and striking workers.

But the direct sources for the concerns explored in this book lie in the more recent past. In 1977 the federal government created a commission of inquiry (the McDonald Commission) to examine the activities of the Royal Canadian Mounted Police. This was after incontrovertible evidence had been made public that the security service of the RCMP had, in pursuit of Québec separatists and left-wing dissidents—and in spite of vehement denials by the government in Parliament—performed many illegal and improper activities, including opening mail, gaining access to tax records, breaking into the offices of a legitimate political party and stealing various items, burning down a barn, and publishing false documents.[1] The opposition parties in Parliament led a prolonged and enthusiastic attack on the government, during which it became apparent that the Solicitor General, the minister responsible for the RCMP, was not aware of the wrongdoings, had been misinformed by the RCMP, and had little if any control over the security service.

The Commission's report, which was made public in 1981, included thorough and detailed proposals for overhauling the security service and its ministerial control. It concluded that Canada should have a civilian security agency outside the RCMP. This agency should be established by an Act of Parliament that would define its mandate, basic functions and powers, and the structure for control and accountability. In 1984, after prolonged and difficult discussion, Parliament passed an act creating the new Canadian Security and Intelligence Service (CSIS).[2]

The structure for the accountability of the new service included an Inspector General to review its operational activities, and a Security Intelligence Review Committee to review the reports of the Director of CSIS, the certificates of the Inspector General, and the general directions of the Minister. The Committee has extensive independent powers of investigation, and hears appeals on issues of security clearance within the government. It also produces an annual report, which is submitted to Parliament and is a public document.

The mandate of the Canadian Security Intelligence Service, as described in the CSIS Act (Section 2), includes the surveillance and assessment of 'threats to the security of Canada'. These include activities involving 'the threat or use of acts of serious violence' and activities 'directed toward undermining by covert unlawful acts, or directed toward or intended ultimately to lead to the destruction or overthrow by violence of, the constitutionally established system of government in Canada'. Such threats do not include, however, 'lawful advocacy, protest or dissent', unless carried on in conjunction with the other activities defined as threats. Though the term 'subversion' does not appear in this description of the mandate of CSIS, nor anywhere else in the Act, counter-subversion was in fact the name of one of the three operational branches of CSIS, the other two being counter-intelligence and counter-terrorism.

Of these three functions it is counter-subversion that holds the greatest risk for undue intrusion into political and intellectual activities. The targeting of groups or individuals as 'subversive' means that they have in the security service's opinion passed beyond lawful advocacy, protest, and dissent into activities that are construed as threats. The careers and political rights of individuals and groups deemed subversive can be harmed, and the range of public discussion curtailed. The Security Intelligence Review Committee (SIRC) found this to be enough of a problem that it made counter-subversion the subject of its first branch-wide study of CSIS. The Committee's 1986-87 report states:

> Counter-intelligence and counter-terrorism offer little room for disagreement. A given foreign nation either spies on us or it does not. No exception can be taken to counter-intelligence aimed at protecting our secrets from those that do.
>
> Similarly, there is no place for terrorism in a country like ours with well-entrenched democratic means for gaining and using power. Any of us could be the innocent victim of a terrorist act. Clearly, those who would use violence to reach their political goals must be detected and stopped.
>
> Counter-subversion is different. The right of peaceful dissent is the bedrock of democracy. Yet there are a few Canadians who proclaim their

belief in the need for violent revolution. And even peaceful dissent may be secretly perverted by foreign powers whose goals are not the goals of most Canadians.

. . . At what point does dissent make an individual or an organization a legitimate target for the Counter-Subversion Branch of CSIS? How much talking about violence does it take to raise a real threat of violent acts? When does contact with foreign powers become detrimental to the interests of Canada?[3]

Following this investigation, SIRC expressed concern that the counter-subversion program cast its net too widely. Its members felt that the Counter-Subversion Branch over-estimated the influence and persuasive powers of potentially subversive groups:

One targeted group, for example, publishes a magazine that deals with a wide range of topics—the arts as well as social policy and other issues—from the perspective of the left.

It is true that some members have advocated violent action by this group, but they have been brushed aside by others.

A good case can be made that the partisans of violence in their group rate investigation as individuals.

But we remain to be convinced that the group itself should be targeted for investigation. It opens the door to unnecessary intrusion on the freedoms and privacy of the most innocuous as well as of the most obnoxious members. It also carries the risk of harm to freedom of speech, one of our fundamental social values.[4]

The Committee also said it was 'perplexed' by some of the threats defined by CSIS. For example, a CSIS report

spoke of a certain organization's 'attack on the anti-communist, pro-US government of El Salvador . . . in direct support of . . . policy objectives to . . . blunt American foreign policy initiatives'. We cannot agree that a non-violent attack on US foreign policy is necessarily a threat to the security of Canada.

On the other hand, there seems to have been minimal CSIS interest in fund-raising inside Canada for the Contra rebels in Nicaragua—although this seems to meet section 2's criterion of 'activities within . . . Canada . . . in support of the . . . use of acts of serious violence against persons or property for the purpose of achieving a political objective within . . . a foreign state'.

This contrast lends weight to our concern . . . that CSIS may too readily accept the foreign policy objectives of our allies as its own and neglect Canadian foreign policy.[5]

This 1986-87 report of SIRC, together with other public and media discussions of CSIS's counter-subversion activities, led to a review of this branch of CSIS by a government-established committee (the Osbaldeston Committee). That review concurred with the Review Committee's conclusion and recommendation:

> There are two paths running through the gray zone in which the Counter-Subversion Branch operates, corresponding to its two major concerns—undue foreign influence and the risk of violence.
>
> As it happens, these are the concerns of two sister branches, Counter-Intelligence and Counter-Terrorism respectively.
>
> We recommend that these two paths be followed to their conclusion. The counter-subversion role should be split between the other two branches. Counter-Intelligence would deal with undue foreign influence, Counter-Terrorism with the risk of violence.
>
> Priorities could be set more rationally, and some of the targeted groups we have cited here might appear more clearly in their real light.
>
> And good intelligence officers who may now feel isolated and ill-appreciated in their counter-subversion role would find themselves in more active environments where their talents would get full rein.[6]

The government accepted this recommendation and dissolved the Counter-Subversion Branch, dividing its personnel and activities between the other two branches.[7]

Simply eliminating the Branch, however, did not eliminate the problem. The Canadian Security Intelligence Service will still find it necessary to make the difficult distinction between legitimate dissent and subversion.

The Security Intelligence Review Committee and the Inspector General also explored another approach to their concern over counter-subversion. They discussed the problem with Canadian scholars with an interest in the field, and out of these discussions arose the idea of examining various important aspects of dissent and the state through a conference at which papers would be presented and discussed by invited experts with the ultimate goal of publishing them in the form of a scholarly book. I accepted the tasks of organizing the conference and editing the book.

Inevitably, work supported by government prompts concern about the independence of researchers. This concern is aggravated when the work of the sponsoring agency itself is largely secret, and the problem in question involves sensitive areas of political and individual rights. In this study these potential difficulties were overcome through a clear and formal arm's-length relationship among the commissioning agencies, the Inspector General and the Security Intelligence Review Committee, and myself as project director. The selection of authors and commentators was entirely my responsibility, as was the editing of this volume. The sponsoring agencies have in no way influenced, or attempted to influence, the direction and content of the papers, which are entirely the responsibility of the authors and editor.

The publication of these papers in book form provides safeguards for both the commissioning agencies and the authors. The commissioning agencies have the assurance that the papers meet academic standards and will be subject to the rigorous processes of scholarly criticism and review. The authors have the assurance that they are sharing in a public discussion rather than contributing to a problem area that already involves too much secrecy. Members of both the academic and the general public have the opportunity to be informed and to contribute to the discussion.

The papers presented at the conference represent a wide range of opinions and topics. In subject matter they divide into three groups. Three papers examine theoretical and legal issues. One, by John Whyte and Allan Macdonald, explores some of the important legal issues in advocacy, protest, and dissent. The second, by Christian Bay, examines civil disobedience, an important form of dissent that can clearly break the law but does not intend to be subversive. The third, by Elizabeth Grace and Colin Leys, explores the concept of subversion, and whether in fact such a category ought to exist apart from the other protections offered by the criminal and civil law.

Four papers examine dissent in a comparative perspective. One, by Athan Theoharis, looks at the actions of the FBI in the United States in its surveillance of dissent. The American example is of particular importance because the United States, as the most powerful country in the Western world, has had a powerful influence on the security services of other Western democracies, and on the assessment of the importance of left-wing, communist, and other threats in the Western world. Aurel Braun's paper examines dissent in the satellite countries of Eastern Europe, where domination by the USSR is even more of a factor than is the power of the United States in the West. Philippe Faucher and Kevin Fitzgibbons explore the problem of dissent and the state in Latin America, where many regimes have resorted to force and violence to maintain order and to suppress dissent. Grant Amyot's contribution on Italy looks at a communist party that is not only an accepted and influential part of normal democratic processes, but is also strongly supportive of the security service and hostile to violent left-wing groups.

Three papers on Canada complete the study. Janine Krieber looks at dissent in Québec, while Reg Whitaker examines left-wing dissent in English-speaking Canada and Stanley Barrett explores right-wing dissent.

The papers were presented at a conference at the Donald Gordon Centre at Queen's University in February 1988. Each received extensive discussion, and the authors, in revising their work for publication, had the benefit not only of these discussions, but also of extensive written comments from the participants. Jock Gunn, Philip Resnick, Peter Russell, and Mildred A. Schwartz provided written critiques of all the papers, and these too were of great help in the processes of editing and revision.

This volume surveys important aspects of the field of dissent and the state. Some issues have perforce been given more attention than others. Violence, whether terrorism, armed insurrection, or revolution, is examined only in passing. The Soviet Union is not examined directly; nor are other democracies, like Britain with Northern Ireland, that for different reasons find themselves using arbitrary, violent, and undemocratic means to keep segments of the population under control. Theories of dissent and the state themselves would require several volumes to explore in depth. But a study must have an end as well as a beginning, and the papers in this volume have been selected to illustrate the important issues of dissent and the state, to cover the main topics and areas, and to serve as an introduction to the field. A list of selected readings prepared by Avigail Eisenberg adds to the papers and sources in this volume, and also offers some suggestions on topics not covered in the papers.

The question that concerned the agencies sponsoring this project is one of action, and it must be answered by the security services and their custodians: on what grounds should a security service make the distinction between acceptable and unacceptable dissent, and in so doing select appropriate targets for their attentions? The papers given at the Kingston conference do not answer this question directly. Rather, they explore the underlying experiences and issues that ought to be taken into account in coming to an answer. These prior questions are (1) How have various regimes, including Canada, made the distinction between acceptable and unacceptable dissent? and (2) What has been the response of regimes to unacceptable dissent? What are the consequences of their responses?

Acceptable and unacceptable dissent: targeting

Every country examined in these papers has, at some time, had to come to a decision on whether a particular form of dissent is acceptable or not—some, most of the time. Dissent in its various forms is an essential part of politics, and politics is an inescapable part of civilized life. In all countries there is a tension between the forces for change and the desire for stability. Among the most important forces for change is dissent by individuals and groups who disagree with government either because they want more change, or because they want less. But there are limits in all states to what those in power consider to be acceptable dissent, and these limits vary enormously from country to country.

This variety in the issues and forms of dissent and the state's response to it can be illustrated by classifying dissent along two dimensions: legal-illegal and legitimate-illegitimate. This gives four categories of dissent: legal-legitimate; legal-illegitimate, illegal-legitimate; and illegal-illegitimate. Those in authority accept and tolerate legal-legitimate dissent, but would not accept illegal-illegitimate dissent. The other two categories are contentious. From a liberal-democratic viewpoint, a goal of government and society should be to include as much as possible in the legal-legitimate category. Electoral politics, political parties, and representative assemblies all legitimize and institutionalize dissent and opposition. But some forms of dissent are not considered legitimate. Others, unable to find expression within an elected assembly, are expressed through extra-parliamentary means. Countries in which democratic electoral politics cannot accommodate important opposition and dissent find themselves in a difficult position. Not only for the ideals of liberal democracy, but also for peaceful survival and gradual change, it should be a goal of government and society to include as much dissent as possible within the legal-legitimate category. There is a presumption in liberal-democratic regimes that freedom of speech, association, and political action are fundamental rights, but in no country are these rights unlimited. And, as the papers on liberal democracies in this volume show, the pressures are powerful to limit rather than expand the types of dissent considered acceptable. In countries that are not liberal democracies, while the grounds for legitimate dissent are often greater, those accepted by the state as legal are even more restricted.

Athan Theoharis's study of the FBI in the United States shows that the FBI, for most of this century, not only intensively monitored dissident political movements and activists—even though it did not have legislative authority to do so—but also, in so doing, often violated the Fourth Amendment ban on unreasonable searches and seizures. The premise of the investigations was that some radical individuals and organizations needed to be monitored not because what they were doing was illegal, but because they might do something illegal in the future. Along with civil-rights groups, left-wing organizations in particular were targets, and apparently FBI officials concluded that efforts, such as those of trade unions, to transform the American economic system were themselves subversive. Right-wing organizations were not in the past subjected to this sort of scrutiny. In addition, the United States imposed legal sanctions against members of the Communist Party. More recently, Americans who opposed President Reagan's Central America policies have been subjected to investigation, and there have been attempts to limit the influence of these groups. The FBI's massive and illegal monitoring of dissent, continuing through the 1980s, has resulted directly from the conservative commitment of federal officials and politicians to contain political change. Professor Theoharis's paper shows that those in authority in the United States have made a substantial and continuing effort to move left-wing and civil-rights-oriented dissent from legitimate to illegitimate, or even illegal.

A stark contrast to the extreme fear of the left wing in the United States is described in Grant Amyot's study of the Italian Communist Party. This party accepts as fully as the other political parties the democratic form of government laid down by the Italian Constitution, is

basic summary of arguments of main Theoharis article

in no sense a menace to democracy, and is an accepted and important part of democratic political processes. It is both legal and legitimate. The Italian Communist Party takes a hard line against left-wing terrorist groups, and has supported extension of police powers to combat them. The Party is firmly rooted in the management of the Italian political system through its role in parliament, local government, the trade unions, and other institutions: 'instead of the system going Communist, the Communists have gone system'.

Reg Whitaker argues that in Canada the Cold War has had a strong influence in determining what dissent was considered acceptable. As in the United States, left-wing groups were particular targets of the security agencies, who focussed on ultimate ideological intentions while ignoring the lack of concrete evidence of revolutionary effect. There was a sort of Cold War mirror logic, in which opposition to 'our side' constituted support for the 'other side' and was thus considered to be disloyal or even subversive. The Canadian state, Whitaker argues, has been unrelentingly hostile to communism and the revolutionary left, as shown by the repressive response to the Winnipeg General Strike of 1919, or the subsequent use of the Criminal Code to prosecute communists. Even in 1939 the head of the RCMP security service argued that communists were a far greater menace than fascism. Whitaker states that, next to the Communist Party itself, labour unions have attracted most of the attention of security services. Nevertheless, with the recent growth of terrorism as a threat, the Cold War mentality of the security establishment has lost its strength and coherence, causing difficulties in establishing legitimacy for the targeting of left-wing groups, and problems in finding a rationale for selecting other appropriate targets.

Janine Krieber examines dissent in Québec with a focus on the dissenting groups within the particular provincial context. At first, in the conservative Québec society, all efforts to change the system, whether through trade unions, intellectual activity, or social organizations, were treated as subversive and 'communist'. The emergence of the separatist and mildly socialist Parti Québécois as a legitimate political party and, later, government created tensions within the radical groups that to some extent mirrored the stresses created within the security service by the same apparent contradiction: the existence of a legitimate political party whose avowed purpose was to overturn the existing system of government.

Stanley Barrett's study shows that the radical right in Canada is not only anti-Semitic but has the aim of rebuilding Canada on a racial basis, with blacks and Jews eliminated—if necessary, by violent means. Anticommunism is a secondary concern of these groups. Two leading spokesmen of the radical right—James Keegstra in Alberta and Ernst Zundel in Ontario—have been found guilty in the courts of spreading hate propaganda, or false news. Their utterances have been found to be illegal, but civil libertarians are still greatly concerned over the legitimacy of such curtailment of freedom of speech by the state. So far, unlike the left, the radical right in Canada has not been an important target for the security service, though police forces keep a watch on its members.

Philippe Faucher and Kevin Fitzgibbons find quite different situations in Latin America. They define dissent as the ideological label ascribed by security services to citizens of widely ranging political leanings. In contrast to opposition, which is tolerated, dissent is unacceptable to the state. The problem in authoritarian Latin American countries, they argue, is that the demands of citizens are not conveyed to the leaders by the political system, and there is little shared understanding of national purpose. Political power is fragile, and it protects itself. These factors make it difficult for regimes to distinguish a real from a potential threat, and as a result the level of tolerated opposition is very limited. At the same time, because society has only a limited capacity to reach a negotiated solution, unresolved and recurring conflicts tend to grow into major turmoil. Agrarian reform, often associated with ethnic conflicts, is a recurring form of dissent and becomes a target of security-force activities. The National Security Doctrine, an extension of the American Cold War mentality, leads to suspicion and targeting of any reformist movement. It also justifies the installation of military or other authoritarian regimes, under which any form of political opposition, including trade-union activity, journalism, or religious social movements, is treated as a threat. There are real tensions and fierce oppositions in the countries examined, and since they cannot be handled within the political system, they become threats to those in power and lead to violent repression. Nevertheless, Latin American countries consistently extol the virtues of democracy. Political repression is conducted in the name of the peace and order necessary to allow democratic politics to work. The range of legal opposition in these authoritarian countries is so restricted as to be almost non-existent; the range of legitimate dissent—prompted by social injustice and offences against human rights—is much greater.

At the conference, discussion of this paper centred around the question of whether the National Security Doctrine and Cold War mentality were not greater causes of the limiting of acceptable dissent than the paper suggested. Faucher and Fitzgibbons argue that they are not, and that the more fundamental causes are to be found in the economic, social, and political structures of Latin America: the National Security Doctrine has simply lent a helping hand to repressive regimes opposed to change.

Aurel Braun finds that dissent in Eastern Europe is directed towards transformation of the system and self-liberation. Here much of the dissent is directed against Soviet domination and in support of historically closer ties with Western Europe. There is also dissent against the monolithic power of the Communist Party and the dominant Marxist ideology. Among the expressions of dissent that are treated as threats by Eastern European states are a wide range of activities including trade unions such as Solidarity in Poland, strikes by Romanian industrial workers, publication by intellectuals in Hungary and Czechoslovakia, and the involvement of young people in peace groups. Braun finds four broad types of dissent—political, economic, national, and religious—of which only a very limited amount is accepted by the regimes. At the same time dissenters have attempted to expand the limits of legal dissent under the various charters of human rights. Some regimes take a tolerant view of dissent as long as they are confident that it can be contained. The range of accepted dissent in these countries appears to be greater than in the Latin American countries examined by Faucher and Fitzgibbons, though narrower than in Canada and the United States. The pressures for change in these countries is great, and the regimes find it difficult to accommodate opposition within legitimate, institutionalized political processes. *Glasnost* in the USSR, and internal pressures in both the USSR and the satellite countries, have recently led to expansion of the range of tolerated dissent.

Christian Bay writes from a rational-humanist perspective that, he says, supplements rather than replaces the prevailing liberal-democratic outlook. He argues that the primary criterion of the legitimacy of any regime or system of government should be its degree of commitment to the protection of human lives by meeting basic human needs. Dissent is consequently legitimate—though it may not be legal—insofar as a regime fails, where it should not, to meet these basic needs. Much discussion arose at the Kingston conference over whether basic human needs could be clearly and usefully defined. Bay himself says that his answers are tentative rather than final. Civil disobedience, he argues, is a means of attempting to reform policies and regimes that fail to meet basic needs; it is not an attempt to overthrow a regime so much as to improve it. Civil disobedience involves breaking the law, and hence is illegal. But in the right sort of cause it is legitimate, is not a threat to the security of the state, and is, consequently, acceptable. Further, Bay argues that civil disobedience is often essential, because even liberal-democratic politics can work in such a way as to deny some groups and individuals the means to meet their basic human needs.

Grace and Leys, in their exploration of the concept of subversion, argue that the term is used to delegitimize ideas and activities opposed to the established order, and hence to legitimize the state's acting against them, even though those ideas and activities are lawful. Subversion as defined by the state is therefore legal but illegitimate. Subversion is largely defined through a supposed link between internal dissent and the threat of world communism; in recent years the concept of 'terrorism' has, they argue, partly replaced Cold War ideology. Subversion is easier to define than is often claimed: it consists in legal activities directed against the existing social, economic, and political order. This is how subversion has been defined by the United States. Canadian security services, as junior and dependent members of the Western intelligence service, are dominated by US values, methods, and policy preferences. Grace and Leys conclude that the historical record shows that the concept of subversion has functioned as a justification for state surveillance of citizens opposed to the status quo, and for repression of their political activities. They argue that there is an inherent contradiction in liberal-democratic freedoms of thought, speech, and association that legitimize the existing socio-economic and political order, because the same freedoms can also threaten this order. The concept of subversion resolves this contradiction, but in so doing corrupts and harms public philosophy and liberal institutions. They conclude that the legal mandate of the Canadian Security Intelligence Service in dealing with 'subversion' should be severely restricted and its counter-subversion activities curtailed.

Apparently denying any sort of justification for a security service, Grace and Leys seem to feel that the police and criminal law offer greater protection to human rights. At the conference, the counter-argument was made that even if subversion and espionage are not accepted as justifications, a security service is needed to protect individuals, such as immigrants from East-Bloc countries, from improper pressures from these countries, as well as to prevent terrorist attacks. Security activities are different from police work, and there is no guarantee that placing them within a police force will avoid the problems identified by Grace and Leys. Hence the problem is one of defining the proper role for a security service, not of arguing the need for one out of existence. The Grace-Leys argument nevertheless poses a severe challenge to security activities: the state should not be concerned with dissent unless it is illegal, and it is wrong to target legal but (state-defined) illegitimate political activities.

Whyte and Macdonald examine the law relating to dissent. They find that it does not directly sanction or prohibit unwanted behaviour by labelling it illegal. Instead, the law permits authorities to investigate, study, and report. This results in indirect penalizing, or what the authors term 'partial sanctioning'. The courts are not used to impose criminal penalties. Rather, hidden penalties such as negative personal reports, or refusal to hire, are used. These sorts of activities do not fit within the liberal-democratic legal tradition. They are outside standard legal and judicial concepts and practices. The authors conclude that Western democracies have probably lost the capacity to bring national security back into the fold of legal concepts. This leads to extreme problems in making a distinction between legal and illegal dissent.

The one type of dissent that was not well examined was the legal-illegitimate variety. This is, conceptually, an odd sort of category. Perhaps the extreme-right activities examined by Stanley Barrett fit into it, though some of these have been found to be illegal by the courts, and others, though offensive, are not illegitimate. The right-wing plots in Italy that originated in part within the secret service also belong in this category. Normally, however, if something is deemed illegitimate by society, governments tend to legislate against it, making it illegal, as has happened (with many protests from civil libertarians) to hate propaganda. Legal-illegitimate appears to be a label most properly applied to government's activities in limiting dissent. Examples are the state terrorism described in Latin America, repression in Eastern-bloc countries, and the continuing persecution of legal left-wing organizations in Western democracies.

The papers illustrate three contrasting approaches to dissent on the part of government. One extreme, found in Latin American countries, is the police-state regime in which no dissent is legitimate or legal. The prime concern of government is to maintain itself in power, and the state uses whatever means it chooses and considers necessary, including widespread offences against fundamental human rights to life and liberty, to eliminate actual or potential dissenters. The ultimate law is the preservation of the state; no law protects the citizens. In the more liberated of the Eastern European countries, by contrast, some dissent is tolerated, and at least some actions of the state are limited and controlled by the law. The Eastern European regimes differ from those of Latin America in that they profess an articulated ideology, a variety of Marxism, and at the same time distinguish between acceptable and unacceptable dissent and defend their actions through defence of that ideology. The Eastern-bloc countries are, however, often arbitrary and beyond legal restraint in their response to some manifestations of dissent. To this extent they also manifest police-state characteristics.

The third sort of regime is the liberal-democratic, in which, in theory, there are two principles distinguishing the regime from the Latin American police-state and Eastern European Marxist models. The first, as Whyte and Macdonald explain, is that constitutional governments should operate under the rule of law and be limited by the law in their interference with individuals and groups. The second is that governments should respect political freedoms, including the advocacy of fundamental changes in society, and ideologies antithetical to those prevailing. The papers on dissent in North America and Italy show that these principles have often been transgressed by governments and security services. Left-wing groups have been targeted not because they represent a serious threat of violence or overthrow of democracy, but because the ideologies they advocate are out of favour. Separatists and the Parti Québécois were targeted because of their belief in a separate

Québec, even when the means they used were peaceful, including a legitimate political party participating in electoral and representative politics.

Some critics from the left side of the political spectrum argue that a particular sort of economic regime—capitalism—is inextricably connected with liberal democracy, and that the one cannot be attacked without attacking the other: both need to be changed. Critics from the right side of the spectrum often argue from the same grounds but reach the opposite conclusion: that both need to be preserved, and that to attack the capitalist structure is to attack the liberal-democratic state itself. The two extremes would appear to support the view of North American security services that left-wing dissent is unacceptable to the state. The papers in this volume suggest that this approach to targeting is far too wide, that inappropriate and innocent groups have too often been targeted, and that the results have been harmful both for individuals and for democratic politics. Perhaps worse, it subverts the basic principles, the *raison d'être*, of democracy. The examination of the Italian Communist Party proves that a functioning liberal democracy can not only tolerate the existence of a powerful, anti-capitalist, and avowedly Marxist party, but in some instances benefit from it.

The response of the state to dissent

One of the main themes of the paper by Athan Theoharis is that in the past the discretion the FBI had in monitoring dissidents, which was supported by presidential directives, led the agency first to monitor personal behaviour, and then to use that information and at the same time to violate legal and constitutional restrictions. The FBI would disseminate information about people, such as alleged communist sympathies, if it were assured that it would not be revealed as the source. It would also inform employers about individuals engaged in non-communist left-wing dissent, presumably with the hope that sanctions would be applied against them. Often this information was gathered illegally, through break-ins, wire-taps, and bugging. The FBI has, up to the present, been interested in political attitudes, and from its conservative perspective has sought to contain political change and the influence of groups such as those opposed to the Reagan administration's Central America policy.

Reg Whitaker argues that the Canadian state's unremitting hostility to communism in the twentieth century led it to overestimate dramatically the revolutionary challenge, and to respond through such repressive measures as small 'wars' against communists by police, the deportation of foreign-born communists and labour organizers, changes to the Criminal Code to outlaw the Communist Party, and the banning of communist publications. Whitaker makes a distinction between political repression such as McCarthyism, which was less visible in

Canada than in the United States, and state repression, which he states was extensive in Canada and directed largely at communism. The security service of the RCMP, for example, by the 1980s performed some 70,000 security clearances a year, not only of government workers but also of workers in defence-related industries. The screening criteria were highly ideological and anti-communist, and until 1984 there was little appeal against them. Even participation in a peace march has been cited as grounds for denial of security clearance. The effect upon left-wing associations of any kind, whether pro-communist or not, was depressing. Communist sympathies were also used by the RCMP as grounds for rejecting immigrants. Hence, even though communism itself has not been illegal in Canada, association with it could be a fatal disability to anyone seeking to become a Canadian. Immigrants and refugees have been politically selected.

A consequence of the strong anti-communist stance of both the security service and the CCF-NDP was that they collaborated to eliminate communists and communist influence. This, Whitaker says, led to a 'domestication' of the left. Although the violent separatist movement had died with the imposition of the War Measures Act in 1970, some subsequent counter-subversion activities of the security service were illegal, and the sanctions were violent. Counter-subversion activities were launched against a target that had become a respectable political party. The decline of the threat of communism has made it difficult, Whitaker concludes, for the security service to find a *raison d'être*. Separatism was no longer an appropriate one, nor has terrorism proven to be. As a result, the political base for repressive state intrusion into Canadian civil society has been weakened. In effect, in the absence of a generally accepted target, the security service has less opportunity to harm the lives of individuals and political activities of the nation.

Stanley Barrett explores the reasons why the Canadian state has consistently ignored the far right. Indeed, the far right often regards the police, with their apparent hostility to visible minorities, as silent partners in the grand design to halt the decline of Western civilization. Nevertheless, Barrett finds that in recent years the police have played a major role in containing Canada's right wing. Undercover police agents, hired infiltrators, and *agents provocateurs* have provided constant surveillance of far-right organizations. Barrett finds a contradiction within the Canadian state in the expectation that official sectors flawed by racist inclinations and an anti-left orientation can respond to new values of openness, liberty, and justice. He concludes that more, not less, state interference in the activities of far-right organizations is warranted.

Grant Amyot's examination of the Italian Communist Party reveals other curious twists in a state's response to right- and left-wing dissent. The Communist Party, itself an accepted part of democratic politics, has never supported attempts to dissolve a reconstituted fascist party (the MSI), even though the latter is outlawed by the constitution. Here the Communist Party has chosen to uphold liberal-democratic principles rather than the letter of the constitution, which bars its traditional enemy. But this tolerance of the fascist political party does not extend to neo-fascist terrorist groups or right-wing plots. Amyot finds that the only serious threats to Italian democracy in the post-war period have come from plots originating wholly or partially within the state, and involving particularly members of the secret services. The Italian Communist Party has been extremely hostile to leftist terrorist groups, and has supported considerable extensions of police powers to handle terrorism.

Janine Krieber does not dwell on the security-service aspects of dissent, but rather on the process through which Québec radicalism found violent resistance not to be viable. With the emergence of the Parti Québécois, radicalism lost much of its steam, becoming a long march through the institutions of politics and administration. This is an important analysis of radical dissent's assimilation into the system, much as has happened in the case of the Italian Communist Party.

Grace and Leys draw a stark and pessimistic conclusion about the activities involved in countering subversion. They argue that the Cold War ideology that has permeated security services negates liberal democracy by identifying persons as threats simply because of their beliefs. In the United States this has led to extensive witch-hunting and repression of dissent in general by intimidation and persecution. This mentality has spilled over into the Canadian security service. Subversion, Grace and Leys argue, belongs to the pathology of liberal-democratic states and harms them through the covert operations of a largely uncontrollable state agency. Perversely, to the extent that this has a 'chilling' effect on popular engagement in radical politics, it helps to ossify the existing order and make it more vulnerable to demands for radical change.

Whyte and Macdonald explore what they call 'partial sanctioning', whereby activities are not actually outlawed but are nevertheless repressed. The result of surveillance of dissenters is that power becomes silent; it ceases to reveal itself in an open fashion, and the legal regime is supplanted by something else. This denies power to the less advantaged in society.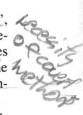

The authors for the most part fit comfortably within the general rubric of liberal-democratic thought. Their arguments are that democracy is served by dissent, and that permitting dissent encourages peaceful change while reducing the chance for violent opposition. They find that generally Western security services have not served the cause of liberal democracy in their opposition to left-wing dissent and their adherence to Cold War ideology. Less state intrusion into dissent would be beneficial.

Stanley Barrett, however, finds the contrary: in the case of the far right, he feels, more state intrusion would be desirable. There is an unresolved contradiction here between Barrett and the others. A perennial issue in liberal democracies is whether the law should be used to prevent things that are merely offensive, or be limited to those that are in fact harmful. The actual practice of modern government is to use the law to control behaviour in many areas, such as some forms of sexual behaviour and substance abuse, where the issues concern offensiveness and taste rather than harm. The result is a situation in which innumerable statutes and clauses of statutes sanction most aspects of human behaviour:

> The complexity of administration in modern societies is such that if all laws and police ordinances were to be universally enforced, all citizens would be criminals. The modern tendency of legislators, as well as administrators, to attempt to improve society by penal sanctions has led to a situation in which anti-social behaviour is combated by rules to make such activities technically illegal as well as socially repugnant. One result of this has been that the law designed to protect society against the rich man in his mansion can also be used to persecute the poor man in his cottage.
>
> Police power in a contemporary setting has largely become the institutionalized use of society's discretionary powers, and the application of the law, although not the law itself, becomes relativistic. . . .
>
> What appears to happen in normal societies is that the exercise of police powers tends to be determined according to an intuitive set of values, the police normally reflecting the values of society. Certain offences are deemed by the police to be so intrinsically harmful or hateful to society that they are automatically pursued with the greatest possible vigour. At the other end of the scale there are a host of trivial offences whose prosecution is purely random. They will be prosecuted if detected, if their authors are known, or, in some cases, if the police authorities wish to make an example. The police put their own gloss on the religious notion of mortal and venial sin.[8]

Using the law to prevent offensive behaviour, as Barrett suggests in the case of abhorrent racially oriented attacks, leaves this sort of discretion to the authorities, whether police or security services. There is then a risk that deviant opinions or sexual behaviour will be equated with subversion or treason. One noted British jurist has proposed precisely this linkage,[9] to which Whyte and Macdonald also allude. Athan Theoharis shows how the FBI has targeted both, and made connections between the two. Grace and Leys argue that authorities should not intrude against left-wing dissent, even if the opinions uttered are offensive to those in power or in advantaged positions in society. They want to reduce the discretion of police and security agencies in a way that would surely limit their ability to sanction the right as well as the left.

In these issues the problems of limiting the powers of a security service to intrude in legitimate political activity are a sub-set of the problems of controlling the police power in modern society. This is one of the great underdeveloped areas of political and legal studies. There are problems in the entire area of police work and police power in liberal democracies that are in urgent need of serious attention.

Aurel Braun finds that Eastern European regimes have not been able to achieve sufficient legitimacy to maintain themselves in power without the use of widespread coercion, which in turn has helped them fritter away whatever legitimacy they had. In these countries, with their professed Marxist creed, dissent seeks to undermine a ruling tradition whose functioning idea has proven to be incapable of mobilizing popular aspirations, and that maintains itself through a process of institutionalized coercion. Hence critical opinions of almost any kind become threatening forms of dissent. In this post-Stalinist era the activities of the secret police are designed to have a 'prophylactic' rather than a 'punitive' effect. This does not exclude the possibility of the state's detaining, imprisoning, exiling, or even killing dissidents. But there is now a much greater emphasis on deterrence, both of individuals and of the population as a whole. Eastern European regimes have also used various forms of co-optation, containment, and co-existence with dissenters. These techniques include pacification through partial inclusion, repressive tolerance, differentiated political justice, and suppression through main force.

The responses of authorities as described by Braun are those of a police state, with no respect for human rights and due legal processes. They are exaggerated versions of the kind of behaviour detailed by the other authors in describing efforts to control dissent in the West. In both East and West, the responses of the state have a chilling effect on politics and dissent. But the sort of suspension of civil liberties found in the West in situations of stress and provocation, such as the October Crisis of 1970 in Québec, or in Italy under aggressive left-wing terrorism, are much more widespread and have become the norm in Eastern Europe. Braun concludes that if Eastern European regimes persist in their unwillingness to allow political pluralism, they have little choice but to continue the battle against dissent. Even the most flexible of regimes are willing to make only tactical concessions: their ultimate objective is to stay in power on their own terms. Aurel Braun does not believe that there can be basic economic reforms in these countries until the communist parties in the region settle for influence rather than dominance. So far they have not solved the problems posed by dissent, and if anything their legitimacy has declined. Whether there can be real pluralism within a socialism acceptable to the regimes is yet to be determined. The present pressures may leading to important changes.

The level of tolerance of dissent found by Aurel Braun in Eastern Europe is much lower than that in Canada and the United States.

Faucher and Fitzgibbons find it to be lower still in Latin America, where widespread violation of human rights is a reality. Used to maintain social control, it is an integral part of the relationship between dissent and the state. Domination has to be forced, even at the cost of undermining the legitimacy of institutions. Faucher and Fitzgibbons find a striking similarity between the mandate given to the Canadian Security Intelligence Service and that of the police in Latin America. The difference is that in Latin America the law has been a false façade, whereas in Canada all parties concerned understand that practice should conform to the law. In Latin America legal safeguards have not prevailed over the system of authority. The political repression conducted there by security services has been institutional terrorism. As the initial, limited, objective of political repression was replaced by the more ambitious project of imposing a system of fear, the security service came to dominate government and civil society. In effect, war was declared, without restriction, on civil society. Not the least of the platoons on the side of authority were clandestine death squads, which performed illegal acts leading to the installation of terror and the conviction that repressive acts would be covered by total impunity.

None of the Latin American regimes examined by Faucher and Fitzgibbons has lasted as long as the Eastern European ones examined by Braun. The violence of such regimes serves ultimately to destroy them: the last victim of the terror is the terror itself. So far, however, a better civil state has not grown out of the ashes of the terror. The Eastern European regimes have been longer-lasting. Some of them have been able to loosen up and accommodate at least some measure of change, reform, and diversity. But they too are under stress, and in the past periods of openness have often been followed by either severe repression or invasion by the USSR.

In comparison with either Eastern Europe or Latin America, the United States, Canada, and Italy appear blissfully peaceful. A wide range of dissent is legitimate and accommodated within accepted political processes; change does occur through politics; the security services and police influence only a small portion of political activity. In conditions of stress, however, liberal democracies move from the relatively free end of the spectrum towards the police-state end. When democracies are subject to continuing and unresolvable stress, the repressive police-state mode of activity tends to dominate. South Africa has moved in this direction in its attempt to limit the rights of blacks; Israel faces tremendous stresses and problems in its efforts to determine what to do with the occupied territory and the peoples of Palestine. The problems in Northern Ireland have affected civil rights throughout the United Kingdom. Latin American democracies collapse because they cannot accommodate dissent. The Christian Bay argument is that regimes must recognize fundamental human rights: otherwise there is a powerful pressure for dissent, which, if suppressed, leads to loss of the regime's legitimacy and widespread violence. National security and the Cold War have already led to unhealthy suppression of dissent in the West.

Liberal democracy, as it has developed in the West, has institutionalized opposition and dissent within the electoral process and representative assemblies. Even in liberal democracies, however, the activities of a security service can harm democracy by preventing some legitimate opinions from being expressed, or by sanctioning individuals and groups engaged in legitimate political activities. This is likely, in the long run, to create greater stress on the regime because problems are submerged and ignored. But Western regimes are fortunate indeed to have made a wide range of dissent and change legitimate and legal through democratic electoral politics. The experience of Eastern European and Latin American regimes shows the political stress, and the violations of human rights, that occur when dissent is not accommodated within political processes. The challenge is not for the state to suppress dissent, but for the state to ameliorate the problems and conditions that cause it. Only then can a regime prove that it is attempting to accommodate the basic human needs and rights that justify its existence. Regimes that do this are, these papers suggest, much more secure and legitimate than those dependent on powerful security services that control and prevent dissent.

An issue that none of the papers deals with directly is the extent to which the problem of dissent and its control by the state is solvable. Some schools of social science argue that conflict is endemic in human society, and that the state will always have to regulate the struggle between interests and groups with competing views of the good life and the role of the state. And as part of the state's regulatory activities it will always have to control and discipline groups whose activities threaten stability and even the state's survival. Hence the issue of distinguishing between acceptable and unacceptable dissent can never disappear; the boundary between them can be readjusted, but the problem will remain. The authors in this volume who are most critical of the present state-security system in Canada and the Western world tend to the more optimistic side. I tend to be more pessimistic. The Air India disaster suggests that there are serious threats to the safety of Canadians from activities that are, or ought to be, targets of security-service attention. The state has legitimate concerns for survival and peaceful change, and a serious risk to democracy comes from radical minorities of left or right who are frequently audacious, violent, and ready to speak for the nation without consulting it. Moderate opinion can be dangerously suppressed by an immoderate fringe. That, certainly, was a large part of the crisis of October 1970 in Canada. Extremism on one side produces polarization and then extremism on the other side. The desires for freedom and order often come into conflict, and the answer is not always on the side of freedom of the individual. On the more optimistic side, I believe that the recent changes in the mandate and accountability of the Canadian security service, and the fact itself that this book has been created, are evidence that the system can respond to criticism, and indeed has changed for the better. Eternal vigilance, not only over aggressors (inside or outside), but also over the custodians of state powers, is the price of freedom. That is one of the strong arguments in favour of the critical tone of many of these papers.

This volume not only covers a wide range of countries and experiences, but also embodies a wide range of viewpoints and attitudes. This introduction has contrasted and highlighted only a few of the important issues and experiences explored by the ten authors. The papers tell their own complex and fascinating stories. The pictures they present are far from comforting.

Dissent and National Security and Dissent Some More

JOHN D. WHYTE AND ALLAN MACDONALD

Introduction

Although the Canadian Security Intelligence Service Act[1] defines behaviour that is hostile to national security, it is not the purpose of the Act to proscribe any such behaviour. At the heart of its concern with threats to national security arising from domestic sources is the charge to the Canadian Security Intelligence Service (CSIS) 'to collect, by investigation or otherwise, to the extent that it is strictly necessary, and to analyze and retain information and intelligence respecting activities that may on reasonable grounds be suspected of constituting threats to the security of Canada . . .'[2] CSIS is required to advise the federal government of such threats.[3] It may also provide security assessments—that is, assessments of individuals' loyalty to Canada and the reliability of that loyalty[4]—to various federal and provincial governmental departments,[5] and may give a federal minister information relating to national security if it is relevant to the minister's responsibilities concerning citizenship and immigration.[6] Finally, in relation to the Act's concern with internal threats to national security, CSIS is empowered to make investigations necessary to provide security assessments and to advise ministers performing responsibilities relating to citizenship and immigration.[7]

The agency's major functions of investigation and information collection in relation to activities that may reasonably be seen as constituting 'threats to the security of Canada' are circumscribed by a statutory definition of such threats.[8] This definition expressly excludes lawful advocacy, protest, and dissent unless they are exercised in conjunction with other activities. The other activities that, under the Act, will taint dissent (and that are not the product of foreign-based espionage or sabotage) are those directed towards (1) the use of serious violence for a political objective or (2) the undermining by covert unlawful acts, or the destroying or overthrowing, or the overthrowing by violence, of the constitutionally established system of government in Canada.

The first thing to be noted in this abridged review of the relevant legislative provisions is the extreme degree of attenuation between the expression of dissent and the most dramatic of the feared outcomes: the destruction or overthrow by violence of government in Canada. The first activity that may legitimately trigger observation, analysis, and reporting under section 12 is activity that supports the *threat* of serious violence made for the purposes of inducing a certain political decision. The second such activity is that directed towards *undermining* (by covert unlawful acts) the system of government that, through one form of constitutionalization or another, has come into place. Finally, the Act is directed to activity that is supported by the *ultimate intention* of violently overthrowing the constitutionally created system of government. It does not matter what the actual effect of the activity is, or what intention can be inferred from the activity itself.

Clearly, among the activities that would fall within these categories and prompt section-12 surveillance is speech activity. The saving clause to the definition of 'threats to the security of Canada'—stating that lawful advocacy, protest, or dissent are not included—does not exempt speech activity, for that clause itself carries the exemption that unlawful advocacy, protest, or dissent can be considered a threat to security if it is carried on *in conjunction with* any of the categories of activity already identified. This phraseology, not unique in proscriptive legislation, raises semantic questions. Must there be two discrete patterns of activity before the responsibilities created by section 12 may be assumed? Must speech activity be conjoined with some other activity of the threatening sort described above? Under this text it would appear that this is not necessary. There would be little point in including an exemption to the exclusion of speech activity from the concerns of the Act if the legislative intention were not to ensure that, in some circumstances, speech activity—the mere expression of dissent—can be sufficient reason to perform section 12's surveillance responsibilities. If, therefore, speech in itself can be a threat to security, the 'in conjunction with' phrase may mean no more than that the speech activity need only, as a matter of content, be connected to one of the described outcomes. On the other hand, it may be that dissent must be connected to some additional activity directed to these outcomes. If the latter is the case, however, what quality must that activity have in order to be 'other' activity? Could it, for instance, be other speech-related activity such as publication, distribution, or organization on the part of an association?

The CSIS Act's second basic feature relates to the quality of regulation provided in it. The Act's primary mechanisms are not proscription and punishment. The sanctioning mandated is more subtle and indirect: because the officers empowered by the Act are required simply to investigate and report, the sanctioning effect becomes incidental, a matter of happenstance. As the late Harry Kalven observed: 'The classic sanction for speech, prior licensing apart, has been the criminal sanction.'[9] Section 12 of the CSIS Act does not create a crime. It merely empowers public administration to act by way of obtaining information and forming views that, when communicated, may affect the ability of residents to enjoy some state benefits—of privacy, employment, citizenship, or subsidy. This consequence of the exercise of the CSIS Act's powers does not constitute a direct sanction. Persons whose activities fall within section 12 are, in an important sense, free to continue those activities. This sort of social control through a public agency has been labelled partial sanctioning.[10] Social control in this form creates a problem of categories. Our legal regime knows (or is coming to know) something about the permissible limits in proscribing speech and other political activities. It is less conscious of the constitutional value of regulation that does not proscribe but simply adds to the bundle of social costs attaching to an activity. State regulation creating disincentives for only some particularly situated persons—applicants for jobs or citizenship, for instance—has no salience in the constitutional balancing of social values; thus partial sanctioning enjoys a privileged position in the face of judicial review and control.

The position of the CSIS Act in relation to political dissent is, first, that the chief regulatory instruments of intelligence gathering, analysis, and advising are appropriate and available in relation to activity that does not go beyond the promotion of certain political visions and ideas; and, second, that the social control imposed through the operation of the Act is not fully amenable to constitutional evaluation. In light of our preliminary assessment that the Act enables, without legal control, the regulation of dissent, it is important that we attempt to come to some understanding of the legal protection for, and the legal validity of, both participation in political dissent and the governmental devices for protecting national security. In other words, the Act appears to provide grounds for concern that deployment of the powers contained in section 12 will not be consonant with the legal protection of expression. Accordingly, it is necessary to examine closely the whole of our legal and constitutional regime and the values underlying it to see how they can be drawn upon to provide a check on the regulation of dissent in pursuit of national security.

Dissent in liberal democracy

For nearly two centuries western democracies have understood that the phenomenon of human choice—that element of imperfect autonomy within individuals—when recognized in the political structure, leads towards certain political forms and social practices.[11] These include democratic politics, limited government, integrity and autonomy for legalist elements, and some degree of liberty to reshape the world, whether in the 'free' marketplace or in the marketplace of ideas. There can be little doubt that our present constitutional arrangement recognizes that liberty as a political value, which when undervalued erodes the basic structures relating to both public and private ordering. It is for this reason that at the level of constitutional ideology we have a high degree of tolerance for private choice and unrestricted private action.

This tolerance is not merely an instrumental phenomenon of the kind underlying the claim that without liberty in relation to speech and association, electoral politics does not work.[12] The very structures of democracy and government under the rule of law make sense only if we understand that our public order is based on a conception of the person, a conception that rests on human liberty and not—as may be the case outside liberalism—on membership, obedience, and service.

If our polity rests on belief in choice, and if our dominant political claim is that collectively we have authority over the life that we lead, it is incumbent upon us to accept that the society in which we live is the consequence of past decisions, and that present decisions will determine what society will be like in the future. This places an awful responsibility on each of us, because wherever we look we see that things are not right. The world imperfectly matches any single person's conception of justice, enlightenment, efficiency, beauty, or grace.

The question is, what is it that each of us is free to do to repair social imperfection? At the outset, every member of society who carries political responsibility is free to identify society's failings. It is not tolerable to base a polity on the concept of choice—hence, on personal responsibility for the way things are—and remove from individuals the voice through which reality can be identified, criticized, and changed. All those people in our society who, for example, believe that we do not care adequately for the world's natural environment, or that we do not truly nurture children and the helpless (or, on the other hand, who see tolerance for others as leading to the loss of standards of civilization) ought to enjoy, as a condition of being a member of a democratic state, the right to proclaim these views.[13]

What, however, does one do about perceptions of social inadequacy that are connected to a particular agenda for reform? It is one thing to be discontented with what is; it is another, more intrusive, thing to know how to improve the world and to urge others to exercise power to achieve that end. Does the promotion of a program for reform enjoy the same protection as the identification that something in the society fails to achieve some stipulated social virtue? What we fear is that the program for reform will include a call to re-order our governmental system. When does a call of that sort amount to dissent? And when is it challenging to the security of the nation?

Discontent proclaimed is in itself a call for reforming action, for disturbing and dismantling the present arrangement and replacing it with some other arrangement that is fairer, purer, more productive, more just. There should be no concept of freedom without a sense of responsibility, and no sense of responsibility without the expression of discontent with the present reality. Hence the connection between dissent and freedom goes beyond the mere recognition of the right to free speech. The concept of liberty does not simply allow dissent; it is the condition that, for some, creates the obligation to dissent and to seek to re-order our social arrangements.

If the security of the nation is threatened by this search for a better world through expression and reform, then the concept of 'security of the nation' is not linked to the most basic values at work in the modern liberal democracy. Yet we know that dissent, and its implicit claim that society needs to be re-ordered, is threatening. This can only be because the re-ordering that is often called for in social criticism strikes too deeply at the institutions and arrangements that we perceive to be indispensable to social order itself. There can be little dissent without a sense of threat, but the latter in itself will produce a strong urge to channel the former. Hence there is inherent in a free and democratic society a conflict between two imperatives: the imperative to seek to reform, and the imperative not to permit social disintegration.

These observations are not simply expressions of abstract political or social theory. They amount to claims of constitutional law. Our nation's most basic constitutional features are liberty, democracy, and the rule of law. Constitutional liberty springs from a concept of personal autonomy. It has produced a sense of individual responsibility for the social fabric that, in turn, has been reflected in democracy. The actions of free individuals in shaping either the private or the public world gain meaning only in the presence of a social order that can guarantee that personal and public decisions will be honoured.[14] The same idea of state-guaranteed stability that makes autonomy meaningful also contains the concept of a social order in which disintegration is held at bay. As explained in the decision of the Supreme Court of Canada in the *Reference re Language Rights Under the Manitoba Act, 1870*:

> The rule of law, a fundamental principle of our Constitution, must mean at least two things. First, that the law is supreme over officials of the government as well as private individuals, and thereby preclusive of the influence of arbitrary power.
>
> . . . Second, the rule of law requires the creation and maintenance of an actual order of positive laws which preserves and embodies the more general principle of normative order. Law and order are indispensable elements of civilized life. 'The Rule of Law in this sense implies . . . simply the existence of public order.' (I. Jennings, *The Law and the Constitution*, 5th ed. (1959), at p. 43.). . . According to Wade and Phillips, *Constitutional Administrative Law*, 9th ed. (1977), at p.89:
>
> . . . the rule of law expresses a preference for law and order within a community rather than anarchy, warfare and constant strife. In

this sense, the rule of law is a philosophical view of society which in the Western tradition is linked with basic democratic notions.[15]

Under this conception of the role of rule of law, it is important not only that there be a legal system in place by which duties and obligations may be imposed on private citizens and public officials alike, but that there be a fixed structure in place supporting the system of law.

The maintenance of a public-order conception of the rule of law extends, then, to the maintenance of governmental institutions and gives force to the CSIS Act's reference, in its description of 'threats to the security of Canada', to 'the constitutionally established system of government'. It is an extension of concern for the rule of law—a doctrine that both limits controls on dissent and permits governmental regulation on behalf of national security—to seek to protect against subversion. The result is that significant tenets of our constitutional law bear on the question of the proper state treatment of dissent and the proper state role in preserving national security.

The nature of constitutionalism

Seeing matters simply in terms of constitutionally established political values, however, and seeing constitutional law as a form of resolution between these values, does not provide an adequate account of what constitutionalism is about. It is not only a system for the expression of values and goals, such as liberty, preserving democratic institutions, and the like; it is a particular structure of resolution. The structure requires that the debate between values be rooted in claims of right. It is, in short, law; it is a system in which courts must determine whether a particular plaintiff's, or applicant's, claim for a remedy is supported by the terms of the legal order. The difference between this process and one that would simply decide on which side the net social benefit lies is that law places the individual claimant's position front and centre and causes the court to focus on the question of whether the individual fits within the constitutional value on which the claim is supported.

This view of legal adjudication as being focussed on a right that is enjoyed by a person or group, and not on a social interest that is in competition with other social interests, stems from the very nature of legalism. Legal adjudication is a process by which specific expectations that have been formally established prior to adjudication (whether by contract or by constitution) are vindicated. The process, like liberalism itself, is rooted in the view that society, with its agencies and instruments, is directed to reflecting human choice.

Inasmuch as constitutional law consists not in mere political accommodation but, rather, in the adjudication of claims, it is required to give full regard to the individual's claim, whether against others or against the state. Legalism and liberalism alike make individualism and the values that promote individual interests the telelogical point of questions of statecraft. This effect is significant because it puts a discounted value on the social interest of preserving the constitutionally established government in Canada. This is not, of course, to say that preserving the system of government counts for nothing; it clearly counts for much when genuinely supported by a people in the exercise of their sovereignty. But it is not immutable, and it is not immune to radical criticism and radical alteration by a polity that is non-coercively mobilized and that expresses a preference for change. Furthermore, the actions that enable a population to exercise its sovereignty—to make choices, no matter how fundamental—are at the heart of our system of constitutional protection.

The business of constitutional law is not merely to reflect the fact that there are two sides to everything—liberty and order—but to reflect in adjudication the values that enjoy legal primacy because they are at the root of the state's reason for being.

National security

Professor Peter Hanks of Monash University has written that 'the concept of national security is elusive and pervasive; its content is value-laden, equivocal and obscure; and it has been pressed into service for a variety of purposes'.[16] In fact, however, it may not be elusive. It may be the most available of political values for the legitimation of political choices[17]—more attractive, even, than justice and charity. Its power comes, at least in part, from its foundational quality: all that we have that is good in a nation—prosperity, a functioning system of justice, a generous welfare apparatus—is contingent on the continuation of the state. Appeals to national integrity succeed in attracting political support as nothing else does.

And yet this anxiety over the durability of the state may not always have been a part of our political life. It seems that our tolerance for concerted and thorough-going political attack was greater in the nineteenth century than it is today.[18] This shift is speculatively accounted for by Professor Rankin:

> developments in technology have mandated the national security state. . . . It has arisen out of the fear of revolution and structural change felt in the Western Alliance and from the economic instability of post-industrial capitalism. Perhaps the most significant cause, however, has been the development of nuclear weapons and advanced military technology. The basic assumption underpinning the state's authority has been eroded in large measure because of qualitative advances in the technology of destruction.[19]

But there are other possible reasons, besides the increased effectiveness of instruments of terror and destruction, for our increasing fixation on the state's vulnerability to subversion from within. Among them are such phenomena as the vast increase in the mobility of persons. Not only can subversives move about quickly—and trans-nationally—and thereby defeat identification and detention (although that is certainly true); the communication between dissident communities can also be extremely direct, and hence supportive and encouraging. Our fear of dissent may also stem from the sense that certain groups—trade unions, associations of social 'undesirables' such as homosexuals, etc.—may find protection in the rule of law.

Furthermore, the recent increase in transnational consciousness has meant not only that dissidents have learnt the effectiveness of petty disruptive practices in the operations of state authority (those who feel oppressed by state structures can learn a lot from the Palestinians on the West Bank), but that the rest of society now appreciates the ease with which subversion can undermine public order. We learn to fear for our nation's security by observing the trials of other nations.

Another cause for fear may be the increase in decontextualized ideology. Throughout the world it is possible to observe that ideologies (and religions) are driving people to purify their social environment to meet conceptions of right without regard for the interests and expectations already in place. This decontextual obtuseness, although noble from the perspective of the righteous, is alarming to the rest of society. Accompanying this phenomenon is an intensified moral responsibility; the world has become full of people who know they carry full responsibility for the moral adequacy of their society and are willing to go to great lengths to ensure that their mandate to improve is achieved. Legality and the interests of others are not primary values in the minds of those who carry this sort of strong moral mission.[20]

A similar moral imperative is at work at both ends of the political spectrum. Successful interruption of constituted political authority comes most often from the conservative end; that is, from those whose political goal is to preserve present, or earlier, political and economic regimes. Their greater efficacy may be the result of the tendency, in the allocation of state instruments of force, for weapons to fall to those whose preference is to preserve the existing arrangement. Such subversion, as practised by armies, police forces, and security services, is driven by a moral conviction that the arrangement that is in place, or that has been in place, is the one that best reflects the true values of the nation and its people. The morality at work is that of saving a people from misguided reformists.

The left, too, can be ruled by a moral sense—that the state is morally bankrupt and that the undoubted coercive power of the state lacks all legitimacy. As David Apter has described the phenomenon:

the common target of terrorism is the legitimacy of the state as given . . .

its moral credibility. Hence, the means, no matter how repugnant, represent judgments. Their outrageousness is a measure of moral seriousness.[21]

Finally, among the speculative reasons for increased concern for national security is the personal, and ultimately national, anxiety produced by rapid change in the social order, the national order, and the international order.

One further and significant explanation for the heightened awareness of national security comes from the Security Intelligence Review Committee in its 1986-87 Annual Report. At one point the report observes:

> It seemed to us that information supplied by friendly foreign intelligence services might too easily be accepted by CSIS at face value; it may not be getting the same critical scrutiny as information from Canadian sources.
>
> Indeed, we sensed that CSIS might be too quick to accept the foreign policy underpinnings of this information instead of recasting it in terms of Canadian policy. Canada has its own national interests, distinct from the interests of any other nation.[22]

Later in the same report, SIRC gave its assessment of the Canadian Security Intelligence Service's counter-subversion operations. After considering a number of Subject Evaluation Reports [SERs] prepared by the Service, it concluded 'that CSIS may too readily accept the foreign policy objectives of our allies as its own and neglect Canadian foreign policy.[23]

Although SIRC provided no explanation for this tendency to adopt the political values (including the value in anxiety about subversion) from other nations, such an explanation is not hard to arrive at: the high level of operational integration between the Canadian Security Intelligence Service and the Central Intelligence Agency of the United States has led to a common perspective on the mission that is to be performed. The fears of the CIA, and the US administration in general, are absorbed by Canadian security services. This is not merely because persons who work together usually come to shared perspectives and values; it is simply impossible to make sense of the operations to which, directly or indirectly, CSIS is party without coming to hold the same view of the world and the same view of political forces as Americans.

The constituent parts of an integrated Western nation's security service cannot help becoming ideologically committed to the same goals as the most dominant of the parts. It may be that the United States has much to fear from both external attacks and internal subversion. (It would indeed be strange if a nation with the international presence of the United States did not have a considerable number of external enemies; it would indeed be strange if a nation with as much economic and political power as the United States did not have enemies within.) It does not follow that Canada has the same national-security concerns.

Nevertheless, evaluation of how genuinely Canada needs to be concerned about internal subversion is impossible in light of the close linkages between security services. This, as much as anything else, accounts for the feeling that Canadian national security is in such jeopardy that we require a distinct and powerful agency with covert and unique regulatory powers.

As a result of this increased sense of threat to national security, we have probably lost the capacity to bring national security back into the fold of legal concepts. Clearly, social disintegration has legal salience, as we have seen in the Supreme Court of Canada's decision in the *Manitoba Language Reference*. But when national security becomes as attached as it seems to have done to inaccessible structures and unexamined relationships and hidden phenomena, both social and political, deciding on the appropriate legal weight to give it in assessing an individual's claim to express dissent becomes highly problematic. In other words, it is difficult to know how to apply the phrase of the first section of the Charter of Rights and Freedoms: 'demonstrably justified in a free and democratic society'. The forces behind our sense of the need to control dissent are not decipherable. Yet that is precisely the task of constitutional law, and the task must be performed unless we wish to accept that, when we come to administer the policy of national security, we have already said farewell to the nation's constitutionalism and to the rule of law.

PART II

The task at hand: a reintroduction

What would it take to bring national security back into the fold of legal concepts? The question immediately appears too ambitious. A more modest question—the one, perhaps, that we ought to ask—is what the legal issues are with respect to the CSIS Act's regulation of 'lawful advocacy, protest or dissent'. Yet even this modest question conceals some presumption. It assumes that the legal regime, like an alert nightwatchman, stands forever on guard against all transgressions of the constituted order. Pictured in such a way, the task of identifying legal issues is tantamount to identifying prowling transgressors—the next step being a simple matter of apprehension.

Matters are not that simple. This paper has, in part, been concerned with the separation between the legal and national-security regimes. The notion that legalism stands watch over only a restricted field of activity runs counter, of course, to our conception of a country governed by the rule of law. It also makes us wonder if anything can be achieved by identifying legal issues—or, better, identifying issues as legal—that arise with respect to an extra-legal order. Our modest question suggests, and even tacitly assures us, that that achievement is possible, that identifying such issues effectively draws the national-security regime—or at least that part of it concerned with advocacy, protest, or dissent—within the confines of legalism. It ignores the distance between regimes; it politely proceeds as though the one can easily be persuaded to the other's point of view. The two saliences in the modest question are legality and 'advocacy, protest or dissent'. Taking into consideration, then, the real possibility that what constitutes the latter may be determined by a different normative order, the question must be re-phrased thus: How can we ensure that what constitutes 'lawful advocacy, protest or dissent' is dictated by the legal regime?

The following section begins to answer this question by reviewing the law with respect to national security. The ostensible purpose of this review is to determine what, in the legal regulation of national-security concerns, has proven authoritative in defining lawful advocacy, protest or dissent. Its main purpose, though, is to provoke further inquiry into what it means to live in a legal regime—to lead a legal life—and what is at stake when that regime is jeopardized by another.

The law review

The task of setting out the law with respect to national security has been made easier by M.L. Friedland's 1979 study 'National Security: The Legal Dimensions'.[24] A major portion of this study is a survey of the then existing law with respect to security matters, the constituent parts of which were the Criminal Code,[25] the Official Secrets Act,[26] and the War Measures Act.[27] Throughout his study Friedland makes recommendations as to how the existing law should be made more consistent. The concern for consistency derives from our conception of the rule of law. In an ideal legal regime there would be no radical difference between, say, *de facto* and *de jure* law application. Furthermore, there would be no justification for *de jure* law's being manipulable to the extent that activity not impugnable under one law should be impugnable under another.

In his concern for consistency Friedland recommends that certain sections of the Official Secrets Act be altered so as to more closely resemble similar sections in the Criminal Code.[28] In order to make a similar comparison today one must compare the Canadian Security Intelligence Service Act with both the Criminal Code and the Canadian Charter of Rights and Freedoms. The purpose of such a study would be to discover the touchstones of the law, as it were, with respect to dissent and national security. If we follow in Friedland's footsteps, the general task is to discover inconsistencies between the Criminal Code and the Canadian Security Intelligence Act. As we learn from Friedland, however, the code itself cannot be understood in isolation. Those sections relevant to dissent and subversion, for example, received early and thorough review by Canadian courts. This review should be appreciated from two very different perspectives. On the one hand, in the grand tradition of bourgeois criminal jurisprudence, there has been great focus upon the subjective element of the crime; for purposes of clarity, one might call this 'the criminal focus'. This is to be distinguished from 'the constitutional focus'. In its review of charges of sedition, for instance, the judiciary has, in parallel fashion, contributed in developing the constitutional doctrines of free speech and opinion. In playing out the tension between these two foci, the judiciary has created a background against which the Canadian Security Intelligence Act must be evaluated.

Section 60 of the Criminal Code reads as follows:

Sedition

Seditious words—Seditious libel—Seditious conspiracy—Seditious intention.

60.(1) Seditious words are words that express a seditious intention.

(2) A seditious libel is a libel that expresses a seditious intention.

(3) A seditious conspiracy is an agreement between two or more persons to carry out a seditious intention.

(4) Without limiting the generality of the meaning of the expression 'seditious intention', every one shall be presumed to have a seditious intention who
(a) teaches or advocates, or
(b) publishes or circulates any writing that advocates the use, without the authority of law, of force as a means of accomplishing a governmental change within Canada.

The criminal law, as we know, has suffered many growing pains in its quest for what constitutes an intention. In section 61, therefore, an exception is added:

61. Notwithstanding subsection 60(4), no person shall be deemed to have a seditious intention by reason only that he intends, in good faith,
(a) to show that Her Majesty has been misled or mistaken in her measures:
(b) to point out errors or defects in
(i) the government or constitution of Canada or a province,
(ii) the Parliament of Canada or the legislature of a province, or
(iii) the administration of justice in Canada;
(c) to procure, by lawful means, the alteration of any matter of government in Canada; or
(d) to point out, for the purpose of removal, matters that produce or tend to produce feelings of hostility and ill-will between different classes of persons in Canada.

A review of the relevant case law reveals the judiciary's efforts to limit what constitutes seditious intent.[29] The tool used in these efforts was the equivalent of today's section 61. Indeed, as early as 1929 that earlier section had so limited the scope of section 60 that a successful charge required either incitement towards violence, or speech accompanied by such violence. As Lord Justice Coleridge was quoted in *R. v. Weir*:

> if (a citizen) thinks that either a despotism, or an oligarchy, or a republic, or even no government at all, is the best way of conducting human affairs, he is at perfect liberty to say so. He may assail politicians, he may attack governments, he may warn the executive of the day against taking a particular course . . . he may seek to show that rebellions, insurrections, outrages, assassinations, and suchlike, are the natural, the deplorable, the inevitable outcome of the policy which he is combating. All that is allowed, because all that is innocuous; but, on the other hand, if he makes use of language calculated to advocate or to incite others to public disorders, to wit, rebellions, insurrections, assassinations, outrages, or any physical force or violence of any kind, then, whatever his intentions, there would be evidence on which a jury might . . . decide that he was guilty of a seditious publication.[30]

As well as being used to qualify seditious intent, section 61 has served as a vehicle to exhort upon the nature of free speech and individual sovereignty. The most famous exhortation is unquestionably that of Mr Justice Rand in *Boucher v. The King*:[31]

> There is no modern authority which holds that the mere effect of tending to create discontent or disaffection among His Majesty's subjects or ill-will or hostility between groups of them, but not tending to issue in illegal conduct, constitutes the crime, and this for obvious reasons. Freedom in thought and speech and disagreement in ideas and beliefs, on every conceivable subject, are of the essence of our life. The clash of critical discussion on political, social and religious subjects has too deeply become the stuff of daily experience to suggest that mere ill-will as a product of controversy can strike down the latter with illegality . . . our compact of free society accepts and absorbs these differences and they are exercised at large within the framework of freedom and order on broader and deeper uniformities as bases of social stability. Similarly in discontent, affection and hostility: as subjective incidents of controversy, they and the ideas which arouse them are part of our living which ultimately serve us in stimulation, in the clarification of thought and, as we believe, in the search for the constitution and truth of things generally.[32]

The legal culture

It is important to consider wherein lies the authority of Rand's judgement. In order to do so we must first exclude that which does not constitute such authority. Rand does not, for instance, rest his judgement on what should or should not constitute subversive behaviour.[33] Is the judgement then anchored by some other concept? The obvious choice here is the concept of freedom. Or is it a particular theory of freedom? Is Rand giving us, as it were, his gloss on liberal theory? And is it this gloss that he offers as authority to silence the criminal law? Or is he relying on some definite constitutional rules or principles? All these questions, it should be noted, stem from the notion that authority rests in some kind of theoretical, or epistemological, structure; that is, that theory is antecedent to and generative of authority.

Judicial authority, we know, is a function of hierarchy. The liberal unpacks hierarchy in value terms; the structuralist does so with discourses of power. But such theories do not inform the hierarchies of which they speak; rather, they tell us how to be informed about them. Leaving theory aside, we know that, somewhere along the way in Rand's decision, the criminal law—or the forces being marshalled under this rubric—is rendered less than dispositive. We have come to call such decisions 'constitutional' in their focus on the 'broader and deeper uniformities as bases of social stability'. The criminal law, in contrast, is neither broad nor deep. In its pursuit for precision, for codification, it divides human activity into component parts. In so doing it excludes—self-consciously, we hope—a great deal. It excludes, for instance, the value that people invest in their activities. In fact, it excludes the entire context in which its isolable, atomic 'criminal' acts occur. In providing such a detailed map of prohibited activity, the criminal law performs a valuable service. This is to pass over, and thereby help to define, questions about our world to be answered in another legal genre: that is, the constitutional one.

To identify what happens in Rand's judgement is not to say that the constitutional genre wins out over the criminal.[34] In other words, there is no transcendental order to which a reader can refer to determine where one genre wins out over the other (or, for that matter, where one begins and the other ends). What happens in Rand's judgement is that the two genres engage in conversation. The criminal law provides as precise a subject as possible. It does so with a rule. In *Boucher*, under what is today section 61 of the Code, the issue was the good faith of the accused pamphleteer. After the issue is established, though, there is still much to say. As Joseph Vining notes:

> That which speaks law's command . . . does not pop out from behind a tree like an eighteenth-century footpad and say something short and crisp about which there can be no question, such as, 'Hand over your purse.'[35]

Upon being restrained by a rule of the criminal law, one gains standing before the court, one becomes a subject to whom a duty is owed. The duty may be characterized in various fashions. It may be the court's duty to account, as it were, for how we order ourselves. Or the duty may be to perform something akin to what, in the law of evidence, we call a judicial view. This, of course, is another way of saying that the court must go into the world in order to fashion its judgement. In any event, the world is immanent in the court's judgement. That is, through the individual—situated as he or she is in the matrix of our practices, in their pools of significance—the world gains entry into the legal discourse.

In Rand's judgement it is the world's dissonance, its political diversity, that proves authoritative. The pamphleteer, in confronting the Criminal Code's embossed authority, must speak in legal terms. These terms, though—freedom of thought, of belief—are only mirrors or, still more transparent, reflections of the world.[36] 'Critical discussion on political, social and religious subjects', says Rand, 'has too deeply become the stuff of daily experience to suggest that mere ill-will as a product of controversy can strike down the latter with illegality. . . .' It is this 'stuff', plainly spoken, that is normative; it is what we do that counts most. The values articulated in the courtroom-those that have found legal significance—emanate from, and are co-extensive with, our lived practices.

More than a fold of concepts, legalism is a culture. First and foremost, it is a culture—an economy—of power. No doubt legalism has served only a few. At its worst it is ideology; it legitimizes the power relationships supposedly existing outside the discourse itself. The picture here is one of determinism. But there are other pictures, even of determinism. In his later work, Michel Foucault paints a complex portrait of power relations. He writes:

> Power discourses are not once and for all subservient to power or raised up against it, any more than silences are. We must make allowance for the complex and unstable process whereby a discourse can be both an instrument and an effect of power, but also a hindrance, a stumbling block, a point of resistance and a starting point for an opposing strategy. Discourse transmits and produces power; it reinforces it, but also undermines and exposes it, renders it fragile and makes it possible to thwart it.[37]

At its best, legalism is a discourse with the capacity to render power fragile. The possibility for such fragility lies in the discourse's distribution of authoritative diads. A review of the case law with respect to advocacy, protest, and dissent reveals that it is not only legal rules that determine what constitutes legal behaviour. Our normative world—lived out and recreated through our practices—generates legal salience. And how, one asks, is this so? How is it that there are sources of legal salience outside the construct of our legal rules? An answer may be fashioned by considering the origins of our legal discourse.

The legal discourse has distinguished itself from others—in the past from the religious and monarchical; today, in a different though related manner, from the hegemony of information gathering and retrieval—in having as its focus and being disposed by the secular, mundane activities of humankind. Legalism blossomed with the rise of mercantile activity. In its role as servant or handmaiden, its purpose was to translate the authoritative customs and practices of trade into legal ones. This same translation process is evident in the transition from English land-use customs into early common law.[38] Such land-use customs had as their source of authority the fact that persons had engaged in them from 'time immemorial'. Situated somewhere in the appeal to time immemorial was, at least in vestigial form, a reference to a transcendent authority. This source of authority, however, was removed from the legal discourse. The appeal became one to an order of human design.

Law has been both born out of and, in reflexive fashion, constitutive of our secular normative order; law is a human artifact and it has gained its ascendancy through its facilitation of human practices. The significance of this can perhaps best be understood if we again conceive of legalism as a discourse of power; that is, as a language, an assortment of values and procedures, through which power is expressed and mediated. Not all power, as we know, is exercised in similar fashion. Different discourses are characterized by the relations they exhibit between values and procedures embraced as authoritative. The legal discourse has its own character, its own composition of saliences. The saliences being vehicles for empowerment in the social order, this composition is also a distribution of opportunities. Fundamental in the legal discourse's composition is the potential for human practices to acquire legal salience. This potential allows for authority to be generated by many and various sources. The result—at least to some degree—is that what constitutes legal authority remains protean in nature.

An important requirement in gaining legal salience is that an activity be open to the world's scrutiny. The present enquiry into our legal culture was prompted by the question of how we can ensure that what constitutes 'lawful advocacy, protest or dissent' is dictated by the legal regime. At least part of the enquiry has consisted in demonstrating that legal authority is not circumscribed within the corpus of our legal rules, that it is generated by and discovered amidst our mundane activities and affairs. Thus in order to ensure that dissent remains regulated by the legal regime, we must maintain it as one of our mundane affairs; that is, we must engage in it openly and regularly.

Attenuation and cultures of control

Engaging in dissent will, of course, bring restraint and, with restraint, further enquiry into what should constitute legal activity. In the history of our law with respect to dissent, such enquiry has resembled a conversation between our proscriptive rules and our mundane practices. The conversation could not take place without either of the partners; it depends upon both the ambition of the dissent and the proscriptions of regulation. For, except in extraordinary circumstances, without proscription there will be no restraint; and without tangible restraint there will be no opportunity, no subject—neither human nor thematic—to provide a response. We will be deprived of the opportunity to participate in a legal culture.

The legal culture can come to an end. This will occur where there is regulation without proscription. But this is only the most vulgar of descriptions; there are subtle variations on the same theme. The same effect is achieved where there is substantial attenuation between a rule and the activity or conditions triggering its application. Between these poles there is a continuum of uncertainty. To what extent, one asks in reference to sections 2 and 12 of the CSIS Act, must dissent attach to some other activity in order to constitute a 'threat to the security of Canada'? Somewhere along the continuum are situated normative words—section 2 offers 'lawful' advocacy, protest, or dissent; section 12 offers 'reasonable grounds' on which activities may be suspected of constituting threats to the security of Canada—suggestive of when section-12 surveillance might occur. But to what—what discourse, what world—do these words attach? They are apparently words of legal significance. In order to have such significance, however, they must be situated in their context; that is, they must be articulated in the ongoing exchange between our proscriptive rules and mundane affairs.

What, one asks, are the legal issues with respect to section-12 surveillance? What is at issue is legalism itself. The legal culture's main locus of enquiry is confrontation. What often provokes such confrontation —especially with respect to dissent—is restraint, or the direct application of power. Surveillance is the indirect application of power.[39] Meted out in indirect fashion, power is difficult—often impossible—to confront, to engage in conversation. Where power becomes silent, where it ceases to reveal itself in an open and engaged fashion, the mantle is passed; the legal regime is supplanted by another.

This new regime—call it what you will—cannot legalize itself, as it were, with words borrowed from the legal regime. As they are situated in the CSIS Act, the words 'lawful' and 'reasonable'—words of a different, perhaps former, culture—are meaningless. So too are the words 'advocacy, protest or dissent'. Inasmuch as the new regime has withdrawn from restraining dissenters, inasmuch as it does not openly acknowledge them, it undermines the legal value, and thus the meaning, of dissent. It here becomes obvious that dissent, even without the appended 'lawful', is a legal word, is part of our legal grammar. Formerly the expression of dissent, even 'illegal' dissent, entitled one to access (if only for punishment) to the legal regime. In effect, this access acknowledged the dissenter's citizenship—even if it meant the removal of citizenship—in that regime: it imbued dissent with meaning. Surveillance acknowledges nothing, and thereby denies the legal significance of human activity. It regulates—and this is its elegant paradox—by inadvertence, by denying the meaning and hence the power of human expression. And what becomes of dissent when it is denied such meaning? It searches for other enclaves of meaning and, in so doing, loses its character and, yes, its life.

Could our social order 're-legalize' itself, as it were, through legal reform? Could 'advocacy, protest or dissent', for example, be altered or situated differently so as to allow greater opportunity for expression consummate with the new rights as entrenched in the Charter? These sorts of questions are expected at such moments: one exposes insufficiencies, re-examines history (and, in so doing, says little), and ends on a hopeful note with suggestions for legislative re-wording or mechanisms for review. That is not enough. To withhold the complete orchestration, we believe, is nihilistic. This is not to deny the reformative power of human agency. Before suggesting reforms, though, it is important to note that agency is expressed not only through legal drafting; that the text called 'legalism'—and, perhaps more so, 'constitutionalism'—runs beyond the printed page. To invest great significance in the formal reform of dissent regulation is to ignore dissent's legal heritage; it is to ignore that within our legal regime the meaning of dissent has not been legislated but has, rather, travelled from the bottom up; it is to ignore the pain suffered in acquiring (and maintaining) legal protection for dissent.

Are there reform alternatives? We tend to be uncomfortable without a list of formal measures, without suggestions regarding how the Charter may bear upon section-12 surveillance. Without such suggestions, where are we left? The degree to which we are left nowhere may be a good indication of how impoverished our legal discourse has become. And its quality will not improve through re-drafting. It will improve only through our bearing witness to our social order, our commenting and criticizing, our getting caught at this witness, and our forcing into the constitutional genre an examination as to why it is we were caught. Only in this manner will we discover, and re-discover, the content of our liberal-democratic values.

And so let us bear some witness. The erotic cannot survive in a pornographic culture; similarly, dissent cannot survive in a culture of control.[40] Pushed underground, hidden in a bottom desk drawer, it assumes the value of things otherworldly. Like all such things, it is an object standing outside our lives for which we fear taking responsibility. And as it is outside our lives, it can serve only to keep us detached from the mundane world to which our lives consistently return us; and in our detachment we remain powerless. Dissent is most often the expression of the less empowered. When these persons become withdrawn or inhibited, dissent turns to frustration, or worse, self-hatred. Unlike dissent, such manifestations have no potential for political mobilization.

Yes, they may find enclaves bestowing meaning and, possibly, redemption; but no, they will not help to reconstitute our social order.

Only the legal regime can empower the dissenter. First, though, the dissenter must give the regime an opportunity to provide such empowerment. Thus the law, or our legal rules, must be broken, and broken again. If reform measures are required, they can be located here. For only in breaking our legal rules can the law be a focus for speech about our social order, about its distribution of opportunities. Speech, of course, will not bring an immediate redistribution of these opportunities. Legal power must always be fought for. To speak, though, is already to win one battle: it is to wrest power from a regime of silence.

Civil Disobedience: The Inner and Outer Limits

CHRISTIAN BAY

I Introduction and overview

In this paper I attempt a constructive critique of some key assumptions in the liberal-democratic political persuasion, which I dare say is a widely shared political belief-system in Canada and most other countries in the so-called 'developed', relatively affluent First World. Let me stress right away that I am not out to try to undermine our electoral system or our present Canadian system of rights and liberties. On the contrary, I hope to help to strengthen our rights by grounding them more firmly in a coherent humanist theory of human rights. I shall call my perspective rational-humanist, for reasons to be explained below; it is intended to supplement, not to replace, the prevailing liberal-democratic outlook.

Democracy in the sense of governance by the majority, or by leaders truly representative of majority wants and demands, cannot be an end in itself, I shall argue. First of all, such a system is probably impossible, as Robert Michels[1] and subsequent generations of behavioural political researchers have shown[2]; it can at best be approximated, and not closely. But should it be, to the extent possible? Perhaps, but not as a first priority.[3] The primary criterion of the legitimacy of any regime or system of government should be its degree of commitment to the protection of human lives—every human life—as demonstrated by its endeavours to meet the most basic needs, the dire needs, of the people most endangered and/or those least privileged. To meet the less basic needs, let alone the preferences and demands of citizens not 'in need', must assume a lower priority.

But why? As Immanuel Kant has argued so powerfully, all human beings should be entitled to be treated as ends, never solely as means.[4] Philosophically, this is for me the first premise; on this point I am dogmatic. But my dogmatism is parsimonious, for I assume that in principle all other normative issues, and all empirical beliefs, should be treated as tentative, subject to future modifications in the light of new argument or experience. Even 'motherhood issues' must be open to question. And while I hold firmly to the 'right to life' of all humans, I have no simple answers to the vexing issues of abortion or euthanasia, at the beginning and end of the life cycle.

By contrast with Kant's humanism, Jeremy Bentham's greatest-happiness principle cannot serve as a basis for political legitimacy; most certainly not when 'of the greatest number' completes the criterion-sentence.[5] Most Canadians might well become incrementally happier if, for example, capital punishment were to be brought back; but from a rational-humanist perspective the life of every criminal, too, must be treated as an end. Human-rights issues, which arise whenever basic kinds of human needs are in jeopardy, must take precedence over democratic issues, those that in principle can be settled by showing how the various alternative solutions would affect the happiness of 'the greatest number'.

This is where the issues of civil disobedience arise, too, when we look for remedies against morally unacceptable outcomes of democratic or otherwise formally legitimate processes of governance. Human-rights theory, as we shall see, anticipates the requirement of acts or campaigns of civil disobedience from time to time, when and if the powers that be treat human-rights issues as if they were democratic issues: in other words, treat issues about people's dire needs as if they were no weightier than issues concerning mere wants or preferences. I shall also discuss the problematic of *uncivil* disobedience—not for the purpose of advocacy, but for the purpose of interpreting realistically what is going on in some less fortunate countries, and occasionally in Canada as well. A better understanding may make for more effective prevention of future uncivil disasters.

One category of utilitarian thought is much closer than Bentham's to the rational-humanist perspective expounded here. Suppose we turn Bentham's criterion-sentence—'the least possible human misery or victimization for the smallest number'—around, and require that the priority always be to assist the very worst-offs first, before reducing the number of those who suffer less extremely.

States are not well suited to decide how to boost the general happiness, for they are ultimately based on coercive power; they should be working to make happiness possible, not required. What legitimate states must do to justify their powers is to reduce human misery. If they do not, or if they fail to do so with effectiveness and with the right priorities, that is when rational-humanists must consider whether appropriate strategies of civil disobedience are available that might be effective as well as prudent. While the task of assisting the exploited and the victimized should be the first objective, there is another point to be made as well: just as ineffective, unjust uses of electoral or other formally legitimate institutions may lead to civil disobedience, so insufficient results of civil disobedience can allow disaffection and anger to grow until we get into situations of uncivil disobedience as well.

Two decades ago I defined 'civil disobedience' as follows: 'any act or process of public defiance of a law or policy enforced by established governmental authorities, insofar as the action is premeditated, understood by the actor(s) to be illegal or of contested legality, carried out and persisted in for limited public ends and by way of carefully chosen and limited means'.[6] For the present purpose of comparison with a concept of 'uncivil' disobedience, a somewhat narrower definition of civil disobedience is called for: 'by way of carefully chosen and limited means that exclude measures that could cause personal injuries or even the loss of life'. Uncivil disobedience will here refer to any act of disobedience or resistance that does not recognize such limits, including, at the extreme, acts of revolutionary terrorism,[7] but not state terrorism or anti-revolutionary terror in defence of the state, regardless of whether the ties between the terrorists and the regime are publicly admitted. There is no assumption made here to the effect that pro-state terrorism, generally speaking, is more to be morally condemned than anti-state terrorism, for the nature of the states may differ, and so may the extent and motivations of foreign intervention. For example, the Reagan administration in the United States has been financing mercenaries trying to bring down a progressive regime in Nicaragua, while supporting with massive military and economic assistance a cruel caricature of a democracy in El Salvador, against a broad coalition of rebels whose main political leaders were driven into exile by right-wing terror.[8] This paper, however, will discuss not terrorism but the broader problems of political disobedience, civil and uncivil.

The idea of subjects' being free to choose to disobey their governments, or even to experiment with strategies of disobedience or open resistance, would have been abhorrent to most ancient and medieval philosophers. Although disobedience was practised by Antigone, the fictional heroine of the Greek tragedy, and by Socrates, in neither case was this a matter of free choice, still less one of having a right to such disobedience: it was a matter of recognizing the command of a higher duty.

Thomas Hobbes represents a watershed in the history of theories of political obligation. He was the first major political thinker to raise the question of a *right* to disobey, and the first one to assume that the authority of the state had to justify itself in terms of serving human purposes. His aversion to violence and anarchy made him rule out as illegitimate almost every possible justification for disobedience and resistance as a citizen's option for choice. But once the issue had been raised, it did not go away, and John Locke, as we will see, advocated a right to rebel against tyrannical regimes.

Liberal writers from Locke to Bentham to Rawls have discussed justifications and limits of political obligations and disobedience, and these discussions continue. With this paper I hope to contribute a few further thoughts on these issues.

In Section II I discuss some philosophical and conceptual preliminaries, chiefly about conceptions of *needs* and *rights* and their bearing on issues of political obligation and civil disobedience. Civil and human rights are distinguished, and priorities among categories of basic human needs are discussed, as well as the proposed conceptual relationship between human rights and human needs. Noted also is the growing worldwide attention, in recent decades, to human-rights issues and problems in many countries.

Next, in Section III, I discuss the *inner limits* of morally legitimate civil disobedience; that is, how to resolve the democratic dilemma that arises whenever rights are invaded by governments or by other political actors who claim a democratic or legal mandate to make such inroads. The dilemma, for each conscientious citizen who is aware of such invasion of rights, his own or others', is whether to comply and urge others to comply with the law, or whether to respectfully disobey and urge others to do the same, unless or until the invasion of rights ceases. A distinction will be made between what I shall call Hobbesian and Lockean conceptions of citizenship.

Section IV brings us to the *outer* limits of the legitimate practice of civil disobedience; that is, to the issue of when or where to draw the line between civil disobedience and *uncivil* resistance or rebellion. I shall not indulge in revolutionary or terrorist fantasies, for (especially in our powder-keg world) I cannot condone the use of lethal weapons against persons for any cause except in self-defence or the defence of others, and then as a last resort—least of all in countries, such as Canada, in which the entire population enjoys a relatively high degree of physical security. But we need to study how and why this security has been achieved, and why people living for example in Sri Lanka, or in Lebanon or South Africa, have been much less fortunate. I cannot condone but neither can I condemn the uses of uncivil disobedience, nor even of insurrectionary violence, in countries in which the regimes or the ruling élites themselves practise terrorism against the life-supporting ecosystem, such action being an evil that governments and national-security establishments are duty-bound to prevent. As Richard E. Rubenstein argues so persuasively in his recent book,[9] if we want to learn well how to reduce the incidence or the risk of terrorism in a given country, then we must study as dispassionately as possible the incentives and motivations of existing terrorist groups, at home and abroad; it is of no help simply to write them off as moral monsters. It could be of help, too, if we did everything possible to reduce the incidence of violations of human rights on the part of our own and allied governments.

In the spirit of the young Rousseau's radical refusal to accept as legitimate any state that unjustly executes even a single person, or keeps even a single innocent person in jail,[10] I shall argue that our commitment to the nation-state should always take second place to our commitment to the victims of power (victimized individuals, classes, ethnic minorities, etc.). I call this position rational-humanist; instead of a worldwide proletarian revolution, I envisage an evolving international order of human rights, gradually expanding in scope and in effectiveness of enforcement, the tempo depending on the strengthening of the political will of citizens in the various regimes and countries that assume responsibilities of international leadership, within and beyond the United Nations and its relevant agencies. In this continuing struggle civil disobedience will play an important part, especially, perhaps, when politically imaginative non-governmental agencies join the fray (examples: Greenpeace, Amnesty International, the Sierra Club). Their activists and supporters practise what I will, with apologies, call Rousseauian citizenship.[11]

The last section, or postscript, will be brief, focussing attention on the new Canadian Charter of Rights and Freedoms, and on the suddenly expanded role of the Canadian courts as protectors and regulators of individual rights in this country. This could be—indeed, can become—a salutary development, even though it could mean a reduced role in this area for the House of Commons and its democratic constituencies. The importance of distinguishing democratic issues from human-rights issues will be reiterated in this concluding section.

II Needs, wants, and political obligation

'The philosopher's interest in political obligation has been mainly in the problem of the *grounds* of political obligation . . . that is, in the question: Why ought we to obey the government?'[12] The prior question, as I shall argue, is *whether* the citizen is obligated to obey the government, under what circumstances, and depending on what kind of government, with what aims and strategies. While Thomas Hobbes represents a watershed in the history of theories of political obligation, as we have seen, he did not address that prior question. Neither did Locke or any other, subsequent liberal writer; at least the *prima facie* obligation to obey the government has been taken for granted. It was Rousseau, as we shall see, who issued the first articulate challenge to the assumptions that, perhaps barring outright tyrannies, almost every established regime or state must be entitled to exercise legitimate political authority over the citizenry, and that each citizen in turn is normally obligated to obey the lawful government.

Before we proceed towards asking that prior question, a couple of philosophical preliminaries are in order, for *how* we ask the question will make a difference. I shall follow Ronald Dworkin in his argument to the effect that there are (at least) three types of political theory. *Goal*-based theories, be they utilitarian or perfectionist, judge regimes and citizens by their degree of commitment to some ultimate conception of a public good; *duty*-based theories assume—for example, with Kant—that the moral will to act right is crucial; finally, *rights*-based theories resemble duty-based theories in that they 'place the individual at the center . . .', but rights-based theories are 'concerned with the independence rather than [with] the conformity [to duty] of individual action'. Dworkin's example of a rights-based theorist is Tom Paine; another example is Dworkin himself, as is implied already in the title of the book from which I have been quoting, *Taking Rights Seriously*.[13]

Dworkin's philosophical point of departure is that moral duties and codes of conduct are important instrumentalities in any civilized society, but have 'no essential value in themselves'.[14] His perspective affirms, and I share this view, that as citizens we have duties and obligations *because* and *to the extent that* we, and all fellow citizens, have rights—not the other way round.

Next question: why is it important to assert that basic rights must be seen to be prior to duties? Surely it is more noble to emphasize our duties to others ahead of claiming our rights against others. It is important to consider, however, that any political or ecclesiastical regime will find it easy and convenient to impose alleged duties and obligations on their subjects, unless the latter have come to develop a sense of having some basic rights, *human* rights, that no regimes, no powers-that-be, are entitled to invade or violate. Expanding human rights is like a vaccination against the arbitrary imposition of duties, on ourselves and others, provided they are the right kinds of rights; not the state-defined civil rights needed to enable people to do their alleged duties, but the universal right of also the less privileged to have rational remedies against unjust demands on them, demands dressed up, perhaps, as patriotic or religious duties.

Goal-based and duty-based political philosophies can readily be called up for compliant service by almost any kind of governmental or other ideologically equipped authority; political and religious hierarchies often mutually reinforce virtually the same demands for individual uncritical subordination. 'Ask not what your country can do for you. Ask what you can do for your country!' These were President John F. Kennedy's ringing words. He did not, however, ask the prior questions: 'What is this country up to? Is this government deserving of our trust?'

How do we go about seeking valid answers to these last questions? Not, I submit, by observing the extent to which the government seeks to expand and reinforce the citizenry's obedience to public duties and alleged obligations. This would be like issuing masses of blank cheques to the government; the door would be left open to authoritarian or totalitarian systems of rule and of political justification. In the absence of a common understanding of basic human rights, why prioritize this duty rather than that? Who says that goal A is worthier, or more pressing, than goal B? Why?

Unlike *ad hoc* selections of human goals, and unlike alleged, perhaps historically grounded, conceptions of duties or obligations, the concept of *rights*, and especially *human rights*, has the important advantage of being compatible, and connectable, with empirical needs concepts: a rights-based political philosophy can be made to serve a most crucial humanist cause, namely to protect the most pressing kinds of human-needs categories: survival and health; solidarity and self-esteem/ identity; and individual freedom and growth.

Not every rights-based political philosophy is grounded in concep-tions of human needs, however. Much rights discourse, including most of Dworkin's, deals with *civil* rights; that is, legal claims, grounded in statutes, in constitutions, or in principles of Common Law or Equity as well as in moral philosophy. Other kinds of rights discourse are ethical or political but do not necessarily relate explicitly (or even implicitly) to conceptions of needs-priorities. Needs 'may have a certain priority with justice; but justice, when needs have been met, and there are still benefits and burdens to be distributed, must also deal with preferences', writes David Braybrooke.[15] But the distinction between needs and pref-erences is of vital moral importance, as Braybrooke affirms. To assert otherwise would, in my view, be not only wrong but monstrous, espe-cially in the context of utilitarian discourse. This kind of position could sanction the tossing of Christians to the lions in ancient Rome, for ex-ample, if this would be for masses of Romans a preferred kind of enter-tainment, objected to by only a relative handful of intended victims.

This example of ethically perverse rights discourse is not, as I shall ar-gue, very far out of line with some of the conventional liberal rights dis-course; or even with liberal *human*-rights discourse, for liberal rights-priorities are most often grounded *not* in the assumption that needs should outweigh preferences, but in the perceived requirements of our private-corporate socio-economic system; and first of all in the demand for optimal freedom to trade and bargain as the proper way to settle competing preference-based or contractual rights-claims. Convention-ally assessed, 'prosperity' for the middle and upper classes is what our 'free' system endeavours to achieve, and, excepting some leftist critics, most North Americans appear to take it for granted that there must be not only 'winners' but 'losers' as well, even in periods of economic growth, when our system works at its best: 'losers' are the people who are chronically out of work, without adequate housing, in poor health, and with low life-expectancy. They are victims of the socio-economic system, as clearly as were some of the Christians in ancient Rome.

If we follow Immanuel Kant[16] in asserting that all human lives must be seen and treated as ends, never merely as means, then we need to follow Plato's Socrates as well,[17] in drawing a sharp line between needs and preferences: for example, between political decisions that appeal to popular desires and those that will actually be of lasting benefit to the people.

Needs and wants (or preferences, desires, interests, perceived needs) may at times coincide. Elementary needs for food and water are usually apparent in clearly expressed wants—unless you happen to be a Gandhi preparing for one of his fasts, or a pious Moslem placed in front of a dish of roast pork. The more real social welfare has been achieved in a society, or the better the standards of mental health, the closer, we may believe, the correspondence between needs and wants will tend to be.

Both concepts are in principle empirical, but only preferences (wants, desires. . .) are readily observable and subject to direct measurement, by survey research, for example; needs may be unconscious, and as often as not they must be inferred. While wants or preferences can multiply indefinitely, real needs are finite and few in number: at the latest count about a dozen altogether; about six having to do with physical functioning and six having to do 'more with (man's or woman's) functioning as a social being'.[18] This count does not claim any finality, of course, for the number depends on terminology and definitions of each component needs-concept. Note that Braybrooke's classification also stipulates a dichotomy between the more broadly based categories of physical and social needs. He hedges on whether or not we can assume any hierarchical ordering between the twelve needs, or even between the two broader needs-categories.

For A.H. Maslow—perhaps the most influential psychologist who has written on needs, at any rate the most influential among political and social scientists—the affirmation of a needs hierarchy is essential. In one of his works[19] he analyzes a proposed dichotomy between deficiency needs and being needs, arguing that the latter will remain latent until the deficiency needs have been met, at least beyond a certain level or threshold (which, to be sure, is difficult to pinpoint or even to conceptualize in an empirically useful way). More influential has been his theory of a five-category needs hierarchy: sustenance, safety, belongingness, self-esteem, and self-actualization needs.[20] Among important empirical studies based on Maslow's five-needs hierarchy are works by Manzer[21] and by Inglehart.[22]

My own preference, at least for the purposes of this paper, is for a reduction of Maslow's five-level hierarchy into three tiers of basic needs: safety and health needs, social well-being needs, and individual freedom needs.[23]

Why is it so important to posit as a working hypothesis that some categories of needs are more basic, more essential for human well-being, than others? First of all, because we in fact must make such distinctions every day when we deal with fellow human beings, as friends, as parents, as lovers, as fellow citizens. And we could not know how to follow Kant's humanist maxim of treating all humans we encounter as ends unless we have at least an implicit way of determining, in conflict situations, how basic the various needs at stake are; it will not do simply to ascertain who complains the loudest, or who is the most articulate in defending his or her claim.

One more point requires a heavy emphasis: basic needs do not go away. If they are repressed, or denied satisfaction, wounds will fester, and the badly oppressed will sooner or later develop a resolve to hit back at their oppressors, or at *someone(s)*, with means as forceful as they can find. This kind of situation is surely a common root cause of crime and, when large numbers are oppressed, *the* most common root cause both of terrorism and its nemesis, counter-terrorism, and of revolution and counter-revolution.[24]

The modern philosophical *problem* of political obligation arose with Hobbes and Locke, we have seen: with Hobbes because he posed the question of limits to political obligation, and with Locke because he argued for a right to rise up in defence of civil rights against tyranny. Both assumed a 'natural' individual liberty voluntarily modified under the terms of a metaphorical social contract (Locke bravely tried to argue for its historicity and may have convinced himself). Each contract was seen as a kind of long-term bargain between 'the People' and the Sovereign. In the Hobbesian contract the deal was irrevocable on the People's side as long as the Sovereign remained in power; in Locke's case the contract was contingent on the Sovereign's continuing respect for the civil rights of the citizenry, their property and liberty rights: an implicit compact to be passed on by 'tacit consent' from each generation to the next.

With the eventual granting of near-universal suffrage, the liberal states of Locke's time have become the liberal-democratic states of our century.[25] Meanwhile, after decades of modern behavioural research it has become abundantly clear that majoritarian democracies may exist in aspiration but do not exist in fact. Rawls only partially acknowledges serious flaws in American-style democracy as damaging to political obligation: 'the duty to comply is problematic for permanent minorities that have suffered from injustice for many years'.[26] As Pateman has observed, modern liberal writers on political obligation have demonstrated 'a singular lack of curiosity'[27] about how well or how badly liberal social-contract theories will serve as a basis for a political obligation depending on the assumption of freely given, informed consent. She also finds it curious how little attention has been given to Rousseau's reasons for rejecting the liberal contract theory.[28]

I shall leave aside here the massive evidence invalidating the allegedly democratic mandate, following elections, as the basis for a moral obligation to obey the government and its legislation, no matter how carefully constitutional procedures are observed, and no matter how in-corruptible our political leaders may be. It should be enough to men-tion a few of the difficulties with hoping to achieve democratic power-sharing in the modern state: think of 'the iron law of oligarchy';[29] of un-equal access to political knowledge;[30] of the massive extent of political passivity, as documented above all in the United States;[31] of power-élite analysis;[32] or of Marxism's and critical theory's evidence of economic and ideological class oppression.[33]

For the purposes of this paper it would be redundant to discuss these various sources of reasons for rejecting the liberal-democratic basis for political obligation because I reject a prior premise: the assumption that majorities have a moral right to prevail on all major contested political issues. I consider majoritarianism a practical and morally acceptable ap-proach to resolving political conflicts only on *democratic issues*;[34] that is, on issues involving competing wants, desires, preferences, interests, etc. Within this wide realm it is indeed imperative to work to improve on, and to preserve, respect, and apply, democratic principles and pro-cedures. But on *human-rights issues* each conscientious citizen should be bound to question majority views and be sure to side with victims of oppression, if there are victims, or with anticipated victims, of a given choice of policy if the majority are to have their way.

The human-rights concepts, theories, and practices now prevailing are not as suitable as they might be for the purpose of distinguishing hu-man-rights issues from democratic issues. This should come as no sur-prise, for specific human-rights claims have evolved historically, as most institutions have, according to politically practical opportunities. Rights claims gathered momentum with the North American State and Federal Bills of Rights around the time of the War of Independence, and in Eu-rope following the French Revolution's Declaration of the Rights of Man and Citizen. And in our own century, especially the second half of it, the emergence of the United Nations and its various human-rights-related global and regional agencies have made a lot of difference, most of it very gratifying, even if, as we might expect, human-rights issues sometimes have been pushed for Cold War purposes rather than for the sake of coming to the aid of victims. New categories of human rights have been proclaimed from time to time, which is to be welcomed in principle, although one human-rights scholar has issued a timely call for 'quality control' of new rights claims, and for restricting mainly to the General Assembly and the World Court and the International Labour Organization the role of adopting United Nations-supported expansions of international human-rights law.[35]

With this new global expansion of human-rights law, and with new in-ternational agencies to press its claims, there will be relatively less at-tention paid to national constitutions and jurisprudence in guiding the World Court and other international agencies supporting human rights.

There will be more influence going the other way as nations attempt to make their national institutions comply more fully with the rules imposed by membership in international agencies. The architects and engineers and the users of the new Canadian Charter of Rights and Freedoms have been and will be paying close attention to the responsibilities inherent in Canada's membership in the United Nations and some of its agencies concerned with human rights.

The one improvement in Canadian and international human-rights law and policies that is most needed, in my judgement, is one that will ultimately place the roots of our political obligation where they belong: in the morally compelling linkage of human-rights priorities with the priorities among the categories of basic human needs. Such a development will allow us some guidance for the purpose of clarifying and justifying the scope and limits of politically responsible and effective civil disobedience—for example, in Canada—with attention to the inner as well as the outer limits of such actions and strategies.

Let me now propose the following definition of 'human right' as a global concept: any entitlement or immunity that must be protected for each and every human being *because* a basic human need will otherwise be in jeopardy.

What are the most basic and general principles of human needs, and what are some of the corresponding categories of human rights, in what order? My answers must be tentative and hypothetical rather than final, though more so with respect to human-rights categories than with respect to the four very broad categories I shall propose for the ordering of human needs. (1) There will hardly be controversy over what I shall call the most basic of all human needs: our stake in collective survival and basic health requirements, like the need of access to non-toxic air, water and nutrition, or protection from nuclear/chemical war; collective needs are individual needs as well. To face individual death with courage and peace of mind is possible; to face the imminence of what Jonathan Schell has called 'the second death' of universal human extinction[36] must be infinitely worse. The most basic human right, I propose, must be the right to optimal protection against ecocide, genocide, nuclear or chemical/bacteriological warfare, and/or mass starvation. How to build respect and universal protection for this first order of human rights raises complex empirical and even conceptual issues, especially when we contemplate that some of the most vulnerable populations will be the future generations and the most defenceless of the now barely surviving forest-dwelling indigenous peoples.[37] (2) Next, surely, we must assume a priority for every individual's and family's own survival need and basic health- and safety-protection needs. Some may be self-sacrificing heroes, but it does not follow that they should be entitled to sacrifice other people's lives without their genuine consent, no matter for what cause. But the implications for priorities of human-rights protection relative to this second level of needs are complex, particularly when we contemplate the issues of national defence and of police protection against such threats as major crimes, and how to prevent and, if necessary, combat terrorism. The most relevant categories of human rights probably should include the following: the right to police protection against murderous crime, including torture; the right to demand that the government pursue peace-building policies with regard to global and regional security as well as to the security of one's own nation; the right of access to the best possible health services and to protection against homelessness and destitution.

The above are all in a sense basic physical needs, of humans as biological beings. Next come (3) the basic needs of men, women, and children as *social* human beings. Needs for dignity, solidarity, self-respect, for example, must be treated with 'equal concern and respect'.[38] The most relevant rights here presumably include the right to protection against racist and sexist discrimination; the right to 'due process of law'; and the right to citizenship and access to critical political knowledge.

Finally, (4), there are the freedom and the growth and development needs of all men, women, and children as *individual* human beings. Examples of the most relevant rights would include the right to choice of education; the right to free speech; the right to sexual, cultural, and religious choice; the right to meaningful and ethically satisfying work and leisure; the right of access to the cultural heritage of one's own and other peoples; the right to personal property, within limits that allow all others to own comparable amounts and kinds of property; and, more generally, the right to exercise all liberties in ways that do not undercut the freedom rights or the other, even more basic rights of others, whether fellow-nationals or fellow human beings elsewhere on this Earth that we all share, and ought to share alike, in the spirit of equal concern and respect.

III   Civil disobedience: the inner limits

'While there are still men who disobey in the name of justice and decency, humanity is not enslaved.' This is how George Woodcock concluded his 1966 CBC lecture series on civil disobedience: 'When the duty to obey without question is accepted, that is the moment of freedom's death'.[39] 'What if everybody disobeyed?' someone is bound to ask, worrying that disobedience, if tolerated, may lead to a breakdown of the public order. The late Willmoore Kendall, as a matter of fact, in a provocative essay endorsed the prosecution, conviction, and subsequent execution of Socrates on precisely these grounds.[40] But for people who worry less about law and order and more about oppression and injustice, the opposite question may seem more urgent: 'What if everybody always obeyed?'.[41]

Not every act of disobedience of the law is political, of course, let alone civil. Let us here leave aside common crimes: the ordinary criminal prefers to break the law surreptitiously, hoping to make financial gains, to obtain access to illicit drugs, to get revenge, or to gain some other kind of private advantage. Let us also for the moment leave aside definitely *non*-civil political crimes, such as political assassinations, bombings, the taking of hostages, torture: acts that are definitely beyond the *outer* moral limits of civil disobedience.

My purpose in this section is to contribute to clarifying the *inner* limits of morally acceptable, or of morally necessary, acts or policies of civil disobedience: where should we draw the line between issues and situations of injustice that justify protests and opposition only within the constraints of the law, and issues and situations that justify, or perhaps even require, a search for the most effective strategy of civil disobedience? This enquiry will endeavour to show what difference it makes when we work within a conception of political obligation founded in a theory of needs-based human rights, as distinct from the most common liberal conceptions of political obligation based on some theory of a tacitly accepted social contract.

Socrates, as his thought is interpreted by Plato, contributes the earliest version of what we today may call the liberal-contract conception as a tacit understanding between citizen and city. In the *Crito* Socrates explains to his friends and would-be rescuers why he thinks that he owes his life to the City that, even more crucially than his parents, has nurtured him as a person and as a civilized citizen. He would betray his City, he asserts, were he to flee now, even though he is about to be executed in a blatant miscarriage of justice.

Locke's contract, as we have seen, elaborates on the Socratic notion of 'tacit consent', reaffirmed by each new generation of citizens, although Locke at the same time allows for the possibility of morally legitimate resistance against a regime indulging in tyrannical acts. But I believe that Locke, had he been in Socrates' place, would have been happy to flee. A leading contemporary liberal theorist, Richard E. Flatham, returns to and indeed endorses the Socratic argument to the effect that a civil disobedient must, morally speaking, 'willingly submit to the penalty that is assigned'; and in this context he quotes with approval a statement by Martin Luther King, Jr, to the effect that a willing acceptance of penalties 'distinguishes . . . civil disobedience from the "uncivil disobedience" of the segregationist . . . [the civil disobedient who willingly accepts the penalty] . . . gives evidence thereby that he so respects that [unjust] law that he belongs in jail until it is changed'.[42]

John Rawls in his influential *A Theory of Justice* adopts another liberal definition of civil disobedience: 'a public, nonviolent, conscientious yet political act contrary to law usually done with the aim of bringing about a change in the law or policies of the government'.[43] He further stipulates (1) that the law that is disobeyed need not be the same one that is attacked as unjust;[44] (2) that the law attacked as unjust may or may not be upheld in the courts;[45] (3) that civil-disobedient activists must be motivated by some shared conception of justice, not solely by self- or group interest;[46] (4) that civil-disobedient acts must be public acts, addressed to the public and visibly in the public domain;[47] and (5) that the acts must be nonviolent.[48] Last but not least, (6) Rawls chooses to distinguish civil disobedience from 'conscientious refusal' (that is, non-compliance with legal orders): for example, conscientious refusal of military service, in countries where such refusal violates the law.[49]

Even with this uncommonly narrow conception of civil disobedience (hereafter, CD), Rawls stipulates that, to be morally justified, CD must be directed to instances of 'substantial and clear injustice' and must be exercised as 'a last resort'.[50] He does indeed worry that overuse of CD may break down respect for the law and the Constitution, and also, surprisingly, may become less effective; he advises dissenting minorities in their own interest to adopt agreements 'to regulate [limit] the overall level of dissent'.[51]

Rawls constricts morally acceptable CD so considerably because his political theory is ultimately *goal*-based:[52] his commanding First Principle of 'justice for institutions' is to seek to achieve, as an equal right for every person, 'the most extensive total system of equal basic liberties compatible with a similar system of liberty for all'.[53] Furthermore, he posits a 'natural duty of justice . . . to support and to further' political and legal institutions that implement his principles of justice.[54] While Rawls uses individual-rights language in stating his First Principle, he speaks of rights in an abstract sense, separated from conceptions of need-priorities.[55]

Another contemporary writer on CD, whose political and legal theory is *rights*-based, is, as we should expect, much more receptive to expanding uses of CD: for Ronald Dworkin, 'taking rights seriously' should be the first concern not only of political morality but of jurisprudence and Constitutional law as well. Not only does he favour the kind of 'constructivist jurisprudence' that endeavours to gradually widen legal protection in American courts for morally but hitherto not yet legally acceptable acts of CD;[56] he also urges non-prosecution to be considered in cases where CD was attempted for morally defensible reasons that could not be sustained legally.[57]

The law, writes Dworkin,

> must state, in its greatest part, the majority's view of the common good. The institution of rights is therefore crucial, because it represents the majority's promise to the minorities that their dignity and equality will be respected. . . . The Government will not re-establish respect for law without giving the law some claim to respect. It cannot do that if it neglects the one feature that distinguishes law from ordered brutality. If the

Government does not take rights seriously, then it does not take law seriously either.[58]

Dworkin too, however, draws the inner limits of CD too tightly, in my view. As a jurist he is concerned with humanizing the law, and especially with humanizing authoritative conceptions of individual legal rights. While he wants the law and legal rights to be brought closer to the dictates of a humanist morality, he is first of all concerned with convincing other jurists, as well as politicians and citizens generally, that the law must accommodate expanding conceptions of moral rights, but in a slow process that avoids ruptures, when possible, with recent legal precedents. But my disagreement on this issue is minor; I would worry a little less about possible ruptures with recent precedents and a little more about reaching morally satisfactory verdicts in each new case, for it should be the task of critical students of jurisprudence to persuade legal scholars and citizens at large that any court's morally flawed verdict should be given a weak status indeed as a precedent for future verdicts.

Second, and more important, Dworkin tends to treat all the various kinds of individual constitutional rights equally as 'trumps',[59] without the kinds of general priority principles that can be discussed or applied when rights-claims are based on relative urgencies of the categories of human needs at stake. The most basic individual right, the one that is more basic than all the rest, Dworkin stipulates, is 'the right to equal concern and respect';[60] a civil right to human dignity, I would paraphrase. But Dworkin does not discuss universal human rights, rights that in principle generate valid moral claims in all countries. The vast disparities in social and economic power within North America become within the global context even more extreme, and should prompt us to ask whether we as concerned citizens of Canada or the United States should not have a right to curb the freedom and power of our giant corporations: to insist that they operate with open books, have public-interest advocates (including environmentalists) on their boards, and be heavily taxed and/or be compelled to share their wealth with, for example, the populations they have displaced, or compelled as past polluters to pay full clean-up costs. Until some of this happens, I would question whether Dworkin's basic right to 'equal concern and respect' should apply to all our corporate executives or to political leaders who help them to hide their crimes against nature and against the health and well-being of present and future human victims of their irresponsibility. This is not an argument against Dworkin's theory of legal rights but a plea that we worry also about the basic human needs and rights beyond Dworkin's legal advocacy on priorities among North American and British legal rights. Perhaps I should add that corporate executives, too, must be deemed innocent until proven guilty.

Respect for 'the Law' and for legally constituted authorities, courts included, is highly desirable whenever such respect is even to a modest degree deserved, as in Canada—especially for members of a generation that has witnessed the Holocaust (even if at a relatively safe distance) and the bombing of open cities, and that at this time observes apparently rising levels of individual and state terrorism in several parts of the world.

For citizens of countries that aspire to democracy and the rule of law there are at least three ways of relating to issues of law and moral/political obligation, which I shall call—with apologies to all three philosophers for vast oversimplifications—Hobbesian, Lockean, and Rousseauian orientations. The first two are in the liberal tradition; the third I like to call rational-humanist; in my view it transcends the liberal tradition.

Hobbesian citizenship practises the maxim that for practical purposes the government is always right. Our taxes are paid as protection-money, and protected we will be, as long as we obey the laws and legal orders as a matter of course. Physical security is the most crucial human need and, except in wartime, it is what we get from the government. Lockean citizenship amounts to another kind of perceived, tacit 'deal': in return for the loyalty of the citizenry, the government promises to protect everybody's liberties and properties according to principles of justice. The Lockean orientation assumes a measure of mutual obligation, as we have seen; if the government violates the rights of citizens, the latter are entitled to disobey or even resist with force, if necessary as a last resort.

How do citizens become Hobbesians or Lockeans? Though they use different terms, Kelman and Lawrence have suggested a part of the answer in their empirical study of the American public's reactions to Lt William Calley's conviction for his part in the March 1968 My Lai massacre in Vietnam.[61] The Hobbesian respondents in their national sample tended to be low in educational attainment and in socio-economic status, and they tended to empathize with Lt Calley as a perceived scapegoat, a low man on the totem pole who had no real choice but to follow orders. The Lockeans (as I call them), who proportionally were better educated and enjoyed higher social status, tended to condemn Calley on the grounds that they thought every citizen should be true to moral principles first of all, and obey the government and other authorities only when the latter would not violate their principles. As free men and women, they felt, we are personally responsible for all our acts, including acts that we are ordered to do.

What about the third orientation to citizenship, which I name after Rousseau?

IV Civil disobedience: the outer limits

There are many ways of reading Rousseau, and my task in this paper is not to try to reconstruct the 'real' Rousseau (or the 'real' Hobbes, or Locke, etc.). Rather, I want to take from Rousseau two or three basic insights that bear on my own conception of the advanced category of citizenship that I call rational-humanist.

Unlike Hobbes, Locke, and most later liberal writers, who conceived of human nature as aggressively, competitively individualist,[62] Rousseau ascribed narrowly selfish and callous human behaviour to *society's* corrupting influence, worsening with advancing civilization and increasing social inequality. Rousseau thought that *compassion* was a 'natural' human virtue, with its beginnings already in the state of nature: 'a disposition suitable to creatures so weak and subject to so many evils as we certainly are. . . .'[63]

Rousseau's humanism was rational in the sense that he drew a contrast between a rational 'general will', on which any republic's sovereignty would depend, and the 'will of all', coming out of liberal processes of political competition and bargaining between contending private and sectional interests. The general will of the 'body politic', writes Rousseau in his 'Discourse on Political Economy', 'tends always to the preservation of the whole and of every part'.[64] He also has a vision of a rational-humanist world order: 'the great city of the world becomes the body politic, whose general will is always the law of nature, and of which the different States and peoples are individual members'[65]—the law of nature not in the sense of the law of the jungle, of course, but in the sense of the dictates and principles of emancipated human reason.

I assume in this paper that political progress in my country, and in the world, consists in moving away, as far and as fast as we can, from the conditions of the jungle. To put it in positive terms, the overall task is to expand and strengthen the protection of human lives, well-being, and liberties, always with priority for those who are worse off under existing conditions. Let us call this the human-rights approach to political emancipation.

Alternatively, there is the liberal-democratic approach, highly favoured in Washington in the waning years of the Reagan administration, but which been around for some time, and is incorporated in the Charter of the North Atlantic Treaty Organization. President Wilson declared on many occasions that the intent of American participation in the (First) World War was 'to make the world safe for democracy'.

As we have learnt, democracy is no panacea, if indeed it is of any help at all in the struggle to reduce violence or to ease the extremes of world poverty. Parliamentary and congressional democracy in countries

like the US, the UK, France, and Israel may have been serving the relatively affluent classes reasonably well, but it has done little for protecting the 'green' and the 'red' human rights (as distinct from the 'blue'
civil liberties): for example, the rights to breathe clean air every day
and to have easy access to uncontaminated water supplies; or the rights
to adequate and affordable nutrition and housing, and to meaningful
employment or self-employment.

Moreover, and often in the name of democracy or human rights,
Americans and Israelis have been saddled with foreign policies that are
contemptuous of other nations' right to live in peace with their neigh-
bours; in addition, Americans specifically have been saddled with (and
many citizens have cheerfully accepted) secretive intelligence agencies
(so-called) engaged in assassination plots and subventions to hired mercenaries in efforts to overthrow foreign governments that allegedly have
been too friendly with the Soviet Union. The Third World's poor are
continually getting the message, in word and deed, that their sufferings
without end are deplored in Washington but that they will be severely
punished if they try to seek relief by way of a socialist revolution. Even
the still (1988) widely popular President Corazon Aquino of the Philippines remains apparently powerless to institute any land-reform program that could convince impoverished peasants that there is hope for
them anywhere but in the Communist Party and the New People's
Army.

Canada is a part of this violent world, and a partner, even a military
supplier, to the biggest military superpower, the biggest bully on our
side of the fence. To me this raises some moral and political issues concerning the outer limits of civil disobedience in this country. Can we
without injustice claim that largely non-violent CD represents the outer
limits to what we as Canadians or as global citizens (in spirit) can do, or
must do, to resist Canadian complicity with present or future US plans
of military, or even nuclear, blackmail against insubordinate foreign
nations?

Deliberate lethal acts of violence against human beings would have to
be the very last resort, even in times of war when we are expected to kill
for our country. Physical violence is the extreme evil that we associate
with the terms of life in the jungle, or in Hobbes's state of nature. Albert Camus eloquently rules out all justifications for complicity in murder, but then turns around and allows for exceptions: in occupied
France, if a collaborator is on his way to Gestapo with a list of names of
Resistance-fighters, then it may be necessary to kill him.[66]

But in times of peace, in relatively non-violent countries like
Canada? We are nowhere near the point, I believe, where uncivil disobedience can be justified. For one thing, political education and democratic participation have not been mobilized to the extent possible, and
we have seen only the bare beginnings of non-violent civil disobedience

so far (Greenpeace has been in the frontline, both in Canada and abroad). The better we learn how to creatively and persuasively demonstrate the strength of our moral concerns, without violence, the further into the future the issue of violent resistance will recede as a practical, let alone a moral, option.

Yet we should avoid easy oversimplification of the issues of violence. With Johan Galtung[67] we should stress the enormous costs in human lives and health that are incurred by the so-called *structural* violence in today's world. There is not only the nuclear-arms race, with all its costs and risks; there is also the weight of an international economic system that breeds opulence and callousness at the top of the social pyramids, and desperate deprivation and hopelessness at the bottom.

For example, consider the following glimpse of the real world, Anno 1987:

> UNICEF estimates that of the 14 million deaths annually of children under the age of five, half could be prevented by implementing low-cost solutions now readily available. At an average cost of $5, for example, a child can be vaccinated against six deadly diseases. Immunization for all those not now protected would save 3.5 million lives a year. To achieve this goal by 1990, UNESCO estimates that only $300 million a year would be needed from external sources. This is less than the cost of 3 hours of world military expenditures at present.[68]

On the whole, though not entirely, Canada has so far escaped the kinds of violent dissent that in less fortunate countries have turned the daily lives of ordinary people into recurring nightmares. The closest thing to a terrorist organization in Canada was the FLQ in Québec, with its plastic bombs and 1970 kidnapping and murder of Pierre Laporte. What ended popular support for the FLQ, it appears, was not the use of the War Measures Act but the emergence of a credible *political* strategy for those who wanted an independent Québec, with the Parti Québécois.[69]

Let us hope that in this country we will continue to settle our differences largely by non-violent political and legal means. Our hopes of achieving this will depend, I believe, on what happens elsewhere in the world, and on how well we come to understand the roots of terrorism and of revolutionary movements in other parts of the world.

We need to become more actively involved—as a nation, as members of non-governmental organizations, and as individual citizens—in efforts to build a safer world; that is to say, a less militarist and a more ecologically and socio-economically safe world. The global public interest, including Canada's, surely is best served by citizenries that abhor all kinds of deliberate uses of physical violence but *abhor equally* the conditions of extreme social or international injustice that breed despair and hatred. This is what my conception of Rousseau-inspired, rational-humanist citizenship is about.

Towards this end we must come to demand from our mass media the insight and the candour to report that some 'friendly governments' in several parts of the world are at present at least as guilty of terrorism as are their boldest, most violent opponents. We must learn to object more strenuously when Canadians or Americans are so quick to damn alleged human rights violations in countries they dislike and so slow to condemn Washington's use of mercenaries to inflict bloodshed on civilians in countries whose governments are deemed hostile (and no wonder!) to the United States.

In conclusion, let us consider whether or not our Canadian Charter of Rights and Freedoms can become an instrument for advancing our understanding, as citizens of Canada and the world, of how to strengthen the prospects for a safer and more just world: for an evolving world order of needs-based human rights.

V A postscript on the Canadian Charter

Unlike the United States Bill of Rights, which is relegated to the place of Amendments to the US Constitution, the Canadian Charter of Rights and Freedoms takes pride of place as the first of the seven parts of the Canadian Constitution, and by far the lengthiest one. Nonetheless, the impact of the US Bill of Rights, for good and for ill, has been and remains highly consequential for the division of powers and for protecting individual and corporate interests and needs south of the border; the Amendments have in this sense been like the tail wagging the dog.

Writing in 1985, Peter Russell surveys 'The First Three Years in Charterland' and finds that, for one thing, the Charter has stimulated a lot of additional employment for the legal profession, but that it is as yet uncertain whether the flood of new litigation will substantially change either the liberties of Canadian citizens or the real division of powers between the federal judiciary and the federal and/or provincial legislative or executive powers; indeed, Russell suggests that 'the Charter of Rights may be having its most significant but most inscrutable impact on the thinking of citizens'.[70] He concludes that it 'will take a generation or more' for the enduring impact of the Charter to be felt.[71]

Among the various organized interest groups that have attempted to litigate with Charter-based claims, with mixed but, for some, not too discouraging results, labour unions appear to have done less well, Russell suggests, and they 'may be beginning to question the value of the Charter'.[72] By way of contrast, though with the benefit of a bit of hindsight, David M. Beatty argues that the rights of labour and of individual workers are likely to make gains as a result of the Charter.[73]

Beatty sees the prospect for co-operative as well as adversarial relationships' developing between the courts and the legislatures on labour-code issues. He expects that cool and cogent legal affidavits prepared for the courts will exert a moderating influence on the partisan political debates; he also anticipates a desire on the part of legislators to avoid seeing their own enactments subsequently invalidated by judicial review.

He further assumes, and on this point I agree with him, that rights-claims based on the human needs of working people add up to a morally stronger case, more often than not, than rights-claims based on corporate interests on the other side.[73] The same goes for the claims of other disadvantaged groups or individuals, in proportion to their status of being in fact underprivileged. That conclusion is sustained by my own attempt, above, to link human-rights priorities with categories of more basic and less basic human needs. I am less optimistic, however, than Beatty appears to be about whether most Canadian judges, legislators, and citizens, generally speaking, can be trusted to stick with the just cause whenever they are confronted with interest-based claims advanced by high-priced lawyers and public-relations experts. I hope, of course, that I am wrong on this issue.

But that depends on whether enough Canadians can mobilize the political will to challenge the political system to take the universality of basic human needs and of needs-based human rights seriously. That means being ready to resort to active civil disobedience, if prudent, when miscarriages of justice occur, and more so when they have become entrenched.

This readiness to prepare for and practise civil disobedience in support of basic rights, with sufficient political will and social awareness, will also have to be applied in efforts towards reducing global injustice, and injustice towards future generations. Whether the Charter will help or hinder such a broadening of the concern of Canadians with human rights, and the requisite strengthening of our political will, remains to be seen.

The likelihood of and the need for civil disobedience in Canada will depend less on Charter-based arguments in the courts than on whether the courts and other branches of government adopt a shared needs-based scheme of priorities for determining which rights-claims are to prevail over competing rights-claims, and on whether it is generally understood, in all three branches of government and in the media, that policy issues always must yield to human-rights issues. Corporations do not have human needs; instead they have interests and demands, many of which have legal protection. That protection should as a matter of public policy always be subject to the conditions that the government deems to be in the public interest. For example, there should be a requirement of open books, available for anyone's inspection; not only should fiscal matters be fully revealed, but there should also be clear and complete data on what any industry takes from and releases into the environment, and what is done each time to protect every person's right (including the right of future persons) to breathe clean air and to drink uncontaminated water. Conflicting *interests* are to be regulated by statutes that reflect democratically based policy preferences, just as conflicting *needs* are to be adjudicated in the courts, unless reconciled informally by genuinely mutual consent or settled by way of progressive legislation.

The ideal Supreme Court judge should be a moral philosopher and a political scientist as well as a jurist. He or she should be looking forward as well as backward: backward, so that the weight of the morally acceptable precedents validates expectations about the current substance of the law as realistic (a constitutional requirement in most countries for criminal law); forward, so that the courts will make sure that future consequences of court decisions are seen to serve the public interest as a secondary concern, after first making sure that the individual human rights at stake have been fully protected.

The Concept of Subversion
and its Implications

ELIZABETH GRACE AND
COLIN LEYS

> National socialism had created a new type of political criminal:
> criminals who had not committed a crime . . . the charge against
> them was not that they actually had distributed political leaflets or
> joined underground parties, but that one day they might.
> —Vasily Grossman, *Life and Fate*[1]

Introduction

The concept of subversion belongs to a succession of concepts associated with the development of the modern state. These concepts, including 'sedition', 'treason', 'subversion', and, recently, 'terrorism', have performed an essentially unchanging function: to delegitimize activities and ideas opposed to the established order, and hence to legitimize the state in acting against them, even though the activities are lawful. The central mechanism of this delegitimization is to portray internal opposition as somehow linked to, and actually or potentially an extension of, an external enemy. The emergence of the liberal-democratic state, which greatly extended the sphere of lawful dissent by affirming a wide range of civil rights and liberties, placed a heavy burden on this mechanism. The concept of subversion met the challenge because of the comprehensive ideology of anti-communism to which it belongs. This ideology, developed most fully in the United States from the 1920s onwards, linked internal dissent to the threat of world communist revolution. With the partial exhaustion of Cold War ideology, the concept of 'terrorism', linking internal dissent to foreign military struggles to which the state is opposed, or to possible threats of violence to the country's individual citizens, whether at home or abroad, has taken up some of the slack.

Many writers on subversion have complained that the term refers to a 'grey area' and is difficult to define.[2] Our view is that it has always referred to a fairly clear reality: legal activities and ideas directed against the existing social, economic and political order (and very seldom against 'democracy', as liberal-democratic states are wont to claim). Any radical activity or idea with the potential to enlist significant popular support may be labelled 'subversive'; the effect of so labelling it is to declare that such an activity or idea aims, directly or indirectly, at the overthrow (by implication, violent) of democracy, and/or that it uses or envisages undemocratic means, and/or that it is 'covert' (in this context, a pejorative term for activities that are entitled to be private, but that the state wants to know about).

There is no question that groups and movements have at various times and places had such aims. But even in the most liberal democracies the law has always made it a criminal offence to use or plan the use of force to achieve political ends, and the police have always had the duty and the powers to prevent such crimes. It is not, therefore, to prevent such activities that the concept of subversion is really needed. It is invoked, rather, in order to *create* a 'grey area' of activities that *are* lawful, but that will be denied protection from state surveillance or harassment by being *declared* illegitimate, on the grounds that they *potentially* have unlawful consequences. In capitalist societies the targets of this delegitimization have been overwhelmingly on the left.

As for the definition of subversion, the difficulty is not in giving it a definition, but that the definitions given conflict with the principles of liberal democracy. Moreover, once the concept is admitted into the law, few if any effective limits can be placed on the 'counter-subversion' activities of the state. This effect is due to the covert nature of such activities, which permits them to be concealed from the elected branch of the state; to the ideology and ethos of security services; and to the necessary vagueness of the language in which the 'counter-subversion' mandate is expressed. State security agencies invariably take a broad view of their mandates. As a result they interest themselves not merely in 'subversive activity' but also in 'potential subversion'; in 'subversives' (i.e., people considered to be engaging in subversive activities, or thought liable to do); in 'subversive' beliefs and attitudes (the holding of which is seen as making one liable to engage in subversive activities); and so on. 'Safeguards' against abuse by security services, such as those adopted in Canada, are valuable and should be strengthened; but the concept of subversion should be removed from the law.

The origins of the modern concept of subversion

Although the early modern state relied primarily on the concepts of treason and sedition, rather than subversion, the language and the ultimate objectives of the treason and sedition laws of England, the United States, and Canada are remarkably similar to the few official definitions of subversion that exist, and to certain recent uses of the term 'terrorism'.[3]

In medieval England, 'treason' most commonly referred to armed attack against the government, but as monarchs increasingly sought absolute power, vague and more repressive uses of the concept were evolved. For example, some of the judicial extensions of the English

Treason Act of 1351 expanded the notion of 'levying war' to comprise riots, and extended the possibility of 'compass[ing] the King's death' to include cases where the King was very clearly in no personal danger.[4] In Canada s.46(2)(a) of the Criminal Code defines using 'force or violence for the purpose of overthrowing the government of Canada or a province' as treason, while s.46(2)(d) provides that everyone commits treason who 'forms an intention' to engage in certain treasonable activities and 'manifests that intention by an overt act' (the overt-act requirement can be satisfied simply by 'open and considered speech').

As England's treason laws became an overly cumbersome instrument of repression, the more subtle and far-reaching concept of 'seditious libel' was created under the Stuarts in the early seventeenth century. Reacting to the invention of the printing press, the Crown's primary aim was to prohibit the publication of discordant opinions.[5] By the 1790s the offence of seditious libel was being employed in England and the United States to discourage the kinds of revolutionary impulses that had culminated in the 1789 revolution in France.[6] Later, in the nineteenth century, the charge of 'seditious conspiracy' was used in the United Kingdom against Chartist and Irish activists.

Section 62 of the Canadian Criminal Code describes three separate sedition offences: first, speaking 'seditious words'; second, publishing 'a seditious libel'; and third, being a 'party to a seditious conspiracy'. Although 'seditious intent' must be proven, this goes undefined in the Code (as we shall see, this emphasis on intentions and goals is also central to the concept of subversion). Even the qualification that no one is to be deemed to have seditious intention by reason only that he or she 'in good faith' criticized the government, or attempted to procure 'by lawful means' the alteration of any matter of government, has proven dispensable: in the heat of the 1919 Winnipeg General Strike, it was struck from the books and was not restored until 1930.

The period following the Russian Revolution of 1917 and the Winnipeg Strike provides valuable insight into the way the charge of 'sedition', like that of subversion in the years that followed, was used as a tool of political repression by the state against radicals on the left. For example, the notorious s.98 of the Canadian Criminal Code enacted in 1919 made it an offence to 'become and continue to be a member' of a seditious or unlawful association, which was defined as

> one . . . whose purpose is to bring about any governmental, industrial, or economic change within Canada by use of force, violence or physical injury to person or property, or by threats of such injury, or which teaches, advocates, advises or defends the use of force, violence, terrorism, or physical injury to person or property, or threats of such injury, in order to accomplish such change.[7]

In the *Rex* v. *Russell* case, the judge summed up what he saw to be the seditious intentions of the strike leaders as

> revolution, the overthrow of the existing form of government in Canada and the introduction of a form of Socialistic or Soviet rule in its place. This was to be accomplished by general strikes, force and terror and, if necessary, by bloodshed.[8]

Thus, on the basis of alleged or even imputed intentions, eight individuals were prosecuted under the sedition provisions for their roles in the Winnipeg strike and six were convicted and sentenced.

Unlike treason and sedition, the word 'subversion' appears to have entered Western colloquial speech fairly recently:[9] that is, after charges of treason and sedition had proven to be dated and unwieldy instruments of political repression in the period of heightened political consciousness and radicalism following the Russian Revolution and during the Depression of the 1930s. The case of the Canadian Communist Party illustrates the unsatisfactory nature of the concept of sedition from the state's point of view: although the Party was declared to be an 'unlawful association' under s.98 of the Criminal Code, its characterization as an association 'whose purpose is to bring about any governmental, industrial or economic change within Canada by use of force, violence or physical injury' was not, strictly speaking, accurate. Sharing the catastrophism of the Comintern, the Party believed that the collapse of capitalism was inevitable and would necessarily be accompanied by violence, whether through crisis-inspired war or through the resort to violence by capital. The Party did not, however, advocate violent methods *per se* to achieve its goals.[10]

Since the era of 'détente' and Eurocommunism, when the ideology of anti-communism lost some of its potency, we have seen the concept of 'terrorism' beginning to be used to achieve results similar to those produced by its predecessors treason, sedition, and subversion. For example, the FBI has restructured its domestic intelligence operations into a new Domestic 'Security-Terrorism' Section of its Criminal Investigative Division, and in 1981 President Reagan pardoned two former FBI officials who planned and supervised unwarranted break-ins during the 1970s on the basis that they were 'men who acted on high principles to bring an end to terrorism that was threatening our nation . . . their actions were necessary to preserve the security interests of our country'.[11] Richard Kobetsky, director of behavioural research for the International Association of Chiefs of Police in the US, has argued that counter-terrorism is 'one of the fastest growing businesses in the country . . . a cash-in opportunity'.[12]

What is noteworthy about 'terrorism' is not only that it once again invokes a link between an external enemy and the 'enemy within', but also that it extends the alleged threat from one to the state to one affecting individual citizens (as air travellers, tourists, etc.), and as a result is likely to be more directly effective in securing the required delegitimization of whatever activities and ideas are successfully labelled as 'terrorist'.

Thus treason, sedition, subversion, and, more recently, terrorism should be seen as forming a continuum of terms whose purpose is to label as a threat to the existing order dissenting political views and the activities to which these views give rise, and *as such* earmark them for state repression. What differentiates these concepts from one another is essentially the historical context in which each has arisen.

The concept of 'subversion' in the United States

The American experience is important to Canadians for at least two reasons. First, the elasticity of the concept of subversion is amply illustrated by the fact that in the United States virtually everything, from the Boy Scouts and Camp Fire Girls to the sexual act, has been described as 'subversive'.[13] Moreover, in the US *every* branch of the state has, at some point or another, joined in the crusade against 'subversives'—the FBI, the CIA, the National Security Agency (NSA), the Army, and the Internal Revenue Service; numerous legislative investigation committees such as the Subversive Activities Control Board; the courts; and even state and municipal governments. Second, because Canada's security service is a junior and very dependent member of a 'Western Intelligence Network' dominated by US values, methods, and policy preferences,[14] the history of subversion in Canada is closely linked to the US case.

Rogin dates the modern history of 'counter-subversion' in the US from the 'red scare' of 1873 to 1878. Responding to the Paris Commune of 1871, the serious economic depression, and labour unrest, city authorities built armouries to protect themselves against working-class uprisings, states revived their militias, and police attacked strikers and unemployed demonstrators. Shortly afterwards, the 1886 Chicago Haymarket Square trial—the first anti-red political trial of nationwide significance—saw eight anarchists convicted of conspiracy to commit a murder, even though none of them was connected with the bombing incident in question.[15]

A distinctive element of the practice of counter-subversion in the US is that in addition to despatching state militia and federal troops regularly to break strikes in the latter nineteenth and early twentieth centuries, the state also employed private corporations and detective agencies to survey radicals and union workers, and even to crush strikes and demonstrations by force.[16] In 1918 the Attorney General's office introduced (without congressional authorization) a General Intelligence Division (GID) of the FBI and placed J. Edgar Hoover at its helm. The GID, whose sole purpose was to infiltrate and collect information on radical organizations, played a central role in the two major 'counter-subversion' offensives of 1919 and 1920: the breaking of the steel strike and the rounding up of thousands of allegedly 'subversive foreigners' for deportation.

In 1924, fearing that the GID might be abusing its powers, Attorney General Harlan Stone abolished this special division and ordered the Bureau to limit its investigations to actual violations of the law. Stone's move was meant to break the FBI's ties with private detective agencies and to put an end to its dissemination of anti-radical propaganda, its undercover spying on labour and radical groups, and its illegal searches, seizures, and wiretapping, as well as its encouragement of anti-radical prosecutions by the state.[17] Theoharis, however, has shown how, on the basis of directives issued by President Roosevelt in 1936 and 1939, Hoover succeeded in convincing successive Presidents and Attorney Generals (from President Truman to Robert Kennedy) that the FBI had been entrusted with an open-ended intelligence mission against domestic subversion unrelated to its law-enforcement responsibilities.[18]

Certainly, by the late 1930s the concept of subversion had become the established, explicit rationale for state surveillance and repression of the left in the US. Thereafter, the history of the ever-expanding notion of subversion becomes a chronicle of repressive legislation and accompanying FBI excesses. Because American anti-communism and fear of 'subversion' have already been so well documented,[19] we shall merely identify some of the basic features of counter-subversion as it has been practised in the US from the late 1930s to the 1980s.

In 1938 the House of Representatives created the House Committee on Un-American Activities (HUAC) to investigate

> (1) the extent, character and objectives of un-American propaganda activities in the United States, (2) the diffusion within the United States of subversive and un-American propaganda that is instigated from foreign countries or of a domestic origin and attacks the principle of the form of government as guaranteed by the Constitution.[20]

This was followed in 1940 by the Aliens Registration, or Smith, Act, which made it illegal to

> knowingly or willfully advocate, abet, advise, or teach the duty, necessity, desirability or propriety of overthrowing or destroying any government in the United States by force or violence, or by the assassination of any officer of any such government.[21]

In addition, the Nationality Act of 1940 provided for the denaturalization of former alien 'communists' (that is, individuals who within the previous ten years had belonged to an organization advocating violent overthrow of government), and the Voorhis Act of 1940 called for the registration of all organizations intending the violent overthrow of any government.

During the infamous McCarthy years, from 1947 to 1954, the state's fear of subversion reached even greater heights. First, in 1947 Truman introduced a loyalty program making all present and prospective federal government employees undergo investigations of their loyalty to the United States and its government.[22] Second, a secret emergency detention program was formally instituted by the Attorney General in 1948 (although Hoover had seen to it that one had unofficially been in place since at least the early 1940s). As a result, Security Index Cards were prepared on communists and 'dangerous individuals' so that in the event of war with the Soviet Union, these persons could immediately be interned. Third, in 1950 the Internal Security, or McCarran, Act established the Subversive Activities Control Board (SACB) to decide whether a group was a 'Communist action', a 'Communist front', or a 'Communist-infiltrated' organization. Groups deemed to be any of these were required not only to file with the Department of Justice a list of their members and the sources of their funds, but to state in their publications and broadcasts that the SACB had made a finding against them. In addition, members of 'action' and 'front' organizations were refused American passports and, of course, employment with the government. Fourth, during the McCarthy period there were many congressional investigations of 'subversives'. Notorious examples include the HUAC, which continued to operate as before, McCarthy's own Subcommittee on Government Operations, and the Internal Security Subcommittee of the Senate Committee on the Judiciary.

The next major 'red scare' in the US occurred from 1967 to 1971 when, in response to anti-war and student protests and urban black ghetto demonstrations, Presidents Johnson and then Nixon directed various government agencies to search out 'communist' and 'foreign influence' in these movements. Apparently it was during this period that the CIA developed its illegal domestic surveillance network. As for the FBI, it expanded its surveillance techniques, infiltrated campuses, planted informers, obtained access to confidential files with the collusion of people such as university administrators, and extended its aggressive and unauthorized 1956 'counter-intelligence' program (COINTELPRO) of disruption and harassment against the remnants of the CP-USA to socialist, new left, black, and (marginally) 'white hate' groups.

In the immediate post-Watergate era several enquiries were undertaken to assess the implications of an unlimited secret domestic intelligence agency for a liberal-democratic nation, and to make recommendations on how to rein in the FBI. In the course of these investigations the extent of the FBI's massive surveillance and countering of dissident political groups was exposed. Theoharis's chapter in this volume describes very clearly the subsequent limitations placed on the FBI by Attorney General Levi's guidelines of 1976 and Ford's and Carter's executive orders of 1976 and 1978 respectively, and the erosion to which these already limited reforms have been subjected by the Reagan administration.[23]

The concept of 'subversion' in Canada

Although the Canadian state never enacted anti-communist legislation comparable to the US Internal Security Act of 1950, and Cold War hysteria in Canada failed to reach the American extremes,[24] until the mid-1930s the state did, as we saw above, make use of extremely confining sedition laws. Moreover, in the Cold War period the Canadian government introduced one of the West's first security-screening programs for the Civil Service, and like the US made plans for the emergency detention of subversives (indeed, a list of persons to be detained in the event of a crisis is believed to be maintained to this day).

Canada's first security-intelligence organization, the Western Frontier Constabulary, was established in 1864 by John A. Macdonald to collect and report information on 'the existence of any plot, conspiracy or organization whereby peace would be endangered, the Queen's Majesty insulted, or her proclamation of neutrality infringed'.[25] Like the Special Branch in Britain, the Constabulary identified as its first targets the Fenians who were believed to be plotting an invasion of the British North American colonies from the United States. A few years later, Commissioners of the newly formed Dominion Police Force supervised a network of undercover agents operating on both sides of the Canadian-American border who provided intelligence reports about Fenian activities and used what became the customary methods of secret police—namely, infiltration, interception of mail, and the following of suspects. Although the Prime Minister gave instructions as to the kind of intelligence the government required, there was no statutory authorization for such intelligence-gathering activities.

In spite of the McDonald Report's claim that there was no 'sustained security intelligence programme' from the 1870s to World War 1, Fenians and anarchists were certainly the objects of surveillance during this time. It is also from this period that Canada's dependence on American intelligence appears to date. Confronted by rumours of American plots to annex the Yukon territory during the gold rush at the turn of the twentieth century, the Canadian government sought intelligence assistance from the American Pinkerton Detective Agency. Later, during the First World War, Canada's Dominion Police hired a number of secret agents from private American detective agencies to aid in preventive measures undertaken against espionage and sabotage.

As in the US and the UK, the years immediately following the Russian Revolution of 1917 proved decisive to the history of counter-subversion in Canada. Fearing that post-war labour unrest such as the Winnipeg General Strike was being nurtured by revolutionary international forces, the federal Cabinet directed the security agencies to look for 'foreign' connections. Consequently, both the Dominion Police and the Royal North-West Mounted Police carried out extensive undercover investigations of Winnipeg's labour movement. In 1920 the Dominion Police Force was merged with the Mounted Police in an effort to centralize and rationalize Canadian security intelligence. Thus, with both federal law-enforcement and intelligence responsibilities, the Royal Canadian Mounted Police (RCMP) became Canada's national police force. During both World Wars the central concerns of Canadian security intelligence included advising the government on the internment of 'enemy aliens' and the surveillance of anti-conscription movements in Québec such as the Jehovah's Witnesses and, of course, communists.

The 1945 Gouzenko revelations of a Soviet espionage network in Canada marked a turning point in the Canadian history of the concept of subversion. In 1946 the Canadian government initiated a program of security screening in the federal public service that was followed by the Americans in 1947 and the British in 1948. Under this program, the RCMP was put in charge of investigating the personal lives and political activities of people seeking certain kinds of government employment. Authorized by a series of Cabinet Directives, the RCMP originally concentrated on membership in or association with communist or fascist organizations, but over the years the criteria for denying a security clearance were extended to include 'separatist sympathies, associations and activities'. Ultimately, the RCMP's equation of separatism with terrorism culminated in 1973 in 'Operation Ham' (the theft and copying of the Parti Québécois membership lists by the RCMP).

With the RCMP operating under regulations stating merely that it was the duty of the force 'to maintain and operate such security and intelligence services as may be required by the Minister', it is hardly surprising that the history of its intelligence mandate was one of steady expansion. In 1936 an 'Intelligence Section' of the Criminal Intelligence Branch (CIB) was established at RCMP Headquarters in Ottawa; by 1970 this had grown into a separate 'Security Service' where intelligence-gathering and 'countering' were assigned to three branches, two of which concentrated on counter-intelligence activities against foreign intelligence agencies while the third, roughly equivalent in size to the two other branches combined, focussed on domestic subversion.

By 1968 it was evident that US Cold War paranoia had also gripped members of the Canadian establishment. The Mackenzie Commission of that year declared that

the forms of Communist subversive activity in Canada are varied, ranging from efforts to develop front organizations to attempts to subvert individuals in government, the mass media, the universities, the trade unions, émigré and ethnic groups and political parties. Such activities are assisted by the fact that the communists are able to exploit and exaggerate existing elements of social unrest and dissent concerned with a variety of appealing causes.[26]

Consequently, the Commissioners' recommendation that a new civilian agency be created outside the RCMP, 'to perform the functions of a Security Service in Canada', did not involve any notion of restricting the scope of domestic intelligence in Canada.

In any event, this new civilian agency failed to materialize, and the RCMP's Counter-Subversion Branch reacted to the rise in political activism in the 1960s and early 1970s by shifting the bulk of its attention away from communists and 'front' organizations and towards new political groups and movements such as 'new left' student radicals and members of ethnic organizations. Violations of the law and the rights of Canadians by the RCMP during these years were extensive. People were intimidated in an effort to make them become informers, confidential files of government departments such as the Department of National Revenue were used in order to build up dossiers on 'subversives', false information was disseminated to discredit and disrupt left-wing groups (e.g., false inflammatory communiques were issued in the name of the FLQ), the premises of left-wing groups were burgled, and mail was illegally opened (this had actually been occurring since 1954).[27]

In response to the much-publicized exposure of these crimes, the Québec Minister of Justice established the Keable Commission in 1977 to investigate the circumstances surrounding the break-in of the offices of the Agence Presse Libre du Québec (APLQ) and the Movement for Defence of Political Prisoners of Quebec (MDPPQ). The following month the federal government, at least in part to contain the damage likely to be done to the RCMP by a critical enquiry taking place in Québec, followed suit with the creation of a Commission of Inquiry Concerning Certain Activities of the Royal Canadian Mounted Police (the McDonald Commission). As we shall see, the findings and recommendations of the McDonald Commission were central to the passage of the Bill to Establish a Canadian Security Intelligence Service in June 1984.

Defining subversion

The historical record thus shows that the concept of subversion has functioned as a justification both for state surveillance of citizens opposed to the status quo, and for varying degrees of repression of their political activities. This can also be seen from an examination of the various attempts that have been made to define 'subversion'. These attempts are of two main kinds.

One comes either from security-service officers or from politicians responsible for or close to them. These definitions are always very wide. A good example is that of Merlyn Rees, the British Home Secretary, in 1978:

> subversive activities are generally regarded as those which threaten the safety or well-being of the state, and which are intended to undermine or overthrow parliamentary democracy by political, industrial or violent means.[28]

Such definitions, with their undefined catch-all words like 'well-being', give security services freedom to 'target' those who the security service believe are hostile to the existing system in virtually any way. Based on very loose definitions of this type, the activities of minority-rights and other single-interest groups of all kinds, not to mention radical political groups and organizations, have been the subject of 'intrusive' surveillance.

Furthermore, security services tend to broaden such 'official' definitions in practice. In the US, as Frank Donner notes,

> [i]ntelligence institutions have extended the boundaries of subversion, first by the application of notions of vicarious, imputed, and derived guilt; second, by a process of cross-fertilization, which proscribes an organization through the individuals associated with it and the individuals through their relationship to the organization; third, by increasing the number of condemned organizations because of parallel programs, mutual objectives, or overlapping leadership; and, fourth, by treating subversion as permanent, irreversible, and indeed hereditary.[29]

A manual of the Australian Security and Intelligence Organisation (ASIO) governing surveillance of MPs said that 'any development which tends to damage the social fabric advances the cause of those whose aim it is to overthrow the constitutional government';[30] and similar extensions by the RCMP Security Service were noted by the McDonald Commission.[31] Anyone who is familiar with the true scale of the membership (let alone the active membership) of 'far left' organizations in Canada can readily infer that the Canadian Security Intelligence Service (CSIS) has similarly expanded the scope of its authority from the fact that in 1986-87 its Counter-Subversion Branch had files on more than 30,000 people.[32] And as Desmond Ball notes, security services in general

> make no distinction between legitimate dissent and illegitimate dissent. If you look at the sorts of activities which have been monitored either by the FBI in the United States or the ASIO in Australia, or the RCMP in Canada, or the equivalent agency in New Zealand . . . [the] spectrum is really very broad indeed. . . They have no criteria for making a distinction between legitimate dissent and subversion.[33]

Ball doubted that any security service could ever be expected to make such a distinction, as CSIS is apparently supposed to do under section 2 of the CSIS Act, let alone a service that is so closely linked with other services that make no such distinction.[34]

The second kind of definition of subversion is to be found in legislation governing (or purporting to govern) security and intelligence agencies. These definitions seek to find grounds for abrogating the civil rights of particular groups or individuals while simultaneously asserting the values of liberal democracy on which those rights are based. The 1981 Report of the McDonald Commission on the RCMP, the 1982 Report of the Special Committee of the Senate on Bill C157 (the Pitfield Committee), and the CSIS Act of 1984 are all cases in point, as is the Australian Security and Intelligence Organization Act of 1979 (to which the Canadian debate frequently referred). These definitions try to distinguish illegitimate activities, or activities that are legal but whose goals are allegedly not, from all other forms of political activity, which are not to be spied or intruded upon. The 'illegitimate' means normally specified is violence or force, and the 'illegitimate' goal is the 'overthrow' of parliamentary democracy and its replacement by, it is implied (though not usually stated), an authoritarian or totalitarian form of government.[35]

But if the activity defined as 'illegitimate' must actually use violence, then the definition covers very few left activists, and in any case such activity is illegal and subject to the normal law-enforcement and prevention powers of the police. And since in reality very few people on the left explicitly or consciously advocate the introduction of an undemocratic form of government, such a goal has to be imputed. Consequently, the definition is usually widened by introducing the concept of (imputed or 'constructive') *intention*, and adding the vague concept of *undermining* alongside the concept of 'overthrowing'.

The definition of subversion in the CSIS Act is the outcome of a process of extension of this kind. The *word* 'subversion', which had been used in the 1975 Cabinet directive to the RCMP (the only formal basis ever provided for the RCMP's 'counter-subversion' activities), was dropped from the CSIS Act. The *concept*, however, remains, clearly formulated in Section 2 of the Act, which defines as one of four 'threats to the security of Canada' (the others being espionage, foreign influence, and terrorism) activities directed towards undermining by covert unlawful acts, or directed towards or intended ultimately to lead to the destruction or overthrow by violence of, the constitutionally established system of government in Canada; but which excludes 'lawful advocacy, protest or dissent', unless carried on in conjunction with such activities (or any of the others covered by the Act). CSIS itself routinely uses the word 'subversion' and until December 1987 had a Counter-Subversion Branch; and the Annual Reports of the Security and Intelligence Review Committee regularly refer to subversion as a proper concern of

CSIS.[36] The absence of the word from the Act is thus of no real significance; we are dealing with a legal definition of subversion.

Before discussing that definition in detail, we should first consider the implications of the fact that 'subversion' refers not to some present injury, but to a 'threat to the security of Canada'. The rationale for focussing on 'threats' is prevention: the government, it is said, is entitled to have advance intelligence of activities that may in future harm Canada's security.[37] But a security agency charged with investigating 'threats' can reasonably argue that it would be failing in its duty if it did not cast its net as widely as possible: 'In 90% of these cases security authorities always err on the side of security: they will always over-react'.[38] Littleton's comment on the effect of legalizing the search for threats is appropriate:

> the task of keeping the state informed of possible subversion necessarily requires surveillance not only of real actions but also of contemplated actions. The paradox is that the kind of state that would systematically attempt to monitor the intentions of its citizens could hardly be characterised as a liberal democracy.[39]

Bearing this in mind, we may briefly consider three of the four definitions of threats to the security of Canada (i.e. those other than espionage) under which CSIS is authorized to 'target' groups or individuals, and hence to secretly follow and videotape them, place informers among them, listen to their phone conversations and open their mail, enter their homes and offices, copy or steal their papers, and so on.

Under subsection 2(b) of the Act CSIS may target activities that it considers 'foreign influenced', 'detrimental to the interests of Canada', and 'clandestine or deceptive'. The official object of this formulation (as expressed by the McDonald Commission, although it proposed the narrower term 'foreign interference') is to legalize the surveillance of 'front organizations', through which foreign interests (normally foreign states such as the USSR) are seen as secretly acting in ways that are harmful to Canada. Not only is it left entirely to CSIS to determine what counts as 'foreign influence', what 'Canada's interests' are, and what is detrimental to them, but there is no further requirement to show that such actions, actually or potentially, threaten the security either of Canadians or of the Canadian state. It is indeed hard to believe that, in reality, the activities of 'front organizations' have ever posed a threat to Canadian security; yet the power of surveillance given here is extremely broad.

Under subsection 2(c) CSIS may put people or organizations under surveillance if it suspects them of doing things that are 'directed toward', or that are 'in support of', the use, or the threat of the use, of 'serious violence against persons or property . . . to achieve a political objective in Canada or a foreign state'. While this is supposed to be a mandate to investigate terrorism, the definition goes well beyond terrorism in the proper sense of the word (the threat or use of terror to achieve a political objective) and covers the use of force generally as well as issues unrelated to the security of Canada or Canadians. It permits CSIS to target people who engage in activities on behalf of military struggles in other countries, such as the struggle against apartheid, however despotic those countries' regimes may be. As SIRC noted in its 1986-87 Report,[40] one internal CSIS report saw opposition to the government of El Salvador, and to US policy there, as *prima facie* evidence of a security threat. On the other hand, the same SIRC Report noted, CSIS appeared to have shown 'minimal' interest in fund-raising in Canada on behalf of the Contras in Nicaragua. This observation testifies both to the scope of the authority given by the definition of terrorism and to CSIS's political bias.

The phrase 'directed toward' also significantly extends the scope of CSIS's power. It could mean that the facts show that the person doing something consciously tries to direct it so as to contribute to a certain result, but it could also mean that regardless of his or her intentions, in the view of CSIS this is the direction it has (i.e., 'constructive' intention); and similar reasoning can be applied to the phrase 'in support of'.

Under subsection 2(d) CSIS is authorized to investigate groups or individuals whose activities are in its opinion 'directed toward' or 'intended ultimately' to lead to the overthrow of the Canadian system of government. (Once again, 'intended ultimately' could mean that those performing the activities intend them to have a certain effect in the long run, or it could mean that in the view of CSIS, the activities correspond to what someone else—for example, in the Kremlin—intends ultimately to happen, even though the persons involved have no such intentions. This permits the targeting of virtually any activities that CSIS sees as serving the purposes of the Politburo, however remotely or indirectly.)

Ostensibly, all these definitions are supposed to exclude 'lawful advocacy, protest or dissent' from state surveillance. But in practice they subject a very wide range of lawful advocacy, protest, and dissent to state surveillance, because all that is required is that such lawful activities be seen as entailing one of the vague 'threats' described in the CSIS Act. (This is, after all, the point of the vagueness.)

Most of the definition of subversion in the Act was drawn from the McDonald Report, but with a crucial difference. The Commissioners had qualms about the last category of activities (those covered by subsection 2[d]), which they labelled 'revolutionary subversion' (and once, 'true subversion'). The label was intended to denote the political activities of people in organizations that 'subscribe' to revolutionary ideologies, i.e., ideologies 'advocating the ultimate overthrow of the liberal democratic system of government'. The Commissioners thought that the government should be able to 'keep track of the growth of such movements and understand the impact they are having on Canadian democracy',[41] but that so long as they used only 'the methods of liberal democracy' to promote their cause, they and their supporters should not be subjected to 'intrusive investigation'.[42] Although the Commissioners considered that, historically, such organizations had not in fact posed a serious threat to Canadian democracy, they were unwilling to remove this category of historically harmless activity from the purview of the security service.

The McDonald Report's repeated attempts to clarify its position on 'revolutionary subversion', or 'true subversion', are not notable for clarity. In one place[43] subversion is simply associated with terrorism as a self-evidently illegitimate activity; in another[44] it is identified with the use or advocacy of violence; in another[45] legitimate dissent is identified as the advocacy of 'unpopular ideas' (which faintly suggests that at the back of the Commissioners' minds was the thought that dissent is legitimate so long as it does not become too popular). In yet another place[46] subversion is identified merely with the '*wish* to overthrow our democratic system'.

Given the importance of the distinction the Commission was trying to draw, this multiplicity of definitions is revealing. In effect, the Commission advocated the use of intrusive methods of surveillance against espionage or terrorism; no surveillance of lawful advocacy, protest, and dissent; and surveillance, but only by non-intrusive methods, of 'revolutionary subversion'. But they failed to define the last of these clearly, because the logic or ideology to which the concept of subversion belongs, a logic pressed on the Commission by many witnesses (and not least by the Security Service itself), was incompatible with the logic and principles of liberal democracy: the logic or ideology of the Cold War.[47]

Cold War ideology presents a Manichean world in which everything that happens is significant only as an aspect of a titanic struggle between the forces of evil, led by the USSR, and the forces of good, led by the US. On this view,

> if you take the ideology of the Cold War seriously, it means that your nation is at war, you have to have a united national effort, and even if it's not actually dropping bombs, it's at war. And when you're at war, you have to have a united national effort, and anybody that steps back and starts questioning that is dangerous and therefore dissent becomes subversion.[48]

Cold War ideology simply contradicts liberal democracy, and overrides it.[49] As the Heritage Foundation's Dr Francis frankly put it, 'it is axiomatic that individual liberties are secondary to the requirements of security and internal civil order'—requirements that Cold Warriors see as omnipresent and urgent.[50] It is not possible simultaneously to uphold both sets of beliefs.

Moreover, Cold War ideology negates liberal democracy by identifying some of one's own fellow-citizens as constituting, by their beliefs or merely by virtue of their place in the system, an actual or potential fifth column of the external enemy in the global struggle.[51] And since the Cold War is ultimately about ideas and values, the 'enemy within' may do as much damage by the ideas it advocates as by any concrete act. Hence thought-control becomes a legitimate state activity. At its height, Cold War ideology led in the US to extensive witch-hunting and the repression of dissent in general by intimidation and persecution. In the post-Watergate era, in spite of the efforts of the New Right, there is more sensitivity about liberal-democratic rights, but a general 'anti-communist' mentality has remained powerful enough to allow the anti-democratic and illiberal concept of subversion to be embodied in Canadian law.

A contributing factor was and is the already-noted relationship that exists between the Canadian and the US security services. The Canadian security service relies heavily on American interpretations of foreign intelligence. In spite of the strong recommendations of the McDonald Commission and SIRC, CSIS has not so far developed a significant capacity of its own for intelligence analysis and hence has not developed a Canadian, as opposed to an American, view of security issues.[52]

One concluding point deserves to be made about Cold War ideology and the concept of subversion. What emerges most clearly from looking at the one period in history—the period of the Comintern, from 1919 to 1943—when Western 'Marxists' were indeed mostly members of communist parties, and when these parties were committed (on paper at least) to pursuing illegal as well as legal methods of work, is the sheer irrelevance, in terms of the real risk of revolution, of the concept of 'the subversive': the seemingly omni-competent individual with an almost miraculous ability to mesmerize and mobilize his or her fellow-citizens to cumulatively weaken public support for liberal democracy and eventually seize power and introduce a dreary and brutal dictatorship under the guise of a socialist utopia. Even in the 1930s it was not such individuals or even, in the end, their parties that threatened the existing order, but acute inequalities and social distress. Today, when most Western 'Marxists' are not members of communist parties (or probably any party), and when most of the major Western communist parties are committed to the electoral road to socialism,[53] the image of 'the subversive' is more irrelevant than ever. But fantasy is seldom dissipated by confrontation with fact; the concept of subversion belongs to the ideology of the Cold War, which is sustained by paranoia. To the paranoid mind, it is the surreptitious activities of a handful of supernaturally potent people—Bolsheviks in 1917, 'subversives' today—and not the maturation of large social changes, and accompanying shifts in popular thinking, that make history.

The McDonald Commissioners approvingly quoted Mr Justice Rand as saying:

> The dangers from the propagation of the Communist dogma lie essentially in the receptivity of the environment. The Canadian social order rests on the enlightened opinion and the reasonable satisfaction of the wants and desires of the people as a whole. . . .[54]

But they did not follow his logic. Instead, in practice, they opened the door to legalized state surveillance of anyone the state's security agents see as a threat according to the ideology of the Cold War—even while purporting to reject the strained and paranoid view of history and the world which that ideology represents. And the CSIS Act adopted the Commission's vague language about 'revolutionary subversion', but not its proposal to restrict surveillance of it to 'non-intrusive' methods.

The reality of counter-subversion

What sorts of activities and thoughts are in practice seen as subversive? The short answer is: primarily anti-capitalist, rather than anti-democratic, activities and ideas. This conclusion has been reached by writers of differing ideological perspectives from a variety of Western countries. In the US, Theoharis concludes, '[i]n effect the FBI officials defined subversion in political terms: adherence to dissident/radical politics, willingness to challenge the status quo, support for disruptive change'.[55] In Britain, according to Bunyan, 'an historical study of the [Special] Branch (and other agencies) shows only one consistent criterion—for "subversion" read "all those actively opposed to the prevailing order" '.[56] And the McDonald Commission, after studying the RCMP Security Service's activities in the 1960s and 1970s (when its targets included the Waffle, labour unions, the Praxis Corporation, the APLQ and the PQ) remarked that it had an 'anti-left bias'.[57]

These judgements are supported by such published evidence as exists. Political surveillance by the FBI in Media, Pennsylvania, in the 1970s comprised 'two cases involving right-wing groups, ten concerning immigrants, and over 200 on left or liberal groups'.[58] The paper by Whitaker in this volume documents the experience of the Canadian left at the hands of the RCMP Security Service.

Such evidence as we have of the activities of CSIS's Counter-Subversion Branch suggests that they differed little if at all from those of its RCMP predecessor.[59] The 1986-87 SIRC Report noted that the Branch was still using an operation manual produced prior to 1984, which was incompatible with the new mandate of CSIS; that it was targeting all those involved in producing a left-wing magazine though only some of these individuals were even alleged to have advocated the use of violence; that in general, it was ' "casting its net too widely", intruding on the lives and activities of too many Canadians'; and that the Branch overestimated 'the influence and persuasive power' of the groups it targeted and 'the likelihood of violence'.[60] Disclosures in Parliament and the press in the fall of 1987 also suggested that CSIS has targeted non-violent peace groups and other left-wing groups (and not merely particular individuals in them). It had an agent in the CNTU who played a central part in a series of conspiracies to bomb premises in the course of a labour dispute. A crude Cold-War outlook has also characterized the CSIS security assessments disclosed in certain security-screening cases that have been appealed to SIRC.[61] Even if we were to assume, with the McDonald Commission, that it is possible to 'draw a line correctly between legitimate dissent and subversion', it is clear that CSIS has not developed the 'sophisticated judgement and political understanding' required for doing so.[62]

The justification for targeting 'subversives' is—sometimes explicitly, always implicitly—that they may help the country's external enemies. The historical record suggests, however, that the surveillance of 'subversives' by Western security services has rarely led to the discovery of foreign espionage. The FBI's 'counter-intelligence program' (COINTELPRO), which seems to have absorbed about half of its resources in the 1960s and early 1970s, uncovered advance information of planned 'subversive or illegal activities' (espionage did not even figure in the results) in only 2 per cent of the investigations sampled by the General Accounting Office of Congress in 1976.[63] A reading of the record provided by Christopher Andrew even for the interwar years, and by Peter Wright (a dedicated enthusiast for counter-subversion) for the postwar years, suggests similarly meagre results for Britain;[64] as for the RCMP Security Service's counter-subversion program, John Sawatsky, a well-informed and dispassionate observer, told the Pitfield Committee:

> My hunch as a reporter is that there is a lot more talk in this area of counter-subversion than there is substance . . . I really do not have any facts to share with the committee on this. The fact is that there really aren't that many facts, and the RCMP Security Service does not seem to have a lot of facts. They have a lot of supposition. . . .[65]

It is hard not to conclude that 'counter-subversion' activities have actually been inspired less by a realistic assessment of threats posed to democracy than by a general anxiety about threats to the existing order. And it is not, finally, a 'paradox' (as some writers have put it) that such known anti-democratic conspiracies as have actually occurred in Western countries have come not from the left, but from security services themselves: in England, for example, two were plotted against the Labour government of Harold Wilson in 1968 and 1974, and another against the risk of a Labour government led by Tony Benn in 1979, and numerous plots have been hatched against successive governments in Italy.[66] (In addition, Andrew establishes fairly conclusively that members of the British 'intelligence community' successfully used the 'Zinoviev letter' to discredit and bring down the first Labour government in 1924.)[67]

'Safeguards'

Until the late 1970s MPs, senators, judges, and the media agreed with the routine and unrestricted surveillance—and until 1984, the routine 'countering'—of radical political activity. What precipitated a reaction was the extension of these practices to the independence movement in Québec. When this movement evolved into a mainstream political party, and then formed a provincial government, the RCMP's treatment of it led to a crisis. The revelation of police 'wrongdoing' against the APLQ and the FLQ and, finally (in Operation Ham), against the PQ itself, was a sensation because these crimes directly or indirectly affected a large and articulate segment of Québec society and, even more importantly, MNAs and the Solicitor-General himself. It suddenly became clear that the secret police had been spying on mainstream party politicians, not just fringe activists, and that there was no way of ensuring that they would not intervene in party politics just as they had always done against the extra-parliamentary left.

As already noted, the McDonald Commission was established to limit the damage, partly by pre-empting (with the help of the Supreme Court) many of the documents that Mr Keable needed for his enquiry in Québec (and preventing him from using some of those he had already obtained); and partly by 'cooling out' the issue by taking four years to produce a report. Then the McDonald Commission's Report, completed in January 1981, was published (in a censored form) by the government only in August of that year, together with two highly partisan legal opinions commissioned by the Minister of Justice, which purported to question its central legal standpoint, arguing that the police could do whatever the law did not expressly forbid them to do.[68] The Report was never tabled for parliamentary debate; instead, a bill (Bill C 157) was introduced to make the security service independent of the RCMP—a bill that in effect greatly expanded the existing Security Service's powers while minimizing its accountability. When this bill met widespread opposition it was referred to a special committee of the Senate (the Pitfield Committee), where its most serious parliamentary opponents, the NDP, were not represented. Finally, in 1984 Bill C 9, which replaced Bill C 157 after it had become clear that the latter could not secure enough legitimacy, was railroaded through all the stages of debate. Apart from the Solicitor General's brief statements refusing to accept any of the amendments that, following brief introductory speeches by him and his Parliamentary Secretary introducing the Second Reading, were proposed by the Opposition, not a single Liberal MP spoke in support of the bill, or sought to reply to the criticisms offered, from the day it was tabled until the day it was passed, by 112 Liberal votes to 60 Conservative and NDP votes, on 21 June 1984.

Bill C 9 was intended to give CSIS a loose mandate and very wide powers. It was designed to keep political control over CSIS to the barest minimum that, presumably, would secure the support of the Liberal caucus for the strategy of forcing the legislation through the House of Commons on the eve of a general election. Nonetheless, the government laid considerable emphasis on the forms of 'safeguard' against abuse of power by CSIS that were built into the bill, stressing that federal judges would have to grant warrants for intrusive forms of surveillance (though not for the use of informers); that an Inspector-General would report annually to the Solicitor General; that a Review Committee would report annually to Parliament; and that Parliament itself would not only be making a law to govern the security service where before there had been none, but would also be reviewing the legislation after five years, following a report from a joint committee of both Houses.[69]

The question of how far federal judges (from whom CSIS must obtain warrants for intrusive methods of surveillance such as wiretaps) are likely to offset CSIS's shortcomings is partly technical; i.e., it is a question of how far they are in a position to assess the validity of the grounds on which warrants are sought. SIRC, while noting that no applications have so far been rejected by judges, said that judges have asked 'searching questions' and sometimes imposed limiting conditions in granting warrants.[70] But the revelation in September 1987 that CSIS had secured a warrant to wiretap a Canadian citizen in Vancouver in 1985 on the basis of false information showed that the warrant mechanism was not an effective safeguard.[71]

There is in any case a further question of whether judges can in general be expected to take a narrower view than CSIS of the proper scope of the activities of the secret police. Canadian judges, including Federal Court judges, have been consistently supportive of the police, including the security police. They have authorized a general level of police wiretapping twenty times higher than that authorized in the US, and in the years 1974 to 1984 refused to issue warrants in only 14 out of over 10,000 requests.[72] A former Supreme Court judge, Mr W.F. Spence, went so far as to say, in his opinion on the McDonald Report solicited by the government,[73] that '[d]oubt must always be resolved in favour of the national security'.[74]

Then there is the Inspector-General, and SIRC. The Inspector-General operates in complete secrecy. It is good to know that the Review Committee is impressed by his 'energy, understanding and thoroughness',[75] but there is no way of evaluating his work as a potential mechanism of control.

SIRC, on the other hand, publishes annual reports that have increasingly supplied useful information and drawn attention to aspects of CSIS that the Committee considers unsatisfactory. But the Committee lacks access to Cabinet papers in the hands of CSIS and has no powers beyond reporting whatever it is not prevented by the Official Secrets Act from revealing.[76] It is appointed by the government after consultation with the leaders of the other major parties in Parliament, which is meant to give it some independence from the government in office at the time of its appointment. On the other hand, its members must be Privy Councillors (normally ex-Cabinet ministers). They tend to reflect the social values and experience of the professional and political milieu from which they are drawn. Although, in reaction to what they have seen as CSIS's excesses, they have sometimes seemed to have doubts about the meaning of 'subversion',[77] they have also asserted firmly that '[s]ome of the threats [sc. of subversion] described by CSIS are clear cut; all loyal Canadians would agree that they deserve the Service's unremitting attention'; but they did not give any indication of what sort of threats these are, and the implication that it would be 'disloyal' to disagree reminds one more of the House Committee on Un-American Activities than of liberalism. In any event, it is clear that the Review Committee does not have the power to make its view of what is subversive prevail over that of CSIS.

The Committee's reports do display a growing impatience with CSIS's indifference to many of their 'urgings' and 'suggestions'; yet they are not written from the standpoint of a body obligated to speak forthrightly and unequivocally on behalf of the rights of the citizen, and entitled by law to the information it requires. Rather, they display a marked anxiety to establish a working relationship with CSIS and to *balance* the rights of citizens to privacy, etc., with the needs of the state.[78] Even in its third Report, the Committee still seemed to feel more obliged to pay slightly fulsome compliments to CSIS than to say plainly that it had been obstructive on some matters and deceptive on others, and that important recommendations in the Committee's earlier reports had been ignored.

The Committee's cautious or diplomatic approach may be defended as necessary for securing support from other branches of the state such as the PMO or particular ministries in its efforts to influence CSIS. This, however, underlines its real powerlessness. The revelations that surfaced in September 1987, and led to the resignation of the Director of CSIS, were not made by the SIRC, the body established to oversee CSIS's operations on behalf of the Canadian Parliament.

This is not to detract from the importance of the Committee's initial work. Under its first chairman, Ron Atkey, SIRC has played a major role in exposing CSIS to much-needed political scrutiny. Even under less determined leadership, the Committee, with its formal powers to obtain information from CSIS and to investigate complaints,[79] and its duty to publish annual reports, is an advance over what exists in many other countries. But its long-term efficacy as a mechanism of democratic control over CSIS must nonetheless be recognized as modest, limited, and particularly vulnerable to the appointment of a less independent-minded and energetic chairperson.

What about the members of Parliament, to whom the Review Committee's reports are directed? What emerges most clearly from the record in 1984 is the silence of the Liberal Party, the ambivalence of the Progressive Conservative Party, and the isolation of the New Democrats on this issue. One Liberal and several Conservatives provided notable exceptions to this general observation. Warren Allmand, a former Liberal Solicitor General, was the sole Liberal backbencher to intervene substantively in the debate on Bill C 9, proposing an amendment to the definitions of 'threats to the security of Canada' that would have narrowed them quite significantly.[80] Ray Hnatyshyn and John Fraser, and former PC Solicitor General Allan Lawrence, led a substantial group of PC backbenchers in joining with the NDP to criticize the bill and the government's strategy of refusing to amend or even debate it. But the Liberal majority, and the front bench of the Conservative opposition, must be taken by their silence to have supported the bill, if not in every detail, at least in all its major provisions: the 'loose' mandate and the wide powers given to CSIS, the lack of parliamentary control, the weakness of the provisions for oversight and review, and the absence of any provision whereby CSIS's activities may be brought before the courts by anyone other than the government itself.[81]

As far as their recorded views on this issue are concerned, MPs are thus mostly unknown quantities. It seems probable that by the time Bill C 9 was introduced, not only had the issue of separatism largely receded, but most MPs had come to feel reassured that after all the fuss, the security service would be unlikely to risk its independence a second time by letting its attention stray into the mainstream of politics—as opposed to the radical fringe, whose rights did not greatly concern them.[82] Pierre Trudeau is on record as saying that he was unable to 'get excited' about the fact that 'some Maoists had their mail opened'. There is, therefore, little grounds for believing that the response of most MPs to the mild criticisms offered in the Annual Reports of SIRC will be to take up the struggle to amend the CSIS Act and force CSIS to abandon attitudes and practices that are in conflict with even the modest restrictions contained in the Act, not to mention the intentions of the McDonald Commission.

Conclusions

The liberal-democratic freedoms of thought, speech, and association legitimize the existing socio-economic and political order, but they also threaten it. The concept of subversion serves to mitigate this contradiction by attenuating the threat while formally retaining the freedoms. It is not a paradox that the periods of greatest expansion of the security service in Canada have been times not of international tension but of internal unrest—the years immediately following the First World War, the Depression era, and the period of 'détente' in the 1960s and 1970s. There is a permanent tension between consent and repression as the basis of modern state power, and intelligence services are among the branches of the state that are geared to its repressive, not its consensual, function, whatever the rhetoric of the CSIS Act and similar legislation elsewhere may imply. It is to allow for, but also to obscure, this fact that a concept such as subversion—creating legal scope for the repressive function—is required. Such a concept should be seen not as an aberration, but as integral to the working of any state based on a contradictory and inegalitarian social order—and perhaps any state at all.

But this is not a reason for acceptance. Integral as it has undoubtedly been, that concept of subversion belongs to the pathology of liberal-democratic states, corrupting their public philosophy and subverting (in the proper sense of the word) their liberal institutions by the covert operations of a largely uncontrollable state agency. To the extent that these operations have, as the McDonald Commission put it, a 'chilling' effect on popular engagement in radical politics, they have an ossifying effect on the existing order, making it more vulnerable to demands for radical change.

The time has come to transcend the doublethink involved in the whole concept of subversion. The history of 'counter-subversion' does not show that it has enhanced the security of either the states or the citizens of the liberal democracies; if anything, it may have made them less secure, by inhibiting the radical impulses from which timely reforms have always come.

The suggestion of SIRC, adopted by the Osbaldeston Committee, accepted by the government, and now implemented, of closing CSIS's counter-subversion branch and absorbing its functions into the counter-espionage and counter-terrorism branches, is not necessarily a step forward, though it may register some loss of efficacy in using subversion as a concept for legitimizing repression. For, as we have noted, the FBI, in response to post-Watergate moves to curb its counter-subversion activities, simply reclassified many of them as counter-terrorist. Since its legal mandate remains unchanged, CSIS will be free to continue, in practice, to target the same people under the more effective legitimization of counter-espionage or counter-terrorism.

The reform that is required is to eliminate the concept of subversion from Canadian law by repealing subsection (d) of section 2 of the CSIS Act and substantially narrowing the scope of subsections (b) and (c) on foreign influence and 'terrorism' respectively.[83] These changes would not end the secret surveillance of dissident opinion by the state. For one thing, some of that surveillance is conducted by the Communications Security Establishment, with its large staff employed to eavesdrop on all electronic communications in Canada and abroad, which is subject to no legislative safeguards of any kind.[84] The RCMP may also have come to duplicate CSIS's activities to some degree, although there is no means of knowing this.[85] And the removal of the concept of subversion from the CSIS Act would not necessarily prevent CSIS itself from secretly continuing to spy on Canadian organizations and individuals as it has hitherto. But removing the concept from the law would remove CSIS's authority for such spying, reduce the probable scope of its 'targeting', and force it to rely more on open sources and much less on intrusive methods, which would become illegal if used for this purpose.

In February 1988 Solicitor General Kelleher announced that CSIS's Counter-Subversion Branch had been made 'non-operational' and that CSIS would 'rely on non-intrusive, open information collection to provide the government with a watching brief' in this area.[86] Far from removing the concept of subversion from the law, however, he stressed that 'the government has the legal responsibility to investigate such groups and individuals [i.e., such as those covered by s.2(d) of the CSIS Act] *if strictly necessary*'.[87] Kelleher also stated that in cases where 'a subversive threat' was judged serious enough by the Director of CSIS and the Solicitor General, 'intrusive investigative techniques' would still be employed. This represented a decision to adopt partially, and by executive order, the original recommendations of the McDonald Commission. But powers that are qualified and contracted in this way can also be expanded in the same manner when times change. As the chapter by Theoharis in this volume clearly shows, this is exactly what has happened in the US, where the Levi guidelines for the FBI laid down under President Carter in 1976 were revised by the Smith Guidelines under President Reagan in 1983, Congress having failed to legislate on this issue. Liberal democracies must, it seems, constantly relearn the lesson that it is never wise to rely only on the politicians who happen to be in office for the long-run protection of liberties.

The FBI and Dissent in the United States

ATHAN G. THEOHARIS

By an executive order issued in July 1908, Attorney General Charles Buonaparte created a new investigative service within the US Department of Justice, the Bureau of Investigation (formally named the Federal Bureau of Investigation in 1935). Buonaparte's order, instituted at a time when Congress was in recess, and following its actions barring Department officials from using appropriated funds to contract for the investigative assistance of Secret Service agents, precipitated a minor political controversy. For although authorized to conduct investigations under the 1870 legislation establishing the Department of Justice, earlier attorneys general had made no attempt to create a departmental investigative service. Instead, whenever requiring investigative agents, they initially contracted with the Pinkerton Detective Agency on a temporary-need basis. Precluded by Congress in 1892 from continuing this relationship with a non-public agency, attorneys general thereafter, again on a temporary-need basis, contracted with the US Secret Service. Fifteen years later, however, responding to the recent disclosure that an investigation conducted by Secret Service Agents had resulted in the indictments of two US Congressmen from Oregon on land-fraud charges, Congress in 1907-1908 adopted appropriation restrictions prohibiting the Justice Department from hiring Secret Service agents. Proponents justified this restriction on states-rights grounds (that law enforcement was a local and state responsibility) and checks-and-balances principles (that by targeting their congressional critics, executive officials could undermine an independent Congress).

Buonaparte's executive order, if authorized under the 1870 statute, contravened the spirit and intent of Congress's appropriations restrictions of 1907-1908. Required to justify his decision, in January 1909 the outgoing attorney general (William Howard Taft won the presidency in November but was not inaugurated until March 1909) also successfully dissuaded congressional leaders from drafting legislation spelling out the parameters of the Bureau's investigative authority. Efficient administration required that the attorney general be accorded needed discretion when initiating investigations, Buonaparte argued. Nor would the Bureau evolve into a secret police that monitored political dissent; its investigations would be strictly confined to violations of federal antitrust and interstate commerce laws. In addition, as the responsible head of the Department, the attorney general would ensure that the Bureau focussed only on violations of federal statutes.

Buonaparte's assurances were convincing, for in 1909 the federal regulatory role was minimal, and thus attorneys general could personally review decisions to initiate investigations. In the following years, however, the Bureau's investigative responsibilities increased radically as Congress enacted a series of laws expanding federal jurisdiction over both business and personal activities (e.g., the White Slave Traffic Act of 1910). And most Americans accepted this expansion as necessary, having concluded not only that crime was also a national responsibility, but that local and state police were incapable of apprehending criminals who either crossed state lines or engaged in activities that had broad national consequences.

This did not mean, however, that the FBI's expanded investigative role was confined to apprehending violators of federal statutes. The FBI intensively monitored dissident political movements and activists (despite First Amendment restrictions and Congress's failure to enact legislation criminalizing 'subversive' activities), and its investigative procedures often violated the Fourth Amendment ban on unreasonable searches and seizures (in the case of bugging and break-in activities).

The impetus to this expanded investigative role came from secret executive directives: in some cases issued by presidents or attorneys general, in others by the FBI director either with the tacit consent of the attorney general or without the latter's knowledge and authorization. Significantly, if the ostensible rationale for these 'intelligence' investigations was the need to safeguard the nation from foreign-directed subversion, in reality after 1940 the FBI increasingly focussed on political dissent and continued to investigate even after uncovering no evidence of foreign direction (some investigations continued for over thirty years). The premise of these investigations was that certain individuals and organizations, because of their radical beliefs and associations, had to be carefully monitored to anticipate or avert possibly illegal or harmful activities in future. The investigative rationale had shifted from prosecutive to preventative; the standard was potential, not actual.

Nor were the resultant investigations limited in scope and purpose, a point underscored by FBI officials' interest in monitoring two prominent Americans and the methods employed to that end. Significantly, owing to their prominence and respectability, these individuals—Eleanor Roosevelt and John Kennedy—should have been immune to such investigative scrutiny.

Mrs Roosevelt may not have been directly targeted for investigation. Nevertheless, FBI officials did not hesitate to amass non-criminal information about her personal and political activities—but only after having ensured that this potentially risky interest could not be discovered.

In January 1942, for example, FBI agents broke into the New York office of the American Youth Congress (AYC) and photocopied Mrs Roosevelt's correspondence with AYC officials. The head of the New York office hand-delivered the duplicate copies of this sensitive correspondence to the office of J. Edgar Hoover, who thereupon demanded that it be 'carefully reviewed & analyzed'. The resulting report, revealing an awareness of the furor its discovery would provoke, was prepared under a special 'blue memorandum' procedure (to permit its undiscoverable destruction), while Assistant Director Louis Nichols maintained in his secret office file the two copies of Mrs Roosevelt's correspondence (this ensured that there would be no retrievable record that the FBI maintained such documents, as would have been the case had the intercepted correspondence been indexed and filed in the FBI's central records system).[1]

From documents pilfered from another break-in of December 1942, this time of the headquarters of the International Students Service (ISS), FBI officials prepared another secret report on Mrs Roosevelt's political activities and attitudes. This report described Mrs Roosevelt as being 'always on hand to use her personal influence on those who threatened to oppose openly the Great Power line' and as having lobbied the Lithuanian delegate to the ISS assembly to cease condemning 'Russian aggression and atrocities in Lithuania' and to sacrifice his 'particular interest "for the larger good of the Assembly" '. Mrs Roosevelt, the report continued, had a 'sincere interest in youth and [realized] the political value of the International Student Assembly both in winning the war and influencing the terms of peace'.[2]

Through another investigation initiated earlier in 1942, FBI officials were seeking to track the activities of individuals challenging prevailing conservative economic and racialist norms. In the course of an investigation ostensibly to survey 'foreign inspired agitation among the Negroes in this country', the FBI's Savannah and Birmingham field offices became apprised of 'other causes of agitation than those which are possibly foreign inspired', and in particular of rumours 'concerning the formation of Eleanor or Eleanor Roosevelt Clubs among the Negroes'. In his report summarizing the preliminary results of these investigations, Assistant Director D. Milton Ladd documented the underlying political concerns of FBI officials:

> Such incidents as Negro maids allegedly demanding their own terms for working and at the same time stating they were members of an Eleanor Roosevelt Club are typical of the rumors. No substantiating information, however, has been received [by the Savannah office] concerning these rumors. However, complaints are received that the cause of the agitation among the Negroes in this country is largely attributed to the encouragement given Negroes by Mrs Roosevelt. . . . attempts in [the Birmingham] area are being made to form Eleanor Clubs by a strange white man and a

large Negro organizer traveling in an automobile. The unverified information indicates that only female domestics are desired for membership. The alleged slogan of the club is 'A White Woman in the Kitchen by Christmas' inferring [sic] that Negroes work only part of the day. Similar clubs are claimed to be in operation in other cities in Alabama.

These concerns, based on the conviction recorded in a New Orleans field office report that 'practically every negro knows of these Clubs and that they are places to patronize', ensured that the rumours were intensively investigated. Promising to keep on top of this matter, Ladd assured Hoover that 'the Bureau has made many inquiries in an effort to obtain specific information concerning the existence of such Clubs, which inquiries have met with negative results'. An undaunted Ladd pledged to continue pressing an FBI informer to 'furnish more specific information concerning his allegation relative to the existence of the "Eleanor Clubs" '.[3]

FBI officials also moved unhesitatingly to collect derogatory information about Mrs Roosevelt's personal life. Alerted to allegations that she was having a sexual affair with a radical youth leader, Joseph Lash, FBI officials sought to preclude discovery of their prurient interest. In this case, the FBI had not directly uncovered this misinformation, having obtained it from the Military Intelligence Division (MID).

Military intelligence agents first learned of Mrs Roosevelt's contacts with Lash in February 1943; at the time Lash was stationed as an army trainee at Chanute Field (near Urbana, Illinois). In the course of this investigation, MID agents (1) monitored and read Lash's correspondence with Mrs Roosevelt and with his wife-to-be Trude Pratt; (2) intercepted his telephone conversation with Mrs Roosevelt; (3) monitored his 5-7 March meetings with Mrs Roosevelt in the Urbana-Lincoln Hotel; (4) bugged his 12-14 March meetings with Trude Pratt in the Urbana-Lincoln Hotel, recording the couple's sexual activities as well as entering their hotel room to read their personal papers; and (5) bugged his meeting with Mrs Roosevelt in her Blackstone Hotel room in Chicago on 27-28 March.

On the day of her departure from Chicago, however, Mrs Roosevelt was briefed by Blackstone Hotel officials that she had been the subject of MID surveillance. Upon returning to Washington in April, the First Lady protested to White House aide Harry Hopkins, who in turn contacted General of the Army George Marshall. In response, Marshall ordered the disbandment of the Army's counter-intelligence corps and the destruction of its domestic-surveillance files. Instead of destroying the documents pertaining to Mrs Roosevelt, however, MID officials in the counter-intelligence corps turned them over to their FBI contact—at the time claiming that Lash's and Mrs Roosevelt's (not Lash's and Trude Pratt's) sexual affair had been recorded and that President Roosevelt, having been briefed on this affair, had ordered the 'dismemberment of the counterintelligence corps, G-2' and further that 'anyone who knew about this case should be immediately relieved of his duties and sent to the South Pacific for action against the Japs until they were killed'.[4]

Except for the fact that Mrs Roosevelt had discovered the MID surveillance of her Chicago trip, this briefing was totally erroneous. And, while MID officials never produced any tapes recording an affair between Lash and Mrs Roosevelt (the only such records involved Lash's affair with Trude Pratt), FBI officials never doubted the accuracy of this allegation. Committed to ensuring that it never become known he was interested in such misinformation, FBI Director Hoover purposely maintained the MID surveillance reports, and his subordinate's summary memorandum reporting this transmission, in his secret office file. This decision further allowed Hoover to make political use of this information whenever he concluded that it was safe to do so.

Such an opportunity presented itself in 1953, with the election of a Republican administration that had its own interest in discrediting the former First Lady. Thus in January 1953 Assistant Director Louis Nichols briefed key Eisenhower campaign aides George Murphy and Francis Alstock on Mrs Roosevelt's 'affair' with Lash in order to strengthen the President-elect's resolve not to reappoint Mrs Roosevelt to the US delegation to the United Nations. So long as Mrs Roosevelt was a member of the UN delegation, Alstock reasoned in response to this briefing, 'she would not become the object of any Congressional investigation, but that sooner or later there was going to be an investigation of her affair with Joe Lash'. Then, in February 1954, Nichols briefed the President on this alleged affair in view of the fact that 'Joe Lash is working for the *New York Post* which has been exceedingly critical of the President as well as of us'.[5]

Just as the MID investigation of Lash's 'subversive' activities uncovered derogatory misinformation about Mrs Roosevelt, so too did an FBI investigation into the 'espionage' activities of Inga Arvad uncover her illicit sexual affair with John F. Kennedy.

A Danish-born beauty who had immigrated to the United States in 1940, Arvad wrote a gossipy daily column for the isolationist *Washington Times-Herald* reporting personal background information on prominent Washingtonians (at the time she was separated from her husband, Paul Fejos, from whom she was soon divorced). Arvad came to the FBI's attention in November 1940 through an unsolicited correspondent and rumours circulating in the Capitol and reported in a syndicated column of one of Washington's newspapers that 'at one time' she had been Hitler's 'publicity agent' and was a current German spy. FBI officials at first ignored these rumours but became interested in them following the Japanese attack on Pearl Harbor and US involvement in war with Germany and Japan. Apparently Arvad herself had piqued this interest when seeking an FBI interview to refute these rumours. During this interview, she explained that prior to immigrating to the United States she had interviewed Hitler (and other Nazi officials) in her capacity as a reporter for a Danish newspaper. Rather than serving to refute these rumours, however, Arvad's FBI interview only aroused Director Hoover's interest. Responding to the briefing, the Director ordered a 'discreet investigation' to ascertain the truth of these allegations, demanding that the report be submitted 'in the near future'.[6]

Arvad's activities and associations were thoroughly investigated. As part of this investigation, FBI agents broke into, bugged, and wiretapped her Washington residence. From their initial monitoring of her activities, FBI agents had discovered her extensive associations with prominent Washingtonians whom she regularly contacted as part of her newspaper assignment. These contacts aroused the suspicions of FBI officials, who concluded that Arvad and her associates 'may be engaged in any subversive or un-American activity'. Accordingly, Hoover sought Attorney General Francis Biddle's approval to wiretap her,[7] claiming that the FBI's 'current' investigation of Arvad as 'an espionage suspect' had determined that 'in the short period she has been in Washington she has established close social and professional contacts with persons holding important positions in the Government departments and bureaus vitally concerned with the national defense'. These 'facts', Hoover continued, indicated 'a definite possibility that she may be engaged in a most subtle type of espionage activities against the United States'.[8]

Biddle approved Hoover's wiretap request. Although the wiretap uncovered no evidence of Arvad's 'subtle' espionage activities, it did uncover information about her personal relationships (whether platonic or sexual) with a number of prominent Washingtonians, some of whom were prewar isolationists and others who had close ties with the Roosevelt administration, notably the financier Bernard Baruch.[9]

Through the Arvad 'espionage' investigation, FBI officials in particular learned that she and then naval ensign John Kennedy (whom FBI reports identified as the son of the former isolationist US Ambassador to Great Britain, Joseph Kennedy) were having a sexual affair. FBI agents' surveillance of Arvad and contacts with Office of Naval Intelligence (ONI) officials first uncovered that during Kennedy's assignment to Washington, DC, and prior to his transfer to Charleston, South Carolina, he had 'spent the night with [Arvad] on several occasions'. Alerted, through the Arvad wiretap, to her plans to visit Kennedy in Charleston, Hoover thereupon ordered the Charleston office to investigate this meeting. The FBI Director urged that this be done with great caution in view of Arvad's employment with the *Times-Herald* and the possibility that, should this ardently anti-New Deal paper learn of this surveillance, it 'would be quick to expose any investigation of the FBI'. Acting discreetly, FBI agents installed a bug in Kennedy's hotel room in Charleston and were able to record that Kennedy and Arvad 'engaged in sexual intercourse on numerous occasions' during the weekends of 6-9 February and 20-23 February 1942. (By then, FBI agents had also learned of Arvad's earlier, 24-25 January visit to Charleston, which they had been unable to bug.) Through the bug of the 20-23 February visit, FBI officials were also privy to Arvad's fears 'about being pregnant as a result of her two previous trips' to Charleston.[10]

Kennedy soon broke off this affair. Moreover, the FBI never uncovered any evidence that Arvad had engaged in 'espionage' or other suspect activities. Nonetheless, the records of this officially classified 'Internal Security-Germany' investigation were not filed in the FBI's central records system, along with those of other FBI espionage cases. To preclude their incorporation in the FBI's central records system, reports on the Arvad investigation were invariably conveyed by special messenger and through 'personal and confidential' letters, and were then deposited in Assistant Director Louis Nichols's office file. Briefed on 13 July 1960, following John Kennedy's nomination as the Democratic presidential candidate, on whatever derogatory information the FBI had compiled on Kennedy, Hoover was reminded of the Arvad affair. The next day the wily FBI Director had the Arvad folder transferred to his secret office file.[11]

The fact that the derogatory information about Mrs Roosevelt and John Kennedy had been maintained in Hoover's office file did not mean that this file was the sole repository of whatever derogatory information the FBI had accumulated on prominent Americans (although 64 of its 164 folders contained such information). The FBI Director could at any time request delivery of specific files or summary memoranda on named individuals. In the case of 'obscene and indecent' information, FBI officials could safely fulfil any such requests from the FBI Director since Hoover had devised in March 1925 another separate records procedure, the Obscene File. To ensure the safe submission and central maintenance of 'obscene and indecent' information, the FBI Director had then ordered that 'any obscene matter of any nature whatsoever' was to be mailed in a sealed envelope clearly marked 'in large type or letters the word "OBSCENE", in order that the nature of the contents may be noted at a glance'. Such captioned submissions were then to be maintained separately in the FBI Laboratory. This file, moreover, was not to be 'exhibited to anyone outside' the FBI without Hoover's or Associate Director Clyde Tolson's 'specific' authorization.[12]

When it was established in 1925, most of the Obscene File consisted of printed pornographic literature. By 1946 its contents included as well 'stag' motion-picture films, free-hand drawings, comic-strip cartoons, playing cards, and photographs. Nor was such material collected simply to enforce relevant anti-obscenity laws. 'Even though no Federal violation exists', Hoover ordered his agents to collect obscene materials 'in order to increase the effectiveness of the Obscene Files'. The FBI Director explained:

> Each obscene literature investigation possesses potential publicity value because of the very nature of the investigation. Every Special Agent in Charge should closely follow obscene matter investigations in order that consideration may be given to obtaining proper publicity in appropriate cases. Where it is contemplated that publicity will result from the Bureau's investigation of an obscene matter case, it is the responsibility of the Special Agent in Charge to make certain that the Bureau is notified in advance of any contemplated arrest, arraignment, or other developments prior to the time that any publicity is released.[13]

The Obscene File procedure, by ensuring the safe submission of such reports, in time was also employed to preclude discovery of the FBI's collection of information about illicit sexual activities—as documented by the following Obscene File submission.

In January 1954, FBI agents intercepted the telephone conversation of John Vitale (an 'Italian hoodlum' residing in St Louis under investigation in a missing ransom case). Vitale had contacted an associate in Detroit to seek his advice on whom to retain as legal counsel for a forthcoming parole hearing. Vitale's Detroit associate recommended Herbert K. Hyde, a man he described as 'getting more powerful all the time' now that Hyde was the 'General Trial Attorney for General Services Administration'. Vitale's Detroit associate conceded that Hyde's job title was not that impressive, but then added that Hyde has 'a good looking wife—he says that Ike [President Eisenhower] has been trying to get into her pants', and further that Hyde 'is scheduled to get a judgship'.

This portion of the Vitale wiretap transcript, because it alleged an illicit sexual affair, was mailed to FBI headquarters under the 'Obscene File' procedure. But because the alleged affair involved an incumbent President, this particular 'Obscene' submission was forwarded to Hoover's media and congressional liaison, Assistant Director Louis Nichols, who thereupon included it in his own office folder on Eisenhower. Alerted to Hyde's possible role and the allegations concerning Mrs Hyde, FBI officials immediately checked the FBI's files on Hyde. A ten-page memorandum was prepared verifying Hyde's General Services Administration employment and other personal information.[14]

Nor were FBI officials interested merely in collecting derogatory political and personal information—information that could not be lawfully used for prosecutive purposes. Unwilling to have this information moulder in the files, FBI officials soon sought other avenues for its use to discredit radical activists, albeit only after ensuring that their political containment activities could not be publicly compromised.

For example, on 28 January 1965, FBI Director Hoover discussed with former CIA Director and Berkeley alumnus John McCone his concerns about student protest activities the previous fall at the University of California-Berkeley (the so-called Free Speech movement). Claiming that the University 'is infiltrated with a lot of communists, both in the student body and the faculty', Hoover learned that McCone was a close friend of a member of the University's Board of Regents (whose name the FBI withheld when releasing this memorandum). His friend, McCone confided, 'is puzzled how to handle the situation and is anxious to get a line on any persons who are communists or have communist associations either on the faculty or in the student body and then at a Board of Regents level handle it without disclosing his source'.

Hoover, more than willing to assist in this extra-legal activity, advised McCone that he would have the Special Agent in Charge (SAC) of the FBI's Los Angeles office, Wesley Grapp, prepare 'a memorandum in the next day or two of public source information of some of these individuals causing trouble at Berkeley'. The FBI Director immediately contacted Grapp, ordering him to give this information to the regent in a private meeting on the condition that this assistance was 'not to be disclosed as having emanated from the FBI'. Expressing his intent to review 'how this works out', Hoover further directed Grapp to find out whether this regent was 'a safe individual to talk to'. Grapp should 'size up' the regent, assess 'whether he is the kind of person we can tell something to off the record and he will not disclose where he got it', and if so, 'we may later give him some information which is not public source'.[15]

The Berkeley incident underscores Hoover's willingness to disseminate information to contain those political movements he found abhorrent, but only if assured that the FBI's assistance could not be discovered. In the Berkeley case, the FBI Director agreed to provide information 'in writing' to an individual he did not personally know to be certifiably reliable because the information 'will be public source and on plain paper and not identified with the FBI'. Were he confident of the individual's reliability, Hoover might agree to leak non-public source information—which information the FBI had been collecting but could not use for prosecutive purposes either because it involved illicit sexual activities (there being no federal law violation) or because it had been illegally obtained (through wiretaps, bugs, or break-ins). How much and what kind of information did the FBI obtain through tapping, bugging, and burglarizing dissident organizations and activists? Are the Berkeley, Roosevelt, and Kennedy cases representative of FBI officials' political activism and interest in containing liberal and radical activists?

These questions can be better answered by reviewing two extremely sensitive (albeit incomplete) files: the Symbol Number Sensitive Source Index (now formally called the National Security Electronic Surveillance Card File) and the Surreptitious Entries file.

The Symbol Number Sensitive Source Index, a card file maintained at FBI headquarters, identifies the symbol numbers assigned to FBI wiretaps and bugs frequently cited in FBI field-office reports. When preparing reports on the results of investigations, FBI agents were required to safeguard their sources of information and thus were not to identify the particular informer or investigative technique. Instead, they were to cite the source by so-called symbol numbers, first identifying the acronym of the field office (Chicago became CHI) and then listing an individual number (e.g., 206). An index maintained at each field office identified the specific sources of its symbol numbers. Culled from these field-office indices, the Symbol Number Source Index maintained at FBI headquarters in Washington records the targets, locations, and dates of installation and discontinuance of those wiretaps and bugs most frequently cited in field-office reports.

Intended to serve as a finding aid, this index can now be employed to identify some of the principal targets of FBI wiretaps and bugs. The inactive (non-pending) section of this index contains some 13,500 cards of the individuals and organizations who, beginning in 1941, were the targets of FBI wiretaps or bugs.[16] In response to my Freedom of Information Act request for this index, the FBI has withheld all cards on individuals on claimed personal-privacy grounds. The released cards on organizations, however, do document that virtually every left-of-centre civil-rights organization and labour union, and every radical group active after the 1940s, had been the target of an FBI tap, bug, or both.

The FBI's surveillance of left-wing unions (ostensibly to ascertain possible communist influence) included wiretapping the CIO Maritime Committee,[17] the Food, Tobacco, Agricultural & Allied Workers of America (CIO),[18] the International Longshoremen's and Warehousemen's Union,[19] the National Maritime Union,[20] the National Union of Marine Cooks & Stewards,[21] and the United Public Workers of America[22] and bugging meetings of the United Automobile Workers,[23] the United Electrical Radio & Machine Workers of America,[24] the United Mine Workers,[25] and the Congress on Industrial Organizations (CIO) Council.[26]

The FBI's electronic coverage of radical unions strongly suggests that FBI officials had concluded that efforts to transform the American economic system were themselves subversive. This conservative purpose also underlay the FBI's coverage of the civil-rights movement—virtually every civil-rights organization challenging racial segregation or seeking to promote equal rights for black Americans was subject to an FBI tap and/or bug. These included the Alabama Peoples Educational Association, the Gandhi Society for Human Rights, the Committee to

Aid the Monroe Defendants, the Southern Conference for Human Welfare, the Black Panther Party, the Nation of Islam, the Universal Negro Improvement Association, the Southern Christian Leadership Conference, the National Association for the Advancement of Colored People (NAACP), the (World War II) March on Washington movement, the African Liberation Day Coordinating Committee, and the Student Non-Violent Coordinating Committee. For example, the March on Washington movement was both tapped and bugged in March and June 1943, at the time of this *ad hoc* organization's announced challenge to the military's policy of racial segregation and to the segregated hiring policies of defence industries. Six months later, in December 1943, a local NAACP chapter was tapped.

While virtually no left-wing organization, no matter how minuscule its membership, escaped FBI tapping or bugging, right-wing organizations eluded similar scrutiny. The sole exceptions were (1) during the 1960s, the Ku Klux Klan; (2) during the World War II period, the American First Party (because of its pro-German orientation) and the Peace Now Movement (because of its advocacy of an immediate negotiated peace with Germany); and (3) within, carefully defined limits, six pro-fascist organizations. It is significant that the FBI's wartime surveillance of right-wing organizations paled in contrast to its massive monitoring of the left (at a time when the United States was aligned with the Soviet Union against Nazi Germany and Fascist Italy) but, as important, that the tap on 'Fascist and Italian matters' was discontinued in June 1941 and another tap on 'Nazi and German matters' was discontinued in December 1941. (Continuance of these wiretaps might have foreclosed any espionage and sabotage prosecutions.)

While the Symbol Number Sensitive Source Index confirms that radical organizations were extensively wiretapped and bugged, such procedures could not uncover all desired information about these organizations. In 1942, accordingly, Director Hoover authorized FBI agents to conduct break-ins (once termed 'black bag jobs,' now called 'surreptitious entries') to acquire the membership and subscription lists, financial records, and correspondence of targeted radical activists and organizations. While recognizing that break-ins were an invaluable investigative technique, Hoover also recognized that they were 'clearly illegal'. Desirous of minimizing any chance that FBI break-ins could be discovered, the Director required his own prior approval before any could be conducted and, further, that there be 'prior planning . . . in that the individual in the field who is making this recommendation is fully assured of complete security'.

When requesting the FBI Director's approval in writing, SACs were to spell out the expected results (justifying the risk) and the procedures to be followed to avert discovery. 'Only stable and dedicated' agents were to be employed in such operations; FBI files were to be consulted for all information about the targeted individual or organization, which information was then to be used to formulate a plan of operation. When formulating this plan, agents were to case the building housing the individual or organization to determine when the operation could be conducted most safely (to know in advance whether a friendly janitor might provide a key, when other occupants were normally absent, and the normal activities of other residents of the building and neighbourhood). Even more careful planning was required for the actual break-in. A special squad normally consisted of eight to ten agents: one agent would act as supervisor and would maintain contact with all the other participants; one or two would tail the suspect, relaying back by walkie-talkie to the other members of the squad any changes in the subject's plans, and possible return; two more would enter the residence or office, one having the responsibility to photograph documents and the other to collect the documents to be copied; and four or five agents would monitor the area outside the targeted building, reporting by walkie-talkie on the activities of other individuals in the area.

This authorization procedure meant that written records were created both of the intention to commit an illegal act and of the FBI Director's approval. Since FBI files could be subject to disclosure in response either to a congressional subpoena or to a court-ordered discovery motion, Hoover devised a special procedure to ensure that break-in request and authorization documents were not indexed and recorded in the targeted individual's/organization's case file. Captioned 'Do Not File', they were to be routed to the FBI Director's office and, following Hoover's approval, were to be filed in the offices of the assistant director having supervisory responsibility for the specific investigation (whether internal-security or criminal). These office files in turn were to be destroyed every six months.

SACs were not to create copies of authorization requests or of other records that 'might at some time prove embarrassing in that it shows cognizance on their part of an illegal entry'. 'There should be no record in any [field office] file concerning authority secured for handling' break-ins, Hoover emphasized; instead, SACs were to maintain 'an informal folder in his personal file or desk and in that folder should be reposited an informal note concerning each particular assignment. These notes should be held until [destroyed after] the next inspection.' Hoover in time modified this procedure, eliminating the requirement that he reauthorize ongoing break-ins of approved targets. In these cases, the original 'informal' memo was to be 'maintained permanently in SAC's office'. Such records, however, should contain 'no reference to Bureau authority', and all reports based on the break-in were to be maintained in the SAC's safe until the semi-annual inspection, after which they were to be destroyed.[27]

Hoover's careful planning had seemingly created a fail-safe system;

and, indeed, despite their frequency, dating from the early 1940s, FBI break-ins went undiscovered. This system broke down in the mid-1970s, owing, ironically, to Hoover's October 1971 decision to transfer a July 1966 memorandum recoding his order banning any future resort to break-ins from his Personal and Confidential File to his Official and Confidential File. Because Hoover's order was written on the bottom of a summary memorandum describing the Do Not File procedure, his decision to transfer this document inadvertently preserved a record of FBI break-in policy. Had Hoover not transferred this memorandum to his Official and Confidential File, it would have been destroyed along with the other contents of the Personal and Confidential File that, immediately after his death in May 1972, and pursuant to his earlier instructions, Helen Gandy, his Administrative Assistant, destroyed. Thus, because Hoover's Official and Confidential File was then incorporated in the FBI's central records system, congressional investigators became apprised of the Do Not File procedure in 1975, when reviewing this formerly secret office file.

Unexpectedly learning of this illegal program, congressional investigators demanded that FBI officials report the number of break-ins conducted between 1942 and 1966. The requested information could not be provided, the officials responded, since the relevant records, maintained in assistant directors' office files, had been destroyed every six months.[28]

Once again Hoover's fail-safe system broke down. All break-in documents had not been destroyed: another office file, this one maintained by Assistant Director Louis Nichols,[29] remains extant, and this file contains documents recording four instances of FBI break-ins. In addition, the 'black bag job' folder of New York SAC Thomas Malone, consisting of the 'informal' memoranda covering the period 1954 through 1973 that he maintained in his safe, inexplicably had not been destroyed. These documents constitute the bulk of the FBI's Surreptitious Entries file. By reviewing these admittedly incomplete break-in records, we can now identify some of the targets and purposes of FBI break-ins.

I have already discussed two of the four most sensitive FBI break-ins recorded in Nichols's office file, those producing information about Eleanor Roosevelt's political activities.[30] The third recorded break-in, which occurred in either 1940 or 1941, involved the Washington-based American Peace Mobilization and the Washington [DC] Committee for Democratic Action. Securing these organizations' membership lists, FBI officials identified certain Department of Justice employees, or their wives, as members. Briefed on this discovery, Hoover thereupon urged Assistant to the Attorney General Matthew McGuire to dismiss these employees because of their membership in these radical organizations. Among those Hoover sought to have purged were then Assistant Solicitor General (later Federal Judge) Charles Fahy, and departmental attorneys Thomas Emerson (later Yale University law professor) and Herbert Wechsler (later Columbia University law professor).[31]

The fourth recorded break-in involved a political controversy that particularly concerned Hoover: the attempts of liberal and radical activists during the early 1940s to raise public doubts about his administration of the Bureau (dubbed by Hoover the 'smear campaign'). The first of these criticisms concerned the FBI's raid leading to the arrest of those American radicals who had recruited volunteers to fight on behalf of the Spanish Loyalists, an action described as indicative of the FBI's having become an 'American OGPU'. The criticisms mounted following the disclosure of the FBI's investigation of West Coast longshoremen's union president Harry Bridges, which included monitoring of his cross-country trip and bugging of his hotel room in New York City. Liberal and radical activists were soon demanding that the Roosevelt administration drop deportation proceedings against Bridges and instead investigate Hoover's FBI.

Embarrassed by these revelations but anxious to contain the resulting political damage, FBI officials sought information about their radical critics' political strategy. Accordingly, in March 1942 FBI agents broke into the office of New York attorney Carol King, who had played a prominent role in defending Bridges during deportation proceedings and in lobbying civil libertarians, trade unionists, and radical activists to support him. Three volumes of 'material' and 'various items' were photocopied and delivered to Hoover's office. Summary memoranda were thereupon prepared recounting the political activities and associations of the individuals identified from these documents as active in this 'smear campaign', the more prominent of whom were Herbert Wechsler, CIO attorney and later Supreme Court Justice Arthur Goldberg, and civil-liberties attorneys Edward Lamb and Louis McCabe.[32]

These four recorded instances leave unanswered the question of whether FBI break-ins were primarily politically motivated and not intended to obtain information about espionage plans or foreign-directed disruption. The larger but nonetheless incomplete 'Surreptitious Entries' file complements these four recorded instances, showing that radical activists were the principal targets of FBI investigations—and that, when it came to the American left, break-ins were not used with restraint. On the one hand, this file confirms that through the break-ins FBI officials sought to identify the membership and political strategies of radical organizations (in the process uncovering little if any evidence of criminal or espionage activities). On the other hand, it documents the almost paranoid obsession of FBI officials with the American left.

A partial list of the targets of FBI break-ins includes the Civil Rights Congress (the date of the break-in cannot be pinpointed, probably June 1953);[33] the Jewish Young Federalists (again, the date cannot be determined, probably June 1954);[34] the Washington office of the Jewish

Culture Society in February 1963;[35] the National Committee to Secure Justice for Morton Sobell (the date cannot be ascertained);[36] the Johnson Forest Group, a splinter faction of the Socialist Workers Party, in October 1953;[37] the Vietnam Veterans Against the War in Vietnam in November 1971;[38] the Washington office of the National Lawyers Guild in December 1949;[39] the Independent Citizens Committee of the Arts, Science and Professions in August 1945;[40] the Veterans of the Abraham Lincoln Brigade in October 1942;[41] the Student Non-Violent Coordinating Committee (twice) in May and (once) in June 1968;[42] the Hellenic American Brotherhood in August 1948;[43] the Emma Lazarus Federation in December 1954 and again in May 1956;[44] the Socialist Workers Party and its youth affiliate the Young Socialist Alliance (too many times to enumerate);[45] the Negro Labor Victory Committee in either July or August 1944;[46] the American section of the World Congress for Peace in June 1949;[47] the Joint Anti-Fascist Refugee Committee in January 1943;[48] the US Festival Committee (planning for the Eighth World Youth Festival) in February and June 1962;[49] the Chicago headquarters of the National Mobilization Committee to End the War in Vietnam in July 1968;[50] the Chicago Committee to Defend the Bill of Rights in November 1966;[51] the business office of Stanley Levison, an adviser to civil-rights leader Martin Luther King, Jr, twenty-nine times between October 1954 and January 1964;[52] the Russian War Relief in September 1944;[53] the League of American Writers in December 1941;[54] the American Slav Congress in July and again in November 1944;[55] the Nationalist Party of Puerto Rico in July 1944;[56] the Muslim Cult of Islam (Black Muslims) in October 1954 and again in February 1955;[57] the Emergency Civil Liberties Committee (later renamed the National Emergency Civil Liberties Committee) in December 1955;[58] the office of the journal *Africa Latin America Asia Revolution* in February 1964;[59] the Fair Play for Cuba Committee in January, May, July, and August 1961, May 1962, and again in April and October 1963;[60] the office of the monthly *Progressive Labor* in August 1962 and again in May 1963;[61] Local 1730 of the International Longshoremen's Association in October 1962;[62] the Proletarian Party in November 1947;[63] the Chinese Hand Laundry Alliance in August 1957;[64] the American Association for Democratic Germany in September 1944;[65] the International Workers Order in July 1944, March 1945, and again in August 1953;[66] and the United Klans of America office in Monroe, Louisiana in March 1966.[67]

Nor were radical activists the sole targets of FBI break-ins. Having been embarrassed by the press's discovery in 1957 that organized crime leaders had convened in Appalachin, New York, without the FBI's advance knowledge, and stung by criticisms that the FBI had been unable to acquire the needed information to indict well-known criminals, Hoover instituted an intensified campaign against crime-syndicate leaders, code-named the Top Hoodlum program. Break-ins were to be employed as part of this program. For example, in December 1957 FBI agents broke into the apartment of a New York crime boss to photocopy his correspondence, papers, and photographs.[68] Unable to obtain desired information about another crime boss, agents broke into the apartment of this hoodlum's girl friend (in May and October 1958) on the belief that he spent 'considerable time' with her. Notes, letters, documents, and photographs were photocopied in the apartment.[69] Having learned that a top hoodlum in Newark had been using his attorney's office to conduct his business and to meet with various criminal associates, in December 1963 agents broke into the attorney's office to photocopy business records and correspondence.[70]

Emboldened by their success in averting discovery of this practice, in time FBI officials began to authorize break-ins during criminal investigations—despite the fact that any information so obtained was tainted and should not have been used for prosecutive purposes. Thus agents broke into (1) the apartment of a suspect in a White Slave Traffic Act investigation, in January 1964;[71] (2) the apartment of a suspect in an investigation of the theft of $400,000 in jewelry from the Americana Hotel in Bal Harbour, Florida, in March 1954;[72] (3) the offices of 'allegedly the largest shylocking operation in the US', in December 1961;[73] (4) a Yonkers office used for recording horse bets during an interstate investigation into illegal gambling operations, in June 1962;[74] (5) the office of a former US attorney under investigation in a bribery case, again in June 1962;[75] (6) the office of the accountant of another individual under investigation to photocopy papers concerning 'stock holdings, income tax returns, and miscellaneous papers re his [the criminal suspect's] concerns and associates', twice in April 1963;[76] (7) the First Commercial Corporation at 424 Madison Avenue in New York City, in December 1961 (the original purpose had been to conduct a survey preparatory to installing a microphone, but agents also photocopied 'as many of the records of the above-named company as could be done in the allotted time' and returned later to photocopy the remaining records);[77] and (8) the office of a New York union local under investigation for criminal influence, in April 1962 (agents photocopied receipts, business cards, personal materials, and a telephone address book).[78]

The FBI's massive surveillance of dissident political activities became known only in the mid-1970s, and primarily as the result of investigations conducted by the House and Senate Select Committees on Intelligence Activities. Since then, FBI files (released in response to Freedom of Information Act requests, including those of the author) have further revealed the scope and political purposes of the FBI's surveillance activities. For the first time the FBI's absolute-secrecy barrier had been breached, a barrier that had effectively foreclosed public access to any FBI document on the premise that national-security interests and the war against crime would be undermined. Instead of undermining a war against criminals and spies, the opportunity to review FBI records has uncovered the massive extent of the FBI's abusive monitoring of dissent.

Able for the first time to understand the bases for these abuses, congressional, journalistic, and academic researchers identified three administrative deficiencies. First, the creation of special categories of files to maintain sensitive FBI records (even though documents in the FBI's central records system were not subject to public release) had effectively neutralized Congress's, the court's, and the press's potential oversight roles. Second, investigations ostensibly initiated for quasi-legitimate foreign intelligence, foreign counter-intelligence, or criminal prosecutive purposes had continued even after no evidence had been uncovered of foreign direction or unlawful activity. And, third, Congress's willingness to defer to attorneys general—on the premise that the FBI was closely monitored to ensure compliance with the law—had proven to be unfounded: attorneys general either did not know, purposely avoided being briefed in order to avoid having to prohibit illegal or questionable activities, or tacitly sanctioned FBI activities that they knew to be politically motivated because they themselves were interested either in learning about or in containing the influence of dissident activists.

The disclosures of past FBI abuses during the mid-1970s led to demands for two possible solutions: either new executive orders should be issued limiting FBI investigations, or Congress should enact a legislative charter spelling out the agency's investigative authority. Of the two, the most effective solution would be the enactment of a legislative charter, insofar as past FBI abuses have been the product of either secret executive directives, the purposeful abuse of executive discretion, or the willingness of high-level Justice Department officials to evade their oversight responsibilities. Indeed, the Senate Select Committee on Intelligence Activities (popularly known as the Church Committee), in its lengthy series of recommendations of April 1976, specifically called for such a charter and offered general guidelines for future FBI investigations.

For a time in the late 1970s, enactment of an FBI legislative charter seemed inevitable; the sole issue in dispute was whether the Congress should spell out precisely what the FBI could and could not do, as opposed to broadly outlining the parameters of the FBI's authority and then relying on the attorney general to establish specific administrative rules and procedures.

The broad congressional division over FBI charter legislation is reflected in the introduction of three radically different measures. One, drafted by the American Civil Liberties Union and proposed by Congressman Herman Badillo, would have limited FBI investigations to uncovering statutory violations; a second, introduced by Senator Edward Kennedy on behalf of the Carter administration, qualified the criminal prosecution standard to permit investigations in the foreign intelligence and foreign counter-intelligence areas; and the third, introduced by Senator Paul Laxalt and championed by Republican conservatives, abandoned any law-enforcement standard and would have permitted FBI investigations of individuals or groups seeking to 'influence or bring about a change in the policy of the United States or any State or subdivision thereof' as well as of 'activity which is likely or has the potential of violating the criminal laws of the United States'.[79]

These fundamental differences militated against quick congressional action—the more so insofar as congressional deliberations coincided with the onset of the 1980 presidential campaign, and in the absence of strong public demand for legislative reform. Serious consideration of any legislation dissipated with Ronald Reagan's election to the presidency in 1980 and the Republicans' success in gaining control of the Senate. Since 1981, accordingly, Congress's role has been at best supervisory, confined to sporadic inquiries of members of Congress as to the scope and purpose of FBI investigative activities—most notably by Congressman Don Edwards (the chairman of the House Judiciary Subcommittee having oversight responsibility over the FBI). Edwards's Subcommittee has conducted public hearings whenever publicized FBI activities have suggested the possibility of abuses. In effect, Congress has deferred to the attorney general, giving him the discretion to determine the scope of FBI investigative activities and to monitor them continuously.

What standards did attorneys general employ after 1975 when authorizing and monitoring FBI investigations in the so-called 'foreign intelligence,' 'domestic security,' and 'terrorism' areas? As the history of the FBI's past monitoring of dissident activities underscored, non-criminal investigations, once initiated, have invariably spilled over into political dissent and, more rarely, personal conduct, based upon two interrelated suspicions (not always on facts): that individuals/organizations were acting as agents of a foreign power, or that they were involved in a conspiracy either to conduct espionage (broadly defined to include industrial secrets) or to promote dissent and disrupt the government.

Can a system based on executive orders, and thus the principles of self-restraint and administrative discretion, preclude future abuses? The known provisions of the recently enacted executive guidelines suggest not—although this question cannot be answered definitively, as the specific guidelines governing FBI foreign intelligence and foreign counter-intelligence investigations issued by Presidents Ford, Carter, and Reagan remain classified. Nonetheless, the publicly released general standards do offer some basis for judgement.

President Ford's foreign intelligence/counter-intelligence guidelines, Executive Order 11905 issued in February 1976, authorized the FBI to 'detect and prevent espionage, sabotage, subversion, and other unlawful activities by or on behalf of foreign powers' subject to the 'supervision of the Attorney General and pursuant to such regulations as the Attorney General may establish'. President Carter's guidelines, Executive Order 12036 of January 1978, imposed tighter restrictions by limiting FBI investigations to 'protect[ion] against espionage and other clandestine intelligence activities, sabotage, international terrorist activities or assassinations conducted for or on behalf of foreign powers, organizations or persons'. In addition, Carter required that the attorney general monitor such investigations, limited the use of intrusive surveillance techniques, and prohibited the dissemination of any information acquired through these investigations unless it was 'reasonably believed' that the individual was acting on behalf of a foreign power. In contrast, the premise of President Reagan's guidelines, Executive Order 12333 of December 1981, was the need both to accord the FBI greater investigative discretion and to relax the attorney general's oversight role. Thus the Reagan guidelines empowered the FBI to 'conduct within the United States, when requested by officials of the intelligence community designated by the President, activities to collect foreign intelligence or support foreign intelligence collection requirements'. Consistent with this policy of having the FBI serve the political interests of other foreign intelligence agencies, Reagan's guidelines abandoned the Carter prohibitions against use of intrusive investigative techniques and restored the more discretionary provisions of Ford's requirements concerning the role of the attorney general: 'under the supervision of the Attorney General and pursuant to such regulations as the Attorney General may establish'. While ostensibly prohibiting investigations 'concerning the domestic activities of United States persons', other sections of Reagan's order qualified this restriction. The FBI was authorized (1) to initiate investigations to protect the 'safety of any persons or organizations, including those who are targets, victims or hostages of international terrorist organizations'; (2) to acquire and disseminate 'information obtained in the course of a lawful foreign intelligence, counterintelligence, international narcotics or international terrorist investigation'; (3) to retain 'incidentally obtained' information 'that may indicate involvement in activities that may violate Federal, state, local or foreign law'; and (4) to acquire information 'necessary for administrative purposes'.[80]

Insofar as the specific standards defining the conduct of 'foreign intelligence' and 'foreign counterintelligence' investigations remain classified, we cannot resolve whether the FBI is either authorized or invited to investigate individuals/organizations actively opposed to controversial foreign-policy decisions, nor, further, whether the sole effect of these restrictions has been to reduce, but not totally preclude, investigations of radical activists. Episodic revelations about particular investiga-

tions strongly suggest that the FBI continues to monitor dissident activities, albeit with greater caution and restraint.

Thus, although Ford's guidelines were relatively more restrictive than
Reagan's, a court case brought by the American Civil Liberties Union
on behalf of a number of dissident organizations confirmed that FBI informers monitoring the US Communist Party, who had formerly been
classified as 'domestic security', were simply reclassified as 'foreign
counterintelligence' under the Ford guidelines. Under Reagan's more
permissive guidelines, moreover, FBI 'foreign intelligence' investigations included asking librarians to watch for library users who might be
either diplomats of hostile powers or gathering information that could
be potentially harmful to the United States and, further, monitoring individuals who had visited El Salvador or Nicaragua or who supported
organizations critical of the Reagan administration's Central America
policy. Queried about the authority for and purpose of these investigations, Acting FBI Director John Otto advised House Judiciary Subcommittee Chairman Don Edwards that '[i]f credible information comes to
the FBI's attention that a group or entity is acting under the direction
and control of a hostile foreign power, the FBI may initiate a counter-
intelligence investigation. Such an investigation could be initiated even
though the activities of the group or entity do not, on their face, violate
a criminal statute.'[81]

Nor is the problem simply that the overbroad 'foreign intelligence'
and 'foreign counterintelligence' guidelines permit investigations spill-
ing over into political dissent. The guidelines governing FBI 'domestic
security' (now broadened to 'domestic security/terrorism') investigations even more strongly suggest that the FBI continues to monitor dissident activities.

In response to congressional revelations of the mid-1970s confirming
that FBI investigations of 'subversive activities' had focussed on political
dissent, and, further, that in the past attorneys general had not effectively monitored FBI investigations, Attorney General Edward Levi attempted to preclude the recurrence of these practices by issuing new
'domestic security' guidelines on 4 March 1976. While unwilling to
adopt a strict law-violation standard, Levi at the same time sought to
ensure (1) that allowing the FBI to initiate investigations of suspected future violations would not result in open-ended investigations that would
continue without regard to criminal conduct, and (2) that after the attorney general had given initial approval, the investigation could not
continue without his reauthorization.

Accordingly, under the Levi guidelines FBI field offices could initiate
'preliminary' investigations 'on their own initiative' on the basis of 'allegations or other information that an individual or a group may be engaged in activities which involve or will involve the violation of federal
law'. Such preliminary investigations, however, were to be limited to a

ninety-day period, and to be confined to verifying or refuting the allegation. In contrast, 'full' investigations had no time limit (although their
continuance required the attorney general's approval) and must be
based on 'specific and articulable facts giving reason to believe that an
individual or a group is or may be engaged in activities which involve
the use of force or violence and which involve or will involve the violation of federal law'.

In addition, Levi's guidelines ensured that attorneys general would
not once again evade their oversight responsibilities either by tacitly authorizing illegal or questionable activities or by conveying the desire not
to be fully briefed. For one, the Department of Justice had to review
'the results of full domestic security investigations at least annually'.
Second, Department of Justice officials must 'determine in writing
whether continued investigation is warranted', and full investigations
'shall not continue beyond one year without the written approval of the
Department'. Third, after securing approval to initiate a full investigation, FBI officials had to 'request that the Department determine in writing whether continued investigation is warranted'.[82]

Imposed by executive order, these restrictions could be modified by
executive order. Indeed, this was done following Reagan's election to
the presidency and his declaration of decidedly different views about FBI
surveillance of dissident activities. Holding expansive opinions on the
'Communist'[83] and 'terrorist' threats, candidate Reagan had called for
the 'unleashing' of the intelligence agencies. Once inaugurated, he
moved quickly to ensure that the FBI monitored dissident activities. The
first step was announced in December 1981, with his executive order revising Carter's 'foreign intelligence' and 'foreign counterintelligence'
standards. Less than two years later, Reagan's attorney general, William French Smith, issued new 'domestic security/terrorism' guidelines,
rescinding those of Attorney General Edward Levi.

Smith's guidelines of 7 March 1983 abandoned Levi's two-part distinction between 'preliminary' and 'full' investigations. FBI investigations were authorized 'when the facts or circumstances reasonably
indicate that two or more persons are engaged in an enterprise [to
further] political or social goals wholly or in part through activities that
involve force or violence and a violation of the criminal laws of the
United States'. But investigations were not to be confined to specific
acts of violence or lawlessness. The FBI was directed as well to 'anticipate or prevent crime' and to initiate investigations whenever individuals or organizations either 'advocate criminal activity or indicate an
apparent intent to engage in crime, particularly crimes of violence'.

In addition, and more ominously, Smith rescinded Levi's carefully
crafted oversight requirements. The FBI director or a designated assistant director was delegated sole responsibility to authorize a 'domestic
security/terrorism' investigation. Limited to a 180-day period, these in-

vestigations could be reauthorized by the director or assistant director. Consistent with this objective of limiting the Department's oversight responsibilities, Smith rescinded Levi's requirement that Justice Department officials review such authorizations annually and then determine 'in writing' whether 'continued' investigation was 'warranted'. Instead, the FBI need only 'notify' the Department's Office of Intelligence Policy and Review whenever initiating a 'domestic security/terrorism' investigation—although Smith did not stipulate that this notification be in writing. The Office of Intelligence Policy and Review would annually review these investigations; its review, however, was confined to the 'results', and the Levi requirement of written annual reauthorization was also dropped. Underscoring Smith's intent to abandon the field and foist responsibility for any adverse reaction should questionable FBI activities be publicly disclosed, the attorney general's role was to be essentially discretionary: he 'may, as he deems necessary, request the FBI to prepare a report on the status of the investigation'.[84]

Not surprisingly, then, the revised guidelines invited FBI officials to expand FBI investigations of 'terrorism' to encompass political dissent. For example, in a recently publicized case, FBI agent John Ryan (assigned to the Peoria, Illinois, office) was fired for refusing to investigate two anti-nuclear groups (the Veterans Fast for Life and Silo Plowshares) under the 'domestic security/terrorism' guidelines. Ryan had refused an order to investigate these groups following the discovery that glue had been put in the locks of Army recruiting offices in Chicago, and that leaflets published by Veterans Fast for Life had been found at this office, while a car of a Silo Plowshares member had been identified as having been at the scene. The acts involved destruction of government property, Ryan conceded, but nonetheless these organizations' activities had 'been consistently non-violent symbolic statements against violence'.[85]

Nor were known FBI investigations of dissidents confined to militant activists. Beginning in 1981, the FBI undertook a massive five-year investigation of individuals and groups opposed to the Reagan administration's Central America policy. Ostensibly initiated on the basis of allegations of terrorism—that the Committee in Solidarity with the People of El Salvador (CISPES) was providing illegal military assistance to the El Salvador rebels—this investigation soon broadened to target other groups and individuals and to amass information relating to their political activities and adherents. Included among the more than one hundred American citizens and groups under surveillance were the National Council of Churches in New York, students and faculty members at Florida State University and seventeen other colleges, the Women's Rape Center in Norfolk, Virginia, the Southern Christian Leadership Conference in Atlanta, the Roman Catholic Maryknoll Sisters in Oklahoma City and Chicago, the Sisters of Mercy in Baltimore, a hospital-workers union in Philadelphia, and United Automobile Workers and National Education Association locals in Cleveland. Unable to develop evidence that CISPES and the other subjects of this massive inquiry were involved in 'terrorism' or acted as agents of foreign powers, FBI agents instead compiled (1) a list of the names of a dozen Philadelphia groups 'actively involved in demonstrations; seminars, marches, etc., regarding the US intervention in Central America', and (2) monitored a Houston peace rally, taking more than one hundred photographs of the demonstrators and recording automobile licence-plate numbers. Queries from agents as to whether 'seemingly legitimate political activity' should be monitored were rebuffed. Indeed, when the FBI's Phoenix office concluded that the Tucson Committee on Human Rights was a non-violent group seeking to educate public opinion on Central American affairs, and thus that 'it does not appear that further investigation is warranted', FBI officials in Washington ordered the Phoenix office to 'consider the possibility that the Tucson Committee may be a front organization for CISPES'.

The extensive deletions in the released FBI documents make it impossible to tell whether FBI agents focussed on activities intended to commit legal acts. The released documents nonetheless confirm that the FBI was interested in political activities and sought to contain these groups' influence. For example, a New Orleans agent wrote that it was 'imperative at this time to formulate some plan of attack against CISPES and specifically against individuals . . . who defiantly display their contempt for the US government by making speeches and propagandizing their cause', while another field office characterized the writings of a church leader as evidence of a 'mind totally sold on the marxist leninist philosophy'.[86]

Because the FBI's investigation of CISPES's alleged support of terrorism began in 1981, when the Levi guidelines were operative, a series of questions arise. Did the 'preliminary' phase of this investigation of allegations of illegal activity uncover (within the prescribed ninety-day period) 'specific and articulable facts' justifying a 'full' investigation? Apparently not, as FBI officials now concede that the investigation was undertaken on the basis of misinformation provided by an FBI informer, Frank Varelli. Why, then, did seasoned FBI officials and the Department of Justice officials responsible for authorizing 'full' investigations conclude that such an investigation was warranted—without 'specific and articulable facts'? Had the Levi guidelines been set aside even before being formally rescinded in March 1983? Furthermore, did FBI officials in 1981 and 1982 brief Justice Department officials about this ongoing investigation and request a determination 'in writing whether continued investigation is warranted'? And did Justice Department officials in 1981 and 1982 authorize, in writing, continuance of this investigation?

The released documents further disclose that this FBI investigation of CISPES was revived on 30 March 1983—understandably, in view of the more permissive Smith standards. In view of the fact that the CISPES investigation thereafter spilled over to other dissident organizations—including the National Council of Churches, the Maryknoll Sisters, and the Southern Christian Leadership Conference—was it the case that the Attorney General encouraged intensified surveillance? Did FBI officials 'notify' the Office of Intelligence Policy and Review of this investigation's expansion to include liberal religious, labour-union, and political organizations? What actions were taken by Justice Department officials in response to these notifications prior to the Department's 1985 determination to terminate the investigation (having concluded that CISPES was engaged in legitimate political activities)? And did the Attorney General at any time request a report on the 'status of these investigations'?

The five-year duration of an investigation uncovering no evidence of criminal activity, and ultimately monitoring political dissent, underscores how the Smith guidelines, and the rationale for the decision to rescind the Levi guidelines, invited the FBI to resume investigations of political dissent, and possibly to resort to illegal investigative techniques.[87]

What then, are the lessons of the American experience for Canadian security policy? The FBI's massive and illegal monitoring of dissent (in the past and resumed in the 1980s) resulted directly from the conservative commitment of federal officials (whether in the White House, the Justice Department, or the FBI) to contain political change. Concomitantly, because they were sensitive to the adverse political consequences should these activities become known, federal officials acted purposefully, if deceitfully, to ensure deniability—whether this meant intentional evasion of their oversight responsibilities on the part of Justice Department and White House officials, or the devising of records procedures by FBI officials to permit the undiscoverable destruction of recognizably sensitive documents. Disturbingly, in view of the revelations during the mid-1970s of both the scope of FBI abuses and the intended ineffectiveness of executive oversight, the Congress to date has failed to enact legislation defining the parameters of FBI investigative authority and thereby reducing the exclusive policy discretion of attorneys general, presidents, and FBI directors. This failure continued even after the Reagan administration, with its published directives of 1981-83, had signalled its intention to expand FBI investigations *and* to minimize departmental oversight. This permissiveness invited both the resumption of FBI monitoring of dissent and the refinement of more failsafe procedures to preclude discovery[88] should ambitious bureaucrats, convinced of their own righteousness and the blindness of the public and Congress, conclude that the nation's security interests are imperilled. By not instituting legislative standards, Congress inadvertently permitted the FBI to resume monitoring dissent and at the same time undermined its own ability to oversee FBI operations.[89]

Dissent and the State in Eastern Europe

AUREL BRAUN

In the late 1980s there is visible turmoil throughout the region commonly referred to as Eastern Europe. In January 1988 demonstrators in Hungary, Poland, and Czechoslovakia protested repression in Romania.[1] The leadership in Czechoslovakia changed in December 1987, and in Hungary in May 1988. All the states in the region are suffering from a variety of economic problems, including inflation, threatened unemployment, and the difficulties of adapting to current and prospective changes in the Soviet Union as Mikhail Gorbachev attempts to pursue his policies of *glasnost* (giving voice), *perestroika* (restructuring or reconstruction), *uskorenie* (acceleration), and *demokratizatcsia* (greater economic and political democracy). In such times dissent can assume particular importance as part of the transformation of the system. It can also be part of a process of self-liberation.

In analyzing developments in this region, however, it may be worthwhile to introduce a note of caution right at the beginning. Since the Second World War, this is certainly not the first time that the region has seen significant turmoil, or that observers in both the East and the West have anticipated major changes. In the mid-to late 1960s, for instance, a number of Western analysts concluded that the region had reached an evolutionary crossroads and that the Soviet Empire was about to disintegrate.[2] But the Soviet/Warsaw Pact invasion of Czechoslovakia in 1968 showed that these expectations were at the very least premature. This is not to suggest that change is not possible, but recent history does show us that change can occur only within certain parameters defined not merely by local needs, but by the interests of the entire socialist system as determined by the Soviet Union and those allied regimes in which it has full confidence.

In the Soviet Union, the July 1988 congress of the Communist Party demonstrated that there is great potential for reform. The vigour with which Gorbachev pushed for change and the politically masterful way in which he managed the meeting showed that it would be a mistake to underestimate the possibilities for altering the system and improving the protection of human rights. Proposed constitutional changes and greater political competition[3] could lead to a significant alteration of the system, which in turn would enlarge the parameters for the Eastern European states.

On the other hand, it would be imprudent to overestimate the scope of the changes envisioned by Gorbachev or the ease with which basic aspects of the socialist system can be altered. Gorbachev's 'revolution' is a change from the top, and at the conference he showed the limits of both his vision of radical reform and his patience. He assured the delegates that the Soviet Union would remain a one-party state and that the Communist Party would retain its traditional role as the 'vanguard of the Soviet system'.[4] He added: 'And in any country the ruling party forms a government—executive power—at all levels.'[5] Other officials in the congress disparaged the notion of a multi-party system. Alexander Yakovlev, one of Gorbachev's closest allies on the Politburo, told a news conference: 'It seems to us that the two-party system that you have in the West is a game.'[6]

Gorbachev also showed at the congress that it was *his* specific vision of *perestroika* and *glasnost* that he wanted implemented. With chilling arrogance he deflated and dismissed the opinions of those who differed with him and indicated that he wanted unquestioning loyalty from his supporters. Leonid I. Abalkin, a senior economic advisor to Gorbachev, differed indirectly with his boss when he suggested that if the Soviet Union was to ensure a democratic organization of social life, there would have to be a real opportunity for non-communism to play a political role.[7] Gorbachev promptly rebuked him for having too little faith in the Communist system. His tone suggested that he considered the line between intellectual digression and personal betrayal perilously thin.[8]

The limits of the reform that Gorbachev envisions and the difficulty of changing the system can also be seen in the question of nationalities. Armenians in the Soviet Union had welcomed *glasnost* and *perestroika* enthusiastically. The Armenian majority in the Nagorno-Karabakh, a region that was incorporated into the Muslim republic of Azerbaijan under Stalin, have sought reunification with the Soviet republic of Armenia. In February 1988 the Nagorno-Karabakh legislature voted to request reunion with Armenia, and in June 1988 the Armenian legislature voted to ask the Supreme Soviet to approve the transfer.[9] Massive demonstrations in Armenia accompanied this request, and there was considerable violence. Gorbachev and the Supreme Soviet, however, rejected the Armenian request.[10] The Soviet leader denounced the Armenian demonstrators, had the capital city of Armenia, Yerevan, surrounded by 150,000 troops to enforce order, and banned Western reporters from the region. He accused Armenian nationalists of 'misusing' *perestroika* and of 'going crazy',[11] and in early July 1988 the Soviet government had Paruir Harikyan, a prominent Armenian nationalist, arrested on charges of fomenting disorder and stripped of his citizenship.[12] Gorbachev and the system, it seems, do not intend to respond to demands for change at the local level when it comes to this issue. The decision was taken from the top. Gorbachev's insistence that his is the only valid and relevant interpretation of *perestroika*, his intransigence, and the intractability of the system, at least on the question of nationalities, have significant implications not only for the Soviet Union but also for Eastern Europe.

This chapter does not purport to be a comprehensive study either of the nature of dissent throughout Eastern Europe or of all the means employed by the regimes in question to deal with it. Rather, it seeks to examine some of the significant aspects and causes of that dissent and of the regimes' responses to it. The nature of dissent varies over the region, and the diversity of the problems each state faces ensures that what happens in one not repeated in another. This diversity underlines the need to clarify definitions and concepts in order to allow a more probative analysis.

Even geography is a source of controversy in this region. 'Dissident' intellectuals have spoken increasingly of a need to think in terms of a 'Central Europe', or *Mitteleuropa*, rather than Eastern Europe. All of these terms are value-laden and, to a considerable degree, political. What is generally called 'Eastern Europe' is not merely a geographic entity stretching from the river Elbe eastward to the Soviet border and from the Baltic Sea to the Adriatic. It is also an area that, with the exception of Yugoslavia and Albania, is dominated by the Soviet Union. Yet several of these states have traditionally been much closer to Western Europe, and as a result the imposition of socialism severed important historical/cultural links. Dissident historians, therefore, make an important point in attempting to re-label the region. While on the one hand it represents an effort to re-establish links, on the other it represents perhaps an even stronger effort to decouple the region from the Soviet Union. The latter is part of a long-term move to differentiate between this region and the Soviet Union by using such labels as 'Asiatic' for the latter, and at times going as far as to call the Soviet bloc itself 'Western Asia'.[13] Dissidents in the region are fully aware of the historical significance of geographic labels and of the impact of geographic differentiation on the evolution—or rather, demise—of the Ottoman and Hapsburg empires.

Nevertheless, these geographic re-definitions may be premature. Soviet domination of the region remains vigorous, and Gorbachevian changes do not, at least yet, point to a radical transformation of the intra-bloc relationship. And despite Western interest in the region, there is no evidence so far of a Western will and ability to restore the kinds of cultural linkages that existed before the Second World War. Moreover, it should be recognized that cultural linkages varied among the states of the region even then, especially in terms of the transmission of Western political ideas. Furthermore, within the region itself social-cultural linkages were limited at best—in some instances, virtually non-existent. Consequently, though it may eventually become more accurate to speak of the region as Central Europe, or at least East-Central Europe, for the time being the term 'Eastern Europe' should do no great violence to an examination of dissident activities and government policies in the area.

It is essential, however, to continue to recognize the diversity of the region. One cannot equate all of Eastern Europe, or lump all the dissidents in the region into one category. National and intellectual histories in the region differ significantly. Popular attitudes to culture and to civil liberties, for instance, are remarkably unlike in Czechoslovakia and Romania. The various governments in the region also differ in what they perceive as threats. Consequently, regimes such as those in Hungary, Yugoslavia, and Poland take a significantly different position from Romania or Albania *vis-à-vis* dissent. The contrast between what happened to striking workers in Yugoslavia and the miners protesting in Romania in 1977 in the Jiu Valley is starkly instructive: the Romanian miners were not heard from again, as the government used mass force to repress the outbreaks. Thus in examining dissent it is vital not to divorce intellectual history from its national, historical, and social bases.

On the other hand, such significant differences should not obscure what is common in the region. For despite its rich cultural and historical diversity, the imposition of socialism following the Second World War has created some essential common features. However one may categorize these governments—whether some appear to be 'inclusion regimes' attempting to control society from 'within',[14] or whether some development schemes appear to offer 'modernization and containment'[15]—the most crucial feature common to all remains a monopoly of party power, and a centralized system of control (coupled with the flow of power from the top down) that fundamentally restricts basic political rights despite the occasional semblance of participation. This is not to suggest, of course, that the same level of participation prevails throughout the region. Clearly political involvement in Hungary, for instance, is significantly greater than in Romania. But as Robert Sharlet has written, genuine participation refers to 'input' rather than 'output', and a pluralism of values would need to be accepted by the political élite as a condition for the existence of political pluralism that in turn is necessary for the protection of genuine political rights.[16]

What is also common in the region is the problem of legitimacy—or, more precisely, the inability of each regime to achieve sufficient legitimacy to maintain itself in power without the use of widespread coercion. Again, the degree of legitimacy of each regime varies according to the role played historically by the native communist party and the method by which it came to power. Thus initially there was a considerably higher level of legitimacy for the regime in Czechoslovakia, for example, than in Poland, although in neither did the regime achieve the legitimacy accorded governments in a pluralistic system. Some regimes, however, were able to enhance their legitimacy by improving their economic performance, as in Hungary (after 1956), or by assuming the mantle of nationalism, as in Romania.

Yet all of these regimes have managed to largely fritter away much of whatever legitimacy they managed to gain for themselves. The inability of the ruling parties in the region to deliver on economic and political promises radically undermined the official Communist tradition. Whatever hopes intellectuals—and, for that matter, workers—had about communism as a functioning idea, capable of mobilizing popular aspirations and of offering a genuine field of activity for democratic reformers, these have evaporated. In the 1950s, at least in Eastern Europe, Marxism had an intellectual appeal that, together with its institutionalized and preponderant political position, ensured that it was virtually the exclusive language of politics and culture. The post-Stalin period saw a major disillusionment with the system and helped bring about the evolution of dissenting or oppositional Marxism, which survived into the 1970s through such voices as those of Rudolf Bahro and Jiri Hajek. Increasingly, however, oppositional or dissenting Marxism has been replaced by 'rights activism' with a 'rights language' that has disposed of most of the baggage of Marxism. 'Rights activism' has spread throughout the region, and though there is no clear co-ordination among the various groups, it is possible to see incipient linkages and, at the very least, a similarity in the types of challenges that they pose to the various regimes. Consensus is growing that Marxism is not the solution but the source of the problem.

There are difficulties, though, beyond the historical diversity of the region, cultural differences, and value-laden geographic terminology. The very term 'dissident' creates difficulties. Though one should quite clearly recognize the common element of 'dissent' in any social system, it is essential to identify the dissent in socialist states, where the ruling tradition that it seeks to undermine is one whose functioning idea has proven to be incapable of mobilizing popular aspirations, and that maintains itself through an institutionalized and coercion-based process. It is not necessary to contrast that system with a system based completely on consent, for that indeed does not exist. Whereas in all social systems there are those who will criticize the contradictions they see around them—and to that extent all dissent is similar—it is really the attitude of the regime that ultimately determines the context within which dissent operates. Thus certain types of non-conformity that would be virtually unnoticed in pluralistic democracies would be treated as subversive activities in Eastern Europe. Given the insistence of these regimes on centralized party control and a single guiding ideology, such non-conformity can only appear subversive. For even when a regime is willing to introduce some reforms, there is a single party mentality at work. Consequently the regime does not tolerate opposition to the core elements of the system and does not yet accept or even contemplate a systemic change.

Perhaps, as Tony Judt has suggested, it would be better to use the term 'opposition' to describe people and movements that function as opponents of the Party and the state in Eastern Europe.[17] This term also creates problems, however, for as Judt admits, it may be confused with a characteristic of the new politics of 'anti-politics' that in some segments of Western society, especially among the young, is little more than the refusal to conform: the insistence upon being 'different' that then is elevated to a form of conscious ideological statement. Hence it may be safer, even in the case of Eastern Europe, to stay with the term 'dissident' as long as one recognizes the diversity of the phenomenon and the differences in the activities of the participants in the various states of the area.

For in Eastern Europe 'dissent' would cover a range of activities from those of the banned trade union Solidarity in Poland, to strikes by Romanian industrial workers in Brasov, to *samizdat* publication by intellectuals in Hungary or Czechoslovakia, to the involvement of young people in Poland in the newly formed peace movement, the Freedom and Peace Group. What is common in all these cases is the perception by the regime that such activities pose a threat. Yet, as noted above, each regime may assess the gravity of such a threat differently, and may use different methods to deal with it.

Dissent continues despite the attempts of the various regimes to develop a socialist consciousness that would bring about consensus. And although there are no organized institutional means to express opposition to the policies of the Communist Party, Eastern European societies, even according to official statements, are hardly conflict-free. In the 1980s especially, 'rights' activists are exploring the limits of proclaimed domestic law to press for a wide range of civil and economic liberties. This approach can be traced back at least to the Helsinki Accords of 1975, but developments in Eastern Europe, together with the actual and proposed changes under Gorbachev in the Soviet Union, have lent the effort a new and special impetus. Yet while the regimes in Eastern Europe may undertake some measures to make themselves more responsive to the plight of the popular base, they do not tolerate challenges to their core security interests, which include, first and foremost, the retention of a monopoly of political power and economic centrality for the Party.

Though the challenges to these regimes vary significantly, it may be possible to identify four broad types of dissent: political, economic, national or nationalist, and religious.[18] There are variations within each type, and often it is impossible or at least extremely difficult to separate them for any but analytic purposes, since acts of dissent frequently involve multiple implications. Nevertheless, most of the time at least one of the broad types of dissent is preponderant and identifiable. Political dissent can range from sharp confrontations to very subtle and nuanced forms of opposition. It can include the activities of hard-line party functionaries who fear that any wave of reform would deprive them of the privileges that they have fought so hard to achieve, or who worry that ultimately the Party itself may be endangered. It can also involve the acts of the opponents of the regime who reject the Marxist-Leninist paradigm in its entirety. In the case of economic dissent, again, the range is considerable, with some challenging merely the direction of economic policies set by the Party and others contending that nothing is acceptable short of the replacement of the economic infrastructure. Nationalist dissent, in turn, can include resistance to Soviet hegemony or Russification as well as opposition to government policies by ethnic minorities within Eastern Europe. In fact, the majority of the Eastern European states have significant ethnic minorities, which have expressed varying degrees of unhappiness. Lastly, religious dissent should be hardly surprising in states where the official policy is to encourage atheism. The degree of dissent, however, varies according to historical traditions and the resiliency and mobilizing powers of domestic religious institutions.

The longevity of the regimes that came to power largely on the coattails of the Red Army, and that have enjoyed little or no popular legitimacy, would tend to indicate a considerable ability to deal with opposition and to cope effectively with dissent. There have been major failures, particularly in Hungary (1956), Czechoslovakia (1968), Poland (1980-81) and the GDR (1953) but in each case the Party has managed to restore most of its power (if not its authority) either by using its own means or by drawing on external help. It is true that on occasion a particular Party has had to be widely purged, as in Czechoslovakia, and fundamental issues remain unresolved. In the end, though, Communist rule has persevered. The regimes in Eastern Europe thus have developed a wide range of tools to cope with dissent, and in some instances they have managed to continually improve and adapt some of these to changing conditions.

Throughout the Soviet bloc, furthermore, regimes deal with dissent differently now than they did in the Stalinist era. As Jeremy Azrael has observed, more of the activities of the secret police are now 'designed to have a "prophylactic" instead of a "punitive" effect'.[19] Though the goals of control remain the same, the methods have had to change substantively. Yet for this more sophisticated approach to succeed, it is important that the state be perceived as having the capability and will to uncover and to act against dissent or unorthodox activity. This is true whether or not it actually does so in every single instance.[20]

A more sophisticated and flexible approach does not exclude *ab initio* attempts by the regime to incapacitate people by removing them from society, whether by detention, imprisonment, exile, or even murder. Nevertheless, this approach places a far greater emphasis than in the past on both individual and general deterrence.[21] In the case of individual deterrence, the regime would retaliate against dissidents and make them hesitant in the future to engage in activities that the Party considered undesirable, or would try to induce them to behave in more appropriate ways. In the case of general deterrence, the regime would seek to make other people wary about becoming involved in the 'undesirable' activities of dissidents, and thus try to shape people's perceptions of what could happen to them if they moved beyond the parameters of 'acceptable' behaviour.

Domestic deterrence, though, is but one tactic employed by the regimes in Eastern Europe. They have used various forms of co-optation, containment, and co-existence. These have been incorporated into the broader strategies of dealing with dissent either singly or in combination. It may be possible to distinguish four broad categories of regime strategy, which in turn have been devised to deal with the four types of dissent we identified earlier: pacification through partial inclusion, repressive tolerance, differentiated political justice, and suppression through main force. Again, regimes in Eastern Europe tend to use a combination of strategies and tactics, and distinctions among them are often blurred.

Political dissent

Dissent from the regime's goals or policies has taken a great many different forms in Eastern Europe, ranging from open opposition to clandestine actions. Though the response of the regimes has differed according to the circumstances, direct opposition challenging the role of the Party or of the leader has proven to be most difficult to tolerate. The monopolistic role of the Party is a key tenet of Leninism, which itself has remained sacrosanct even under Gorbachev. Despite multicandidate elections in the Soviet Union in March 1989 and the victory of a number of nationalist candidates in the Baltic republics, Gorbachev has steadfastly opposed the creation of a multi-party system. Following the election, in a speech to senior news editors, he also reminded everyone that the Soviet press was expected to hew to the Communist Party line.[22] The retention of Leninism as the legitimizing ideology thus makes systemic reform extraordinarily difficult, if not impossible.

In Poland the creation of the mass union Solidarity was viewed as a direct challenge to the Party. The creation of such a union did in fact deny the vanguard role of the Party in presenting the interests of the workers, and the events of 1980-81 were therefore viewed as a challenge to the core security interests of socialism by both the leadership of

Wojciech Jaruzelski and the Soviet Union. Consequently, the regime perceived the 10-million-strong union as a threat of a magnitude that necessitated suppression through main force. Mass arrests and the imposition of martial law in 1981 were designed to crush the union movement. The regime did succeed in breaking Solidarity as an organization, but not as political opposition. It has been far less successful than Hungary in its attempts at 'normalization', even though the Kadar regime used more brutal repression than martial law following the 1956 uprising. In some ways Poland has also been less successful than the Czechoslovak regime, which at least stabilized the country (granted, at a very high cost) after 1968, when the Warsaw Pact used suppression through main force to deal with what Moscow perceived as a threat to socialism. And in 1989 the Jaruzelski regime has been forced to enter into negotiations with Solidarity on re-legalizing the union.

Romania too has used main force to suppress violent demonstrations against the regime in 1977 and in 1987. The miners' strike in 1977 in the Jiu River Valley took on a political overtone when the workers denounced the regime and attacked officials. The Ceausescu regime suppressed the strike through the use of main force and arrested and deported the strike leaders.[23] In November 1987 a protest by several thousand workers at the Steagul Rosu truck and machine works in Brasov also began spontaneously quickly acquired political overtones.[24] The workers denounced Ceausescu himself and some attacked and ransacked the mayor's office. The demonstration was stopped only when the regime called in the militia and riot police, who arrested a large number of demonstrators.[25]

In most instances, though, the East European regimes have been able—and have chosen—to respond to political dissent by other means. The Czechoslovak regime's mode of dealing with the Charter 77 group (formed in January 1977) represents a newer approach to dissent. In part, the creation of Charter 77 was prompted by the 1976 trials and conviction of a group of rock musicians, the Plastic People of the Universe, who, together with their supporters, had been accused of 'disturbance of the peace'.[26] But the formation of Charter 77 was not simply a response to a particular act of suppression by the Czechoslovak government. From the beginning there was a great diversity of views among the signatories, who included ex-communists and liberals, intellectuals and workers. It had a significant and immediate impact, and it generated a great deal of sympathy in the West, particularly in Western Europe. At first the members sought to be *non-political*, tried to establish a dialogue with the regime, and denied that they represented an opposition. That in all of this they were unsuccessful should not be entirely surprising, for as Gordon Skilling, in his authoritative book on Charter 77, states, the name of the group referred not merely to a document but to a movement for human rights.[27] Significantly, the Charter declaration contained the following passage:

> Charter 77 is a free, informal, open community of people of different convictions, different faiths and different professions united by the will to strive individually and collectively, for the respect of civic and human rights in our country and throughout the world—rights accorded to all men by the two mentioned international covenants [the International Covenant on Civil and Political Rights and International Covenant on Economic, Social and Cultural Rights signed by Czechoslovakia in 1968 and confirmed at Helsinki in 1975], by the Final Act of the Helsinki Conference and by numerous other international documents opposing war, violence and social or spiritual oppression, and which are comprehensively laid down in the United Nations' Universal Declaration of Human Rights.[28]

In its emphasis on 'rights' language, the Declaration represented an evolution in dissent. It referred to both domestic and international legality, and by invoking the two human-rights covenants and the Helsinki Final Act, its drafters placed themselves and their demands within an international context and made themselves part of a worldwide movement for human rights. The challenge to a regime intent on tight control and centralization was potentially enormous. Though the Chartists ruled out violence or terrorist acts, and would use even passive resistance only on rare occasions, thereby restricting their activities to speeches and writing, there could be little doubt as to the nature of the challenge. Charter 77 was a call to full and active citizenship. Vaclav Havel, a leading dissident, declared that Charter 77 was 'an attempt to *live in the truth*', and that truth 'plays the role of a power factor and a direct political force'.[29] Another member wrote that it 'destroyed the carefully erected facade of socialist consolidation'.[30] For all its efforts to avoid confrontation, therefore, in its insistence on civil rights Charter 77 struck at the very foundation of Eastern European-style socialism. Ultimately, it involved a rejection of Leninism.

Despite the more than one thousand signatories and the potential explosiveness of such dissent, the Czechoslovak regime chose, as noted, not to seek suppression through main force. But it did not treat the challenge lightly. It employed a whole panoply of other means against Charter 77, including a form of differentiated political justice. In the first year of the Charter the regime did not punish persons for dissident activity directly. Though it contended that Charter 77 was illegal, individuals were not at first indicted for their role in drafting, signing, or distributing it, or for acting as group spokesmen.[31] Even in 1979, when the regime moved much more directly against Chartists, arresting sixteen (all of whom were members of the Committee for the Defence of the Unjustly Persecuted [VONS]),[32] the trials were designed to deter others rather than as a direct mass suppression.

Of course, the government did engage in a variety of other activities against Chartists, including 'unofficial' acts of violence ranging from beatings in the streets or in the woods outside the cities, to the throwing of poison pellets into the gardens of dissidents.[33] It also encouraged emigration through threats and by either annulling the citizenship of activists visiting abroad or simply denying re-entry and then stripping them of their citizenship.[34]

None of these tactics, however, was sufficient to crush Charter 77, which continues its activities today. As the group has clearly been a significant irritant to the government, it may at first be somewhat puzzling that the latter has not used greater force to suppress it. Here, however, as elsewhere in Eastern Europe, it is important not to confuse the *potential* threat of a dissident movement with the *actual* danger that it poses to the regime. Despite the bravery, the imagination, and the persistence of the members of Charter 77 in seeking to enhance the protection of civil rights and to build civil society, the group has not won the large-scale endorsement of the population. Unlike Solidarity in Poland, it has never become a mass movement. Accordingly, the Czechoslovak government has recognized that Charter 77 is not a great threat either to its own stability or to the process of consolidation in which it has been engaged since the Warsaw Pact invasion of the country in 1968. It has concluded that it would be able to contain the challenge, and that therefore suppression by main force is unnecessary.

Still, the Czechoslovak regime remains vigilant in all matters relating to dissent, and continues to use a type of differentiated political justice. Dissent in the arts, whether in literature or in music, has been viewed by Prague as ultimately representing a political threat, and rock and jazz in particular have been carefully monitored. Though the regime has long waged a battle with rock, it has indicated a willingness to accept such music if it does not threaten the Communist cultural monopoly. In 1986, for instance, it allowed a rock festival to be held in Prague under official sponsorship but with the participation of many underground rock groups.[35] On the other hand, certain rock and jazz groups have been persecuted, as have members of the former jazz section of the Czech Union of Musicians. Although it had several thousand members, and its periodicals had reached a readership of no fewer than 100,000, the section was disbanded in 1983. It protested against the dissolution at the European Cultural Forum at Budapest in 1985, and planned another protest action to coincide with the Conference on Security and Cooperation in Europe (CSCE) session in Vienna in November 1986.[36] Moving selectively, the government had the Chairman of the Jazz Section and six other members arrested,[37] though the courts gave them sentences considerably lighter than those sought by the State prosecutor.[38]

In fact, in all its actions directed against dissent, the Czechoslovak government has been selective. It has subjected the leading personalities of human-rights groups to questioning and harassment, arrested some, and confined others to insane asylums.[39] And it has been even harsher, as we will see, in its treatment of those engaged in unauthorized religious activities.[40]

Other regimes in the Soviet bloc have also employed differentiated political justice to deal with dissent. In Poland, although the Jaruzelski regime has crushed the structure of the Solidarity union, as noted, it has not managed to destroy the Solidarity movement. When US Vice-President George Bush visited Warsaw in September 1987 and laid a wreath at the graveside of Father Jerzy Popieluszko, a pro-Solidarity priest murdered by security police officers in 1984, thousands of onlookers chanted, 'We want Lech [Walesa] not Wojciech [Jaruzelski].'[41] Furthermore, a rich underground literature has flourished in Poland, with many works on literature, politics, and music coming out in *samizdat* form. In order to deal with what it views as an unruly society, the regime has employed tough measures directed against some 'problematic' individuals followed by equally sudden retreats with calls for some form of reconciliation.

In 1986, for example, the regime put five members of the Confederation of Independent Poland (known by its Polish acronym KPN) on trial. KPN had attempted to function as an opposition political party and had demanded free elections and the abolishment of the Communist system by the non-violent means of the ballot box.[42] In May 1986 the regime also managed to arrest Zbigniew Bujak, a Solidarity leader who for four-and-a-half years had headed the Underground Provisional Coordinating Commission (the TKK committee of the outlawed Solidarity).[43]

Yet, despite the arrest of Bujak, TKK continued its activities on a national scale and managed to mount several large-scale public demonstrations. The Warsaw regime therefore attempted other means of containment. On 11 September 1986 it announced that it would free all prisoners, including Bujak, but not those charged with espionage, terrorism, sabotage, or treason.[44] With this amnesty the regime also released about 20,000 common criminals out of a prison population estimated to exceed 100,000.[45] But members of certain political dissenting groups, such as the Independent Pacifist Movement, were not initially released. Though the amnesty was a welcome development to most dissidents, it presented problems. As in all three previous amnesties, the accused political prisoners had no right to reject clemency or to demand a trial to prove their innocence. Following the amnesty, moreover, the regime continued to harass various leaders in the dissident movement, though it allowed Walesa to speak out. The latter claimed that TKK had a right to resist and that this was 'guaranteed by the Polish Constitution as well as by International Conventions signed by Poland'.[46] Here again, notice the use of 'rights' language.

The Yugoslav regime too has used differentiated political justice (together with a number of other methods) to handle political dissent. In 1985, for instance, it charged a total of 415 individuals with political crimes, though of these only 62 were accused of posing a counter-revolutionary threat to society or conspiring to commit acts of enemy activity.[47] The majority, according to the regime, were tried for promoting national and religious hatred.

Among the less harsh methods used by Eastern European governments are pacification through partial inclusion and repressive tolerance. Both domestically and externally, it has been important for some of these regimes to create the impression of participation and relative freedom. The attitude of the young has been of particular concern. Even in Albania the regime has acknowledged that there are problems: in 1987 it voiced its concern over a younger generation that persists in adopting 'alien' styles and on occasion 'thumbs its nose' at party and state tutelage.[48] Thus in addition to practising a differentiated political justice, the Albanian regime has sought to co-opt the youth of the country both through political education and Party involvement and through the use of material incentives.

In Czechoslovakia, too, there has been significant concern with the young. Complaining of the lack of social awareness among the young, the former Party leader Gustav Husak stressed the need to involve this segment of the population in the fabric of politics in order to ward off attempts to introduce what he called harmful trends from the West.[49] As noted above, one of the measures taken by the Prague regime was to allow a rock festival under official sponsorship.

In the GDR one of the methods employed by the regime to co-opt the young has been the holding of paramilitary sports contests every summer. These have included exercises with rifles, hand grenades, machine guns, and radio communications, as well as a general militarization of the school curriculum. The Free German Youth (FDJ), patterned after the Soviet Komosomol, now numbers 2.3 million young people (out of a population of under 17 million).[50]

In many instances, Eastern European countries have taken advantage of the willingness of at least some of the intelligentsia to co-operate or at least to co-exist with the regime. This is particularly the case in the GDR, where the intelligentsia has experienced no popular-democratic anti-Stalinist uprising (with the possible exception of 1953) and has been willing to co-exist and often even to compromise with the government.[51] Similarly in Romania, the docility and the accommodating attitudes of the intelligentsia have worked in favour of the Ceausescu regime in its attempts to stifle political dissent.

Some regimes have taken a more tolerant view of political dissent as long as they feel confident that opposition can be contained. For the most part, they practise a repressive tolerance whereby they define the parameters within which dissent can operate and then show considerable flexibility. The Hungarian regime has been especially adept at using repressive tolerance. Reform-minded dissenters have been able to publish relatively openly such 'illegal' tracts as the *Beszelo* and *Hirmondo* and have even published abroad in Western journals. Hungarian films have on occasion been critical of the regime, though usually in a rather oblique fashion. The regime has even tolerated a group of intellectuals calling themselves the National Democratic Forum, who have openly expressed their hope for the creation of a pluralistic regime. By and large, what the Hungarian government has attempted is to combine the strategies of co-optation and repressive tolerance in order to replace the harsh censorship of Stalinism, integrating the intellectuals into the establishment and relying more on willing collaboration.

But until recently the institutional challenge that these dissidents posed to the Hungarian regime was minimal. Though many intellectuals and some of the more politically sensitive workers are sympathetic to the dissidents, who number no more than a few hundred, the message of dissent has not yet spread effectively throughout the population. For years, therefore, the regime did not have to fear a Solidarity-like development in the country. It is not that the working class in Hungary is not potentially volatile,[52] but rather that the dissident intelligentsia, heavily sociological in its style, and suggesting solutions that lie somewhere between 'individualism' and 'collectivism', has not been very adept at reaching the general population.

The Hungarian regime—first under Kadar, now under Grosz—has taken concrete steps to define the parameters for dissent. Whenever it has felt that dissidents have become too vocal or too active in opposition to government policies, it has not hesitated to resort to some form of harassment ranging from the denial of exit visas to outright crackdowns such as the one on 11 March 1987, when police raided at least three apartments in Budapest and confiscated large quantities of underground dissident publications.[53] And despite the appearance of freedom in films, this medium too is tightly controlled. Film-makers must inform the Ministry of Culture about *all* the projects they are planning and resubmit them when they are completed. As a result, film director Andras Kovacs has said, even films critical of the authorities reveal official positions by showing the limits of expression.[54] It is little wonder that Miklos Haraszti, one of Hungary's leading dissidents and a highly respected writer, has called the country a 'velvet prison'.[55]

But all this may change. Unable to revive the economy without popular involvement, the Hungarian and Polish regimes have had to agree to major political concessions. In January 1989 the Hungarian parliament passed two laws giving citizens the right to demonstrate and form associations, including independent political parties.[56] But until another law regulating the operations of new political entities is passed in the summer of 1989, the new political parties and dozens of independent political groups formed in recent months cannot enter candidates in parliamentary or local elections. The regime's public commitment to the creation of a multi-party system is encouraging, but it is still not clear what type of legislation will be put into place and what kind of competition will be allowed for the 1990 parliamentary elections. There are already reports from Budapest that the Communist Party is trying to convince the opposition groups to agree to rig the 1990 elections so as to ensure a Communist majority in parliament. In return, the opposition would be allowed some minor posts in government.[57] Yet even if these reports turn out to be unfounded—if the elections are free and the Communist Party is significantly challenged (or even defeated)—it is yet to be seen whether parliament itself will wield substantive power in formulating core political and economic policies in the country.

In Poland there is also movement towards greater political pluralism. In August 1988 Jozef Czyrek, the Party's chief ideological officer, not only proposed talks with the opposition but also called for 'socialist pluralism', which he defined as 'respecting the political consequences of the diversity of interests, views, and orientations in our society'.[58] He added, however, that the Party would not tolerate 'confrontational pluralism'. Under increased pressure, the regime has agreed to further concessions, and at the end of March 1989 the Central Committee approved a whole set of measures to increase political pluralism, including the creation of a senate (upper house) in parliament that is to be democratically elected.[59] The upper chamber would have delegates from each of the 49 Polish administrative provinces. This is part of the Central Committee's decision to create 'a citizens' society and a state based on *socialist* parliamentary democracy and the rule of law'.[60] But there is no agreement with Solidarity (which is being relegalized) on the sharing of power between the upper house and the presidency. And, perhaps even more important, the regime has insisted that in the 460-member lower house the opposition parties be restricted to 35 per cent of the seats in the next parliament.[61]

In some ways it may be more difficult for most of these regimes to cope with dissent from hard-liners within the Party. If Gorbachev is able to continue policies of *glasnost* and *perestroika*, there should at least be more flexibility both in the Soviet Union and in Eastern Europe. In Hungary and Czechoslovakia the regimes have shown some ability in dealing with hard-liners. In Hungary a former hard-liner, Karoly Grosz, has been co-opted and as Party leader has shown a remarkable degree of pragmatism; in Czechoslovakia Milos Jakes, who has taken over from Husak as head of the Party, is another former hard-liner who is beginning to show at least some limited signs of pragmatism. But resistance to change is strong among bureaucrats. These privileged officials support all hard-line *apparatchiks* who oppose greater political and economic flexibility. If substantive reforms are introduced, the Eastern European regimes will need to address this 'dissent from within', for ultimately the success of such programs will depend to a considerable degree on their acquiescence.

Economic dissent

Though some economic dissenters frame their criticism of government policy in political terms and challenge the legitimacy of the Party, they are a very small minority among those who differ with the economic policies of Eastern European regimes. Most economic dissenters tend to object merely to the direction of the regime's economic policies. In some ways, therefore, economic dissenters present a more subtle challenge to the regimes. But such opposition also provides them with certain opportunities for accommodation. Decentralization and the creation of second economies allow for the possibility of co-existence between the regime and the populace. Moreover, they facilitate attempts by the regime to contain dissent or even to co-opt some dissidents. The magnitude, the nature, and the impact of economic dissent vary from state to state in the region, but in general the goal of the dissidents appears to be to move toward greater liberalization, further application of market principles under socialist conditions, greater limitation on the administrative bureaucracy, and improvements in economic relations with the advanced Western democracies.

Hungary is a good example of a regime willing to accept economic co-existence in order to ensure containment. The reforms that began with the introduction of the New Economic Mechanism (NEM) in 1968 have brought market forces into play to a greater extent than in other socialist states. Private enterprise has been allowed to flourish in certain areas of the economy, and many citizens are engaged in second—some, even third—jobs in the non-government sector. Kadar recognized that in order to increase productivity, private plots in agriculture and entrepreneurial industrial production should be encouraged, and that greater flexibility was required in the service sector. Therefore he not only allowed a greater measure of private enterprise than in other socialist states, but also turned a blind eye to the emergence of a second, unofficial, economy. Through this policy of economic co-existence the regime not only managed to substantially increase productivity and better satisfy the needs of Hungarian consumers, but also enhanced its legitimacy and thereby improved its ability to contain dissent.

Yet despite these significant domestic achievements, and the favourable image it enjoys abroad, Hungary's economic system suffers from severe stresses. Basically, it remains a centrally planned and controlled economy whose performance has been declining significantly in the 1980s. The report on the sixth five-year plan (1981-85) provided a statistically revealing picture of the problems of economic development.[62]

National income had increased by only 7 per cent instead of the planned 14 to 17 per cent (and had in fact fallen by 1 per cent in 1985). Industrial production rose by 12 per cent over the five years as compared to planned growth of 19 to 22 per cent. The terms of trade deteriorated by 8.2 per cent. Real wages declined by 5 per cent during the period, although per capita real income rose 7 to 8 per cent in large part because of second jobs, private enterprise, and additional social benefits. The pace of privatization did accelerate, though, with 12 per cent of shops and 40 per cent of catering establishments transferred to contractual operations.

There are limits, however, to what Hungary can do in terms of economic accommodation, and the constraints are external as well as internal. Externally, Hungary not only faces political guidelines from the Soviet Union, but as a member of the Council for Mutual Economic Assistance (CMEA) must gear a great deal of its production to trade with the socialist bloc; it is also dependent on the Soviet Union for most of its raw materials. Internally, decentralization and the introduction of some market forces have created social problems as income differentials have widened and as inflation and the threat of unemployment have increased. The reforms introduced in the financial sector, creating a bond market and a two-tier banking system, have brought about only modest changes and few, if any, concrete benefits for the population. The bankruptcy law, designed to provide for the liquidation or reorganization of insolvent enterprises, has become a significant threat to workers' economic security, even though a safety net is provided and relatively few workers have been directly threatened.[63] A Western-style value-added tax and a new income-tax law that affects people whose income has never before been taxable have hardly helped economic coexistence.

There is considerable debate in Hungary on how to cope with the major economic slowdown of the past few years. The decision-making élite in the Party agree on the need for belt-tightening and limiting, if not ending, heavy subsidies to highly uneconomic heavy industrial enterprises. But it is difficult to change existing economic mechanisms. Some economists believe that only fundamental change, 'an escape forward', can help.[64] This is unlikely, however, because such ideas have implications beyond the economic sphere and would necessarily involve 'dangerous' political corollaries. Relief seems a long way off, and even Hungarian officials acknowledge it. In 1987 Laszlo Antal, a senior Finance Ministry economist, forecast that in 1988 incomes would be cut by up to 10 per cent, while prices were likely to increase by 14 to 15 per cent.[65] In 1988 Karoly Grosz promised more austerity measures and stated that it would take ten years to implement his program of 'consolidation and revival'.[66] Contradictions continue to plague Hungarian efforts at change. Attempts to increase economic efficiency have resulted instead in releasing hidden inflation. In January 1989, for instance, the government had to announce further substantial price increases of 17 per cent on food, 24 per cent on cars, and 60 to 80 per cent on public transportation.[67] And the Hungarian Communist Party daily, *Népszabadsag*, has admitted that the average real wage has sunk to the level of 1973.[68] Together with growing unemployment as the regime addresses the issue of inefficient enterprises, this is increasing social tensions.

Two other regimes in the region have also seemed inclined to seek economic accommodation with the opposition within acceptable political parameters. But in both Poland and Yugoslavia prevailing economic conditions are such that they may work as constraints on the regime's ability to make those accommodations. In Poland economic accommodation is especially important as the declaration of martial law in 1981 destroyed virtually all the remaining legitimacy that the regime may have had. Unfortunately, although Jaruzelski is an enthusiastic supporter of Gorbachev's policies of *glasnost* and *perestroika*, he must grapple with a virtually bankrupt economy. Unable to achieve political stabilization, Jaruzelski cannot introduce fundamental economic reforms or significant market measures, and true price liberalization would bring about a decentralization that would dangerously loosen the Party's tenuous control over Poland's turbulent society. And yet, though the government can ill afford the further alienation of the Polish people, it has had little choice but to introduce certain measures that increase discontent.

The government has thus put forth only half-measures, and these simply have not been adequate to cope with the ills of the Polish economy. Even the economic changes proposed by Jaruzelski and submitted to a popular referendum on 29 November 1987 did not represent the 'deep changes' in the economic and political system touted by the regime. It is true that the purpose of the referendum was to gain the acceptance of the population for measures to reorganize the Polish economy, including steps to expand private enterprise, to make state-run enterprises more independent of central authority, and to raise wages and prices.[69] According to the regime there was to be more freedom for individuals to establish businesses in the private sector, and these economic steps were to be followed by appropriate political measures;[70] after two to three years of relative economic hardship, the standard of living would improve steadily over the longer term. Government and party sources were careful, however, to stress that the proposed changes would not alter the constitutionally mandated 'leading role' of the Communist Party, or Poland's close alliance with the Soviet Union.[71] The retention of the same political framework would, of course, limit the scope of economic change, and it is not surprising that the outlawed Solidarity union urged the population to boycott the referendum.[72]

In the first referendum in forty-one years, the regime failed to gain popular approval.[73] Nevertheless it has gone ahead with a good many price increases, ranging as high as 200 per cent on some items.[74] Unable to achieve economic consensus, the regime continues to attempt to muddle through. Unlike Janos Kadar's government in Hungary following the 1956 revolution, the Polish regime does not have the economic means to bribe society by offering it a higher standard of living. On the contrary, it has proved to be quite inept at stopping the downward spiral. In 1986 inflation had already reached 19 per cent,[75] and the policy of assigning large funds to specific projects and structural changes could at best produce increased consumption only after two or three decades. By 1988 some estimates put inflation in Poland at 100 per cent.[76] The standard of living is lower than a decade ago.[77] Most likely the economy is going to continue to decline, and as one Polish commentator noted, by the year 2000 Poland will probably find itself 'outside the European economy'.[78] Consequently, as J.F. Brown has suggested, the gulf between the rulers and the ruled is not being bridged.[79]

Yugoslavia is another Eastern European state where, although the regime has been willing to practise economic co-existence, grave economic conditions have prevented it from doing so successfully. Its experiments with some market-style reforms, industrial democracy, and a federal approach have yielded some benefits, but in the main they have created economic chaos. In 1987, for instance, inflation reached more than 120 per cent, the foreign debt climbed to $20 billion (US), unemployment increased to 18 per cent, the regime failed to meet debt payments, and there were more than one thousand strikes.[80] The various economic packages introduced by the regime have all failed, and exports have declined.[81] Even though the strikes were illegal, the government tolerated them because they served as a safety valve. By March 1989 inflation had reached 346 per cent, and the new Prime Minister, Ante Markovic, warned that it could reach 1000 per cent unless a radical reform program is implemented.[82] Attempts to roll back and to freeze prices in the past, though, have been unsuccessful, and the economic problems have further aggravated not only regional disparities, but political difficulties in the poorer provinces, especially Kosovo. The ethnic Albanians in that province have long complained of neglect by the federal government, and the unemployment rate of 30 per cent—as high as 50 per cent among young people[83]—has greatly increased tensions.

Widespread corruption and scandals involving high-ranking politicians and managers have added to Yugoslavia's economic malaise.[84] As in Poland, these economic troubles help to fuel inflationary tendencies and contribute to a growing attitude of detachment from public affairs.

In both countries this disengagement is reflected in a tendency to hoard goods that goes beyond the actual need to beat inflation, an abdication of responsibility for public property, and extremely poor performance at work.

Other regimes, however, have taken a different tack in dealing with economic dissent. The GDR, which has provided its citizens with the highest standard of living in the socialist world, has rejected reforms that include greater decentralization. Although Erich Honecker tolerates a modicum of private enterprise both in the services and in agriculture, he and his regime have indicated repeatedly that they do not wish to follow the Hungarian model or replicate Gorbachev's attempts at *glasnost* or *perestroika*. He has declared quite openly that the GDR is not about to follow Soviet-style economic reforms.[85] Other officials, echoing this line, have contended that GDR successes mean that they do not need to follow the experiences of other socialist countries.[86] And, given that in some respects the GDR's economy is held up as a model by some socialist economists, there may appear to be little need for reform.[87] On the other hand, there still is a vast gap between the GDR's economy and those of the Western democracies, particularly of West Germany. The GDR retains a highly labour-intensive system with low capital productivity, inadequate scientific and technological progress, spiralling costs for material inputs, and wasteful use of resources.[88] In a sense, the GDR regime has been fortunate in that, so far, it has not had to face significant economic dissent. Should it do so in the future, however, the regime's current approach suggests that it would much more likely attempt to contain dissent through differentiated political justice or even suppression by main force than through economic co-existence.

Other socialist states, such as Romania and Albania, have also refused to accept economic co-existence, even though their economies are performing poorly. In some ways Romania shows the greatest rigidity, for its economy, unlike the GDR's, is in shambles. There are shortages of all consumer goods, including most staples,[89] yet the country exports large quantities of meat for hard currency. A grossly inefficient heavy industry continues to consume most of the country's investment resources, and much of the rest is eaten up by prestige projects designed to glorify the rule of Nicolae Ceausescu. There is almost a surreal quality to the regime's approach to economic matters. Unrest and alienation are attributed exclusively to 'unsuitable' Western influences.[90] Instead of economic liberalization, the standard response of the Ceausescu regime is tighter control and more centralization. Ceausescu himself has categorically rejected any move towards a market-oriented economy.[91] To some degree the regime has benefitted from the remarkable patience, even docility, of the population. Whenever there have been blatant manifestations of opposition, however, including economic dissent, the regime has acted sharply and violently. Romania's approach has been to employ either differentiated political justice or suppression by main force, as in the case of the demonstrations in Brasov in 1987.

In comparison to the Romanian situation, even the response of the Albanian regime to economic dissent has been more positive. The government has acknowledged the need for economic incentives, and has declared that workers should be granted appropriate rewards and recognition.[92] This is not to suggest that the regime of Ramiz Alia is intent on widespread economic reform, but even this Stalinist state has in some ways shown greater flexibility than Romania. In sum, throughout Eastern Europe, even under the best of circumstances (as in Hungary), economic dissent is still contained: the issues that give rise to it have not been resolved.

Nationalist dissent

In a region of multi-ethnic states, few of the regimes have much to be proud of in terms of handling ethnic-minority issues. Given that there is a general problem as far as human and civil rights are concerned, all segments of society are to some extent limited in their capacity to influence the regime. Yet even developments that may not be primarily directed at altering or limiting the rights of national minorities may eventually be perceived as such by the latter because of unforeseen or even unintended consequences of current policies. Since perception is a seminal element in political functions, it must be taken into account even if it is at variance with actual developments. It is also important to recognize that for minorities, nationality rights are different from individual rights. As Mary Ellen Fischer has suggested, 'nationality rights are essentially collective rights, since nationality is a form of communal existence'.[93] Thus a member of a national minority is affected not only by the deprivation of his or her individual rights, but also by restrictions on group autonomy. Whether this is caused directly or indirectly by the policies of a regime, it tends to be viewed as a violation of that person's individual rights.[94]

In addition to the problem of dealing with national minorities, all the Eastern European states have been affected by the policies of the USSR, which has employed 'socialist internationalism' and Sovietization and/or Russification to increase its power and control over the region since the end of the Second World War. Whereas in the immediate post-war period the regimes were unquestionably loyal to Moscow, gradually—beginning with Yugoslavia's 'revisionism' in 1948—there was a re-emergence of nationalism, or at least an attempt to build socialism in particular national settings. As the USSR's interventions in various states and the Brezhnev doctrine of limited sovereignty have shown, the USSR has been reluctant to accept national roads to socialism if the deviations endanger socialist control. There is still, however, a need to build legitimacy for those regimes, and appeals to nationalism have been among the more successful approaches to that end. Therefore, despite its desire to maintain cohesion in the bloc, Moscow has had to demonstrate greater flexibility in order to allow its members greater viability—even though anti-Soviet or anti-Russian nationalism has tended to sound alarm bells in Moscow.

Ethnic hostilities preceded the rise of communist regimes in Eastern Europe, and those regimes have had little success in resolving them. A number of states in the region have an advantage in that they are relatively homogeneous: Poland, the GDR, and Hungary have few minorities, and they are not concentrated as majorities in particular regions. The method for achieving such ethnic homogeneity, however, has sometimes betrayed the worst type of xenophobia. At the end of the Second World War, Poland expelled millions of ethnic Germans, and following the March 1968 student riots in Warsaw it embarked on a virulent anti-Semitic campaign, which drove up to 20,000 Jews from the country. Now, however, although a number of prominent Polish dissidents are Jewish, the Jaruzelski regime has been careful to condemn anti-Semitism, and on 18 February 1988 the Party weekly *Polityka*, in a front-page article, called the 1968 campaign an embarrassment to Poland.[95] Some cynics have suggested that this simply represents an effort on the part of the government to improve Poland's image as it seeks foreign credit for its faltering economy, but such an admission of past mistakes is nevertheless unusual. Hungary too has tried to pursue a policy of ethnic co-existence with its German and Romanian national minorities—in part to maintain good relations with West Germany, but also to underline its benign treatment of Romanians, in contrast to the Bucharest regime's harsh treatment of its large Hungarian minority.

In many ways the task of the Eastern European regimes is more difficult when there is a large ethnic minority that cannot be expelled or absorbed into the majority group. In Romania, Hungarians (Magyars) constitute by far the largest ethnic minority; they are concentrated in Transylvania, which for about a thousand years had belonged to Hungary. The fate of this minority has been of grave concern not only to the government of Hungary, but also to human-rights activists around the world. To some degree the problems faced by this minority group reflect the perhaps unintended consequences of policies formulated by Bucharest. First, the Ceausescu regime has tried to entrench itself in power by assigning important positions to family members—all of whom are, of course, ethnic Romanians—and, second, it has sought to enhance its legitimacy by assuming the mantle of Romanian nationalism. One may argue, as Kenneth Jowitt has, that here a Communist-type of 'familialism' has occurred that is related both to the routinization of the Party and to the rationalization of society,[96] which then generates a 'right to rule' mentality within the élite families.

A good deal of the dissatisfaction of the Hungarian minority, however, is due to deliberate policies of the Romanian regime that are discriminatory in nature. The regime has made a conscious effort to deprive the Hungarians of educational opportunities in their own language and to prevent them from exercising political autonomy by restricting their participation in the political process and restructuring the political/regional units in the country.[97] Bucharest has also begun to implement Ceausescu's plan to bulldoze 7000 villages and replace them with 558 'agricultural industrial centres'.[98] A great many of these villages are populated by ethnic Hungarians who see the destruction of their homes as another attempt at cultural assimilation. The well-known Western human-rights monitoring group Helsinki Watch has also accused the Romanian regime of using the resettlement plans as a tool for destroying the separate cultural identity of the Hungarian minority.[99]

Romania has also employed the strongest measures to contain Hungarian dissent. Hungarian strikers in the Jiu Valley in 1977 were treated considerably more harshly than Romanian ones, and many were exiled to distant areas of the country that had no Hungarian minority. The singling out of the Hungarians for such treatment has caused great friction between Romania and Hungary. The two countries have strongly criticized each other, and Budapest has even contemplated granting refugee status to the tens of thousands of ethnic Hungarians who fled Romania.[100] Gorbachev himself became involved in the dispute during his visit to Bucharest in 1987, when he made an oblique reference to complaints by Hungary that Romania was mistreating ethnic Hungarians.[101]

Yugoslavia has used both suppression through main force and repressive tolerance to deal with nationalist dissent, especially among the Albanians of Kosovo, where the riots of 1986 were put down by mass police action. But in the same year Belgrade also allowed a three-day debate in the province, with more than a thousand speakers, in order to defuse tensions between the Serbs and the Albanian nationalists.[102] The Albanians constitute the majority of the population in Kosovo and continue to demand republican status within the Yugoslav federation as well as economic improvements.

Although as a multi-ethnic state Yugoslavia has made an effort to accommodate certain ethnic aspirations, it has cracked down sharply on any activities that it felt threatened the federation. In 1986, for example, district courts handed out prison sentences to forty-six Albanians charged with trying to create an Albanian republic in Yugoslavia, and another twenty-seven members of a dissident Albanian Marxist-Leninist group were sentenced for 'anti-Yugoslav' activities.[103]

Attempts by Serbia to increase its control over Kosovo and by the ambitious Serbian leader Slobodan Milosevic to enhance his power by playing on Serbian nationalism have made matters much worse. In

March 1989 both the Serbian parliament and the Kosovo legislature approved constitutional changes, demanded by the Serbians, that will significantly limit the automony of Kosovo, where ethnic Albanians comprise 85 per cent of the population.[104] A series of Albanian protests and strikes against the constitutional amendments culminated in full-scale riots in Kosovo. In the bloodshed that followed more than a score of people were killed, according to official sources.[105] Only a massive show of force by the Yugoslav army brought about a measure of calm. But continued economic problems and seemingly irreconcilable Serbian and Albanian nationalist demands continue to fuel instability and repression.

Bulgaria, which has a large ethnic Turkish minority comprising at least 10 per cent of the total population, has sought to resolve what it perceives to be an ethnic problem through assimilation. The Turkish minority has a far higher birthrate than the Bulgarians, and is predominantly Islamic. In December 1984 Sofia began a huge campaign of assimilation that was often violently resisted by the Turks. According to an Amnesty International report, within four months the regime had forced 900,000 Bulgarian citizens of Turkish origin to adopt Bulgarian names.[106] Moreover, it seems that Bulgarian security forces killed at least 100 people in outbreaks of violence that accompanied the name-changing campaign and imprisoned at least 250 individuals.[107]

There have been minority problems as well in Czechoslovakia and Albania. In the former, animosities between the two main groups, the Czech majority and the Slovak minority, are traditional, but the 1980s have seen an increase in the difficulties that the Hungarian minority—of around 600,000 people—has encountered. An unofficial committee for the defence of the rights of the Hungarian minority in Czechoslovakia has been set up, and incidents of racial tension have been reported, including arson attacks on the cultural centres of the Hungarian minority in Bratislava.[108] In Albania too the government had made attempts to assimilate non-Albanian speaking minorities, a policy especially directed at the Greek minority. The regime has passed a number of laws to force the change of individual and village names in Greek areas.[109]

Nationalist opposition in the form of anti-Russianism or anti-Sovietism (the two often being equated in Eastern Europe) has been manifested most starkly in Romania and Poland, but with somewhat different effects. Though there is some historical anti-Russian feeling in Romania, the Ceausescu regime has deliberately encouraged the phenomenon as a means of generating popular support. Poland has a history of virulent anti-Russianism, but the regime has tried to discourage this in order to avoid confrontations with the Soviet Union. Ironically, the Ceausescu regime has so thoroughly discredited itself in the eyes of the population that anti-Russianism, with which it has been associated, has dissipated. In Poland, despite the efforts of the Jaruzelski regime to foster better ties with the Soviet Union, anti-Soviet and anti-Russian feelings have grown because the population blames many of the country's ills on Moscow.

Religious dissent

Marxism-Leninism is basically an anti-religious doctrine. In Eastern Europe, therefore, the regimes have encouraged atheism, and party ideology has been based on the philosophy of dialectical materialism. Nevertheless, none of the regimes in the region, including that in Tirana—which has proudly proclaimed Albania to be the first officially atheistic country in the world—has succeeded in completely eradicating religion and its influence among the population. Still, the importance of religion varies throughout the region, as does the attitude of each regime to religious dissent.

Nowhere does religion appear to have a stronger hold than in Poland, where it claims the allegiance of the vast majority of the population and where the Church is also a symbol of the country's historic continuity. Despite various attempts on the part of the government to suppress the Church, it has not only survived but flourished, and has often managed to protect the faithful. And the election of Karol Cardinal Wojtyla of Krakow as Pope John Paul II in 1978 further strengthened the Church in his native country. Nevertheless, the regime has never given up in its efforts to intimidate the Church, and some members of the Polish security forces have taken extreme measures, as in 1984, when they brutally murdered the pro-Solidarity priest Father Popieluszko.

Yet even though the regime, through the official press, continues to attack the Church, and tries to formulate schemes to discredit it,[110] Jaruzelski has also employed strategies of repressive tolerance and co-existence. Since the regime is aware, even openly admits, that the majority (up to 90 per cent) of Polish citizens are believers, it has found it useful to try to work out a *modus vivendi* with the Church.[111] Of course there is to be no ideological reconciliation between the Party and the Church, for in a sense each seeks ideological monopoly. Moreover, the Church tends to combine religion and nationalism in contending that the right to express Christian values is a testimony to Poland's national sovereignty, and that Marxism-Leninism runs counter to the country's millennium-old cultural values. But it is not always antagonistic towards the Communist authorities. Although continuing to support Solidarity, under Jozef Cardinal Glemp, as the Primate of Poland, the Church urged moderation following the imposition of martial law in 1981, and summits between Glemp and Jaruzelski have produced some compromises. In 1986 the two parties agreed to work together to combat 'social pathology' and to maintain the 'patriotic ties joining Poles abroad to their country'.[112] Both condemned Western economic sanctions against Poland and called for their removal.[113]

In Czechoslovakia state and Church relations were relatively calm in the 1960s, but by the mid-1970s the Party once again began to take very harsh measures against the religious institutions, particularly the Catholic Church. Unauthorized religious activities, for instance, have come to be repressed even more harshly than activities in defence of human rights.[114] The regime has placed some churchgoers under surveillance, and others, deemed to be 'threats' to the regime, were put in psychiatric institutions.[115] Frequently Czechoslovak authorities have withdrawn the vocational licences of individual priests and thus have made even more acute the already critical shortage of ecclesiastical personnel.[116] Those priests who lose their licences face up to two years in prison if they wear clerical garb or preach in a church. Yet, despite these attempts at suppressing religion, the number of churchgoers has increased. In July 1987 100,000 people descended on the Shrine of Our Lady in Levoca in North Eastern Slovakia, and in February 1988 more than 300,000 Czechoslovak Catholics signed an appeal to their government to guarantee the Roman Catholic Church's fundamental rights.[117]

In Romania the regime has also taken a very hard line against organized religion. A good deal of the repression has been directed against Evangelical Christians and some of the lower-level Orthodox clergy who have taken an activist role in defending Church rights.[118] Evangelical Christians have been arrested and tried, and those engaging in clandestine efforts to import Bibles have often been beaten.[119]

In Albania the situation is, if anything, even worse. Religious practice was outlawed by the Tirana regime in 1967. Albanians who have left the country illegally have claimed that religious observance, even in private homes, continues to be severely repressed,[120] and numerous priests and monks have died in prison or been executed.[121]

Despite these measures, religious belief and dissent continue in Eastern Europe. Whether the regimes have tried to allow for some co-existence with organized religion, as in Poland and Hungary, or whether they have sought to co-opt members of the clergy, as in the GDR —where the regime has attempted to manipulate the Evangelical Church—or employed brutal suppression, as in Romania and Albania, religious dissent has not only continued but has become even more intertwined with political, economic, and nationalist dissent. From the perspective of these regimes, therefore, despite their attempts at suppression, the dangers of religious dissent have increased.

Conclusion

For the Eastern European regimes the battle against dissent continues. If they persist in their unwillingness to allow political pluralism, they have little choice. As long as they insist on party dominance instead of mere influence, they will need to either deter or suppress dissent that aims at transforming society. It would be a mistake to equate the policies of all the regimes in the region. A willingness to co-exist with some types of dissent, to employ more selective and sophisticated means of containing it, does make a difference. The difference in the ways the Hungarian and the Romanian regimes, for instance, deal with the various forms of dissent are important, and trends or tendencies that show greater flexibility are especially noteworthy.

Still, the overall record in Eastern Europe is an unhappy one. Even in the best of circumstances, the regimes seem to be willing to make only tactical concessions. For ultimately their objective is to stay in power—and on their terms. In that respect they do not necessarily differ from other political parties, except that they do not fully recognize the legitimacy of any movement that challenges this goal. Though they may be willing to de-Stalinize, they have adamantly refused to de-Leninize. The desire to remain in power may not predetermine all basic economic activity, but even in countries such as Hungary it is a very powerful influence. It is therefore unlikely that basic economic reforms can occur unless there is fundamental political reform. And that can only happen with the re-emergence—or emergence—of a true civil society.

The Communist parties in the region would need to adapt their doctrine to changing conditions and settle for influence rather than dominance in a process that would be rather similar to the erosion of Franco's power in the last few years of his rule. In that situation there was transcendence. Both the rulers and the ruled accepted and lived with certain myths. Franco and his supporters lived with the myth of dominance, or at least primacy, when in fact they now exercised no more than influence. The populace and underground movements accepted this myth, though they were beginning to exercise substantive power. Thus during this phase of development all parties engaged in an intricate political choreography. Eventually, however, with Franco's death there was a systemic change to true political pluralism. The Eastern European regimes may be unwilling to embark on this road. On the other hand, after four decades in power they have not resolved the problems of dissent, or the fundamental economic, political, and social issues that have given rise to them. If anything, their legitimacy has declined. At the very least, in order to remain in power by means other than the threat of Soviet military intervention, the various Communist parties need to ensure that their countries' economies perform sufficiently well to provide the population with a reasonable standard of living. Economic difficulties, therefore, may force these regimes to become more flexible. But better economic performance ultimately depends on answering at least some of the questions posed by political, economic, nationalist, and religious dissent.

Dissent and the State in Latin America

PHILIPPE FAUCHER AND
KEVIN FITZGIBBONS

> He that is a righteous master of his house
> Will be a righteous statesman. To transgress
> Or twist the law to one's own pleasure, presume
> To order where one should obey, is sinful,
> And I will have none of it.
> He whom the state appoints must be obeyed
> To the smallest matter, be it right—or wrong.
> And he that rules his household, without a doubt,
> Will make the wisest king, or, for that matter,
> The staunchest subject. He will be the man
> You can depend on in the storm of war.
> The faithfullest comrade in the day of battle.
> There is no more deadly peril than disobedience;
> states are devoured by it, homes laid in ruins,
> Armies defeated, victory turned to rout.
> While simple obedience saves the lives of hundreds
> Of honest folk. Therefore, I hold to the law,
> And will never betray it.
>
> — Sophocles, *Antigone*

'When *I* use a word,' Humpty Dumpty said, in rather a scornful tone, 'it means just what I choose it to mean—neither more nor less.'

'The question is,' said Alice, 'whether you *can* make words mean so many things.'

'The question is,' said Humpty Dumpty, 'which is to be master—that's all.'

— Lewis Carroll, *Through the Looking-Glass*

While reading in preparation for this paper, we came across some very stimulating abstract considerations on legal order and legitimacy, on revolutionary legitimacy and human rights. Other documents presented concrete evidence on censorship, 'disappearance', and torture. It rapidly became evident that the topic we had agreed to write on is one of paralyzing complexity, calling for knowledge that covers legal and political philosophy as well as history and sociology. Because of the very serious implications of the topic, it also appeared that total clarity of thought and transparency of purpose were more than ever imperative.

138

One can certainly not assume that the reader is sharing a common framework; implicit assumptions are definitively out of order.

Working from a simple and operational definition of dissent, we will concentrate on trying to show what distinguishes Latin American systems of government from our own liberal democracies, the manner in which their opponents are treated, and, in particular, why their modes of coercion are different from ours.

Our central argument is contained in the operational definition of dissent that we have adopted. *Dissent can be understood as the ideological label ascribed by security forces to social conducts and/or opinions held by citizens of diverging political leaning.* It follows from our definition that dissent cannot be recognized by a determined behaviour of social actors, but rather by the limits (of either an ethical or a formal nature) set to what is considered acceptable social and political behaviour. The object of this paper is to try to better understand what those limits have been in the geographical and cultural arena of Latin America.

Modern political history in the region has been marked by constant political violence and social unrest. In the late seventies military governments were dominant, and the civilian democracies that have taken their place in Peru, Argentina, Uruguay, Brazil, and Bolivia are still making strenuous efforts at consolidation. So far, intellectual ingenuity has not produced a convincing explanation to help us understand the constant recurrence of violence and military intervention. Instead of looking for one single causal explanation, we believe that a multi-causal analysis combining historical, ideological, cultural, and institutional approaches, where determinants combine and support each other, should help us have a better understanding of the phenomenon.

We are strongly opposed to interpretations of political dissent and violence as imported phenomena. It is true that the authorities have adopted a strong anti-Marxist posture in the region. But even considering the existence of Cuba, the strong rhetoric and frequent repression of left-wing organizations do not mean that the Soviet penetration is more important in Latin America than it is in Western Europe. On the other hand, the Cold War, the constant American influence, and direct US participation in the training of the region's military and police forces have given great visibility to the foreign influence in the repression of dissent. Ideology breeds on social reality, and in our opinion it is quite wrong to blame foreign influences for dissent or the imposition of social control.

To the question of why dissent and violence prevail in the region, the answer—given our preference for internal factors of explanation— should consider the dimension of the political space available for authorized debate. As we will demonstrate, the level of tolerance in Latin America is extremely limited. In our society, because power is relatively diluted, social agents are forced into negotiation and compromise, because it is understood that no one can win in an open confrontation. On the other hand, strongly concentrated social and economic control tends to stifle opposition when relations of domination are actively enforced. As our hypothesis, we submit that *the level of social violence is directly related to the challenge experienced or anticipated to the traditional (vertical) relations of social domination.*

The way authoritarian rule operates can be instructive. There is a broad range of conduct that can be covered by the general label of dissent: from wearing one's hair too long, to marching behind a forbidden flag, to directly participating in subversive acts. The difference between opposition and dissent is given in part by the formal legal framework, but also by the intensity of the repression. This duality will be examined in Part II.

It is not possible to reflect on dissent in Latin America without being concerned by the fundamental issue of human rights and by the horror of psychological and physical repression. Violation of human rights is a social reality, and is being used to maintain social control. It is therefore an integral part of the relationship between dissent and the state.

Political repression operates according to a definite logic that has been exposed and documented. The institutional production of fear has proven to be an effective and relatively inexpensive instrument of social control. Political domination is based on discrimination between winners and losers. For a regime to base its stability on fear, it has to produce that fear. The evolution of repression and its relation to dissent will be treated in Part III.

Having rejected both cultural and geo-political global explanations of dissent, we are left with the specific national dynamic as our main explanatory variable. This means that in order to avoid superficial generalization, one must consider the internal situation of particular countries. We have selected three—Argentina, Chile, and Guatemala —to make our claim; intentionally, we have chosen two countries that are among the most economically advanced, that have been governed by civilians for significant periods of time, that have had political systems and parties covering a wide spectrum of ideologies, and in which opposition, dissent, and subversion have manifested themselves in all possible manners.

Guatemala stands out as a different case. For decades a latent civil war has been taking place, in which the Indian majority has been fighting for survival against the white minority. Over this background of ethnic violence a more modern form of ideological political conflict, with its known ingredients of unions and students, has superimposed itself, creating a complex entanglement.

The conclusion will offer a reflection on the reality of citizenship in the countries examined, as a means of establishing the specificity of Latin America states in dealing with dissent.

I DISSENT: ITS CHARACTERISTICS AND SPECIFICITY IN THE LATIN AMERICAN ENVIRONMENT

Understanding dissent in the Latin American context involves a study of the specific political environment within which it is defined. Dissent is a social product of the political system, invariably presenting itself as a claim for freedom and justice, and perceived as a challenge to order and legality. However precisely the legislator defines the limits of social peace and national security, the understanding of dissent carries both a negative connotation (that which is outside the norm) and an implicit one (that which constitutes a potential threat). Dissent is not found by considering expressions of political opposition, but rather through the limits set by the legal structure and its official (tolerated) interpretation.[1] In order to define and establish the complete framework of dissent, therefore, one must examine the prevalent understanding of what restrictions must be imposed on personal liberty in order to guarantee social peace.

Latin American societies have often been labelled authoritarian. Many studies have used cultural, historical, or structural perspectives in an effort to comprehend the authoritarianism common in the region.[2] But we believe that the simple measure of the state's repressive capacity cannot explain the extent and manifestation of dissent. Authoritarian 'tradition' cannot be considered a *cause* of dissent. If this were true, a liberal democracy would not experience dissent, which is obviously not the case. It is not in the nature of Latin American societies to be violent, any more than it is in ours to be peaceful. All human collectivities have a disturbing potential for violence; the difference lies in the dynamic between manifestations of opposition and the government response.

A lack of social cohesion and an exclusionist political system, we suggest, are the breeding grounds of dissent. According to Alain Rouquié, the concentration of economic and social power, the strong cleavages, and the perennial presence of structures of domination have established a pattern of authoritarian rule:

> Horizontal social ties (free and between equals) are not only seen as rare or at least difficult but the nature of relations between the élite and the masses is virtually immutable: repressive, paternalistic and monopolized—with nuances and gradations even within a given country. By this we mean that the exclusion mechanisms are ambivalent and are experienced jointly and successively in the obligatory mode of cooptation and marginalization.[3]

In an environment of strong regional, cultural, ethnic, religious, economic, and ideological cleavages, dependent development provokes a radical disarticulation of social agents. Classes are not in a position to function directly as political actors where there is no link between the mode of production and social development. The political system does not necessarily convey the demands of those who define themselves as economic producers, and there is generally no collective understanding of what development process the country is (or should be) engaged in. Underdeveloped societies are frequently strongly divided, with little collective understanding of a national purpose. That is what Touraine means when he claims that there are discrepancies between the system of social control (in its political and ideological dimensions) and the accumulation process. This is the basic condition of a dependent society.[4]

Where horizontal cleavages prevail, social classes are the fundamental actors. The working class and the bourgeoisie are defined by their integration into the dominant mode of production. Where vertical relations are prevalent, the power base is found mostly in inherited authority and force. Society is divided between those who have authority and direct access to the use of force, and those who have little alternative but to obey. In Latin America the main actors are the oligarchy and, for lack of a better term, *el pueblo* (the people).[5] By oligarchy we do not mean here the traditional group of landowners, but an élite that lives on speculation rather than entrepreneurship, for whom politics is a means to guarantee its gains and repress opposition, and not an instrument of collective social and economic development. Because the oligarchy has no capacity to act in a coherent fashion at the collective level, it is not a social class but rather a group of loosely connected individuals, motivated by the desire for personal gain and defence of their status and privileges.[6]

Power structures are maintained and reproduced through clientelism both in political parties and in social organizations such as trade unions. Vertical social relations therefore restrict the possibility of horizontal class solidarity. With co-optation comes the iron rule of conformity. For the excluded, marginality is associated with social annihilation (the rights associated with citizenship are negated), resulting in dissent and, all too often, violence.[7]

The concentration of social power associated with a low consensus level allows a limited group of social actors to impose its political will on society. Regime legitimacy is limited, and institutions are weak. It follows that it is quite common for a new government to systematically revoke the legislation of its predecessor, thus increasing uncertainty. In a system where minority rule is the norm and where exclusion is the only alternative to holding power, government cannot operate through negotiation and compromise.

On the contrary, total power is fragile and must constantly protect itself.[8] In a vertically structured society where social relations are based on authority and tradition, and enforced by exclusion and violence, the major threat comes from the emergence of 'modern' horizontal (class) relations. Democracy—if it means the recognition of the right to vote, to participate, and to form associations—is a threat:

> Enlarged participation is perceived as a threat to the system of domination. The enlargement of the electorate, first of all, because it implies the loss of élite control . . . and the acceptance of legal equality—one man, one vote—ignoring individual roles. The autonomous individual overrides the 'person' and quantity takes precedence over quality. Secondly, because associative horizontal groupings modify the power structure and pose a direct threat to the system of domination.[9]

Domination has to be enforced where co-optation fails; exclusion must prevail, even at the cost of undermining the legality of the institutions in place:

> Within each Latin American society, taking into account its structure and history, there are varying thresholds of intolerance between dominating and dominated groups, where the intrusion of public force is unacceptable. All policy touching these sensitive zones illegitimizes the government which promotes it. In general, all that affects vertical social relations is considered subversive and unacceptable by all those who benefit from the status quo. Horizontal relations between equals, the free organization of the lower classes, can be sufficient to disqualify the government which tolerated them.[10]

By comparison, where social cohesion is high and political institutions are solid, opposition is not considered a threat, and dissent can be dealt with in a manner both firm and restrained. The major challenge that remains is to limit the institutional autonomy of the security forces—in other words, not to allow a small group within society, sharing a common institutional interest, to have a free rein in the operational definition of dissent and the means to control it.

Given the low social cohesion associated with Latin American societies, two attitudes towards dissent can be explained. First, it is difficult for the regime to distinguish a real from a potential threat; any manifestation of opposition may result in a coalition capable of successfully challenging those in power. Therefore the type and level of tolerated opposition are necessarily very limited.

Second, given such a society's limited capacity to reach a negotiated solution, it is not uncommon to see unresolved and recurring conflicts develop into major turmoil. The classic case in point is certainly the elusive agrarian reform. In an unstable social context, any institutional reaction may increase adverse mobilization, and governments, given their incapacity to generate strong civil support, will refrain from taking the appropriate measures of control. This is interpreted by organized opposition, and rightly, as a sign of weakness of the group in power.

Social movements are pushed, through exclusion, into the use of violence. They adopt the accents of a national liberation movement where foreign intervention is more direct, as in Central America, and may use for support the ethnic identity of the Indian population.[11]

When repression strikes, it is already too late. The government has lost its ability to impose order by calling for collective control, and the voices demanding retaliation easily win over those that ask for conciliation. Manifestations of social conflict are translated into issues of national security överriding any concerns for constitutional civil rights. The inability of the government to maintain order is used by the security forces to increase their institutional autonomy and to impose their particular understanding of what constitutes a threat to the security of the country. Society then faces two major threats. One is the politization of the security forces, which leads to the use of legal violence to support one side in a conflict of interests. The other is the militarization of society, characterized by absolute domination and total political exclusion.

Much attention has been given to the National Security Doctrine elaborated in the late nineteenth and early twentieth centuries in Brazil, Argentina, and Chile, which took its inspiration from such conservative Catholic organizations as *Opus Dei* in Spain and the French *Action française*, combined with a strong anti-Marxist (American-inspired, Cold War) flavour. The emergence of this doctrine coincided with the process of professionalization of the armed forces, the creation of advanced military academies, and the introduction of the new social sciences into the advanced military training curricula. Essentially, the Doctrine affirms that modern war cannot be limited to foreign territories, that all countries are pawns in the total and fundamental antagonism between the United States and the Soviet Union, and that subversive war respects no borders. The military must be aware and prepared to conduct war on all fronts—economic, political, financial, psychological, and scientific—in addition to its more traditional military responsibilities.

The Doctrine then goes on to imply that for each front an appropriate strategy has to be designed, and that there are gradations of conflicts that require the appropriate level of mobilization and repressive action. The policy for the preservation of internal security simply requires that action be taken to neutralize any activity that undermines unity, integrity, and the established social and economic order. Since internal conflict, by distracting the authorities from their true mission, creates conditions favourable to the enemy, any kind of social protest can be attributed directly or indirectly to subversion and communist infiltration. In the words of Brazilian Gen. Golbery do Couto e Silva, an influential strategist and one of the leaders of the military conspiracy that led to the 1964 coup:

Internal Security, which is an integral part of National Security, is concerned with the antagonisms and pressures that manifest themselves within the country. It is not relevant to consider the internal, external or external/internal origins of these antagonisms or pressures; its nature —political, economic, social or military—is of no concern, as are of no significance its various manifestations: violence, subversion, corruption, ideological infiltration, economic domination, social disintegration, or loss of sovereignty. On all occasions when antagonisms or pressures occur within national boundaries, the task to overcome, neutralize and reduce them is part of the actions planned and executed which comprise the Internal Security policy.[12]

The equivalent rhetoric prevails over the whole sub-continent with the full support of the North American, including Canadian, security forces.

Chile is another illustration. The Doctrine, with its intended vagueness, has been written into the laws and the Constitution, and serves as the mandatory ideological cement in the training of the military and police forces. According to the junta's declaration of 23 December 1973, the primary national objectives were independence, territorial integrity, Christianity, and development for the common general good. The major obstacles to the achievement of these goals were communist subversion and, more interestingly, uncontrolled pluralism. The specific role of the military in power was to restore public order, eradicate the communist threat, and install a 'new protected democracy'.

As can be expected, the Doctrine has been widely denounced inside and outside Latin America, by academics, Church and union leaders, students, and civilian politicians (who, according to the Doctrine, are all suspected of pro-Marxist leanings, therefore providing an empirical confirmation of the world-conspiracy theory), for giving the military a ready rationale for open support of politically conservative and socially repressive governments, or for a more direct take-over of the state.

The National Security Doctrine is certainly important for observers wishing to appreciate the ideological reference used by security forces. It also provides an additional confirmation of the overwhelming influence of the American Cold War ideology in the sub-continent. But the Doctrine cannot be used to explain the particular activities performed by Latin American security forces.[13] First, it does not help our understanding of dissent to trace the profound influence exerted by the United States and the direct involvement of its armed forces in the indoctrination of Latin American officers. On the one hand, it is undeniable that the United States has historically demonstrated that it believes it has the right to intervene at will in the sub-continent. On the other hand, however, given the uniformity of the Doctrine, it cannot help us explain the wide variety in repression found in Central America. The observed diversity of dissent and repression can only be associated with the level of internal conflicts within each country, the relative strength of social interests, and the breakdown of the political system.

The policies followed by the military, once in power, differ widely from one country to the other; therefore the Doctrine does not help us to predict or better understand the politics of the military. For instance, the Peruvian military, which took power in 1968, also claimed to have its own brand of National Security Doctrine,[14] implemented an economic and social policy, aimed at the modernization of the country's productive structure, that was in many respects more progressive than the civilian government it had overthrown.[15] This is certainly in absolute contrast to the actions of the military in Argentina and Chile.

Second, beyond the rhetoric and pretensions, the Doctrine is not fundamentally different from the very crude rationale regularly fed to European and North American military and security forces, and occasionally transmitted to selected civilians. Invoking 'national security' as a justification to jail and torture does not require more than a vague and superficial definition, together with a profound conviction that permanent war is required. All those outside Latin America who have denounced the National Security Doctrine would certainly be appalled at what they could find in their own houses, if they only cared to look.[16]

Third, it is not the Doctrine that matters most, but the way it is interpreted. The interpretation is not left to the fancy of the security forces. It is more a social outcome, an act of mediation between what is required, what is possible, and what is acceptable. Given the assumed homogeneity[17] of military doctrine in Latin America, the differences in action are striking. They are due to the diversities in influence and in relative strength of civilian societies.

When it comes to security matters, intellectual questioning and epistemological doubt are, in some sectors of society, associated with quiche: real men don't eat such denatured food. Those not part of the 'intelligence community' are always suspect of being naïve, of not perceiving the real dangers facing our society and institutions. Security forces justify their constant state of alert by maintaining that Latin America is indeed facing a serious threat of communist infiltration.

Evidence does not support this line of reasoning. Left-wing radicalism is undoubtedly more widely diffused than in Canada, and political violence is a major concern. But the urgency of the threat bears no relation to the overwhelming display of repressive force. This statement can be supported by three considerations. First, neither violence nor repression can be linked exclusively to political radicalism; they are also the result of more fundamental social conditions derived from political domination and concentration of economic and social power. Second, those who fall victim to repression not only come from all social and economic backgrounds, but have very diverse political inclinations.

Third, as will become clear when we present the situation in different countries, repression rapidly acquires a dynamic of its own, and continues with full intensity even after subversive groups have been physically eliminated and parties dissolved, their most prominent members in exile or under close surveillance.

It follows from the preceding presentation that dissent must be studied in the social context within which it emerged, and cannot, should not, be analyzed on the basis of concepts derived from a different tradition; nor should its study be influenced by self-justifying ideology. Given the predominance of vertical social relations in Latin American countries, it is no surprise that dissent and institutional violence reach levels that have only exceptionally been experienced in our society. Latin American nations are fragile social constructs in which conventions and guarantees are periodically questioned and shattered. Fear is common, for no one is safe from being either the selected target or the casual victim of the other side's ultimate rage and despair.

II   AUTHORITARIAN REGIMES: THE LEGAL REPRESSIVE FRAMEWORK

One will learn little about dissent and the state by examining the legal framework in which security forces are expected to operate. In Latin America, advanced safeguards are incorporated in all constitutions and legal codes. The similarities between the mandate given to the Canadian Security Intelligence Service and the limits imposed by law upon the activities of the intelligence services and police in the sub-continent are striking. In Latin America, law is but a façade behind which government officials stand in international forums as proof of their profound attachment to human rights, whereas in our country all concerned parties understand that the practice should conform to the law (notwithstanding some differences in interpretation).

What can be observed in authoritarian regimes is a profound discrepancy between the democratic ideology and the reality of social relations that are characterized by the institutionalized imposition of a system of inequality between individuals. Legal safeguards cannot prevail over the system of authority. Judicial norms are not congruent with the social system and cannot be enforced. The constant flouting of these basic guarantees has been tirelessly denounced by such organizations as Amnesty International.

If security forces are given a free hand to use whatever they see as needed for the efficient fulfilment of their mandate, why do military governments, upon taking power, insist on formalizing their usurpation through a new custom-made legality? Such 'legitimacy' is not effective, because legitimacy cannot simply be decreed. The constant constitutional changes, the permanent reintroduction of emergency measures, are manifestations of repressive authority. They are loud signals to would-be opponents that the legal system 'from now on' is meant to re-inforce the power structure. But the schizophrenic discrepancy between the ideological legality and the social reality is always maintained. Whatever repressive legal language is adopted, and however wide a range of powers is granted them, security forces will always tend to go further, demonstrating that there is no limit to the violence they are ready to use in defending the status quo. Rouquié is quite correct in writing that the 'conservative convulsions' so common in the region (and much more frequent than the episodic revolutionary turmoil) serve to exclude, at great social cost, the 'dangerous classes'.[18]

After a successful coup, one of the first concerns of those in power is to close the political system to all opposing parties and organizations. Exclusion is enforced, and prominent opponents are eliminated. The reason for the closing of the political system, with parties outlawed and elections abolished, is that the conditions for negotiation do not exist. Those holding opposite views on fundamental social issues are not pre-pared to compromise. As a result, debates end up in clashes, or issues are avoided.[19]

In the authoritarian regime, once the illegitimate legal safeguards have been systematically ignored, the authorities become concerned with preventing eventual retaliation from those they persecuted.[20] This is the reason for the amnesty laws that are systematically decreed after a few years of military rule. Their purpose is to exempt the security forces from the code of social conduct imposed on the general population. This protection is systematically present on the agenda when the au-thoritarian government has resolved to hand power over to its succes-sors (the outcome of this negotiation can vary). That such a decree should be promulgated is an indication both of the atrocities that have been committed under the guise of political control, and the very pro-found and irreconcilable differences in a society divided between win-ners and losers. This is why we feel justified in speaking of the political repression conducted by the security forces as 'institutional terrorism'.

III   DEALING WITH OPPOSITION AND DISSENT: THE TERRORIST STATE

There is a logic that develops in the use of force. The initial limited ob-jective of political repression is soon replaced by the more ambitious project of imposing a system of fear. The reasons for this change in course are complex and will vary widely in quality and intensity from one country to another. Nevertheless, we believe that there is a pattern, of which we will present the major characteristics.[21]

Following a succession of stages, fear progressively becomes a system of government. The first preoccupation is to dismantle the prevailing political system. Parties, unions, militant and professional organizations are abolished, disbanded, outlawed, or reconstituted. Clearly, all those considered to be opponents, real or potential, have to be cut off from their base and isolated. In the case of armed resistance, war measures are immediately decreed with the ritual invocation of the National Security Doctrine.

This is a period of strong tension and intense fear, when anyone may find himself facing the tragic dilemma of having to choose sides.[22] Reports of repression are severely restricted, and in their absence rumours soon spread. Solidarity groups try to organize, concerned by the suspension of human rights. They also become the targets of either official intimidation or outright repression by parallel security forces. Opponents are described by government officials as a 'social cancer' that must be eliminated in order to restore peace and tranquillity.[23]

The collectivity, initially concerned for those who fall victim, is soon pervaded with a feeling of uncertainty. Systems of collective support have been destroyed, individuals are isolated. Mistrust and fear set in, destroying all social networks in their progress. It is not an accident that the Church soon becomes the only institution that manages (sometimes at considerable risk) to remain the only tolerated rallying institution.

Once the enemy has been destroyed, one would expect normality to resume. But this is not the observed pattern. In Argentina and Chile (and also in Brazil), armed struggle has been wiped out within a matter of months by security forces. By all counts, the number of individuals directly involved in the conflict has been limited, and most left-wing organizations (and the Communist Party most clearly) have been very prompt in dissociating themselves from violent action. Nevertheless, repression has been maintained virtually on full alert.

Once the urgency that sparked the coup has passed, authoritarian regimes look for consolidation. Both external and internal resistance soon reappear, and popular support for the regime, requiring meaningful mobilization, is not a practical possibility. Traditional élites look with suspicion at the usurpers and withhold their support. Among the internal difficulties that arise is the evident lack of any political program or social project on the part of those in power other than to abolish politics altogether. Security forces use their privileged position to influence other areas of government; they have an obvious vested interest in seeing that their services are continuously required to quell subversion. This pressure creates tension within the military, challenging the integrity of the institution.

In a society where the law is not respected as the collective norm (you do justice to your friends and apply the law to your enemies), the continuation of repression beyond the initial mission of controlling the active members of subversive groups is profoundly unsettling. The security forces usually come from a different social background than the political élite. They do not share the same culture and set of values as the élite, and therefore are looked upon as outsiders—a threat. Security forces are dangerous in such an environment because they are not incorporated in the clientelist system of shared favours and patronage that acts as the cement of the vertical social-relations network. The system works as long as everyone has an authority overhead. In exchange for one's episodic but unwavering support, power is shared and its influence used on one's behalf. Security forces are not part of the system; they have a large degree of autonomy, combined with almost unlimited resources; and, most dangerous of all, it soon appears that they are in the game to serve their own particular interests, and no one is in a position to stop them.

The bourgeoisie and middle class become concerned when they realize that the unwritten code of repression applies not only to the subversion of workers and peasants, but also to the intellectual 'deviation'—previously tolerated—among the élites. This anxiety turns into fear when the privileged groups realize that they also have been excluded, that their link with the state apparatus has been cut off. They are struck with sudden and total impotence. This realization usually coincides with the strongest representations for the respect of human rights, in a campaign meant to alert international opinion.

It soon becomes evident that in the absence of a program, and lacking support, the regime has no other concern than to perpetuate itself. Repression is still used to weaken resistance and maintain social fragmentation, and it continues to operate alternately with threat as the security forces try to exorcise their growing fear (see note 20). It is very clear today in Chile (as was the case in Brazil with the assassination of the journalist Vladimir Herzog and the metallurgist Mancel Fiel Filho in 1975, and later with the Rio-Centro bomb affair) that the episodic uncovering of subversive activities is used by the government to maintain authoritarian rule. It is obviously in the interest of the authorities to exaggerate the threat, and some evidence even suggests that police forces have been instrumental in fabricating plots to justify their repressive acts and gain more autonomy. As Gen. Pinochet once declared: 'It is essentially the persistent and serious nature of terrorist activity that constitutes the greatest obstacle to the restoration of democracy in Chile.'[24] One might add that it is improbable that 'terrorist activities' will diminish as long as Gen. Pinochet and his regime remain in power.

When collective support and institutional recognition are lacking, fear is produced by the authoritarian state as a central element in its system of domination and social control. Dissent is claimed to be the justification for fear, but the real cause is the climate of constant uncertainty produced through arbitrary repression, censorship, propaganda, and, most of all, the absolute impunity enjoyed by the official and clandestine security forces.

IV ARGENTINA

Argentina differs significantly from other countries in Latin America in two respects. First, political violence was constant from 1955 to 1983, reaching endemic proportions from 1969 through 1976. Second, the elected government of President Raúl Alfonsín brought to public trial military leaders who had presided over gross violations of human rights.

When the military took power in March 1976, it was with the intention of putting an end to years of political confusion and social disruption. Reports on the repression that took place during the 'dirty war' (*la guerra sucia*) give accounts of 8,906 cases of unresolved 'disappearances', along with evidence of homicide, rape, torture, illegal detention, robbery, and falsification of official documents.[25]

The five years leading up to the coup of 24 March 1976 were marked by violent social tensions between right and left factions in the Peronist party, the emergence of well-organized rural and urban insurgency, the appearance of right-wing gangs, and violent labour relations. Many of these tensions can be traced back to the regime of Juan Perón, a charismatic populist dictator ousted in a coup in 1955. His ambivalent support of both the working classes and the oligarchy created irreconcilable extremist factions among his followers, and these factions were to be the focus of violence upon his return from exile in June 1973.

An enormous crowd of supporters gathered at the airport to welcome him back from Spain. Before his plane landed, the crowd turned into two warring armies, and in the fighting that followed over 200 people were killed. Many point to this event as the beginning of the 'dirty war'.[26] Perón immediately sided with the right wing of his party, and the period of violent confrontation and repression had begun. In September 1973 Perón resumed the presidency until his death in July of the following year. His successor and widow, 'Isabelita', was soon overwhelmed by the national chaos of mounting public violence and severe economic decline. She was deposed in March 1976 by a three-man military junta who were at that time generally welcomed as being the only force in the country capable of restoring public order.

Upon taking power, the junta announced the five-point 'National Reorganization Process' in which it assumed all executive, legislative, and constitutional powers. The National Congress and the Provincial Legislatures were dissolved, and all governors, municipal leaders, and Supreme Court judges were replaced by government appointees, quite often military personnel.

The official and clandestine repressive framework

The vast majority of government anti-subversive activities occurred under the regime of the first junta (March 1976 to March 1981) headed by Gen. Videla. The state of siege declared by Isabelita Perón in November 1974 was finally lifted in October 1983.

The main instrument of the anti-subversive strategy were the *Grupos de Tareas* (GTs). These units came under the direct control of naval intelligence with its headquarters in the *Escuela de Mecánica de la Armada* (ESMA) in Buenos Aires. GTs were located throughout the country and were divided into three departments: Intelligence, Operations, and Logistics.

The Intelligence Service was headed by naval officials responsible for identifying targets of repression and detaining political prisoners for interrogation. The primary function of the Operations Service was to carry out the business of abductions and harassment of political targets identified by the Intelligence Branch. The actual kidnapping groups operated in units commonly known as *patotas*. The Logistics Service was in charge of supplying materiel such as arms and vehicles for the other branches as well as the control of finances. GTs operated out of what were known as *Centros clandistinos de detención* (CCDs). The Sábato Commission identified over 340 that were in use over this period.

The operations of these groups were highly systematic. Targets were identified by the Intelligence Service, which passed on the information to the Operations Branch. The latter in turn was responsible for harassing or abducting the people so identified, or members of their families. The government officials and the security forces systematically refused to confirm the detention of these people, and no official records were kept. When prisoners died, their bodies were either disposed of in mass unmarked graves, dropped from aircraft over the ocean or the Rio de la Plata, or set up as casualties in shoot-outs with government forces. Americas Watch estimates that between fifteen and thirty thousand people disappeared over seven years of military rule.[27]

Before the 1976 coup, there existed one right-wing gang of note: the *Alianza Anti-Communista Argentina* (AAA). This extremely violent group operated in the first half of the 1970s and claimed responsibility for as many as 300 assassinations in 1974. Although no members were ever captured or identified, it is believed that the AAA was made up of right-wing Peronist extremists, off-duty police and military officials, and criminal hired hands of large landowners and the urban bourgeoisie. Contrary to the situation in Guatemala and Chile, their activities tended to decline with the military's arrival in power.

Opposition and dissent

In the years preceding the 1976 coup, armed insurgency was highly present in Argentina and posed a serious threat to the government. The *Montoneros* were an avowed extreme leftist faction of the Peronist party, based primarily in Buenos Aires. This relatively small group claimed responsibility for as many as 800 assassinations between 1970 and 1975. Their targets were government officials, right-wing Peronists, important industrialists, and military and police personnel. In 1970 they abducted and murdered former president Gen. Aramburu, the leader of the 1955 coup that had ousted Perón. Most observers agree that the *Montoneros* were completely eradicated within the first six months following the 1976 coup, even though the government continued to accuse them of sabotage for several years afterwards.

The *Ejército Popular Revolutionario* was a smaller group that operated in the rural areas of northwestern Argentina, close to the Bolivian border. They were similar to many other insurgent movements in that they were rural guerrillas with a military field command modelled after that of Che Guevara. Their strategy was to attack military and police outposts, sabotage infrastructure, and gain control of certain guerrilla fronts or *focos* with the support of the local population. In February 1975 the President asked the military to intervene in the province of Tucumán, and in a few months the movement was crushed.

All sectors of the population were affected by the *guerra sucia*. The most active in protest and the most heavily repressed were the trade unions, which held considerable power and refused to buckle under to the austerity measures of the military and Peronist governments in the early 1970s. The period leading up to the coup was marked by a series of lengthy and often violent strikes in virtually all sectors, which paralyzed the economy for months. According to the Sábato Commission, blue- and white-collar workers together accounted for almost half (48 per cent) of the disappearances between 1976 and 1983.[28]

During this period a number of civil- and human-rights groups emerged to put pressure on the government to release those detained, to help families with *habeas corpus* writs, and to draw international attention to government abuses. The best known of these groups, *Las Madres de la Plaza de Mayo*, was formed in 1976 by fourteen mothers of disappeared persons. Every Thursday they quietly demonstrated in front of the Government Palace demanding to know the whereabouts of their children. By 1980 their numbers had grown to several hundred, and they attracted attention from around the world. Several of these women themselves became targeted for repression. Today this group continues to be a force in the country, demanding to know the whereabouts of the children born in captivity and later adopted.

The question of accountability

After the military disaster of the Falklands invasion, the armed forces had no choice but to leave power in disgrace, with very little room to negotiate their exit. A fourth junta was established to oversee the transfer of power to civilians and to supervise the elections. In 1983 the government of Gen. Bignone published its *Final Document of the Military Junta on the War against Subversion and Terrorism*, in which it admitted to 'certain excesses' in the war against subversion and justified its actions as being in the interest of national security and social order. It also stated that, for administrative purposes, all those who had disappeared over the previous eight years should be considered dead.

On 23 September 1983 the junta published an amnesty law (*Ley de Pacificatión Nacional*), in which all crimes committed by government forces in the line of duty were pardoned and all investigations into the disappearances were suspended.

The civilian government of Raúl Alfonsín was sworn in on 10 December 1983. Alfonsín, the leader of the Radical Party and founding member of the *Centro de Estudios Legales y Sociales* (the centre worked on behalf of the families to pressure the government to release its prisoners), had campaigned for making the military accountable for its deeds during the *guerra sucia*. He made two commitments to the nation: to investigate the 'disappearances' and to prosecute those responsible. Once elected, he created CONADEP to investigate the cases of the 'disappeared' and appointed as president of the commission Ernesto Sábato, a highly respected writer and critic of the military regime. Although the commission was not a judicial body, and could not pass judgement on individual responsibility, it proved two major points: first, that the activities of the government forces during the military rule were illegal, and that crimes such as torture, homicide, kidnapping, robbery, and rape were widespread throughout the country; and second, that this was an organized, systematic strategy operating with the knowledge and under the control of government leaders.

On 27 December 1983 Alfonsin passed a law revoking the *Ley de Pacificación Nacional* on the grounds that it was unconstitutional. The trial of nine commanders of the armed forces and prominent leaders of the juntas began on 22 April 1985. Although the rules of procedure were military, the trial was conducted in a civilian court, the Military Supreme Tribunal, the court of first instance, having refused to conduct the trial. Of the nine leaders four were acquitted and five were found guilty, with sentences ranging from life imprisonment to less than five years on counts of multiple homicide, detention, torture, and robbery.

The next step was the prosecution of the minor officers and agents under the principal of 'due obedience', according to which subordinates could be prosecuted for acts of atrocity that they were fully aware were illegal. In February 1987 the law known as *Punto Final* was passed, allowing a sixty-day period for all remaining charges to be laid against subordinate officers. When the period was up and over 300 officers had been charged, the military revolted and refused to turn over any more officers for trial. Alfonsin compromised and in June of 1987 published the *Law of Due Obedience*, which granted immunity, except for charges of rape and the abduction of children, up to the rank of Colonel.

Although political violence and repression have abated in Argentina since 1983, Alfonsín's relations with the military over the past two years have been complicated. Three military rebellions (April 1987, January 1988, December 1988) have forced the president to make major concessions concerning the future prosecution of military officers (under the law of due obedience), higher wages, and removal of the army Chief-of-Staff. There has, however, been no amnesty for those already condemned by criminal courts. Seventeen officers are still awaiting trial.

Since 1987 the government has proceeded with the privatization of the defence industry and has named a civilian, Horacio Jaunarena, as Minister of Defence. Although the military seems to be accepting its diminished role in civilian politics, the pre-1983 right-wing elements are still very influential in the military apparatus, and intelligence services have not been dismantled. In September 1987 a kidnap ring was exposed in security services.

Social protest has been on the rise. On 10 September 1988, a protest by the *Confederatión General del Trabajo* (CGT) turned into a violent confrontation in the Plaza de Mayo, with over a hundred injured, including many police officers. There has also been a resurgence of right-wing terrorism (fire-bomb attacks on offices of the radical party, the *Unión Cívica Radical* [UCR] in June 1988).

The most serious development was the assault on the military barracks at La Tablada on 23 January 1989, in which close to forty people died. After initially confused reports, it was finally confirmed that the *Movimiento Todos por la Patria* (MTP), a previously unknown group of about fifty armed insurgents with links to the abolished ELP, was responsible.

The UCR's chances of winning the elections to be held on 14 May 1989 are slim. Alfonsín's credibility has been tarnished with the poor economic performance of the country and his inability to deal effectively with the military. No major military reform has taken place, and the old guard is still intact. A recent retired officers' communiqué (July 1988) shows that the National Security Doctrine is still on the agenda: 'The country is fast moving towards a state of total decadence as a result of the infiltration at all levels of an abhorrent idea, Marxism.'[29]

V CHILE

For Chile the most obvious point of departure is the military coup of September 1973, when the armed forces led by Gen. Augusto Pinochet violently overthrew the elected government of Salvador Allende. From that day on Chile has been ruled by a military junta under an uninterrupted series of 'states of exception' imposed on the civilian population. Open disregard for human rights and civil liberties has been justified under the National Security Doctrine.

The political opposition and repression are both concentrated primarily in the urban areas and to some extent in the mines. Unlike the conflict in Guatemala, Chile's cannot be divided along racial lines, nor can it be understood by looking exclusively at class struggle.

It has often been said that Chile has had one of the longest traditions of democracy; that its institutions were solid, modern, and pluralistic, and its military highly professionalized.[30] Despite this democratic legacy, the people of Chile have endured one of the harshest and longest lasting military dictatorships in the Western hemisphere.

Nevertheless, on 5 October 1988, under the 1980 constitution (transitory article 29) the Chilean people, backed by a sixteen-party coalition, rejected another eight-year term for Gen. Pinochet in a national plebiscite (54.6 per cent 'no'; 43.4 per cent 'yes'). Open elections will be held on 14 December 1989 and power will be transferred to the new president on 11 March 1990.

The official and clandestine repressive framework

Probably because of its 'modernity', Chile has developed a sophisticated legal system that serves to define and limit the political space allowed by the regime in place. In 1973 the National Congress was dissolved, as were the Constitutional Courts. All mayors and municipal councillors were appointed directly by the military, and many were military personnel. The major legal mechanism for increasing the discretionary powers of government forces and restricting personal and civil liberties is the *Estado de excepción*. This can be applied simultaneously on three levels. The State of Siege (*Estado de sitio*), the most severe measure, was applied on two occasions, from 1973 to 1979, and for eight months between 1984 and 1985. It amounts to a declaration of internal war, in which government powers are absolute and such civil liberties as the rights to *habeas corpus*, assembly, expression, and information are suspended. The authorities are empowered to enforce exile and internal banishment (up to three months).

The State of Emergency, in effect throughout the Pinochet regime, was lifted only six weeks before the October 1988 plebiscite. It has the same provisions as the State of Siege, in a 'restricted' rather than 'suspended' form. The State of Danger of Disturbance of Internal Peace, established under the 1980 Constitution (Interim Article 24), provides temporary powers to the authorities to detain a prisoner for five days without charge and fifteen days in cases of 'serious terrorist acts'—all by administrative order, bypassing the courts. These provisions have been applied in particular during periods of mass protest and raids on *poblaciones* (urban slums) and university campuses. Although Chilean law contains ample provisions for the protection of fundamental rights, the apparent legal safeguards stating the extent and limits of government powers have been rendered ineffective by the constant flouting of procedures by the security forces.[31]

In contrast to the situations in Argentina and Guatemala, in Chile the military, despite being in full and exclusive control of the government apparatus, has not been highly involved in the actual application of the repressive strategy. Its activities have mostly been restricted to the first phase in the immediate post-coup restoring of general order. Since then the military has been called in as support for internal security and police forces for quelling mass protest demonstrations. Nevertheless, an increasing direct participation of the army in internal-security activities, most notably in raids on *poblaciones* and university campuses, was reported up to the 1988 plebiscite.[32]

The internal-security forces have been the major instrument of repression. These groups have existed under two names: first DINA (1973-1980) and then CNI (*Central nacional de investigaciones*). The service, under the direct jurisdiction of the President, is empowered to arrest without warrant, to detain without charge, to detain incommunicado, and to detain on its own premises.

The national police (*Carabineros*) come under the jurisdiction of the Ministry of the Interior, and have much the same power as the CNI. The special unit DICOMCAR was in charge of intelligence and political control; it was officially disbanded in 1986 after four of its members were charged with the murder of three political activists (none was ever prosecuted).

The judiciary has been considered an important instrument of repression because of its role in interpreting the law and the handling of cases. One of the major points to be made is that the vast majority of political offences have been tried by military tribunals. The process for dealing with *habeas corpus* writs has been notoriously slow, and of the several thousand petitions that have been presented since 1973, by 1988 only four have been approved by the court, and in only one case was the prisoner actually released. On the other hand, not one member of the military, police, or internal-security forces has ever been convicted of a crime involving human-rights violations.

Death squads have re-emerged since 1983. Somewhat active in the first years of the regime, they had become less important in the late 1970s. Although the identity of their members is unknown, it is safe to assume that they enjoy close connections with the armed forces and therefore with the government. They appear to be well equipped, handling arms that seem to be military property, and operate freely in broad daylight as well as during curfew hours. These groups, commonly called *los desconocidos*, have a variety of names: ACHA (*Acción Chilena Anti-Communista*), FNC (*Frente Nacionalista de Combate*), BOA, MONA, and *Commando 11 de Septiembre*. Their basic role has been to intimidate common citizens associated with church groups, trade unions, student associations, community organizations, and political opposition. In 1985 there were sixty-five abductions attributed to these groups, and at least three murders.[33] All reports leading up to the 1988 plebiscite indicated that the repressive apparatus has remained intact. Since the 'no' vote there has been a gradual opening of the military regime, and reports of human-rights violations have diminished.

Opposition and dissent

Although the military came to power with the support of the oligarchy and many sectors of the middle class, in the past four years they appear to have lost much of their support, especially among the middle class. Today, as shown in the 1988 plebiscite, opposition is widespread and comes from virtually all sectors of society. Armed insurgencies have taken place, but have been minimal in comparison with similar actions in Peru or Colombia. Most opposition has come from groups calling for a return to democracy and an end to human-rights violations. Aside from the armed-insurgency groups, the major sources of dissent have been unions, journalists, human-rights and church groups, community workers, students, and the inhabitants of shantytowns.

The two main armed opposition groups in Chile are the FPMR (*Frente patriótico Manuel Rodriguez*) and MIR (*Movimiento de izquierda revolutionario*). Although not considered to be very large organizations, they have been responsible for acts of sabotage (bombing of public infrastructure such as hydro-electric installations, government buildings, etc.), the kidnapping of government personnel, and attacks on government forces. The FPMR was accused of the assassination attempt on Gen. Pinochet in September 1984, in which five bodyguards were killed and Pinochet was slightly injured. Its activities intensified in 1987, but a truce was declared before the plebiscite.

Trade unions in Chile have been subjected to harassment and intimidation since the first days of the coup because of their connections with the leftist parties and their support of Allende. One of the major targets has been the Chilean Copperworkers' Federation (CTC). The Teachers Union (AGEH) has also been singled out.

Among the human-rights groups, the two major domestic organizations are the *Vicaria de Solidaridad*, which has direct connections with the Catholic Church, and the Chilean Human Rights Commission, which primarily denounces violations of human rights and provides legal aid for political prisoners and families of the disappeared. These groups have also been intimidated by the authorities.

Since 1982, university campuses have emerged as areas of high political tension. Protest demonstrations have been repressed, and student leaders and activists abducted and arrested. The main issues have been university autonomy (the university rectors have been military personnel since 1973), civil liberties, and human rights.

The National Civic Assembly is probably the group most indicative of the climate of political protest today. A non-partisan coalition formed in April 1986, it has managed to mobilize broad sectors of the population, from trade unions to teachers' associations, from slum-dwellers' groups to professional associations. In July 1986 it organized a two-day general strike and large protest marches throughout the country, in the course of which over 1,000 people were arrested in Santiago and eight killed.[34]

The inhabitants of the *poblaciones* have been the hardest hit by the economic recession and the cuts in social expenditures imposed by the government. The most significant developments in dissent and repression have been the mass protests organized in these communities and the mass raids and arrests and indiscriminate shootings that have been common occurrences in the recent government strategy to maintain public order.

Protest and repression: strategies and practices

One of the most specific practices used by the government has been the extensive imposition of restrictions on freedom of movement. Through the banishment policy, opponents are sent to isolated parts of the country, either the extreme south or the desert in the north, for periods of up to three months. Forced exile and the stripping of nationality has been another practice. Many citizens who either were expelled during the first years following the coup or who emigrated were not allowed to return. A list of banned citizens has been published periodically; in the edition of 15 May 1986, 3,717 names appeared.

Two strategies that have emerged since 1983 have been the increased use of clandestine right-wing groups and the practice of mass arrests during demonstrations and pre-emptive raids. Clandestine groups are responsible for most of the cases of enforced disappearances (there are close to 1,000 officially unresolved cases before the courts today). Abduction is another tactic often used. The authorities gave themselves a legal cover with the Amnesty Decree-Law No. 2191 of 18 April 1978, which guarantees amnesty to any police or security agent considered accessory to disappearances.

In the four years leading up to October 1988, mass arrests during public demonstrations and during raids on *poblaciones* were widely reported. Over the first nine months of 1986, 31,084 people were reportedly detained, 9,155 of whom were arrested during demonstrations while a further 21,205 were detained in sweeps. This was a marked increase from a total of 8,946 arrests in 1985.[35] The general practice during raids has been to arrest all men as well as some women between the ages of 16 and 60 and to take them to stadiums for further investigation. The majority are released, but those remaining are taken into detention and interrogation centres. Raids have been used as intimidation practices before planned demonstrations and as reprisals afterwards. The indiscriminate shooting of people during demonstrations and raids has also been reported.

The political activity that has taken place since the regime lifted the ban on political parties in 1987 has shown that Pinochet has been unable to depoliticize civilian life. Today the possible scenario for the elections, providing that party coalitions are allowed, is for five major groups, two on the left and three on the right. The centre-left coalition led by the Christian Democrats seems to have the best chance of winning over a more divided right.

VI GUATEMALA

Of all the countries in South America experiencing problems of social upheaval in the difficult passage from military rule to democracy, Guatemala stands out as having one of the poorest human-rights records in the past decade. Since 1982, over 200,000 political refugees have crossed the border into Mexico.

Social and political situation

Guatemala is the largest and most populous country in Central America, with close to 8 million inhabitants, of whom over 55 per cent are Indians, descended from the Quiche-Maya culture. The majority of the Indian population lives in the mountainous central highlands in small remote villages or on marginal patches of farmland that are generally unfit for sustaining a family. Literacy levels are among the lowest in Latin America, and infant mortality, as well as death from curable diseases and undernourishment, is widespread. Quite often non-Spanish-speaking and easily identified by their customs and traditional dress, the Guatemalan Indians are the most oppressed group in Guatemala. Most instances of armed insurgency have come from the rural areas where the indigenous population is highest.

The Guatemalan oligarchy is considered to be one of the wealthiest in Central America, having built up immense fortunes from the agrarian export sector, most notably in coffee and sugar cane. Two per cent of the population controls over 80 per cent of the arable land.

The central political factor has been the armed forces, which ruled the country after a military coup in 1954 brought down the elected, reformist Arbenz government. With the exception of a brief four-year period (1966-70), until the 1986 election of President Cerezo, the head of state was a military general.

Guatemalan politics is still dominated by the traditional oligarchy, for whom the military acted as caretakers and bore the exclusive responsibility for internal security. The authorized political system is largely dominated by conservative parties (National Liberation Movement,

Popular Democratic Front, Christian Democratic Party), while more radical alternatives to the status quo are reduced to clandestinity.

Christian Democrat Vinicio Cerezo assumed the presidency in January 1986. Although the change from military rule is welcome, after more than three years in power the new administration has been incapable of challenging the dominant position held by the military, even within the context of the new regional peace plan.[36]

The official and clandestine repressive framework

Because of the ongoing subversive activities in the rural areas, military rules of war have prevailed, leaving very little political space available for open debate or even for peace-seeking initiatives. Until the election of President Cerezo, Guatemala lived under a system of constant and institutionalized terror.

Legal restraints on repression were never enforced and the few legal provisions, such as the Fundamental Statute (which replaced the suspended Constitution between 1982 and the the 1986 election of President Cerezo) were never respected. Gen. Rios Montt, who took power in March 1982, waited three months before declaring a State of Siege and suspending the 1965 Constitution. By decree he suspended all political activity, imposed press censorship, and reintroduced the death penalty.

Decree 46-82 established special military tribunals that were empowered to impose the death penalty on civilians in the military court system. Proceedings were officially secret, and there was no requirement to make public the identity of those detained, nor the sentences handed down.

The National Police is officially in charge of leading the counterinsurgency operations. The National Police come under the direction of the Ministry of the Interior, which from 1954 to 1986 was headed by a member of the military.

The unit most frequently linked to counter-insurgency operations was the DIT (*Departamento de Investigaciones Técnicas*), formed under the regime of Rios Montt and disbanded in 1986. This unit existed under a variety of names over the years, staffed by essentially the same personnel.

The Rural Military Police (PMA), which has taken its orders from the local military G2 (Central Intelligence Service) as well as from the DIT command, is a more decentralized unit, less highly trained and professional than the élite military or internal security forces.

Patrullas de autodefensa (PAC) are civilian defence patrols formed under the regime of Lucas Garcia in 1978 and expanded as a major component of the Rios Montt 'beans and bullets' program in 1982. They are formed by local men in modern villages to control the movements of residents and to watch for guerrilla activities. These units are headed by a civilian Military Commissioner, generally a retired military officer who takes his orders from the local G2 commander. Although this service is officially voluntary, local peasants are intimidated into joining under threat of death. Today they number some 900,000.

The Death Squads (*esquadrones de la muerte*) are clandestine rightwing terrorist groups responsible for extrajudicial killing, abductions, disappearances, and torture. These groups originated in Guatemala and were used for the first time in the counter-insurgency campaign in the 1960s. Now they have become widespread in troublesome areas throughout Latin America, most notably in El Salvador and Colombia. In Guatemala, death-squad activities were most notable during the regime of Lucas Garcia and later under Mejia Victores. The official government position is that they are 'extremist groups beyond government control'.[37] It is generally accepted that these groups are an integral part of the military and internal security apparatus. Membership is of course totally secret, but generally these groups are considered to be staffed by off-duty military and police, civilians connected with the government, and local criminals.

Opposition and dissent

Given the unrestrained repression in Guatemala, until the 1986 elections there was practically no space for opposition. Traditional civil organizations have emerged as champions of social justice and human rights. Trade unions, students, members of the liberal professions, human-rights organizations, and sections of the clergy have all been trying, at considerable risk, to end the stalemate of reciprocal violence.

Some Roman Catholic clergy working in small villages and involved in grass-roots development have been considered subversive because of their leadership role in programs such as rural co-operatives. Trade unions have been another obvious target for repression under the claim of communist infiltration, eliminating any possibility of negotiated settlement of working conditions.

Intellectual opposition has been heavily repressed, and the University of San Carlos has been singled out in particular. In the early 1980s the Economics Department was described as a 'centre of subversion' by police authorities. Student members of the *Asociación de Estudantes Universitarios* disappeared and were killed. Journalists, doctors, and lawyers who were suspected of sympathy with subversion have also been targeted.

Armed opposition has been a constant in the modern history of Guatemala, re-emerging in the more remote areas of the central highlands during the 1970s.[38] Unlike the *landino*[39] rebellions of the late 1960s, the guerrilla movement in the late 1970s and early 1980s attracted a high level of participation and support from the Indian population. The four groups most often identified were the *Organización del Pueblo en*

Armas (ORPA), the *Fuerzas Armadas Revolutionarias* (FAR), the *Partido Guatemalteco Trabajador* (PGT), and the *Ejército Guerrillero de los Pobres* (EGP), the latter being largest and most active. In 1982 the four groups merged into the more centralized *Unidad Revolucionaria Nacional Guatemalteca* (URNG).

The basic operations of these groups were for the most part confined to remote rural areas and consisted in acts of sabotage against infrastructure and attacks on local police and military installations. Revolutionary education was another level of their operations, with the primary objectives of winning over the local population to their view of revolutionary action and soliciting support in the form of food and shelter. In the late 1970s and early 1980s, this movement gathered force, becoming better equipped and more daring. Estimates give the total of active members in these groups to be in the order of three to five thousand in 1981. Since the huge national counter-insurgency program under Rios Montt in 1983, armed insurgency has ceased to be considered a serious threat to government. Nevertheless, the URNG has resurfaced (especially in El Petén and Solalá) and has been the target of three major military offensives since 1987.

Protest and repression: strategies and practices

From 1978 to 1986 each of the three military governments implemented a distinct repressive strategy. The regime of Gen. Lucas Garcia was noted mostly for a haphazard and indiscriminate use of secret death squads for the elimination of political forces and suspected subversives. These groups operated quite openly (certainly an element in the terror that the government wished to instil) and without restriction, both day and night. Their cars (similar to the infamous black Ford Falcons used in Argentina and Brazil) were quite often easily recognizable in the streets of Guatemala City. This was also a period in which guerrilla activity became more widespread and intense in the central mountains. The Lucas Garcia regime was responsible for putting into place most of the elements used in the 'scorched-earth policy' later in force under the Rios Montt regime.

It was during the brief stay of Rios Montt, from March 1982 to August 1983, that the counter-insurgency campaign reached its highest level of intensity. His regime was particularly characterized by massive rural displacement and mass murder.[40] Rios Montt came to power, in a coup supported by the US government, with a mandate to clean up Guatemala's image—tainted by the blatant excesses of his predecessor—and to wage an all-out counter-insurgency operation. This program was known as the 'beans and bullets' strategy, or 'scorched-earth policy'. The President clamped down on death-squad activities in the capital and embarked on an extensive campaign to move communities in sensitive areas into model villages, where the rural population could be more closely controlled and the logistic support system of the guerrillas cut off. The most significant manifestation of this policy was the massive and indiscriminate killing of non-combatant rural Indians. Over 400 villages were destroyed, and close to ten thousand people lost their lives.

At the same time, Rios Montt initiated a series of rural development programs (the National Security and Development Plan) in these model villages with the double objective of winning over the Indian population and convincing the international community of his concern for human rights.

Gen. Mejia Victores took power in a coup in August 1983. His regime was noted for the re-emergence of death-squad activities in a more selective manner than under Lucas Garcia. Many disappearances and killings were more carefully planned to look like accidents. Over eighty disappearances occurred in the first month of this government, the major targets being the University of San Carlos, trade unions, rural leaders, and the newly emerged human-rights movement.

As might be suspected, the military and para-military forces acted with total impunity. But in order to raise yet another legal barrier against any civilian government that might think to challenge its claim, the military government made a final gesture before turning power over to an elected civilian president. The final law passed by the military before the inauguration of President Cerezo was Decree law 08-86, absolving the military of all excesses in the counter-insurgency campaign between 23 March 1982 and 14 January 1986, the period covering the regimes of Rios Montt and Mejia Victores.[41] The decree has not been revoked by the new civilian administration.[42]

Political instability and violence have increased dramatically over the past year. Human-rights violations have escalated, guerrilla warfare has re-emerged in the past two years, and social protest on both the right and the left seems to be isolating the Christian Democratic government of President Cerezo. The government has been forced to back down on a modest (by international standards) tax reform voted in in late 1987. Price controls on basic foodstuffs were lifted and social unrest broke out in August 1988.

Despite Cerezo's leading role in the regional Peace Plan, he was forced to postpone meetings with URNG representatives after an initial meeting in Madrid in October 1987. The repatriation of refugees has been slow (some 1,200 out of close to 200,000 in 1987). The military is in complete control of operations in the rural areas and has launched three major offensives in less than two years (June 1987, Sept. 1988, Dec. 1988). Civilian patrols are still intact and there have been several accounts of murders attributed to these groups. Death-squad activity has intensified in the cities, and reports of massacres in rural areas (twenty-two people in November 1988) are resurfacing. President

Cerezo publicly admitted that there were 1,706 disappearances in 1988. In December 1987 alone, seventy-eight extrajudicial killings and fifteen kidnappings were reported by human-rights groups.

VII CONCLUSION

We have argued in this paper that it is the quantity and severity of repression relative to manifestations of opposition that determines the nature and the intensity of dissent. This, in our opinion, is where the specificity of Latin America lies. We certainly do not wish to give the impression that all actions of security forces are arbitrary, and that dissent and subversion do not exist as such. There obviously are real tensions, and oppositions are fierce. As we argued in the first section, what is recognized as dissent is political and social opposition of a particular nature: i.e., that challenges the system of social domination based on vertical relations. It must be remembered that, from a sociological point of view, the existence of unions does not mean that the conditions exist for a working class to play an active role in society.[43] If unions can be integrated into the system of social control, they will not represent a threat. But they may also thrive by reinforcing the horizontal (class) solidarity of their constituents.[44] They will then most certainly be considered as opposition, and eventually as subversive.

It flows from our hypothesis that where vertical relations dominate, social deviation will be the most severely repressed and security forces will enjoy the highest level of absolute impunity. This is confirmed by our presentation of Guatemala, which is certainly the most violent and repressive of the three countries examined here. We have observed a mix of ethnic and traditional violence that is more social than political. There is in Guatemala a latent civil war, for which American security considerations are not without responsibility.

In Argentina, as a result of a long history of social conflict that by 1976 was deteriorating into near chaos, the military government declared war without restriction on civil society. The generals took it upon themselves to purge society of all subversive elements. Because of their institutional weakness, repression was decentralized, conducted by both official and clandestine organizations, which resulted in an unprecedented multiplication of victims. The resulting 'excesses' of *la guerra sucia* severely damaged the national integrity. That is why the restoration of legitimate authority in Argentina has been contingent on the prosecution of all those who violated the laws, and why impunity could not be tolerated.

Chile is our best illustration of a modern terrorist state: a system based on low-intensity terror, with a manipulative strategy used to maintain order within both the military as an institution and the civilian political class. It offers perhaps some of the most disturbing lessons for a country such as our own, where despite a long democratic tradition and a sophisticated political apparatus, the level of tolerance for opposition can break down under the stress of political and economic crisis. One need only think back to the tolerance level displayed by the Canadian government during the October Crisis of 1970 to draw some uncomfortable parallels.

It has, of course, been intentional on our part to draw parallels between such countries as Guatemala on the one hand, and Argentina and Chile on the other, on the issue of dissent. Although these countries are quite distinct, and their political processes quite specific, we nevertheless wanted to show the similarities in the manifestations of dissent and repression under military rule. Also, an argument can be made to the effect that in these countries, with their economic crises and neo-liberal economic policies that have been responsible for destroying whatever limited industrial productive capacity once existed, the economic élites have reinforced their power, thus increasing social and political inequalities. Given the events of the past fifteen years, one can defend the idea that the societies of both Argentina and Chile are today more hierarchical and less pluralistic than they were in the first half of this century. The apparent ideological and political modernity of these societies can no more be invoked as a distinctive feature. Repression reproduces socio-economic inequalities and restricts citizens' rights. In the countries studied here as well as others in the hemisphere, the rich and powerful have amply demonstrated their incapacity as a social class to provide leadership and to work collectively towards nation-building and economic development. Given these observable similarities, it is no surprise that repression and dissent manifest themselves in similar fashion.

Repression uses a great variety of techniques and strategies. It has very wide resources, enjoys a very broad level of autonomy, and has the fundamental advantage of defining its own rules. In general, there is a great discrepancy between the actions of the opposition and the retaliation orchestrated by the repressive forces. Clandestine repressive groups have appeared throughout Latin America. They are very much a product of situations in which groups within society feel that they are authorized to take justice into their own hands. They are also a manifestation of the fundamental cleavage between the legal ideology and the social reality. Death squads are instrumental; they serve as a buffer between repression and governmental responsibility. They perform illegal acts without directly engaging the official responsibility of the state, thus contributing to the installation of terror and the conviction that repressive acts are covered by total impunity.

Does this mean that Latin American countries are fundamentally undemocratic? The most common perspective, influenced by stories of coups, generals, *caudillos*, electoral fraud, and violence, assumes the authoritarian nature of Latin America. But another case can also be made:

> If one were to describe the most striking aspect of Latin American political life it would most certainly not be either coups, nor putsches nor the *continuismo* of Presidents-for-Life, nor electoral fraud but the unwavering, platonic attachment to representative institutions of western-style democracies.[45]

Latin American political culture is profoundly marked by its constant and systematic reference to democratic ideals. Even the official discourse of the most authoritarian governments contains constant references to democracy. Political repression is conducted in the name of the peace and order judged indispensable to allow for a democratic opening of the political process. This does not mean that there is consensus as to what a democratic system is. Where transition to civilian rule has occurred, it can be shown that political opening has meant the return of the old political élite,[46] without allowing for much change in the inefficient and unequal organization and representation of the popular masses.

Recognition and respect for the human rights and obligations of the citizen, based on a set of values and attitudes conferred on each individual at birth, is essential in Latin America. The pervasive bartering of favours and use of threat among unequal partners are in opposition to these values, and must be abandoned in favour of a more open system of debate, allowing for change while respecting social order.

It is surprising to realize that so few have really given up all hope of a peaceful change, that so few have turned to open subversion against a political system that has rejected and persecuted them. To use a sociological comparison, one might say that political dissent is much less common than social marginalization. Ernesto 'Che' Guevara is no more an inspiring hero in Latin America than Louis Riel is in Canada.

How does our limited knowledge of dissent and the state in Latin America help us to address this same problem in our Canadian environment? First, it shows that there are very real dangers involved in the manipulation of violence. In those countries where such a thing is possible, it should be considered as a privilege for the general public, and for intellectuals in particular, to be as active in preventing problems as they are in denouncing them.

Second, Latin America reminds us that the process of adjustment between security forces and the collectivity they are supposed to protect is continual. The socially acceptable limits to individual and collective political freedom must be the subject of regular and open debate. It is essential for all citizens to be reassured that their rights will be respected, and to make the issue of internal security a collective endeavour.

Third, and most important, the Latin American experience tragically demonstrates that no small group, whatever its competence, should be given the exclusive opportunity to define what it considers a threat to society and what means should be used to eradicate it. Democracy—in the sense of public debate and a relative degree of openness—is indispensable. Social cohesion will be reinforced and institutions better protected when the population is genuinely convinced that security forces are not acting on behalf of particular interests (least of all their own), but are truly protecting the collectivity, using an accepted and realistic definition of what constitutes a threat. No plea for secrecy and efficiency is a match for the collective benefits of responsible openness.

Via Italiana al Socialismo: The Italian Communist Party and Democracy

G. GRANT AMYOT

In 1987 Joseph LaPalombara, Arnold Wolfers Professor of Political Science at Yale University, long-time authority on Italian politics, *and* First Secretary of the US Embassy in Rome in the early 1980s, wrote:

> The evidence is by now *beyond reasonable doubt* that the PCI has long since abandoned whatever Leninist, Stalinist, revolutionary, or dictatorial intentions it once may have had. . . . where one is not blinded by ideology or motivated by opportunism, it requires an act of will not to recognize that the only thing even mildly menacing about the Communist party today is its name.[1]

Such a clear statement from so authoritative and unimpeachable a source ought to be sufficient to close the issue. LaPalombara's opinion could be backed up by similar statements by the leading academic students of the Italian Communist Party (PCI) and by non-Communist Italian politicians, including the leaders of the PCI's principal rival, the Christian Democratic party (DC).[2] Furthermore, in the two years since he wrote it, the PCI has moved faster than ever before towards the adoption of a fully social-democratic stance.

Nevertheless, as LaPalombara also points out, there are many people, both inside and outside Italy, who have an interest in painting the Communist Party as ultimately opposed to democracy and the constitution, and willing to use violent means to overthrow them. Besides the visceral anti-communists, there are those politicians who benefit from the unwritten convention that has excluded the PCI from participating in government as a coalition partner since 1947, thus increasing their own bargaining power and likelihood of entering the cabinet, and who find it profitable to attack the party as 'undemocratic' at election time. There are also those who fear that a government with PCI participation would adopt policies that they oppose: the wealthy and privileged may fear measures that might somehow reduce their incomes and wealth, while Italy's NATO allies are apprehensive about the foreign and defence policies of such a government. They find it convenient to equate the defence of their own interests with the defence of democracy itself, however little justification there may be for such an identification.

These critics, lacking evidence, fall back on the argument that the PCI's espousal of democracy is simply a ruse or tactic, and that at a suitable opportunity it will 'throw down the mask' and attempt a violent revolution.[3]

It will be the aim of this paper to demonstrate that the Italian Communist Party accepts the democratic form of government laid down by the Italian Constitution, and does so as fully as the other democratic parties, without any reservations or *arrière-pensées*. I shall do this not only by referring to the party's own statements on the subject, but also by tracing the evolution of its strategy so as to show that its commitment to democracy has solid foundations and cannot be dismissed as a ruse. Since, as we have seen, mine is a position very widely accepted today, I shall emphasize the distinctive features of this strategic evolution as I see them, and then go on to outline the type of democracy that the PCI supports by referring to some major issues, including the party's position on the USSR, its attitude towards neo-fascism, its stance on left-wing terrorism, and its current proposals for reforming Italy's democratic institutions. This extended discussion should put flesh on the bones of the PCI's commitment to democracy, reinforcing the main thesis of the paper. I shall also try to assess its overall view of Italian democracy in the light of the numerous rightist plots of the last twenty-five years.

Finally, since the interest of the Italian case lies in the fact that the PCI is presented as the prime example of a Marxist party that accepts and supports the democratic framework, I shall consider whether the party has 'largely buried Karl Marx'[4] at the same time as it has embraced democracy. Has the party become completely 'social-democratized', as many have held in the light of its recent evolution, or has it retained a distinctly Marxist character? Such a question, like that about its commitment to democracy, cannot be answered simply by reference to official pronouncements, but requires a consideration of the PCI's actual practice, its social make-up, and its place in the Italian political system.

I THE EVOLUTION OF THE PCI'S STRATEGY

The Comintern and revolution

When the PCI was founded at Livorno in January 1921, it was as a member of the Third (Communist) International, explicitly committed to the Leninist conception of revolution outlined in the Twenty-One Conditions.[5] In essence, Lenin grafted the experience of the Russian Revolution onto the older theory, dominant in the socialist parties of the Second International (1889-1914), that capitalism was bound to break down in a catastrophic crisis. This collapse was to occur as a result of the economic contradictions of capitalism that Marx had identified. At the same time, the proletarianization of the middle class, predicted by Marx, would ensure that at the time of crisis the working class would be the vast majority of the population, and would be ready to follow the lead of the socialist party and seize power.[6]

Although the Russian Revolution was an extremely complex historical event, this theory could be stretched to fit it: there had been a catastrophic crisis of the tsarist empire, precipitated by a war that could be traced back to imperialism and the economic contradictions of capitalism that gave rise to it.[7] Lenin and the Bolsheviks added only one element to the older theory: the necessity for a vanguard party, which could lead the masses in the moment of crisis towards the seizure of state power. The Comintern prescribed the Russian model of the party and of revolutionary strategy for the Western European Communist parties as well, as it believed the World War had ushered in a revolutionary period for the whole world.

This model was applied by the European parties from 1919 to 1934 with singularly little success, until the rise to power of Hitler led the leaders of the Comintern to introduce a radically different strategy, the Popular Front. Consecrated by the 7th Congress of the Comintern in 1935, this strategy has, with some qualifications and brief suspensions, been the basic line of every Communist party almost up to the present day. The Popular Front involved for the first time an alliance of Communists not only with other working-class parties and with the peasantry, but also with sectors of the middle class and even of the capitalist class, and the platform of this alliance was not the introduction of socialism but the defence of democracy against Fascism. The new line was the product both of Soviet foreign-policy concerns and of tendencies within the European parties, including notably the PCI.[8]

The Popular Front implied a two-stage strategy for the Western European parties. Since monopoly capital (and, in countries such as Italy, large landowners) was seen as the fundamental social basis of Fascism, the first stage would be a government composed of all the anti-monopoly forces, from the workers to non-monopolistic business, with a 'democratic' program of reforms stopping well short of socialism. This was what both the Spanish and the French Popular Front governments actually did, and the Communists were among the most insistent that these governments should not go too far and frighten away the middle-class parties and voters that supported them. Only later, in a second stage not very clearly linked to the first, would the transition to socialism occur.

After the defeat of Fascism in the Second World War, the Popular Front strategy was continued, with the monopolies and large landowners as the enemies and virtually all other social classes as potential allies. The dissolution of the Comintern in 1943 made it difficult in any case to formalize any new line. Since the two stages did not cohere well, individual parties tended to stress one or the other, depending on their history and circumstances. Some, generally the more 'pro-Soviet' parties, tended to lay more emphasis on the ultimate goal of socialism, while others, the future 'Eurocommunist' parties, concentrated almost exclusively on the forging of broad alliances for the attainment of a Popular-Front type of government, while socialism receded further and further into an indefinite future.

The adoption of the Popular Front line in 1935 entailed no immediate revision of the parties' formal theory or ideology, however. It was only gradually, over the following decades, that the Eurocommunist parties brought their positions on other issues, such as 'bourgeois' democracy and the nature of the Soviet Union, into line with their actual policy of alliances. The resistance to these doctrinal changes was strong, because many militants had been formed in the period when the USSR was seen as a model and 'orthodox' Marxism-Leninism was presented as the party ideology. But when they occurred they were a matter of bringing theory into line with long-standing practice.

Togliatti and the Italian road to socialism

One of the major proponents of the Popular Front line within the Comintern was Palmiro Togliatti, Secretary General of the PCI from 1926 to 1964. Togliatti's thought also moulded the strategy of the PCI, which he dubbed the 'Italian road to socialism' (*via italiana al socialismo*). He and the rest of the PCI leadership were influenced above all by the defeat of the working-class movement and the victory of Fascism in Italy after the First World War. In his view, the principal reason for the Fascist victory was the fact that Mussolini and his supporters had been able to win over the middle class, principally the self-employed petty bourgeoisie. Drawing in part on Marx's analyses of French politics in 1848-52, Togliatti suggested that the contest between the two principal forces in modern society, the bourgeoisie and the proletariat, would be decided in favour of the class that won over the third element, the petty bourgeoisie, to its side. Hence the centrality of the 'policy of alliances' for the Communist Party. The Italian Socialist Party, the principal left-wing force in 1918-22, had had no specific programs for the middle classes and had instead driven them into the Fascist camp by preaching about their impending proletarianization. This was especially true in the countryside, where the smallholders and sharecroppers provided much of the early support for Fascism. The Socialists had also repelled veterans of all classes with their anti-militarist propaganda and condemnation of all who had supported the war effort, and, with their pronounced anti-clericalism, the Catholics as well.

The rise of Fascism also led Togliatti to conclude that economic and social crisis did not always favour the left and, indeed, was more likely to drive the middle strata to the right. Hence his conclusion that the PCI should strive for positive solutions to the country's problems, rather than stand by or pursue a *politique du pire*. As he said in 1944:

> In the past we have often been faced with dangerous situations, created by the policy of the ruling classes. For the most part, however, we and the other parties which represented the working masses were content to denounce the consequences of this policy and to say to the people: look, learn, see the faults of your rulers and of the regime under which you live. It was, in substance, the position of an association of propagandists for a different and better regime. But today can we limit ourselves to a position of this sort?
>
> . . . If we limited ourselves to taking such a position, we would be making a great mistake.[9]

Already in the mid-1920s Togliatti and other PCI leaders had suggested that the fall of Fascism might be the product of a broad, multi-class 'people's revolution', rather than the socialist revolution that the Comintern's catastrophic perspective foresaw. Hence they championed the slogan of a 'constituent assembly' or 'republican assembly' in order to win petty-bourgeois support. Togliatti supported Bukharin, who believed that capitalism was entering a rather long phase of consolidation, within the Comintern, and opposed the 'class against class' slogan adopted after Bukharin's defeat in 1929. In spite of attempts by Stalin to unseat him, he remained leader of the party during the ultra-left 'third period' (1929-34), and then, as Vice-Secretary-General of the Comintern, had a major role in the formulation of the Popular Front strategy and delivered the second major report to the 7th Congress. As Comintern representative in Spain during the Civil War, he saw the Spanish Republic as a prototype of the first-stage 'Popular Front' government.[10]

The Communists prided themselves on being the most consistent and active anti-fascist opposition group during the years of the regime. When it fell in 1943, their militants were released from prison, and after the armistice of 8 September they were the first to organize the armed Resistance movement behind the German lines. The Resistance was a formative experience for the PCI, and remains a powerful myth for its members as for other Italians. In the Resistance, as they had since 1935, the Communists were aiming at the formation of a broad alliance of all anti-fascist forces to achieve not socialism, but a 'progressive democracy,' as the first stage of a Popular Front government was called. In the immediate situation, they argued for the unity of all forces prepared to fight the Germans and their Fascist allies. When Togliatti returned to Italy from Moscow in April 1944, he reversed the party's position on the formation of a coalition government, stating that he was prepared to work even with monarchists to pursue the war against Germany, and settle the 'institutional question' (monarchy v. republic) after the war.

The new 'line of Salerno' shocked those Communists (and other leftists) who saw the monarchy, which had kept Mussolini in power for twenty-one years, as tainted with the crimes of Fascism, but it was typical of Togliatti and his constant search for unity with a broad spectrum of anti-fascist forces.

As the leading party of the Resistance movement (40 to 50 per cent of all partisans fought in Communist units)[11] and as one of the three major parties in the provisional government from 1944 to 1947, the PCI adhered rigidly to the two-stage approach. The leadership under Togliatti opposed any groups within the party who wished to turn the Resistance into a socialist revolution. Even those who sought to use the occasion for radical but non-socialist reforms were told that these would have to wait until after the defeat of Nazism and the calling of a constituent assembly.[12] Thus the partisans turned over their arms to the Allied forces after the end of the war, and attempts to turn the local Committees of National Liberation into the basis of a new state structure were abandoned as the old system of control by prefects and central ministries was re-established, with only a few changes in personnel. Even such reforms as the redrafting of the legal codes introduced under Fascism were postponed, and never undertaken until many years later. The overwhelming emphasis in PCI policy in this period was on unity with all the other anti-fascist forces. While it is certainly true that this line was in keeping with Moscow's policy of adhering to the Yalta division of Europe into spheres of influence, Togliatti had his own very strong reasons for embracing it, as we have seen above. (That the PCI's line was a result of its own autonomous elaboration is shown by the fact that in Greece, in the same period, the wishes of the USSR did not prevent the Communists from attempting to keep power after the departure of the Germans, even though Stalin had recognized Greece as part of the British sphere of influence.)[13]

The culmination of the Resistance and reconstruction period, from the Communist point of view, was the drafting of the republican Constitution by the Constituent Assembly elected in 1946. It was the product of joint work and negotiation between the PCI and the two other major parties, the Christian Democrats and the Socialists. Today it is still one of the world's most modern constitutions: it is a blueprint for an advanced form of democracy, although one in which private capitalism is explicitly recognized and guaranteed.[14] It contains a full series of personal rights and freedoms, as well as a number of programmatic norms that enjoin the Republic to guarantee the right to work, the health and education of the citizens, and the family, and to eliminate the social and economic inequalities that 'prevent the full development of the human person and the effective participation of all working people in the political, economic and social organization of the country' (Art. 3). It also affirms solemnly, if to limited practical effect, that 'Italy is a democratic

Republic, founded on labour' (Art. 1).[15] Togliatti was prepared to accept several concessions to the Catholics, including the incorporation into the Constitution of the Lateran Pacts, which gave the Church a special status in Italy (Art. 7). Because of its role in the Resistance and the Constituent Assembly, the PCI can rightly see itself as among the founders of Italian democracy. The more advanced provisions of the Constitution, such as Article 3 and other provisions allowing agrarian reform and the nationalization of monopolies and other enterprises, have even been cited by the Communists as 'an important conquest on the Italian road to socialism'.[16]

As a result of opposition from the right wing and business interests in Italy, perhaps abetted by the United States,[17] the Communists and Socialists were expelled from the governing coalition in May 1947. In spite of the heightened tensions of the Cold War and the Korean War, however, Togliatti kept the PCI on the course he had set for it. Spontaneous upsurges of unrest, such as the demonstrations and occasional acts of violence that broke out after an attempt on Togliatti's life in 1948, were quickly ended by firm action on the part of the PCI leadership. Togliatti continued to criticize the mentality of some of the rank and file, particularly ex-partisans, who looked forward to a revolutionary moment (the famous 'X hour'). Nor did the more orthodox Vice-Secretary-General, Pietro Secchia, often incorrectly labelled a 'Stalinist', encourage the insurrectionary perspective.[18] Even though Communists had some reason to fear that the party would be driven into clandestinity again as a result of international tensions, no concrete plans existed even for defensive violence.[19]

Instead, Togliatti continued to insist on the long-term perspective of unity between the parties representing the working class, the middle class, and the non-monopolistic bourgeoisie (principally the Communists, Socialists, and Christian Democrats). The platform was now not simply anti-fascism, control of the monopolies, and land reform to break up the large estates: it also included peace and opposition to American influence in Italy.[20] He also combatted those who thought the party's main task was to husband and augment its strength for some future moment rather than to propose solutions and intermediate objectives that could be realized in the present through alliances with other classes and political forces. In 1951 Stalin offered Togliatti the Secretary-Generalship of the Cominform, the successor to the Comintern; though the invitation was peremptory, Togliatti was eventually able to turn it down. This episode suggests that Stalin was not altogether pleased at Togliatti's conduct of PCI policy, and would have preferred to have Secchia at the helm of the Italian party.[21]

After Stalin's death, Togliatti intensified his campaign against those who did not accept his emphasis on alliances and intermediate objectives, and in 1955 he removed Secchia from his post. The dramatic events of 1956 allowed him to expound even more openly the positions he had held and had been promoting within the party for many years. In this sense I, unlike some scholars, believe that there is substantial continuity in the PCI's line before and after 1956.[22]

The 20th Congress of the Soviet party and Khrushchev's secret speech denouncing Stalin opened the way to a stormy debate throughout the Communist movement. In Italy, PCI leaders for the first time guaranteed explicitly that a plurality of parties would exist both in the intermediate stage of progressive democracy and under socialism.[23] This had already been implicit in the concept of progressive democracy. At the same time, however, the party revised the older concept of the dictatorship of the proletariat, which seemed in contrast with the current line. After some debate, and suggestions that although the dictatorship of the proletariat was a necessary phase, it could take different forms, the Programmatic Declaration passed by the 8th Congress of the PCI (December 1956) implicitly rejected such a dictatorship: it stated that a transition to socialism within the framework of the Constitution was possible. While there could theoretically be a violent reaction by the ruling class (this was Lenin's justification for the dictatorship of the proletariat), the Declaration stated that it would be extremely unlikely in the face of a broad coalition of workers and the middle classes that isolated the reactionary elements.[24] Significantly, in its promises to the middle classes the Declaration went considerably beyond simple allegiance to the democratic principle of majority rule: 'for decisive middle-class groups the passage to new socialist or socialist-type relations will take place only on the basis of their economic advantage and of free consent.'[25]

Berlinguer and the historic compromise

The events of 1956 marked the revision of the PCI's theoretical position on the transition to socialism and the dictatorship of the proletariat to match its practice. By the time of Togliatti's death in 1964, his line had been fully consolidated within the party, and the last pockets of serious resistance eliminated. The traumatic experience of Fascism had deeply influenced Togliatti and with him a whole generation of Communist leaders, who thereafter never overestimated the strength of their own forces or underestimated those of the enemy. This appreciation coloured their attitude for decades afterward, as it still does today, and led them to opt naturally for defensive responses to new developments and above all to give absolute priority to the policy of alliances with the middle strata and the parties that represented them. The PCI's profound commitment to this policy was prior, both temporally and conceptually, to its commitment to the democratic framework—almost inevitably so, since the Popular Front was born when no such framework existed in Italy. But the acceptance and indeed championing of democracy flowed naturally from it, as Togliatti believed that the PCI could not hope to advance towards socialism without the support of both the workers and the middle classes—a good deal more than a bare majority of the population. Furthermore, the PCI was unlikely to attract broad middle-class support or win recognition as a legitimate governing force from the other parties unless it made its commitment to democracy plain, in theory as well as in practice.

From 1944 on Togliatti used the formidable resources at his disposal to propagate his position in its many forms, from the celebration of the Resistance as a moment of unity between Communists and the antifascist middle classes to the reinterpretation of Gramsci's thought as an intellectual justification for the policy of alliances.[26] In the end, the sectarian and orthodox elements in the party were marginalized, and the Italian road to socialism became common sense for two generations of Communists.

The pervasive effect of this Togliattian mind-set of the PCI leadership is well illustrated by the genesis of the policy of the 'historic compromise' adopted in 1972. While the student and worker agitation of 1968-70 had given the country a powerful push to the left, it had also given rise to a right-wing backlash, evident in the riots of late 1970 in Reggio Calabria, where right-wing extremists seized the leadership of a localist protest, and the striking electoral gains of the neo-fascist Italian Social Movement (MSI), which advanced from 6.6 per cent to 16.3 per cent of the popular vote in the Sicilian regional elections of 1971, and in the national elections of 1972 reached the record level of 8.7 per cent. Moreover, in 1969 neo-fascist terrorists launched the so-called 'strategy of tension' with the bombing at the Banca Nazionale dell'Agricoltura in Milan, which was made to appear the work of left-wing groups. There were rumours of attempted coups d'état, as well as disturbing signs that some elements of the state apparatus were conniving at the strategy of tension.[27] This situation was more than enough to drive the PCI leadership, now under Enrico Berlinguer, to adopt a defensive approach aimed above all at staving off a fascistic reaction, rather than take advantage of the new situation to move aggressively towards socialism. At the 13th Congress of the party (Milan, 1972), Berlinguer proposed a new strategy of collaboration between the PCI, PSI, and DC, later dubbed the 'historic compromise'.

The coup in Chile in September 1973 led Berlinguer to restate with great clarity the policy of the historic compromise and the PCI's attitude towards democracy in general.[28] With many citations of Togliatti, he reaffirmed the centrality of alliances with the middle strata for the party:

> It is completely evident . . . that whether the weight of these
> [intermediate] social forces is shifted to the side of the working class or

against it is decisive for the success of democratic development and of the advance towards socialism.

   . . . The central political problem in Italy has been, and remains more than ever, precisely that of avoiding the creation of a stable and organic union between the centre and the right, of a broad front of the clerico-fascist type . . . .[29]

And he continued: 'But it would be completely illusory to think that, even if the parties and forces of the left succeeded in reaching 51 per cent of the votes and of the parliamentary seats . . . this fact would guarantee the survival and the achievements of a government that represented this 51 per cent.'[30] This statement demonstrates that the PCI does not have a simple majoritarian conception of democracy, but believes a strategic majority is necessary for any major social change.

Berlinguer also rebutted the ultra-left argument that the Chilean coup proved that the right would abandon the democratic framework if it felt it necessary, and that therefore the left had to prepare for an eventual violent confrontation. On the contrary, the left should attempt to forestall such a danger by 'hold[ing] firmly in our hands the cause of the defence of freedoms and of democratic progress' and organizing a broad alliance to isolate the most reactionary groups: 'The possibility of a recourse to reactionary violence "must not therefore lead [us]", as comrade Longo [Luigi Longo, PCI Secretary-General 1964-72] affirmed, "to have a duality in perspective and practical preparation." '[31] And Berlinguer cited as proof of the wisdom of the party's approach the numerous successful struggles it had waged against the right in Italy since 1947.

This brief account of the evolution of the PCI's outlook has demonstrated that its commitment to democracy arises not from a tactical calculation, but from its long-term strategy. By concentrating on strategy and theory, I have left to one side, for the time being, the social and political reality of the party, which has now been operating within the democratic framework of modern Italy for forty-three years, and by this fact alone has become an integral part of the political system. It has always shared in government at the local and regional levels, and, even from the opposition benches, has a considerable role in law-making.[32] During the 'historic compromise' period it briefly entered the governmental majority, though not the cabinet: it supported Giulio Andreotti's Christian Democratic government by its abstention from 1976 to 1978, and became a full-fledged member of the majority from 1978 to 1979. This participation in the workings of Italian democracy has had a profound effect on the PCI's ethos and outlook. I have also omitted a detailed consideration of the substantial softening of the PCI's line on a whole series of issues, from foreign policy to industrial policy. This was another aspect of the revision of the party's earlier positions that proceeded in tandem with its explicit recognition of the democratic framework and from the same motivations.

II THE PCI AND THE SOVIET UNION

As the PCI revised its theory and doctrine to match its democratic practice, it also had to revise its attitude towards the USSR and the other Soviet-bloc states. It was inconsistent to promise that the PCI would maintain democratic freedoms in a socialist society and at the same time present the Soviet Union as a model to be imitated. Furthermore, middle-class voters and other parties were unlikely to have confidence in the Communists unless they took their distance from the countries of 'actually existing socialism': until they did so convincingly, the reality of these countries was one of the best propaganda tools of their enemies. But beyond these considerations, as Joan Barth Urban argues, the PCI was also motivated by sincere conviction that a democratic society was superior when it condemned the Soviet system.[33]

On the other hand, sentimental attachment to the USSR (or to the brilliant image of it once presented in PCI propaganda) was strong among the membership; much of it dated from the Resistance period, when the slogan 'Big moustache [Stalin] is coming' was often repeated and chalked on walls by Communist partisans. Every denunciation of Stalin and the Soviet Union shook the party's rank and file and led to resignations. After 1956 there was also the danger that the USSR would exploit this situation by supporting and funding a dissident pro-Soviet faction or breakaway group. (In fact, the Soviet Union, which had ceased to support the PCI directly years before, sent at least two billion lire [US$3.25 million] to assist the small Socialist Party of Proletarian Unity when it was founded in 1964.)[34] Such a tactic has been employed in more recent years against the Spanish Communist Party.

Khrushchev's secret speech provided the stimulus for Togliatti to publicly differentiate the Italian road to socialism from the Soviet. In an interview with *Nuovi argomenti* (May-June 1956), he stated that there could be national roads to socialism, and that in the capitalist countries it was possible to move towards socialism 'in the presence of a plurality of parties and by the initiative of some of these'.[35] Moreover, he did not limit himself to distinguishing the Italian case from the Soviet, but also criticized Khrushchev's explanation of the crimes and suffocation of democracy of the Stalin era as the product of the 'personality cult' alone. Instead, he said it was necessary to study carefully the social, political, and economic roots of Stalinism, in particular the centralization and military methods made necessary by the Civil War and the way in which the first Five-Year Plan and collectivization were implemented.[36]

Togliatti went on to champion the concept of 'polycentrism' within the international Communist movement, arguing that, just as there was no longer any one model of socialism, there was no longer any 'leading state'. He resisted any attempts by the Soviets to recreate a form of international Communist organization after the demise of the Cominform.[37] Within the PCI, Khrushchev's further revelations at the 22nd Congress of the CPSU (1961) led to a renewed campaign against the residual 'orthodox' elements in the party apparatus, and stimulated further reflection on the cause of the degeneration of socialism in the USSR. The more thoughtful PCI leaders did not simply dismiss the Soviet experience as irrelevant because it occurred in very different and unrepeatable circumstances, but sought to learn from it how to avoid a similar tragedy in Italy—for instance, by reinforcing autonomous local governments and movements and organizations in civil society, as a defence against the danger of a monolithic party-state.[38]

Unlike the 1956 Hungarian invasion—on which the Italian Communists had equivocated before eventually supporting the Soviet action—the Soviet invasion of Czechoslovakia in 1968 led to a prompt condemnation by the PCI.[39] While admitting that the invasion was not simply an 'error', but arose from the objective contradictions of the Soviet bloc, nevertheless Berlinguer was not prepared to accept the call from more radical party members to reject the USSR's claim to be a socialist state.[40]

Tensions between the PCI and the USSR mounted after 1968, particularly when the party came out in support of Italy's membership in NATO in 1972 and took the lead in the 'Eurocommunist' movement in the mid-1970s. Berlinguer increasingly saw the need to distance his party from the international Communist movement. As events elsewhere in Europe unfolded, it became evident that the USSR preferred weak pro-Soviet parties to strong Eurocommunist ones, and would even act to undermine the latter.[41] Indeed, Berlinguer stated that one reason for the PCI's acceptance of NATO was that it provided a 'shield' against any possible Soviet intervention against a democratic socialist government in Italy, and represented a choice of the Western democratic camp as opposed to the undemocratic Soviet model.[42]

The declaration of martial law in Poland in December 1981 provided the occasion for the decisive 'rip' (*strappo*) between the PCI and the USSR that Berlinguer wanted. Condemning the action of the Polish government and the USSR's role, he stated that 'the innovative impulse that had its origin in the October Revolution has been exhausted'.[43] These positions touched off polemics with Moscow and controversy within the PCI, but they were reaffirmed at the 16th Congress in 1983. There the amendments proposed by Armando Cossutta, a member of the Executive who disagreed with the *strappo*, received scant support, so that 'the PCI leadership no longer had to worry unduly about pro-Soviet loyalties among party activists'.[44]

The reforming actions of Mikhail Gorbachev have certainly aroused interest and support in the PCI, but have not led the party to fundamentally revise its former judgements. Indeed, the Soviets have instead moved a considerable distance towards the PCI's positions, even to the point of accepting Berlinguer's drastic judgement that the Revolution has exhausted its 'innovative impulse'.[45] This change in the Soviet attitude accounts for the noticeable *rapprochement* between the PCI and the Soviet Union in the last few years. As Alessandro Natta, then Secretary-General, stressed while welcoming the return of Andrei Sakharov from exile in December 1986, the PCI will not reconsider its 'choice of camp' in favour of Western democracy. Recent PCI documents on defence policy have similarly stressed that the PCI's support for NATO signifies adherence to the Western values of democracy and pluralism.[46]

III THE PCI AND NEO-FASCISM

The issue of neo-fascism illustrates in an interesting way the precise nature and contours of the PCI's commitment to democracy. While the Italian Constitution is one of the most democratic in the world, it does limit democratic freedoms in one respect. Its twelfth transitional provision (para. 1) states: 'The reorganization, in any form, of the dissolved fascist party is prohibited.' This provision goes beyond the other parts of the Constitution that directly regulate political parties, Article 49 ('All citizens have the right to associate freely in parties to participate with democratic methods in determining national policy') and Article 18, para. 2 ('Secret associations and those which pursue, even indirectly, political ends by means of organizations of a military character are prohibited'), and rules out a fascist party even if it operates openly, uses only democratic methods, and has a non-military character.[47] This restriction is arguably contrary to the principles of liberal democracy, although it is certainly understandable in the light of Italy's recent history.

The PCI, as illustrated above, has made anti-fascism a cardinal point of its policy and of its mass appeal. Anti-fascism has been presented, even in the most recent period, as the basis of an alliance with the middle classes and the parties that represent them (notably the DC) for the defence of Italian democracy. And the PCI's anti-fascist record, from 1921 to the present, is the most impressive of all the Italian parties'. Yet, faced with a relatively large party, the MSI (Italian Social Movement), that quite arguably fits the definition of a reconstitution of the fascist party set out in the law implementing Transitional Provision XII (law no. 645 of 20 June 1952, the 'Scelba Law'),[48] the PCI has ceased to support attempts to dissolve it through either an act of parliament or a decision of the judiciary or the Minister of the Interior.[49]

The Communist party in this case has chosen to uphold a liberal-democratic principle rather than the letter of the Constitution, even though the Constitution appears to ban one of its traditional enemies. There are several reasons for this stance. First, the MSI, because it is seen as anti-constitutional, could never participate in a governmental coalition without bringing discredit and defeat on the government it supported (as Prime Minister Tambroni discovered in 1960). Therefore it 'freezes' 12 to 15 per cent of the right-wing vote, making that portion useless as far as the formation of a government is concerned. Second, if the MSI were banned, its voters and activists would probably attempt to form another party or—worse from the Communist point of view—enter the DC and shift the balance of forces within that party to the right (facilitating the 'clerico-fascist' bloc that Berlinguer feared). Third, the PCI's appeals for anti-fascist unity are much more convincing if there is a real neo-fascist party in existence. Fourth, the PCI fears that dissolving the MSI would simply drive its more dangerous elements underground: it is better that they operate in the open.

But beyond these political calculations, the PCI's attitude stems also from the basic democratic conviction that it is wrong and ultimately self-defeating to ban a party, however distasteful, that represents 2.3 million voters and a tradition rooted in Italian history that cannot be eradicated by simple repression. The underlying conviction of the PCI leaders is that the MSI as a party must be combatted by political means—argument and debate—rather than by laws and prison sentences. They rightly see it as far less dangerous to Italian democracy than the various secret right-wing conspiracies that have come to light in the past twenty-five years.

IV   THE PCI AND TERRORISM

An examination of the PCI's attitude towards terrorism, particularly left-wing terrorism, does not strengthen its democratic credentials in a similar manner. But in its willingness to sanction broad police powers that limited personal freedoms and to support prosecutors who imprisoned large numbers of people on charges they could not support with direct evidence, the PCI was in the company of most of the other political parties.

The PCI has typically displayed a very hostile and intolerant attitude towards groups that claim to be on its left. This was in part because of a residue of Stalinist tradition, but principally because such groups could only hinder the implementation of the policy of alliances by denouncing it to the PCI's rank and file and/or by frightening off potential middle-class allies. Furthermore, taking a tough stand against far-left movements was almost a necessity for the PCI if it wished to be accepted by middle-class voters or the DC. Even before the first episodes of leftist terrorism, the PCI condemned harshly the 'extra-parliamentary' left groups that emerged after 1968 in the universities and factories, labelling them 'extremist', 'anarchist', and 'anti-democratic', and hinting that right-wing provocateurs might be behind them.[50]

It was therefore not surprising that the PCI should take an extremely hard line against the left-wing terrorist groups when they emerged from 1972 on. At first, like many other observers, the Communists thought that some episodes—such as the death of left-wing publisher Giangiacomo Feltrinelli while placing an explosive charge on a power pylon—were right-wing provocations, like the 1969 bombings. This attitude was understandable, given the PCI's pervasive fear of obscure plots against democracy at that time. But once it was clear that the Red Brigades and other terrorist organizations of the left actually did exist, the PCI spared no venom in its attacks. One example may suffice, an editorial in the party daily attacking those who called the Red Brigades 'comrades who have erred':

> The 'comrades in error' are in reality . . . primarily enemies of the working class. They differ from the fascists in nothing but words , and not always even these. To collaborate with them signifies to collaborate in the undoing of society and the preparation of days of oppression.[51]

When Aldo Moro, Chairman of the DC, was kidnapped by the Red Brigades in March 1978, the PCI immediately took a position of extreme 'firmness', opposing any negotiation or any concession whatever to the terrorists. Given that they were at that moment seeking democratic legitimacy so that they could enter the majority, they had little choice.

The Communists argued that Italian democracy would be fatally weakened if it descended to bargaining with the Red Brigades. They also feared that concessions might lead to a rightist, authoritarian government.[52] This apprehension was in keeping with the defensive mentality that we noted above. In any case, they believed that the terrorists' intention was to provoke an extreme, repressive backlash by the state and the polarization of society—exactly what the PCI had always feared. They also suspected that the Red Brigades might be in some way manoeuvred or financed by outside forces (the US or the USSR) that wished to prevent the PCI's entry into the government: the timing of the kidnapping (during the debate in parliament that was to lead to the PCI's entering the majority) reinforced these suspicions. It should be added that Moro was the Christian Democratic leader who had worked the most tenaciously for the acceptance of the PCI as part of the majority.

The Communists were especially concerned to dispel any notion that the Red Brigades were in any way connected to their party, or that it bore any responsibility, even indirect, for their actions. (Only a minority of the terrorists were ex-Communists, but some still tried to make a connection between the Red Brigades and the more radical Communist rhetoric of the Stalin era.) It is interesting to speculate on why political terrorism has emerged in some advanced countries and not in others: in the Italian case, a plethora of explanations has been advanced, and it is even doubtful that explanations using the tools of social science, as opposed to those of psychiatry, are possible.[53] But the sense of betrayal felt by some youth as the PCI became more moderate undoubtedly played a role, particularly when the PCI was supporting the Christian Democratic Andreotti cabinet (1976-79). The inefficiency, if not deliberate neglect, of the police forces is certainly another factor that must be taken into account. Many questions have been raised, for instance, about their inability to find Moro during his captivity; the major police forces involved were headed by members of the secret Propaganda 2 (P2) Masonic lodge, whose aim was to prevent the PCI's entry into the government.[54] The reduction in terrorist violence in recent years suggests that the police can work effectively when not held back, and that terrorism is not endemic to Italy.

Having taken the above positions, the PCI accepted and supported the considerable extensions of police powers contained in the Reale law of 1975 and the Cossiga law of 1979. While it voted against the former in parliament, by 1978, when the law was put to a referendum at the request of the small Radical Party, the party supported it. It also supported the Cossiga law in a 1981 referendum. Among other provisions, these laws broadened the definition of the crime of attempting a terrorist act to include many ill-defined 'preparatory acts'; allowed the issuing of search warrants for whole blocks of flats; extended the period for which suspects could be held before being brought before a magistrate; lengthened the permitted periods of pre-trial detention (in some cases to ten years); and made it more difficult to prosecute police officers for acts committed while on duty (e.g., firing at fleeing suspects). According to many legal scholars, many provisions of these laws are contrary to the Constitution's guarantees of individual freedoms.[55] But the PCI dismissed such exponents of constitutional guarantees (*garantismo*) in the name of the struggle against terrorism, the enemy of democracy.

The PCI also supported the judiciary when the latter pursued suspected terrorists vigorously. The most famous case in point was that of Professor Antonio Negri, of the University of Padua, and others accused by the prosecutor of, among other things, complicity in the kidnapping and murder of Moro. Negri, a leading intellectual of the extreme left, had likely been involved in certain episodes of violence perpetrated in Padua by *Autonomia operaia* (Workers' Autonomy), but this more serious charge was supported by little direct evidence. Nevertheless, he was held in pre-trial detention for four years until elected to parliament on the Radical list in 1983. The PCI was the most strenuous defender of the prosecutor, and indeed had been active in providing him with evidence against Negri and *Autonomia*.[56] This case exemplified the party's extreme zeal in pursuing anyone suspected of complicity with terrorism, even in the absence of solid proof. But, as we have said, in this the PCI was not alone.

V THE PCI AND INSTITUTIONAL REFORM

Further insight into the PCI's attitude towards democracy can be gleaned from an examination of its proposals for the reform of some of the institutions of Italian democracy. This subject is especially topical, since a recent meeting of the Central Committee (November 1987) proposed such reform as the possible basis for an agreement with one or both of the DC and the Socialists.[57]

The Communists have generally been unwilling to contemplate changes in the Constitution, fighting instead for its complete implementation (e.g., the creation of regional governments, delayed until 1970) and defending the prerogatives of parliament *vis-à-vis* the executive.[58] The party admitted, however, at the November 1987 Central Committee, that its own exclusion from office since 1947 is not the only reason for the inadequacies of democratic institutions in Italy; it is also genuinely worried over the weakness and inefficiency of the state, and over the exercise of power by secret groups, such as the P2 Masonic lodge, that that weakness has facilitated.

The Central Committee therefore agreed to consider institutional reforms such as a correction or modification of the system of proportional representation (PR). (The PCI fought the 1953 election against a DC attempt to limit the effect of PR; the outcome of the election blocked the proposed change.) It also suggested the use of the constructive vote of non-confidence, as in West Germany, and a series of other proposals also aimed at making governments more stable and efficient. This departure, which may be the prelude to the first significant amendments to the Constitution since 1948, demonstrates the PCI's solicitude for the proper functioning of the institutions of parliamentary democracy. It is prepared to contemplate a move towards a system with a clearer distinction between majority and opposition, and real alternation in power. Indeed, since his election in June 1988, the PCI's new Secretary-General, Achille Occhetto, has repeatedly insisted that the 'consociative phase' in the history of Italian democracy, when all political forces supposedly had a share of power, is over, and that the PCI must play a more clearly oppositional role. This has led him to propose the formation of a Communist 'shadow cabinet'. These moves have been interpreted as indicating acceptance by the PCI of the role of official opposition within the present system, as opposed to former role of formal opposition to the capitalist system itself.

VI THE PCI AND THE NATURE OF ITALIAN DEMOCRACY

Reviewing the Italian Communists' history and current policies, we can identify a significant connecting thread: the conviction that, in modern capitalist states, it is the masses rather than minorities that make history. Togliatti recognized this in characterizing Fascism as a reactionary *mass* movement that succeeded because it won over large numbers of the middle classes, and not simply because it used violence and fraud against its opponents.[59] And Antonio Gramsci, his predecessor as party leader, was developing at the same time, in his *Prison Notebooks*, his famous distinction between 'war of position' and 'war of movement': he drew analogies between the war of movement—swift actions by small, disciplined forces—and the Russian Revolution, and between the war of position—the slow, patient siege of the enemy's fortifications, as in the trench warfare of the First World War—and the conquest of ideological hegemony that he believed was the only possible strategy for the revolutionary left in modern Western Europe. For Gramsci, revolution was no longer a minority affair, but needed the active consent of the majority.[60]

In the recent past, too, Communist leaders have demonstrated their belief that force cannot succeed, whichever side uses it. For instance, they have refused to invoke the repressive violence of the state against the neo-fascist MSI, judging it to be a mass phenomenon that can be dealt with only by political means. On the other hand, they have been quite willing to support repressive measures against terrorism, which they correctly perceive as a minority movement. As we have seen, they have also taken the optimistic view that a coup such as occurred in Chile cannot succeed if it is opposed by a mass movement uniting the working and middle classes.

How well founded is this view? In fact, the only serious threats to Italian democracy in the post-war period have come not from the PCI, but from the political right. The aim of these manoeuvres has usually been not the outright overthrow of the Constitution, but a shift to the right in the political climate, government policy, or government personnel, coupled on occasion with constitutional changes that would institute a more authoritarian regime. The means used have ranged from the threat of a coup d'état to corruption, influence-peddling, and blackmail—all illegal activities that undermine and distort the democratic process.

In the first of these right-wing plots, the commander of the secret service (SIFAR: Armed Forces Information Service), General Giovanni De Lorenzo, prepared a contingency plan for the arrest and removal to Sardinia of some three thousand political leaders, mostly of the left. It is unlikely that he actually intended to carry out this plan, but it did serve a useful purpose at a time (1964) when the Socialist Party was being admitted to the cabinet after seventeen years in opposition, and the right was fearful of the consequences of this 'opening to the left'. The threat posed by De Lorenzo did serve to make the new government less left-wing than it otherwise would have been.[61]

From 1969 to 1974 a series of actions, known collectively as the 'strategy of tension', were carried out with the intention of shifting public opinion and the political situation to the right and of exploiting the backlash to the student and worker *contestazione* of 1968-70. While the material executors were usually neo-fascists, the strategy of tension was planned by more obscure forces, including some officers of the secret services who were in contact with the US Embassy. In December 1969 a bomb exploded in a branch of the Banca Nazionale dell'Agricoltura in Milan, killing sixteen people. It had in fact been set by neo-fascist extremists, but at the time the police blamed anarchists, and the episode was used to foment a law-and-order campaign dubbed by some of its leaders the 'silent majority'. Other provocations ensued, with the object of creating an atmosphere of disorder that would evoke a call for a strong government. There were also at least two plotted coups, during one of which a large part of the Ministry of the Interior was secretly occupied for several hours. One could argue that the strategy of tension was immensely successful in ensuring that the PCI adopted the defensive line of the historic compromise.

The P2 secret Masonic lodge, headed by Licio Gelli, constituted the third and perhaps the most dangerous of these shadowy right-wing plots. Gelli used his influence over government appointments, banking and credit, and the media, as well as the power to blackmail that came from the SIFAR dossiers given to him by De Lorenzo's successor, to further the personal interests of the lodge's members and his own political aims. These were to keep the Communists out of the cabinet and, eventually, to establish a stronger, presidential regime. There are suspicions that Gelli may have been involved in organizing the 'strategy of tension', but his activities intensified in the late 1970s. The lodge had some one thousand members, drawn from the upper ranks of the bureaucracy, the armed forces, and the secret service, as well as industry and the political parties. When it was discovered in 1981, it was dissolved as a secret association under Article 18 of the Constitution.

Several conditions have allowed these threats to Italian democracy to arise. In the first place, the Christian Democratic regime has protected and entrenched many very conservative interests, inside and outside the state apparatus, which feel themselves gravely threatened by any reform or movement to the left. Second, the state apparatus itself is relatively weak, divided and corrupted by the patronage practised by the DC; therefore it is open to penetration by parallel centres of power. Third, the Fascist legacy has meant that there are willing operatives available to these right-wing groups. And, finally, the US government and the CIA have certainly been aware of some of these plots and in contact with the plotters. One can easily deduce that the latter have received support and encouragement from that quarter.[62]

Although it has taken the lead in denouncing these serious threats, the PCI remains convinced that Italian democracy is fundamentally sound and unlikely to be overthrown by force. It is no doubt encouraged in this view by Italy's membership in the EEC, which is a kind of international guarantee of its democratic constitution. More generally, the Communists have observed that all the advanced capitalist states are democracies, even those with weak democratic traditions, and they reason, in Marxian fashion, that there is a causal link between the socio-economic structure and the political system of these states.

A similar logic has been behind the evolution of many other Communist parties in advanced capitalist states towards Eurocommunism, a brand of Communism that fully accepts the democratic framework.[63] They have shared the belief that politics in the modern era is an affair of masses rather than minorities. Even though none of them has had the unique experience of Fascism and the Resistance, they have appreciated intellectually that the PCI has evolved a position that could be applied more generally, and is the most viable for a Communist party in modern capitalism. Furthermore, many of them have gone through historical experiences that convinced them, as Fascism did the PCI, of the need to fully embrace and develop the Popular Front strategy. The Communist parties of Great Britain, Australia, Sweden, Spain, and Japan, among others, have adopted the Eurocommunist perspective. The French Communist Party took the same road for a few years, then retreated somewhat to a more pro-Soviet stance.

Even the Communist parties that have not adjusted their theory to their practice by embracing Eurocommunism—most notably the Portuguese Communist Party and the Greek Communist Party (Exterior)—do not, in their day-to-day activity, differ greatly from the Eurocommunist parties. They are not concretely engaged in planning insurrection or political violence. They too adhere to the Popular Front strategy; their main difference with the Eurocommunists concerns the transition to the second stage of socialism, which is still a theoretical issue (and, of course, their attitude to the Soviet Union). Furthermore, these large Communist parties, by virtue of their participation in democratic politics, are subject to some of the same subtle influence that such participation exercises on the PCI.

VII   IS THE PCI STILL A MARXIST PARTY?

In the light of the above evolution, many observers have concluded that the PCI has become so thoroughly integrated into the Italian political and socio-economic system that it is no longer in any sense a Marxist party, nor even a party that aims at socialism, but simply a party of social reform. Most, if not all, of the world's social-democratic and labour parties fall into this category, even those, like the Swedish SAP, that still formally refer to themselves as Marxist, and there is currently much soul-searching in the PCI on precisely this point. In favour of this view one could cite the moderate election platforms that the party presents, which involve no nationalizations and very little to frighten Italian business; its willingness to support austerity measures that directly hurt its principal constituency, the working class, in 1976-79; and the presence of a very strong right-wing tendency within the party (the *miglioristi*) that wishes to push it even further in a social-democratic direction.[64] In the past year Occhetto has taken several steps to further 'laicize' the party and weaken its links to its Communist heritage: for instance, he has openly criticized Togliatti for co-responsibility in Stalin's crimes, and the document prepared for the 18th Congress (March 1989) makes virtually no use of Marxist concepts such as class or class struggle. It presents socialism not as a 'system', but as the fullest extension of democracy to all spheres, including the economy.

With the end of the historic compromise, the PCI finally left behind the Popular Front strategy, and, in the 1980s, felt the wave of disillusionment with the results of the radicalism of the 1970s and the new vigour of Italian capitalism and free-market ideology. Under Occhetto, it acted deliberately to reduce the 'difference' that has always distinguished it from other parties. By the time of the 18th Congress, a change in the party's name and symbol and its entry into the Socialist International and the Socialist group in the European parliament were being seriously discussed; the last two innovations, at least, may be only a matter of time.[65]

Moreover, the party has become firmly rooted in the management of the Italian political system through its role in parliament, local government, the trade unions, and a myriad of other institutions—in the words of one wag, instead of the system going Communist, the Communists have gone system. One can also note a definite increase in the middle-class presence among the party membership and cadres over the past fifteen years.[66] Many of these—the 'children of Berlinguer'—were formed by the party's moderate line of the historic compromise period.

But while it may seem otiose to debate over the attribution of labels, there is also much evidence to suggest that the PCI is more than simply a party of social reform: while firmly committed to the democratic framework, it has not been simply 'social-democratized'. In the first place, the Italian social and political situation has never furnished the conditions for a true social democracy: a consensus on a developed welfare state, Keynesian fiscal policy, and regulated wage bargaining. The overall situation is too backward, because of the resistance of entrenched social groups, particularly the petty bourgeoisie, to such a 'Keynesian welfare state'.[67] The primary vehicle for this conservative resistance is

the Christian Democratic party, which has, in forty-three years of uninterrupted power, occupied the largest part of the state and the vast network of public enterprises and institutions. In Italy, then, even reforms
can be revolutionary in their impact, because they shake the entire social and political system. (This is what Togliatti had in mind when he
spoke of 'structural reforms'.) Rather than stabilizing the situation,
they set it in motion and open up further prospects for change. The PCI
realized that this was the situation when it abandoned the historic compromise policy in 1980 and made the denunciation of the 'DC system of
power' its major campaign theme. This marked a shift to the left by the
party after a period of seemingly irreversible movement to the right.

Second, the PCI's analysis of the Italian situation, however defensive a
policy it may generate, has been, at least until very recently, couched in
a Marxist framework. For the Communists, as we saw above, social
classes have been the principal actors on the political stage, and their
struggle the stuff of politics. The PCI did not adopt the policy of alliances
out of electoral calculation, as Przeworski and Sprague argue that social-democratic parties do,[68] but as a result of their assessment of the
class forces present in Italy (and at a time when there were no free elections in any case). Moreover, this broadly Marxist view of society is not
restricted to party leaders and intellectuals, but is part of the world-
view of the masses of the PCI's members and many of its voters.

Finally, the PCI, in spite of its strenuous pursuit of middle-class allies,
remains overwhelmingly a party of the working class. The manual
working class provides at least 70 per cent of its electoral support.[69]
Many social-democratic parties are also primarily working-class parties
in this sense, but the Italian working class has demonstrated a high degree of class consciousness over the past two decades, which makes it
more difficult for the PCI to act simply as a party of social reform.

The PCI, then, can fairly claim to be a Marxist party that is firmly
committed to the democratic framework as it currently exists in Italy.
This commitment is, as we have seen, the product of Italian history and
Italian conditions. Though others have followed, the PCI was the first,
and remains by far the largest, Communist party to combine Marxism
and democracy in a coherent strategic perspective.

Left-wing Dissent and the State: Canada in the Cold War Era

REG WHITAKER

The subjects of this study are, first, the left in Canada since the end of the Second World War and, second, state surveillance, infiltration, disruption, and repression of left-wing activities. In reality, the two subjects go together; neither can be properly understood without consideration of the other.

For the purposes of this study, the 'left' is defined as including all organized forms of political activity that have as their object change toward greater egalitarianism, a redistribution of resources from capital to labour or from rich to poor, and the transformation of private ownership of the means of production to public ownership—with the ultimate aim of achieving a classless society. In this definition, the means are less important than the ends. Some groups may have emphasized parliamentary and constitutional methods of achieving change, others have emphasized the necessity of extra-parliamentary or revolutionary methods, and others still have adopted both methods, sometimes simultaneously, sometimes serially. What distinguish them as left-wing are their aims, not their methods.

Political activity in Canada over the postwar decades has been characterized by the overarching influence of the international Cold War. The tendency to define all left-wing political activity within broad Cold War terms (pro- or anti-Soviet, pro- or anti-American) has added not only an additional dimension to the traditional left-right conflict in politics, but also a further split *within* the left along the Cold War fissure: some on the left lined up in support of the anti-Soviet alliance; others took a stand in solidarity with the Soviet bloc. Moreover, the international setting has added another aspect to left-wing dissent: 'peace' has been broadly defined through much of this era as a left-wing issue when it is being used as a challenge to existing state policies in defence and foreign affairs.

At the end of the Second World War, the Canadian left could be broadly defined as flowing in two partially separate but mutually antagonistic streams. The first and larger stream was that of the Co-operative Commonwealth Federation (CCF), representing a unique blend of social democracy somewhat similar to that of the British Labour Party with a distinctive agrarian radicalism—electoralist in orientation but maintaining a strong presence in the trade-union movement and other popular associations, as well as in academic circles. The second and smaller stream was that surrounding the Labour Progressive (Communist) Party; its activists within the trade-union movement; its various associated (or 'front') organizations among youth, women, tenants, ethnic and other groups; and its (very small) intelligentsia.

The differences between these two streams and the causes of their mutual antagonism were obviously rooted in ideology. The Communists were committed to the 'scientific' Marxism characteristic of the Stalin era and to a revolutionary program that looked toward the abolition of capitalism and the establishment of socialism through the 'dictatorship of the proletariat'. Although there were some Marxist strains (mainly from British Columbia) to be found within the CCF, the broader ideological thrust of that party was towards reformist social democracy —seeking the gradual transformation of capitalism through an expanded political and economic role for the state that would encompass greater public ownership, redistribution of wealth, an enlarged welfare state, and state planning for a mixed economy. This much is evident from what the CCF and Communist Party said about their aims and principles.

Less clear, and more controversial, is the interpretation of some other key aspects of the programs of these two parties. The first has to do with *means* as opposed to *ends*. It is the orthodox wisdom of social-democratic, as well as non-socialist, writers that the Communists differed from the CCF in that they were committed to violent, revolutionary means, whereas the CCF adhered to constitutional parliamentarism. The latter characterization is undoubtedly true, but the former represents a serious oversimplification of a relatively complex position. There appears to be no evidence that the Communists ever actually conspired to effect the violent or revolutionary overthrow of the Canadian state. The only legal victories won against the Communists by the state were on the terrain of abstract ideas (as in the prosecutions against the party leaders under the notorious Section 98 of the Criminal Code in the *Rex* v. *Buck et al.* trial of 1931), or under narrow, specific criteria established by emergency powers (as when the party opposed the war effort from 1939 into 1941, while the extraordinary Defence of Canada Regulations were in effect), or for espionage or espionage-related offences by individuals associated with the party (in the single instance of the trials arising out of the 1946 Gouzenko affair). Nor is there any evidence from within the party itself that its leaders ever attempted, or even discussed attempting, to overthrow the state in any immediate or concrete sense (rhetoric aside).

Nor did the party actually *advocate* the overthrow of the state in the sense of inciting followers to take up arms or violently assault the state's institutions and personnel.[1] To the Communists, revolution always seemed a goal for a future stage of class struggle. For the present the tactics were mainly parliamentary in focus, with the occasional addition of peaceful and legal extra-parliamentary tactics—'mass' propaganda campaigns given expression in leaflets, petitions, demonstrations, etc.; support for strike activities; and attempts to disseminate ideas through party newspapers, publications, and occasional party-sponsored cultural events. None of these activities were in themselves 'revolutionary', even though they were intended to fit into a long-term political strategy that foresaw the sharpening of the class struggle and the eventual development of a truly revolutionary situation. As such, of course, they could be, and were, seen by the security forces as subversive actions seeking to undermine constitutional government from within. Subversion might be understood as a preparatory stage in the process of revolutionary overthrow of government, but the two concepts are, or ought to be, distinct.

In the eyes of their opponents, especially the social democrats, a certain odium surrounded Communist infiltration of non-Communist activities or associations. Infiltration was viewed as the undermining from within of free institutions by conspirators who concealed their true affiliations and motives. This perception became particularly acute after 1935, when the Moscow line directed Communist parties around the world towards a 'united front' against fascism, and again after the Nazi invasion of the USSR in 1941. The strategy of 'boring from within' did no doubt contain elements of clandestinity and deception. It is scarcely surprising that the CCF would react with hostility towards covert actions by a rival on its left.

Yet once again, matters are rather more complex than the conventional wisdom allows. First, attempts to expand party influence through participation in such associations as trade unions, civil-liberties associations, peace movements, and issue-oriented citizens' groups are perfectly normal tactics of left-wing parties. Indeed, the social-democratic left was just as interested in such 'infiltration', which it practised with particular success in the labour movement—as, for that matter, did the Liberal Party. Second, to the limited extent that the Communists did so surreptitiously, their behaviour was hardly unconnected with the illegitimacy in which they were viewed by the state and the broader society: the charge of conspiracy is something of a self-fulfilling prophecy. From another point of view, the state security establishment has always held an exaggerated idea of the damage to liberal institutions that a few dedicated Communists could allegedly wreak. That one or two larger-than-life Reds on the executive of a large organization could easily subvert and twist that organization to their ends is a romantic idea that owes more to the fevered imaginations of witch-hunters than to mundane experience. The fear of Communist infiltration, however exaggerated, did exercise a distorting influence on the social-democratic left. Dissent from within social-democratic ranks that happened to coincide with policy positions taken by the Communists was often branded pro-Communist; dissenters were sometimes purged or expelled. In this way, policy issues on the left were transformed into loyalty tests.

To the state security service, ultimate ideological intentions overrode the lack of concrete evidence of revolutionary effect. In this there was a curious complicity between the Canadian state and the Communists. Both dramatically overestimated the revolutionary challenge posed by Canadian Communism. This overestimate skewed the pattern of politics on the left in fundamental ways, the effects of which are still being felt today. Another form of complicity lay in the emphasis that both sides placed on the close and subordinate connection between the Canadian Communists and the Soviet Union. The state maintained that the Communists were mere tools of Moscow, while for their part the Communists seemed bent on fulfilling this description by acting as persistent apologists for the Soviet Union. Broader 'front' activities, such as the CPC-influenced peace movement, were drawn into Soviet apologetics. The political effect in the context of the Cold War was to discredit many left or progressive ideas among their potential constituents. The ramifications went far beyond the fate of the Communist Party to affect the left in general, including the social democrats.

The Cold War imposed a kind of mirror-logic upon its protagonists. By definition, opposition to 'our side' constituted support for the 'other side'—and was thus disloyal, even subversive. To the extent that some dissenters could be found who willingly fitted the stereotype of apologist for the 'other side', all dissent could be broadly discredited as subversive. The wounds thus inflicted on the left could be crippling. That some were inflicted by the state and others were self-inflicted is a matter of historical irony.

The Communists had been a primary target of the state security apparatus from their very origin in the aftermath of the Russian Revolution. To correct one common misconception, it is important to recognize the deep historical roots of official hostility to Communism. It has been said that the spy scandal of 1945-46 suddenly awoke official Ottawa to the true nature of the subversive threat posed by international Communism, a threat of which it had remained blissfully innocent until Igor Gouzenko tore off the deceptive mask of the Soviet state. Nothing could be further from the truth.

Among the highlights of the state's unrelenting hostility to Communism and the revolutionary left are the following: the repressive response of the state to the Winnipeg General Strike of 1919; the passage of s.98 of the Criminal Code in the wake of the strike and the prosecutions brought against Communist leaders under that section in 1931; the small 'wars' fought against Communists by police in major cities in the 1920s and 1930s; the deportations of foreign-born Communists and labour organizers between the wars, and especially in the early 1930s; the passage of the notorious 'Padlock Law' in Québec in the late 1930s, and the failure of the federal government to disallow such a flagrantly illiberal and probably unconstitutional law; and the outlawing of the Communist Party and associated front organizations, the banning of Communist publications, and the internment of Communists under emergency powers during the Second World War. The official historian of the RCMP has written recently that during the interwar years, the 'principal target of RCMP intelligence . . . was the Communist Party of Canada and its front organizations'. Even pro-Nazi and pro-fascist groups were no more than a 'secondary objective'.[2] Charles Rivett-Carnac, head of the RCMP's security service,[3] advised the government in early 1939 that Communists represented a menace far worse than fascism. Fascism, he insisted, did not require the 'overthrow of the present economic order—and its administrative machinery'. As proof, he pointed out that 'a modified form of capitalism now exists' in the Nazi Reich. 'Fascism', he concluded, 'is the reaction of the middle classes to the Communist danger and, as perhaps you are aware, the Communists describe it as "the last refuge of capitalism"'.[4] The Commissioner of the RCMP went on public record in 1941 as asserting that Reds were more dangerous than fascists, even during a war against fascism.[5]

Strong and consistent anti-Communism was thus a longstanding feature of the Canadian state prior to the Cold War. Communism was officially seen as an illegitimate participant in Canadian public life, to be at worst watchfully tolerated, and at best repressed when the opportunity arose. It is in this context that the espionage affair of 1945-46 and the ensuing shift to a quasi-official Cold War ideology can most appropriately be understood.

The documents removed from the Soviet Embassy in Ottawa in 1945 by Igor Gouzenko revealed that the USSR was carrying on espionage against its Canadian ally, and that Canadians with ideological sympathy for Communism were being recruited as agents. This is not to suggest that all those detained by the RCMP were actually guilty (as the Taschereau-Kellock Royal Commission publicly indicated but the courts failed in many cases to substantiate); but the basic outline of activity is clear from the Commission report and from the documents and testimony used by the Commission.[6] What is most interesting is how the government handled this information, and the uses to which the facts were put.

The most outspoken anti-Soviet official in External Affairs, Arnold Smith, was given the task of writing and editing the text of the report. Smith did so in a way that maximized the domestic anti-Communist impact of the affair. With the way already prepared by sensational international and domestic press reporting, any brush with Communism—the possession of 'Communist' books or magazines; association with known Communists; participation in 'study groups' led by Communists; membership in groups in which Communists also participated; even expression of ideas deemed to be pro-Communist—could be seen as *prima facie* evidence of disloyalty. In the aftermath of the spy affair, and against the darkening background of worsening relations between the wartime allies, Communism was widely equated with subversion.

The Liberal government in Ottawa, for reasons that will be touched upon later, did not choose to exploit the Communist issue in quite the same way as the Truman Democrats in Washington—with sharply different consequences for the domestic politics of the two countries. As I have elsewhere argued, comparative study suggests that there are two forms of repression, analytically distinct but almost always related in practice: *state repression* includes forms of coercive control exercised through the official state apparatus—the 'legitimate' use of force in the Weberian sense; *political repression* refers to the exercise of coercion outside the state system proper, but originating in the wider political system (parties, interest groups, private associations).[7] McCarthyism, as a generic phenomenon, is a form of political repression in which opposition politicians using the Communist issue exploit the political system against the state apparatus itself. McCarthyism was a highly visible manifestation in the first postwar decade, mainly in the US, but to an extent in Australia as well. In Britain, and to a degree in Canada, political repression was less visible. The relative absence of McCarthyism, as such, in Canada should not be taken as evidence that anti-Communism was not central to Canadian internal-security policy.[8] In the Canadian state sphere, anti-Communist repression was, and is, extensive. Its *form*, as state rather than political repression, has misled many observers into making dubious generalizations about the more liberal and politically tolerant culture of Canada as opposed to the US. Such generalizations may or may not be accurate in the broadly defined area of political culture, but in the instance of the state repression of left-wing dissent they cannot be supported.

The Royal Commission gave only one of its 733 pages to specific policy implications. Of seven recommendations three spoke in general terms of tighter government security measures to be 'co-ordinated and rendered as uniform as possible'.[9] Out of these recommendations grew the formidable machinery of the government's internal-security system. At the top was the Security Panel, where senior public servants with an interest in security matters, military intelligence officials, and representatives of the RCMP security service regularly met to plan policy and co-ordinate security operations. At the heart of the security process lay the screening of public servants and applicants to the public service by the RCMP. The number of security clearances began at a rate of about 2000 per month in the late 1940s and rose in the early 1950s to stabilize at between 4000 and 5000 per month by the mid-1950s. By the 1980s these numbers were higher yet, reaching some 70,000 per year, or just under 6000 per month.[10] This process also broadened out to cover workers in defence-related industries and in the 1950s even to seamen on Great Lakes ships. For public servants adversely affected by security assessments, there was no appeal in a substantive sense until 1984, when the Security Intelligence Review Committee (SIRC) was created under the Canadian Security Intelligence Service (CSIS) Act.

The screening criteria applied by the RCMP under successive cabinet directives from 1948 until 1986 were highly ideological and decisively anti-Communist in their thrust. Discussions surrounding the drafting of these directives leave no more doubt as to their specific target than does their language. The 1952 directive, for instance, which was to remain substantially in effect for a decade, declared that 'a person who is a member of the Communist party, or who by his words shows himself to believe in marxism-leninism, or any other ideology which advocates the overthrow of government by force, should not be permitted to enter the public service. Such persons discovered within the public service must not be allowed access to classified information, and their continued employment by the government may be undesirable.'[11] The Mackenzie Royal Commission on Security, which reported in 1968, found no quarrel with these criteria, and indeed even asserted that the threat of Communism was sufficiently central to the definition of Canadian national security as to justify the use of what they called 'the admittedly simplistic terms "Communism" and "Communist"'. The later McDonald Commission was more blunt on this point: the security-clearance criteria that they found in effect in 1981 reflected a Cold War mentality and were, in their view, inadequate. It was not until 1986 that a new government security policy finally wrote 'Communism' as such out of the clearance criteria, to be replaced by a more functional, and not specifically political, test of reliability and trustworthiness on the part of public servants.[12]

For four decades anti-Communism was thus the official governing principle of an extensive internal-security system with impact upon a substantial number of Canadians. This is of much greater significance than might appear on the surface. For one thing, it situated the security service in a close relationship with the senior public service and established the former's continuing presence in ongoing discussion of security policy at the focal point of the Security Panel and its successor bodies. The conservative anti-Communist ideology of the security service (which all observers have remarked) was given particular resonance within the councils of government by the service's privileged place in a key area of administration.

At the same time, the demands of security screening offered another set of opportunities to the security service. It is standard procedure in counter-intelligence that when an agent is discovered, it will, where appropriate, be preferable to 'turn' or 'double' that agent rather than to reveal his existence publicly. By analogy, when a subject of security screening tests positive, there is always an opportunity to transform that person into a source of information on the group or association that led to the positive result. To such individuals, of course, the alternative may well be the loss of their jobs and the end of their careers, so the incentive to co-operate is not inconsiderable. The security service has always denied that it does this, but public servants or former public servants who have run into 'security' problems indicate that fishing for names, with the implied promise of not proceeding in exchange for co-operation, is quite common.[13] Thus the screening system offers the security service special opportunities to gain footholds within the kind of left-wing groups that it has traditionally seen as subversive.

From the individual's point of view, the process is not only unpleasant but also deeply ambiguous. Apart from outright membership in the Communist Party, it has never been clear precisely which associations might lead to difficulties. Unlike the US, which for a time maintained the Attorney General's list of subversive organizations (a kind of official proscription list), Canada has always shied away from officially branding groups as subversive or disloyal. Secret lists were maintained by the security establishment, but these could offer no guide for the perplexed public servant. As recently as 1987 a Federal Court judge cited, *inter alia*, as reasonable grounds for denial of security clearance, evidence that a public servant had 'participated in a peace march'.[14] The effect, of course, upon left-wing associations of any kind, whether pro-Communist or not, can be quite depressing—which may well be part of the subtext of the official security discourse.

Canadian public servants had until recently few rights in relation to security matters—for example, they lacked a genuine appeal process and other elements of natural justice. Unions were toothless or tamed in the 1950s and 1960s, and though no longer toothless with the advent of collective bargaining, public-service unions remain relatively domesticated in regard to security issues. It was an oft-stated official principle that a public-service job was a 'privilege, not a right'. This innocuous-sounding maxim (a mere truism in one sense) in practice could be used to justify repressive controls over the political activities of public servants. In effect, one group of Canadians could be walled off from full democratic citizenship.

They were not the only ones. Another, much larger, group has also felt the touch of state repression without adequate protection in rights. Immigrants to Canada—5.6 million since the war—have been perceived as a massive potential threat to Canada's security.[15] This threat, despite an influx of Nazi war criminals and criminal collaborators,[16] was always defined as coming from the left. Political screening of immigrants began systematically in the late 1940s, and continues unabated today. Screening focussed in the first decades almost exclusively on those with Communist associations. In 1958 the RCMP reported to the Minister of Immigration that from 1946 to 1958 a total of just under 30,000 applications for immigration had been rejected on security grounds; the Mounties helpfully pointed out that '21,000 is said to be the highest membership the Communist Party in Canada has ever been able to obtain'.[17]

This single-minded preoccupation with the left has been only partially allayed in the 1980s by concern with terrorism, which does not always come clothed in the colour red. Nor did the political controls stop with immigration. Barring left-wing visitors to Canada has been a long-standing practice, and screening of citizenship applications has provided the security service with a second line of defence against those who might have slipped through as landed immigrants. Refugee policy has shown a persistent political bias: almost 80 per cent of all refugees accepted in Canada since the war have come from Communist states, while refugees from right-wing anti-Communist states have fared relatively poorly by comparison.

Underlying all this has been an explicit principle, similar to the one applied to public servants: immigration to Canada is a privilege, not a right. In the name of this principle, a pronounced political bias against the left has been exercised by the Canadian state, a bias that could not have been exercised so persistently and effectively if the objects of the bias had been people with full rights of democratic citizenship. Indeed, one of the particular ironies remarked upon from time to time, even by government officials, was that immigrants were being treated according to criteria that could not be applied against Canadian citizens—that is, Communism, as such, was not illegal in Canada, but alleged association with it could be a fatal disability to anyone seeking to become a Canadian. This bias has thus been a doubly effective means of state repression in a country like Canada, which has been heavily dependent upon immigration. First, new Canadians have been politically selected; second, an indirect control is in effect exercised upon Canadian civil society as the political criteria imposed upon immigrants tend to be diffused into the institutions in which immigrants participate. Moreover, immigration- and citizenship-screening has offered the security service an opportunity to plant sources among whatever left-wing ethnic organizations remain active after forty years of the Cold War.[18]

State repression has gone hand in hand with an official aversion to McCarthyism or anything that smacked of freelance witch-hunting. Although political repression was practised in some private sectors with state approval—the anti-Communist purges in the trade unions being the most obvious example—the Canadian way was to strictly curtail McCarthyism as such. Moreover, the federal government rejected the American and Australian examples of trying to legislate directly against Communism. Yet anti-Communism was used by state officials against opponents, or even potential opponents, of state policy. How the state élites steered carefully and, on the whole, successfully between the Scylla and Charybdis of this issue is an interesting study in itself. In the United States the Truman Democrats tried to use the Red Scare to gain domestic backing for their international Cold War commitments; they succeeded in stirring up the fires of a witch-hunt in which they themselves were ultimately consumed. In Canada the Liberals avoided that fate while gaining domestic consent for a greatly expanded diplomatic and military role in the world.

The Liberals were not reluctant to use emotional anti-Communist rhetoric when it suited their purposes. Indeed, the so-called 'debate' over the Canadian role in the Marshall Plan and NATO was an exercise in the brittle and aggressive politics of loyalty. Those who supported these initiatives were branded as disloyal and pro-Communist and did so at their peril. Louis St Laurent and Lester Pearson were particularly extreme in their rhetoric. This tone was carried over into official denunciations of the Canadian Peace Congress, in the early 1950s, as a tool for Moscow. During the Korean War a cabinet meeting was actually held to decide whether to try the Congress leader, Dr James Endicott, for treason. There was in this behaviour a threat of political rationality. Determined to bring Canada on side for collective security under American leadership—for what the Liberals took to be good reasons, in terms of both internationalism and the Canadian national interest—the St Laurent/Pearson team faced two major domestic sources of potential opposition. The English Canadian Tories had traditionally been pro-British and cool to the Americans, while Québec had been strongly isolationist and opposed to international military commitments of any kind. Anti-Communism was the key to bringing both conservative English Canadians and deeply anti-Communist Québec Catholics around to support of the new international commitment. The strategy worked, and worked so well that later historians have tended to miss its significance. When the dispatch of Canadian troops to Korea was announced in 1950, there was scarcely a murmur of protest from Québec. This represented a triumph of Liberal strategy.

The strategy was not without dangers. The spectacle of the Un-American Activities Committee and Senator Joseph McCarthy was not a pleasant one for Canadians to contemplate, especially for Liberals who might well become targets for US-style charges of coddling Communists in government. George Drew, the former Ontario premier, and Maurice Duplessis of Québec both sported impeccable anti-Communist credentials (Duplessis had authored the infamous Padlock Law in the late 1930s). Drew, as Opposition Leader in Ottawa, tried to develop a McCarthy-style following by belabouring the Communist issue. But no McCarthyist movement could get off the ground in Canada. In part this may have been due to the British style of parliamentary government, which allows less scope for independent political entrepreneurship than American congressional institutions (although Australia in this era suggests that parliamentary institutions are not in themselves proof against the rise of political repression).[19] But the Liberal Party was well-placed to avert excesses. Québec was for historical reasons tied directly to the federal Liberals. A Catholic prime minister from Québec, Louis St Laurent, could rein in his Québec members when anti-Communism threatened to get out of hand. And there was no chance at all that Drew, the blustering Tory from Protestant Ontario, could ever shape a workable right-wing alliance with French-speaking Catholics. So anti-Communism remained largely under Liberal state control.[20]

There was only one major slip, and this came from American pressures. Diplomat Herbert Norman was twice named by American sources as an alleged security risk. The first time, in 1950, he was intensively investigated by the security service and External Affairs. Pearson's department cleared him. With the image of what the witch-hunt had done to the US State Department before their eyes, the External Affairs establishment was quick to protect one of their own. In 1957 Norman committed suicide in Cairo after a US Senate committee again dragged his name before the public. The Liberal government reacted with anger toward the Americans (as did the Canadian public and press). The Norman affair defined the limit of anti-Communism permissible within the Canadian system. Thirty years later, an academic intent upon demonstrating that Norman (and Lester Pearson to boot) was a Soviet spy, inspired a right-wing Tory backbencher to press for disclosure of secret documents on the case that would allegedly reveal Norman's culpability. The Tory Minister of External Affairs rejected the request as 'unnecessary and unworthy'.[21]

In the Norman case there was some tension between the government and the security service, which had leaked misleading information on Norman to the FBI, from whence it fell into the hands of the Senate committee. But this case offers a misleading guide to the normal relations between the security service nad the Liberal government's philosophy of maintaining anti-Communism under tight state control. The security service did not like McCarthyism any more than the Liberals did, perceiving it (no doubt correctly) as a threat to authority. In 1955 the head of the security service, Clifford Harvison (later RCMP Commissioner), in a lengthy memorandum to the Commissioner, touched upon the attitude of Parliament to security and intelligence:

> at times there has been a reluctance to accept the need for a security service. Members have shown a very stong and proper interest in protecting the rights of the individual and an understandable aversion toward the necessary intrigue and secrecy of intelligence work. Widely publicized reports of the work of civilian anti-subversive organizations investigating Communism in the USA have in no way served to allay the fears of

Members that anti-subversive activities may get out of hand if not closely controlled.[22]

In addition to its direct role in regard to public servants and immigrants, the security service has also been active against the left in what has been known as counter-subversion. Documented in some detail in the McDonald Commission and in John Sawatsky's investigative journalism on the security service,[23] counter-subversion activities have proven to be not only controversial but acutely embarrassing to the government. The real push towards civilianization of the security service came from the revelation of counter-subversion measures in the 1970s that were illegal and in some cases involved violence. The CSIS Act of 1984 tried to define threats to the security of Canada in terms that omitted mention of subversion as such, as well as excluding 'lawful advocacy, protest and dissent' from the scope of CSIS's legitimate concern. Finally, in 1987, following the release of the Osbaldeston Report to the Solicitor General, it was announced that the counter-subversion branch of CSIS would be closed, and the number of counter-subversion targets reduced and reallocated under the counter-espionage and counter-terrorism branches.[24]

Yet for the past forty years counter-subversion has been integral to the security service's definition of its role. Counter-terrorism has only recently come to the fore; counter-sabotage (once a security-service function) was always an exercise without a target. Since the Gouzenko revelations fell on the RCMP from the sky, counter-espionage has, of course, been a central preoccupation. In the nature of this trade, public notice of 'successes' may not coincide with actual effectiveness.[25] But counter-subversion has, for better or worse, always had relatively high public visibility. Perhaps this activity has held its place in security-service operations for reasons that have to do with the fundamental philosophy and self-definition of that service. The RCMP were the watchdogs of the state, the thin red (but not Red!) line at the edge of civilization where the law was enforced and order formed out of disorder. In the twentieth century the spectre of revolution began to haunt the Mounties.[26] Crime was the everyday tactical challenge to the practice of law and order, but revolution was the strategic challenge to the very notion of order itself. The Communists, who apparently embodied twin threats to the existing order—overthrow both of capitalist property and of the state—were the ultimate enemy. As Superintendent Rivett-Carnac, then head of the security service, explained to his immediate superior in early 1947, just as the Cold War was coming into clear focus:

The safeguarding of the internal security of the Dominion, bearing in mind the promise of events in the international field and the situation regarding subversive activity as a National and International problem, appears to assume a position of predominance over all other subjects, not only now but more especially in the future. With regard to this point there seems little room for discussion, and it is as well, perhaps, to bear this carefully in mind from the standpoint of our own very definite responsibilities in the matter.[27]

From the evidence of security-service documentation that I have been able to obtain, it does not appear that any very sophisticated understanding of the nature of Communism was developed within the service. In particular, an exaggerated impression of the potential of Communists for disruption was endemic—a reflection of widespread fears in Western societies in the late 1940s and early 1950s, which tended to persist longer among the 'specialists' than among the public. Although the Communists never did fulfil the Mounties' expectations that they would foment mass disorder or carry out acts profoundly damaging to Canada, their *definitional* status as 'subversive' generally proved adequate for control and surveillance purposes.

To appreciate this point, a short excursus on the security service's surveillance of labour unions is helpful. Although direct access to what the service once called its 'subversive indices' has not been granted by CSIS, the intelligence bulletins circulated among members of the service give some indication that unions were considered important subversive threats.[28] Next to the Communist Party itself, it appears that labour unions attracted the most attention. Revelations in 1987 of CSIS infiltration of trade unions roused some strong criticism, and probably helped push the government towards its decision to wind up the counter-subversion branch.[29] Yet analysis of what the security service was up to in penetrating unions must be careful not to miss the police's own perception of its objectives in this area.

It is interesting to note that even in communications among themselves, the security people insisted from time to time that trade unions were legitimate associations, and that even strikes were normally legal activities—not in themselves a proper concern for the security service. Their own justification for surveillance was not that trade unionism as such was subversive, but rather that *Communists* working within trade unions were subversive. This was in fact more or less the rationale advanced by Solicitor General James Kelleher in 1987, when recent revelations of union infiltration were acknowledged; SIRC's independent study of the issue came to a similar conclusion.[30] Depending upon the perspective of the observer, this proposition may or may not make much difference. Objectively, security-service activities within trade unions targeting Communists result in a profile of surveillance and infiltration similar to that which would result from targeting the union movement itself. On the other hand, the security service was making a philosophical distinction that turns out to have significant consequences for locating the precise relations between the Canadian state and the left.

The trade-union movement in its non-communist majority has collaborated with the state in stigmatizing Communist unionists as subversive and illegitimate. This collaboration has obviously taken the clandestine form of co-operation of certain officials with the security service. Given the service's insistence on protecting the identity of its sources, we can say very little about this specifically other than to note, as a general statement, that such co-operation must have been extensive over the years. In any event, the overt collaboration of the trade-union movement is on the public record. In the late 1940s and early 1950s a number of affiliates of both the Canadian Congress of Labour (CCL) and the Trades and Labour Congress (TLC) carried out extensive purges of Communist organizers and officials. Either anti-communist officials seized control of affiliates and locals or the latter were disaffiliated or suspended and replaced by anti-Communist rivals. Perhaps the most dramatic and controversial example was the violent struggle on the waterfront between the Communist-led Canadian Seamen's Union (CSU) and the Seafarers International (SIU) led by the notorious American labour thug Hal Banks. This struggle, concluding in the total victory of the SIU, involved not only the active intervention against the CSU of the Canadian state, in both its executive and judicial manifestations, but the intervention of the TLC as well.[31]

Both the security service and the anti-Communist majority within the labour movement were in apparent agreement on the principle that Communism in unions was subversive. This was essentially a definitional equation. It is striking that the security service seems never to have addressed the question of just what dangers to security were actually posed by Communist unionists. The argument that they were attempting to use the union movement for their own ulterior party motives could just as well have been directed at CCF-NDP unionists—but never was.[32] The idea that Communists could somehow turn the objectives of union members away from wages and working conditions towards revolution or fanatic support of the USSR flies in the face of everything that is known about the conditions of success for union organizers: if they do not deliver in terms of contracts, they are likely to be unsuccessful. To the extent that Communist unionists were successful, it was because they were good trade unionists, not revolutionaries.

One Communist-led union that outlasted the first Cold War era was the United Electrical Workers. When reporters nosed around UE members asking about Communism, the rank and file had a standard response: they would take a dollar bill from their wallets, scrutinize it carefully and then announce that they could find no hammer and sickle on it. There is little evidence that the UE rank and file have been educated in Communism or, in many cases, have even been aware of the politics of their leadership. Indeed, one ex-Communist organizer for UE noted in an interview that the Communist Party itself had no trade-union policy and no idea what to do with the party members within the unions. My research into the security-screening program in defence-related industries has revealed that in the early 1950s the UE quietly agreed not to challenge the imposition of security screening against their members even though Communists were the major target of screening.[33]

The security service asked no more searching questions about the actual effects of Communism than did the social democrats or even, ironically enough, the Communists themselves.[34] *Identification* was considered sufficient. What is important here is that the non-communist or social-democratic left was actively assisting the state in the construction of the legitimate limits of left-wing dissent. Sometimes this assistance extended to direct complicity in the imposition of state controls over union activity, as in the 1949 Reid Robinson affair when the CCF and mainstream trade unionists in effect joined with mining capital and right-wing business elements in a successful pressure campaign on the government to bar Communists from entering Canada to organize union activities.[35] Even if this co-operation was limited to tacit agreement with the anti-communist standards of the security service, the effect was the same. The left was participating in its own domestication by the state.

Stepping outside the trade-union movement, the social-democratic left was more widely complicit in this process. The role of the CCF-NDP as Cold War social democrats was the Canadian equivalent of the crucial role played by the Cold War liberals in the United States in the shaping of the American national-security state.[36] In the 'debate' over the Marshall Plan and NATO the CCF fully accepted the apocalyptic logic of the Cold War and treated the issues as loyalty tests. Those who failed were simply expelled—including some sitting members of provincial legislatures. Similar treatment was meted out to those who joined the peace movement of that era, or who criticized Canada's military role in the Korean War. The fears of a Communist takeover expressed by the leadership seem grossly exaggerated in retrospect (there were hardly enough Communists in the country to manage it). What the party really feared was not so much a takeover as being identified with radical ideas tarred by the Red brush. There was no debate as such in Canadian society over the beginnings of the Cold War in the late 1940s and early 1950s. The social-democratic party contributed to the loyalty-oath atmosphere that precluded debate.

The CCF leadership actively advanced the cause of Cold War social democracy. M.J. Coldwell, party leader in the 1940s and 1950s, was a bitter anti-communist and enthusiastic Cold Warrior who later became a conservative pillar of the three-member Mackenzie Royal

Commission on Security, which reported in 1968.[37] David Lewis's political orientation was shaped by the long years of struggle with the Communists; as leader in the 1970s, he responded to internal party dissent in
much the way his predecessors had.[38] In the 1970s the NDP caucus in
Parliament was rather reticent concerning the RCMP security-service
scandals of that decade, apparently fearing a pro-RCMP backlash in public opinion.

For its part, the security service has over the years been quite careful
not to include the NDP, or the CCF before it, within its direct mandate.
From time to time mistakes are made and bad publicity generated, but
these seem to be the exceptions that prove the rule. The one known major surveillance operation mounted against the NDP in recent decades
targeted the left-wing Waffle movement in the early 1970s.[39] Condemned as inappropriate by the McDonald Commission, this operation
focussed on a party faction that was itself ultimately expelled by the
leadership, thus confirming the relationship of the social-democratic left
to the state that had been set long before.

By the late 1960s and early 1970s the old Cold War patterns had obviously come unstuck. The Sino-Soviet split sundered the monolithic
structure of the world Communist movement. Pro-Peking parties soon
appeared to parallel the old Moscow-line parties. The split ramified into
other areas as the so-called Communist-front organizations sometimes
splintered as well (for example, Dr Endicott, the charismatic founder of
the Canadian Peace Congress, was expelled for his pro-Chinese views).
'Marxism' as a philosophical and political tendency was liberated from
the ties to Moscow and to the party line that had been typical during the
1930s and 1940s, and began a new career as a popular intellectual current among young Canadian academics and political activists. Efforts to
develop a non-aligned progressive politics expanded dramatically
throughout the 1960s, devolving out into new peace groupings, New
Left and student movements, feminist groups, diverse vanguardist
workers' parties, environmental activists, anarchist tendencies, etc. The
Cold War mentality of the 1950s had ill prepared the security service for
grappling with these developments, but nowhere was their failure more
pronounced, and nowhere more dramatic in its effects, than in Québec,
with the rise of the independence movement.

The October Crisis of 1970 fundamentally transformed the Canadian
state's perception of national security and of the nature of the threats to
it. The security service had been unprepared for the emergence of an
armed urban terrorist group capable of challenging, even momentarily,
the state's legitimacy. The *indépendentiste* movement is not the subject
of this essay, but suffice it to say that the movement jolted the dominant
security paradigm so severely that it has never recovered the coherence
it once had. That a *real*, *concrete* threat to order could come from
within, yet be undirected by Moscow and uninformed by traditional

Communist Party discipline, was a shock to the old paradigm. That this threat was posed by a small and unrepresentative extremist wing of a much larger movement that was parliamentarist and moderate in its methods seems to have momentarily escaped a government panicked by the kidnappings and the murder of a minister of the Crown. As a result, the security service was directed towards a whole new field of *subversion* in which 'separatism' was construed as a violent movement requiring active 'countering'. The Trudeau government probably shares much more of the blame for the disastrous results of this new policy than it admitted or than the McDonald Commission allowed in its opaque third volume on *Certain RCMP Activities and the Question of Governmental Knowledge*.[40] But the historical irony is that the violent separatist movement died with the overwhelming state reaction of the War Measures Act; the next half-decade saw excessive, intrusive (and illegal) counter-subversion activities launched against a movement that in its dominant and effective manifestation had taken strong root not as a subversive force but as a respectable legal political movement, which was to come to office in Québec only six years after the October Crisis. At this point the role of the security service became the ground for a political confrontation between the Ottawa Liberals and the Québec *péquistes*, and a bone of contention between rival federal and provincial commissions of inquiry.[41]

Having narrowly escaped civilianization in the aftermath of the 1968 Mackenzie Commission, the RCMP security service laid the groundwork for its own organizational demise by its activities of the 1970s. Civilianization has created some unique problems of its own, but the CSIS scandals of the late 1980s[42] appear sufficiently similar to those of its predecessor agency to suggest that the civilianization issue is really a diversion from the main point. The crisis of the RCMP security service, the passage of the CSIS Act in 1984, and the subsequent CSIS crises are more interesting when seen as a commentary on a deeper, ongoing crisis in the definition of national security, rooted in changing political values and perceptions of Canadian society.

Certainly the Cold War mentality has lost much of its hold upon Canadian attitudes. Perceptions of the USSR may oscillate with the winds of superpower diplomacy, but the domestic ramifications of these oscillations become fainter with the passing years. For the first time in the postwar era, the NDP has sparked a debate on Cold War alliances, by actively questioning Canada's membership in NATO, without unleashing a McCarthyite backlash. The carefully constructed definition of Communism as the paradigmatic threat to domestic security has fallen into disrepair. Domestic Communism neither poses a threat nor is widely seen to pose a threat. Espionage has lost much of its dangerous allure; the expulsion of Soviet-bloc diplomats no longer rates more than a day's notice in the media. And in any event, espionage has always been a crime against the state and thus mainly an affair of state élites. The shock of the Gouzenko affair has long since passed into a public perception of the business-as-usual of international affairs. Terrorism is a perceived (and widely feared) threat to public security, but the terrorist menace is diffuse and not readily identifiable with a single group acting as an arm of a single hostile foreign power armed with a monolithic ideology, as in the old Cold War paradigm. The net result is that the idea of subversion has gone out of focus.

The growing lack of clarity in the background against which national-security policy is formed is deepened by two major developments in Canadian society over the past two decades. One is the growing democratization of Canadian life, symbolized by the declining deference to authority and the rising clamour and contestation of public life. Direct representation of views on public policy is today sought by a much wider spectrum of the population than was the case twenty or thirty years ago. The old reliance on élite accommodation has been undergoing considerable strain as a result. Closely related to this is the widely noted development of what has been called a 'rights culture'. The coming into force of the Charter of Rights is both a cause and a result of a new assertive rights-consciousness as an attribute of active citizenship. The walling-off of classes of persons with reduced rights against the national-security state—particularly public servants and immigrants—is rendered more difficult as Charter cases (such as *Singh* v. *the Minister of Employment and Immigration*, which allows non-citizens to claim the protections of the Charter) reverberate through the legal system.

My research into the making and administration of national-security policy over the past forty years has led me to a somewhat unexpected observation. When the state had the freest hand in constructing its controls, public opinion was rarely, if ever, invoked within the councils of government as justification. By the 1970s public opinion began making a more concrete appearance in security-policy discussions—almost always as a liberal constraint upon repressive state actions.[43] This tendency spilled over into public notoriety when the first draft of the CSIS bill in 1983 led to a storm of public disapproval, virtually all of which came from a critical liberal perspective.[44]

Through an intricate manoeuvre with the Senate, the government retreated and liberalized the bill. The debate over the mandate of CSIS, and especially the definition of the threats to security, is especially interesting in this regard. The successful insistence of public advocacy groups that 'lawful advocacy, protest and dissent' be exempted from the mandate of the security agency, along with the inclusion of 'violence' in the definition of the intention to overthrow government, was not only important in itself but symbolic of changing public attitudes. In this light it comes as no surprise that a recent study of Canadian attitudes towards intrusive state surveillance of subversion finds greater degrees of illiberalism the closer one comes to the state élites.[45]

A second clear reflection of the changed context is the public reception of SIRC. Despite the intense hostility evidenced by CSIS itself, SIRC appears to have a good press and, so far as can be seen, public approval for its critical scrutiny of CSIS. Certainly, after the fiasco of the first Director's resignation and the acceptance of the Osbaldeston Report, SIRC has apparently strengthened its hand. This could not have been the case so long as the old Cold War paradigm continued to hold sway, and with it the old perception of subversion. CSIS under the direction of Ted Finn did not seem to grasp this changed reality.[46] Since Finn's departure it is being compelled to adapt to the new reality.

CSIS has been seen by the public to be particularly ineffective in relation to the one threat to security that evokes strong public concern: terrorism. Terrorism is widely perceived, with much justice, as a crime that strikes not at the state directly but at the state through the public, particularly through attacks on innocent persons. Although the threat of terrorism has been used in the past as an excuse for chasing old hares of left-wing subversion (as in Québec following the October Crisis), this tactic has become increasingly obsolete by the late 1980s. The conspiracy theory linking Moscow with international terrorism collapsed with the farcical 'Bulgarian Connection' trial of the Pope's attempted assassin. The Senate Committee that investigated terrorism in Canada reported in 1987 that 'right-wing/racist' groups with US connections posed more of a threat than left-wing terrorism.[47] Canada has never produced anything like the left-wing terrorist movements characteristic of Europe in the 1970s and 1980s (Red Army Faction, Red Brigades, Action Directe).[48] The terrorist acts that have taken place on Canadian soil have been associated with foreign causes not readily categorized in left/right or Cold War terms. Yet such acts as the 1985 destruction of the Air India plane, with its appalling human carnage, offer a target for security operations that no doubt sustain wide support in Canadian society. There is a potential new paradigm for national-security policy here, but it has so far eluded the grasp of the security establishment, especially with the public notice given to divisions between CSIS and the RCMP over counter-terrorism operations.[49]

In the meantime, the decline of the old paradigm can be expected to further erode the legitimacy of CSIS in its relation to the left. The almost symbiotic relationship pointed out earlier in this paper between the security service, the labour movement, and the social-democratic party is unlikely to continue once the threat of Communist subversion has receded. All three institutions were in tacit agreement on the Communist issue; without that focus, it is likely that relations with the security service will be more naturally antagonistic. In short, the emancipation of the left from the grip of the Cold War mould has shaken loose one link-age between the state and the associations of civil society.

The conjuncture of the late twentieth century in Canada offers unique opportunities for the enlargement of the space for autonomous development of oppositional forces. Whether those opportunities will be seized is, of course, a question of politics (and economics) that lies outside the scope of this essay. But those who cherish freedom can take heart that, even with the technological refinement of the means of state repression in the post-1984 world, the political basis for repressive state intrusion into Canadian civil society is, in certain crucial ways, weaker than at any time in the postwar era.

Protest and Fringe Groups in Québec

JANINE KRIEBER

I belong to no faction; I will fight them all. They will never be extinguished except by institutions that produce guarantees, that set the limits of authority and irrevocably submit human pride to the yoke of public freedom.

— Saint-Just, speech in defence of Robespierre

Now that the second half of this decade has arrived, Québec is examining itself. Citizens and experts are gauging the weight of the state, its corporations, and the privileges of its public servants. The achievements of the Quiet Revolution are being questioned. Already in 1979, in a series of articles published in *Le Devoir*, Nathalie Petrowsky told of a nostalgic hunt for the old militants: where are they now?[1] In 1987 Jean-Marc Piotte gave a pessimistic report on 'social struggles',[2] and at the National Film Board Jacques Leduc produced a series of documentaries that, perhaps even unintentionally, portrayed the empty lives of the last people still clinging to the concept of a class struggle, survivors of a bygone era.[3] Even the intellectual beacons have allowed their uncertainties to show: Léon Dion said in 1987 that he was still seeking the Québec that many people thought they had found.[4]

Hesitation and uncertainty are the marks of a society defining itself. Québec has just barely emerged from a long period of transition or, as the forerunners and originators of the Quiet Revolution liked to call it, 'catching up'. Everything has happened very quickly since the end of the war. Former rebels formed first the official opposition and then the government, leaving in their wake the impatient activists of the radical fringe. In the space of a very short time, Québec has completely institutionalized an ideology of protest—a 'revolution' in the most mechanical sense of the word.

The product of groups competing for power, ideologies have their importance in the transformation of societies. Discursive strategies that motivate and justify political action, they are used to identify, to denounce, and to rally.[5] In the interplay of alliances and separations—always explained and justified in one way or another—political action groups identify themselves through their respective positions *vis-à-vis* a number of meaningful ideological cores.[6] Passed on through the language, these cores have a narrative effect on the writing of history. We will look at the various positions that make up the process of change marked by the accession to political institutions of a neo-nationalist ideology born of extra-parliamentary protest. A corollary of this institutionalization is the appearance of a new radical dimension on the fringes of the modern protest movement, a radical dimension that in the 1960s was divided between the educational approach to independence of the journal *Parti pris* and the violent option represented by the FLQ.

Ideologies in modern Québec will long be defined in relation to the central nationalist core. Canada and Québec, social and liberal: these issues always converge on the national question, a veritable battlefield where everyone tries to impose his or her own notions of the true and the desirable, to the exclusion of all other approaches. We will see how alliances have been made and unmade on the basis of a modernist nationalist ideology that was a marginalized minority in the very early 1950s, that was enriched by a social program through the Quiet Revolution and the turmoil of the 1960s, and that, finally, ended in failure when bound by the constraints of power.

What is a protest movement?

Definitions are always a trap. There are dozens of typologies of protest movements. Each one, following an examination of political attitudes, has tried to classify so-called deviant or a-institutional behaviour according to a number of factors. From minimal participation to revolutionary war, there is a certain continuum in that all are manifestations of a single phenomenon: political commitment. To shed some light on these various behaviours, we have selected the classification suggested by Gérard Bergeron, since he makes a distinction between 'social' units (*us*) and units of the 'state' (*them*). Thus within the *polity* there can be six social behaviours, which the author terms 'infrafunctional behaviours': contribution, participation, opposition, protest, dissent, and rebellion.[7]

In this typology, protest appears as the midpoint between contribution—the minimal political act that is characteristic of the great majority of people—and rebellion, which by its very nature can involve only a small minority. Protest is more than opposition, since it rejects the 'system', which it sees as the material structure that determines the government and the opposition alike. Protest is less than dissent, because it lacks ideological unity. This splintered quality is essential to an understanding of the process during the period of Québec history that interests us. In fact, a rapid redefinition of the political spectrum took place over a period of approximately twenty years—from 1960 to 1980, from the Quiet Revolution to the referendum. By refusing to recognize the legitimacy of the groups in power, the protest movement did not yet deny the ethical foundations of the regime in a dispassionate analysis and an attitude of withdrawal. It employed a number of eloquent ideological signs to mobilize as many people as possible.

The protest movement has two characteristics: (1) a distinct style, and (2) sporadic action. The reason protest is so difficult to grasp as a unique phenomenon is that it is always balancing between society and politics. A minority that wants to be taken for a majority, it demands the right to speak on behalf of society as a whole, a society frustrated by political immobility. It draws its mobilizing legitimacy from both its apparent spontaneity and its generalized and altruistic ideological messages. This discursive strategy means that protest action can be reinterpreted as the 'profound will of the people'.[8] Protest groups, most often a minority, act on behalf of the ethics of the majority. Styles of behaviour, street demonstrations, wildcat strikes, noisy public rallies—all create this apparent spontaneity that allows the activist minority to speak on behalf of the majority.

While stability is the hallmark of the majority, change is typical of minorities:

> It is the characteristic of a majority to wish to remain a majority. But a minority that has decided to become 'active' is not always satisfied with the role of official opposition. It is at that point that opponents, oppressed or with no future and no past, become protesters, dissenters, or rebels.[9]

It is on the actions of these minorities, which assume the mantle of the democratic will, that the social 'project' capable of provoking protest is founded. For a minority to be able to reach the level of visibility and influence that will give it the appearance of a majority—the source of legitimacy in politics—it must develop a number of persuasion strategies. Moscovici tried to isolate the determining variables of persuasion that constitute influence.[10] In one work, he showed that *style* is the only variable that can be independent.[11]

Moscovici admits that he found no satisfactory explanation for the effectiveness of style. But he nevertheless succeeds in isolating a development model, a taxonomy of social groups:[12]

1. **Differentiation phase**: '. . . in the beginning, a deviant minority group acts in a rigid manner, which allows it to consolidate in the shelter of a well-defined unit.'

2. **Flexibility phase**: 'a more flexible behaviour, resulting from the fact that its [the group's] internal structure is defined and separate from its external environment. Its new 'equitable' style allows it to maintain its consistency, and at the same time to form alliances . . . so as to enlarge its sphere of influence, without thereby running the risk of breaking apart. . .'

3. **Conformity phase**: '. . . the necessity emerges for [the group] to take increasing account of the diversity of the external environment, to be more

and more flexible and less and less consistent, i.e., subject to the needs of its internal environment. This continues until it is no longer either a minority or truly deviant, acting much less through innovation than through conformity.'

The above is a simple model of group transformation, based on the effectiveness of the persuasion strategies used. It should be noted here that this process can in no way be considered deterministic. The transition from one phase to another depends on the success of the strategies applied by each player at various times. The phases can, however, be identified fairly easily in the contemporary history of protest in Québec.

1. **Differentiation phase, 1948-1959**. The rejection of tradition grew under the Duplessis government, marked by a radical re-interpretation of history and extra-parliamentary political action. In this phase two sets of ideologico-factual poles served as the foundation for the rejection that would distinguish the 'progressive' protest movement from its 'conservative' environment. The publication of the *Refus global* manifesto, in 1948, and the asbestos strike in 1949 would allow a scattered protest movement to form around common ideological axes: modernist nationalism and reformist liberalism.

2. **Flexibility phase, 1960-1976**. This phase was marked by two stages. (a) The Quiet Revolution was a period of institutionalization, during which the protest movement entered the opposition and formed the government, when the unity acquired in the first phase gave rise to new élites, in the vacuum left by the decline of the Duplessis regime. It was at this point that cracks began to appear in that unity, and the divergent trends, expressed through discourse, broke on the rocks of the issues of nationhood, social policy, and the means to be used to achieve independence. (b) When the independence protest movement managed to structure itself sufficiently to take a place in the institutionally legitimized political game, it suffered considerable internal disintegration, leaving behind it the disappointed remnants of the Quiet Revolution. The presence of splinter groups can be considered a by-product of institutionalization, a result of the functional impact of conflict on the cohesiveness of groups, as observed by Coser.[13] Marginalized, muzzled, exasperated by the half-heartedness of former companions at the barricades, one of those minorities found that the temptation to resort to violence, as a strategy to achieve visibility, was strong: the FLQ.

3. **Conformity phase, 1976-1982**, followed by the decline of the issue of nationhood. In the flexibility phase the PQ effectively managed to dissociate itself from violent radical groups, while maintaining a difficult dual alliance with the unions and their social progressivism and with impatient separatist groups. But the constraints of power, the soon-limited budgets, the failure of the referendum, and, finally, the economic crisis revealed deep ideological divisions. During this third phase the PQ,

while it was in power, attempted to maintain its position as a structure within which there was still room for protest. But thereafter its role as manager of the state increasingly distanced it from the demands that could still be made by groups outside its control. In an attempt to unite incompatible positions, the sovereignty discourse became more and more convoluted and vague, in the face of activist fringes where Marxism had taken hold.

We will concentrate on the first two of these three phases, which involved particularly intense protest activities in Québec. We will conclude by returning to the third phase, which characterizes the current political situation.

The rejection of tradition and extra-parliamentary protest (1948-1959)

If we approach the issue of protest as an archaeologist would, the deepest layer, which helps to explain the current situation, is located between approximately 1945 and 1960. More specifically, it began in 1948, the year in which the *Refus global* manifesto was published, and ended with the death of Duplessis, in 1959. It was a period of economic expansion[14] and strong demographic growth.[15] In spite of this growth, there were major ethnic and geographic divisions. French-Canadians remained disadvantaged as compared with other groups, and the Montreal region experienced much more rapid growth and modernization than the rest of the province. The public image of French-Canadians (not yet considered Québécois) was still that of poor peasants, barely literate, dominated by an omnipotent clergy and a legal élite servile to 'foreign' interests. That image has more to do with traditional visions of family life than with reality, but it would become the central theme that justified—by way of contrast—a modernizing and progressive nationalism. Here we see almost the archetype of the narrative effect. If the *Refus global*—which was in fact written by an extremely small minority group—had such an impact, it was because it produced the exaggerated reaction necessary for a protest movement to appear.

This era was totally dominated by the strongly personalized government of Duplessis, who was elected for the first time in 1944 and remained in power until his death in 1959. Economically, socially, and politically conservative, Duplessism settled over Québec following a period of rapid reforms brought in by the Godbout government,[16] and isolated the province from the major Western trends of the time, in particular the emergence of the welfare state. The ideas of the Union Nationale party—a mixture of corporatism, religious traditionalism, and nationalist conservatism—were able to attract many of the traditional élites in the liberal professions and the clergy who felt themselves threatened by the modernization process. The results of the 1944 election established the supremacy of the conservative hinterland over the modernist city.[17]

Québec in this phase was thus characterized by immobility—what was later termed the 'great darkness'. The ideology of the Quiet Revolution mythicized this period. But this seeming immobility did not entirely succeed in masking the stirrings of excitement outside political institutions. In 1948 the Borduas group declared itself by publishing its manifesto. Intellectuals started speaking out in favour of modernity, and unionism, although threatened with eternal damnation, began developing on solid foundations. Duplessis labelled all these voices raised in opposition to the powers of the traditional minorities 'communist'. This label added to the impression that national security was threatened by an alliance between certain groups and 'foreign powers'. Thus deprived of its right to legitimate discourse, the opposition developed outside the institutions, in groups of thinkers and through politically committed journals—the traditional situation of extra-parliamentarism.

It is no longer a new idea that the seeming immobility of the 1940s and 1950s hid the complex reality of social tensions that had been artificially ejected from politics. An outmoded electoral map that gave an inordinate amount of power to the less-and-less populated hinterland was not enough to muzzle a modernist urban élite that focussed its efforts on cultural, social, and economic demands.

As early as 1948, the *Refus global* pointed to the existence of a minority that condemned the Church's stranglehold on people, thought, and creativity. Proclaiming the primacy of man as individual, Paul-Emile Borduas promoted a liberating anarchy in denouncing traditionalist nationalism, the ideological pillar of Duplessism:

> modest French-Canadian families, workers or petty bourgeois, from their arrival in this country to the present time, who have remained French and Catholic in resistance to the conqueror, through unthinking attachment to the past, through pleasure, sentimental pride and other necessities.[18]

The manifesto denounced, criticized, and rejected the French-Canadian community that had turned inward to preserve itself. Caught up in the enthusiasm that marked the rebirth of an intellectual culture, Borduas ran the risk of nihilism: 'For you, the rationally ordered (like everything at the fond heart of decadence) scramble for the spoils; for us, the unpredictable passion; for us, the total risk in total rejection.'[19]

In this way was created an element essential for rallying extra-political forces: the primacy of action; to act because, in the circumstances, not to act would be intolerable. This was one of the very first steps in the idealization of the People, whose spontaneous action cannot but be a source of positive creativity: 'In the imaginable future, we foresee man, once freed of his useless chains, realizing in the unexpected, necessary order of spontaneity, in splendid anarchy, the fullness of his individual gifts.'[20]

For the thinkers of the new culture, the choices were clear: either shameful submission or total freedom. This Manichaean division of the world of political activity was essential for revolt. It was through this framework, of which the manifesto is an archetype, that the extra-parliamentary movement discovered its founding unity of differentiation—the line separating the *them* (clerical and conservative) from the *us* inspired by the sole objective of Liberty.

Borduas' position can be considered the magnetic centre of this first phase. It summarized everything, in exaggerated form, until the second magnetic pole appeared: the new dimension of unionism, of which the archetype was the 1949 asbestos strike. Union activity was fundamental to both the unification and, later, the break-up of the various protest movements. It achieved in fact what Borduas had advanced only as an abstraction: the primacy of action. Until 1960 intellectuals paraded under their placards, accompanying strikers; between 1960 and 1970 the ritual was repeated, and young intellectuals fell under police truncheons alongside Murray Hill taxi drivers.

The magnetic power of these two pivotal events managed to erase the conflicts between the different concepts of the Québec nation, to create the illusion of a unified approach to the objective of affirming and modernizing French Canada. But despite the apparent unanimity of the protesting ideologies, two ideological poles were already in collision: reformist liberalism and modernist nationalism. Groups would be attracted to these two dominant currents, united in their fight against Duplessis. Intellectuals, writers, journalists,[21] and university professors would work to develop this new social doctrine that challenged the lines drawn by the Church.

Social upheaval (1960-1976)

The flexibility phase comprised two steps, each with its own characteristics. First there was the Quiet Revolution, when, despite diverging points of view, a relative consensus reigned with regard to the need to modernize the Québec state. Very soon, however, divisions appeared: on the right, where liberalism was concentrating its energies on a centralizing view of Canada, and on the left, with the Rassemblement pour l'Indépendance National (RIN) and the mouthpiece of the fringes, the journal *Parti pris*; and finally, at the far edge, the FLQ.

The death of Duplessis, followed by a short period of indecision, left a political vacuum into which rushed the new nationalism that had been discussed, weighed, and structured in the previous period. It had had the chance to mature and become a true political ideology with a 'program' ready for implementation. This was to be the 'Quiet Revolution'. Protest movements from the previous phase quickly besieged the province's institutions, creating a fine unanimity in the early years of reform: 'To carry out its reform plan, the "hell of a team" . . . benefits from a real consensus among the new labour, management, intellectual, and political élites, which all agree on the need to modernize institutions.'[22]

But this consensus would not withstand the social, political, and economic tensions to come. Very early in the decade, factions that had been hidden by the anti-Duplessism of the previous phase, and lost in the general turmoil of modernizing the Québec state, would become increasingly distinct, taking on the role of critics of political institutions. Thus the journal *Cité libre*—the spearhead of the protest movement in the preceding phase, and an essential medium in the construction of the social project realized through the Quiet Revolution—distanced itself in its 1964 manifesto:

> We are citizens radically opposed to the situation that appears to be taking root in Canada and in our province. We condemn the indifference of the public and private sectors with regard to the numerous problems facing us. We assert our disagreement with most of the solutions popular among our political leaders. . . In Québec, the 'Quiet Revolution' —which certainly has some achievements to its credit—has already ground to a halt, out of breath. The reform movement appears less committed, and there is a risk of its wandering far off course. Cries of emotion often obscure the voice of reason, and appeals to racial considerations are heard instead of objective analysis of reality.[23]

While the two ideologies formulated in the first phase—federalist liberalism and modernist nationalism—confronted each other in the institutions, the brand-new education system was rapidly affected by the growing wave of what would later be termed the 'student revolt'. A new élite took power, but was followed by another generation for whom progress meant not modernization but revolution.[24] An early and—because it expressed all the symbols of the revolutionary left—important factor in this trend took shape in the *Revue socialiste*, founded by Raoul Roy[25] in 1959. The first issue explained how the failure to distinguish between revolution and independence would lay the groundwork for the break-up of the nationalist movement:

> There is no social, political or economic dualism in the human being. For instance, a [French] Canadian worker is both a proletarian and a [French] Canadian. It is utopian to claim to save the body, i.e., the proletarian, while ignoring the soul, that is, the national culture. [French] Canadian workers, exploited by a two-faced oligarchy, monopolist-imperialist and colonialist-foreign, must fight on two fronts against this oppression, founded on class, capitalism, and nationalism, and not neglect either of them.[26]

This concept of a war on two fronts would gain tremendous popularity. It was this ideological core that would make it possible to adapt a number of symbols from the international protest movement[27] to the Québec context. On the fringes of nationalism, new ideological intellectuals emerged to denounce the fickleness of the élites and reveal the new treason.

When, following the differentiation phase, the original modernizing nationalism managed to gain political legitimacy, it had to soften certain of its criticisms and demands. The extremes, which it had been possible to keep in place through the abstract nature of the project and the common interest in protest, pulled away from the main body to enter, in turn, their own differentiation phases.

In the 1960s these minorities took their cue from the international student protest movement: third-worldism, anti-imperialist pacifism, and revolutionary romanticism. The international protest discourse was applied to the particular context of Québec to define new approaches to the issue of nationhood.

At about the same time as the *Cité libre* manifesto appeared, in 1964, *Parti pris*, after one year of publication,[28] brought out its own. The magazine first defined its position *vis-à-vis* the FLQ:

> The left wing of the separatist movement has surpassed itself, giving birth to the FLQ, and then the ALQ. These movements have a total revolutionary commitment: they seek a national liberation struggle led by the lower classes. But their wishes are not yet reality; the lower classes are neither ready to act, nor educated, nor politicized. The groundwork for the revolution has not been laid.[29]

Parti pris took as its vocation to politicize and raise the consciousness of the lower classes through education. It is interest to note that Latouche, in a footnote, directly relates this interest in research and education to the impact of the educational reforms effected by the very group in power whose élitist, capitalist, and exploitative tendencies *Parti pris* denounced:

> We are now at the point of creating a true revolutionary and socialist popular party, creating it with the assent and assistance of the lower classes that we have to reach. It will be a long and arduous task, but it is a step on the road to revolution.[30]

And so one front took the place of the other. Almost imperceptibly, the revolution had assumed greater importance than nationhood. In fact, *Parti pris* would be the pole drawing the militant Québec left towards an independent socialist state.

We will not examine in detail the events of the second half of the decade.[31] Increasing student and labour mobilization, the emergence of a municipal opposition in Montreal, a world's fair, the visit by General De Gaulle,[32] 'Vive le Québec libre' . . .; socialism in all its forms, marked by varying degrees of nationalism, student unionism, counterculture, terrorism—the groups formed and dissolved until the October Crisis, whose importance cannot be calculated by the number of deaths and prisoners—nor the stadium, nor the velodrome, which in any case did not yet exist—but by its impact on the collective memory. October (a wonderful revolutionary symbol) was the achievement of the second generation of the FLQ, the one that proclaimed the primacy of revolution.

Indeed, the violent nationalist movement itself also underwent changes throughout this period. Three manifestos reveal its path over the field of revolt—over what we are obliged to call, according to the revolutionaries themselves, the *two fronts of the struggle*. The first dates from 1963, and essentially consists of variations on the theme of colonial dependency, the root of all evil in Québec:

> In Québec, as in all other colonized countries, the oppressor categorically denies its imperialism, with the support of our so-called national élite, which is more interested in protecting its personal economic interests than in serving the vital interests of the Québec nation. It persists in denying the evidence, and spends its time creating a multitude of false problems, with the aim of distracting the subjugated people from the only essential one: INDEPENDENCE.[33]

This first generation of the FLQ[34] was thus situated in the nationalist camp, a sympathetic environment for it. For many nationalist intellectuals, the unacceptability of the means—bombs, theft, provocation—was overridden by the legitimacy of the ends of the revolt. This was the period of the primacy of separatism, which was to force many to take a clear stand.

By 1970, the various groups had almost finished sorting themselves out. The Parti Québécois was born of the Mouvement Souveraineté-association, and absorbed some major fringes of the separatist and progressive groups. This creation of a political party dedicated to both nationalism and workers, with a 'soft' social-democratic approach —*reformist*, according to some—provoked a veritable earthquake within the RIN. The latter considered itself a party of the masses, like the great European socialist movements. But it would be overtaken by the rallying ability of the strong, mediagenic personality of René Lévesque, who knew how to employ an ideology (sovereignty-association) so vague and ambiguous that it could mean anything when applied to the issue of Québec nationhood. It was in this context, as the turmoil subsided and positions solidified, that the fringe groups became more rigid in their marginality and had to seek a new identity in greater radicalism.

Three months prior to the October Crisis, the FLQ tried to make public a new manifesto. It had to redefine its political position because its natural constituency, the nationalist and progressive intellectual group, had been drawn into the political institutions by the Parti Québécois. This manifesto set out a new position justifying the rejection of institutionalization. The first 1970 manifesto stated its position clearly. The 'long march through the institutions'[35] was impossible, because the institutions were basically violent, and violence could be met only with violence:

> We wish to respond to the provocation of the established order. We wish to respond to the blackmail practised by businessmen who feel that they can maintain the current political and economic system by sowing fear of change in the hearts of the people. To the type of bombs thrown by Royal Trust, we respond with real ones. We are simply meeting their violence with counter-violence. We are defending ourselves against the ongoing attacks of anti-worker and anti-Québec forces—financial syndicates, big business, chambers of commerce, and others supported by the Liberal party of Trudeau and Bourassa.[36]

This was the first time that this position, which was not new among marginal groups, had been set out in such a clear and rational way. This new statement of its intentions placed the FLQ on the same ideological path as the violent groups in America and Europe. In the early 1960s, the model had been taken from the Third World, the struggle against colonialism, and the obligatory readings from Fanon and Guevara. Now the model was action. The Americans had denounced the 'crimes' committed in the 'Babylon' of the West, and the FLQ naturally took a place on the front line: 'We fight all forms of racism, discrimination, or segregation. . . . We express our solidarity with American blacks and with Puerto Ricans combating Yankee capitalism.'[37]

So now the confining and inward-looking nationalism condemned by protesting intellectuals in the Duplessis era was outmoded, replaced by a new solidarity with oppressed peoples. The groups in revolt naturally fed on the legends born of the wave of protest among Western youth. By the end of the 1960s, street politics had become calmer, leaving in its wake a constellation of splinter groups disconnected from their society. Some would take action at any cost. The model had already been developed, discussed, and weighed through analysis and discussion of the activities of the Tupamaros and the theses of Marighella.

There were many ideological signs promoting violent action; a mountain of politico-sociological analyses produced a favourable form of organization. The Leninist concept of the avant-garde—revised and corrected by Mao—the Marcusian analyses of the hidden violence of capitalism, Fanon's certainty that murder was a liberating act: everything came together in the early 1970s to convince those disappointed in the student revolt that the only possible outlet was spectacular action.

But the newspapers to which the group sent its manifesto were totally uninterested in the issue, which in any case was not news. A few months later, the second 1970 manifesto would be heard in every Québec living room, read in a suitable monotone on state television. This strategy of media visibility was baptized 'terrorism'.

The October Crisis was, in fact, only the last convulsion of a marginal fringe in its death throes. On the international scene, the student revolt had calmed, and young Québec adults, better educated, had broken with political militancy and were preparing to apply the new watchword: 'the long march through the institutions'. There were Maoists in the teachers' unions, preachers of Marxism in the social-science faculties, sometimes even disciples of Stalinist egalitarianism. They would be largely responsible for the rigid positions assumed in the socio-economic demands of the first half of the 1970s, until the electoral victory of the PQ posed a tactical problem[38] that would not really be solved until the decrees of 1982.[39]

Conclusion: the conformity phase, or the betrayal of the people

In this exploration of protest movements in Québec, we have seen some ideologies come into existence and, transmitted by groups, take their place in protest movements, the official opposition, and the government, while others split up and died. The conformity phase emerged with the victory of the PQ and the stabilization of institutions in the two-party system. The violent option had not resurfaced, despite the provocations, and the radical groups, particularly the Marxists, survived within only the protective cocoon of educational institutions and some trade unions. The turmoil was gently subsiding—until the beginning of the 1980s, which would be a period of disillusionment for extra-institutional militancy:

> Most militants are severe, unpitying, implacable in their criticism of the past. The hopes they worked to realize have dissipated, as Québec is still one of the ten Canadian provinces, women continue to suffer discrimination, and workers are still exploited by capitalists. The militants sacrificed their pleasures, sometimes their studies or career plans, for lost causes.[40]

The result of the 1980 referendum suddenly defused the populist discourse on nationalism with a socialist approach. Seventeen years after the founding of *Parti pris*, which had taken on the task of awakening popular awareness, the People had not yet chosen the appointed path of independence, let alone socialism.

The crisis and the decrees of 1982 revealed a state that was no longer the driving force behind Québec society, but rather a barrier to its development. With its mass of public servants, the enormous machine founded as a step towards liberation had begun to cost too much. From that point on, the globalizing ideologies founded on voluntarist progress gave way to splinter groups organized around sectoral demands. Tenants fought to remain in their apartments; welfare recipients, to receive bread and butter; soft hearts, for an end to the fur trade. Faced with the new hard times, everyone fell back on his or her own needs, and the generalized altruism that had been apparent in the demands of the middle class in the 1960s was no more than a memory. Evidence of this is that in the social analysis of the left, some have replaced the concept of 'class struggle' with that of 'social movements'.[41] Perhaps, behind a restored façade, one could find in this the highly liberal notion of 'pressure groups'. For the moment, the social analysis is adapting to splintered militancies, but there is nothing to say that nationalism could not surge up again and become the magnetic centre of these partial ideologies.

Political discourse is central to the understanding and evaluation of political strategies. In itself it is not sufficient to explain history, but, as we have seen through the successive steps in the transformation of the protest movement, it does determine the evolutionary framework for individuals who decide and who take action. Some militants may be proponents of what Camus called 'metaphysical revolt'. This concept, of mythical—Promethean—origin, seeks a justice above human justice, and a legitimacy that exceeds the law. In the final analysis, it is this recurring centre, whether it claims to speak in the name of the Nation, of God, or of historical necessity, that succeeds in justifying political murder.

The Far Right in Canada

STANLEY BARRETT

Introduction

One of Canada's best-kept secrets is the degree of racism and anti-Semitism that has existed in the country during the past century. Much of this—and no doubt the most significant part—has been institutionalized into the fabric of Canadian society and thus relatively invisible (if only by virtue of being considered 'normal'), reflected indirectly in immigration patterns and employment opportunities. At different periods, however, racism and anti-Semitism have been anything but covert, constituting the *raison d'être* for a host of fascist-oriented groups, such as the Ku Klux Klan in the early 1980s.

This paper will focus on the formally organized radical right in Canada, especially in the post-Second-World-War period. The Ku Klux Klan and comparable organizations like the Western Guard, the Nationalist Party, and the Aryan Nations are fundamentally committed to the defence of Western Christian civilization. In their view, white people have been subjected to a massive, insidious attack by black people and Jews. Their aim is nothing less than to rebuild the nation on a racial basis—by violent means if necessary—with blacks repatriated and Jews eliminated.

The presence in Canada of organizations such as the Ku Klux Klan raises complex questions about freedom of speech and legitimacy of non-establishment political protest. This paper is guided by an implicit assumption: dissent not only is compatible with democracy, but indeed is an essential ingredient. Yet dissent is never unbounded. Like freedom of speech, it necessarily must accommodate other values, such as individual worth regardless of racial criteria. That the world-view of the radical right makes no room for the latter value—in fact, white supremacists often dismiss liberal democracy as nothing more than a Jewish invention inimical to the interests of gentiles—is reason enough to oppose it. One of the big questions in this paper is whether the opposition should include a 'secret police force'—the Canadian Security and Intelligence Service (CSIS) or otherwise. Given the elaborate institutional framework of Canada's other police forces (including their intelligence branches), of the legal system, and of the grassroots organizations that emerge to confront crises such as those generated by dedicated white supremacists, one may question the necessity for a secret police at all. Even if this remark is considered naïve in view of the numerous internal and external threats that face the modern nation state, and we are stuck with the Canadian Security and Intelligence Service, I hope that this paper will make one thing clear: it is the far right—not the far left—that arguably poses the greater danger to the country, at least from the standpoint of the quality of its democratic system.

Organizations and members

There have been four distinct periods of organized right-wing activity in Canada: the Ku Klux Klan in the 1920s, a fascist thrust preceding World War Two, an incipient neo-Nazi presence in the 1960s, and full-blown neo-fascism in the 1970s and 1980s. The Ku Klux Klan was founded in Tennessee in 1865 by six former Confederate soldiers. The name 'The Merry Six' had been considered,[1] but one of the men, who had studied Greek, suggested *kuklos*, meaning band or circle; the final rendition was the Ku Klux Klan. The early American Klansmen saw themselves as a moral force, upholding law and order. But as Forster and Epstein have stated: 'The Klan's chief aim was to intimidate the Negro into absolute submission, to drive out the "carpetbaggers" and to destroy every vestige of Negro political power in the Southern states.'[2] The defence of the moral order translated into propping up the status quo, which brought the Klan the implicit support of the white majority. Throughout 1866, bands of nightriders dressed in white robes terrorized the black population, as well as whites who did not toe the line. By 1868 the Klan's estimated membership was 550,000. Although by the turn of the century the organization had been reduced to a small remnant—partly as a result of government legislation that made hooded nightriders illegal, and partly because of infiltration by government agents—in 1915 it underwent a dramatic revival. Whereas in the 1860s it had been primarily anti-black, the 'new' Klan was also opposed to Catholics, Jews, organized labour, communism, and foreigners. It was during this period that the intimidating practice of cross-burning (Klansmen prefer the expression 'cross-lighting') was introduced, as well as a woman's auxiliary called 'Kamelia'. By 1923 an estimated three to six million people had joined the Klan:[3] 15 to 20 per cent and 25 to 30 per cent of the total adult male population and the Protestant population respectively. During that period the Klan had not only spread beyond the South, but also had become as much an urban as a rural phenomenon. Leading citizens and businessmen were members, as were a disproportionate number of policemen and clergymen.[4] In several states, and at all levels of public office, the Klan exercised influence. Indeed, three former presidents of the United States were reputed to have been Klansmen.[5]

Winks suggests that the original Klan of the 1860s may have had some followers in Ontario,[6] although the facts are not conclusive. What is certain is that the US Klan's second wave swept over the border into

Canada. In 1921 solicitations for Klan membership appeared in newspapers in British Columbia,[7] and a klavern (or den) was established in Montreal.[8] During the 1920s there were three separate Klan organizations in Canada: the Ku Klux Klan of Canada, the Kanadian Ku Klux Klan, and the Ku Klux Klan of the British Empire. The Klan's presence was particularly pronounced in Ontario, British Columbia, Alberta, and Saskatchewan. Promoting anti-Catholic sentiments, the Ontario Klan established local units in several towns and cities, including St Thomas, Sault Ste Marie, Belleville, Kingston, and Ottawa. One newspaper estimated the Toronto Klan alone to have 8,000 members[9]—no doubt a gross exaggeration. In the town of Barrie, St Mary's Roman Catholic Church was bombed by a Klansman, and in Oakville the Klan held a parade and burned a cross on the main street. A pastor from a Hamilton church took part, and Hamilton itself was the scene of cross-burnings.[10]

In 1924 a Klan klavern was established in Vancouver.[11] The BC Klan claimed a membership of more than 10,000 (again, probably a gross overestimate), including five MLAs.[12] In that province the Klan merely latched on to existing strong anti-Asian sentiments and the demand that East Indian, Chinese, and Japanese immigrants be repatriated. The targets were different in Alberta and Saskatchewan. Immigrants from Central and Eastern Europe were singled out, as well as French-Canadian settlers, and anti-Catholicism (with an undercurrent of anti-Semitism) became the Klan's rallying cry. The Klan's greatest success at the time, undoubtedly, was in Saskatchewan, where an estimated 40,000 people joined the infamous organization. Even if Kyba is correct that the membership was more in the range of 15,000,[13] that is still remarkable. The number of Protestant ministers who had joined the Saskatchewan Klan (at least twenty-six) is equally remarkable, as was the Klan's impact on the 1929 election. As Kyba has remarked, it was thought by some people that the KKK had become in effect a radical wing of the Conservative party.[14] Sher points out that the Klan worked hand in hand with the Conservatives to help defeat the ruling Liberal administration.[15] Nevertheless, it must be stressed that the Klan also had its appeal to Liberal supporters.[16] As Calderwood has observed, no single political party in Saskatchewan had a monopoly on Klan membership.[17]

The Ku Klux Klan adventure in Canada was as short-lived as it was dramatic, and by the 1930s it had become a spent force. Yet there was little time to celebrate, for as the Klan shrunk, a fascist and Nazi movement expanded. Québec had the largest and oldest Canadian Jewish community in the 1930s, and it was there that the most virulent fascist organization took root.[18] This was Adrian Arcand's Parti National Social Chrétien. Arcand portrayed Hitler as the champion of Christianity, advocated fascism as the solution to the world's problems, and contended that liberal democracy was a Jewish invention—merely the dictatorship of money powers. By 1937 Arcand claimed that in Montreal alone he had more than 80,000 followers. While this certainly was a wild exaggeration, his membership lists for that year do reveal the names of 700 card-carrying followers.[19] One of the most prominent subalterns was a medical practitioner named Dr Lambert, whose claim to fame was the compilation of the pernicious tract *The Key to the Mystery*. This document, a diatribe against Jews, was still being distributed in the 1980s by the current leader of the Western Guard, John Ross Taylor.

Arcand had close links with the Conservatives and the Union Nationale. In 1934 he was a paid publicist in R.B. Bennett's Conservative party in Québec. A year later, according to Weinfeld, he was minister of labour in Duplessis's Union Nationale government; he was also the editor of one of the party's semi-official publications.[20] By the late 1930s, Arcand had become a somewhat celebrated figure. Newspapers outside Québec began to pay attention to him, and often were laudatory in their evaluation. *The Globe and Mail* of 2 December 1937, for example, referred to him as 'the brilliant young French Canadian'. Even commentators in the United States became aware of his stature in Québec. When Arcand made a trip to New York in 1937 and spoke at a rally staged by the German-American Bund, *The Nation*, *Foreign Affairs*, and *Life* published articles about him. Immediately prior to the Second World War he was in communication with fascists in other countries, such as Mosley in Britain, and according to Betcherman he received financial backing from some of them.[21] Around that time, too, Arcand attempted to expand his organization beyond Québec. In Ontario it was to be called the National Christian Party of Canada, although in later years it became known as the National Unity Party. But Arcand's hopes for a vibrant fascist presence in Canada disintegrated in the face of the war, for the duration of which he was interned, along with other prominent fascists, in a New Brunswick concentration camp.

Although Arcand was the most prominent and influential fascist in Québec, there were other organizations in that province with similar goals, including as Les Jeune-Canada and the Fédération des Clubs Ouvriers,[22] as well as the *achat chez nous* movement, a campaign against Jewish goods and businesses. It must not be thought, however, that fascism was confined to Québec. As Betcherman has stated, fascists in other provinces, especially Ontario, were even more numerous and better organized than in Québec.[23] In Toronto swastika clubs began to emerge, leading to the notorious Christie Pits incident in 1933, when members of the Balmy Beach Swastika Club and other Gentiles clashed with Jewish students and factory workers.[24] Jewish shops along Bloor Street were vandalized and Jews in nearby neighbourhoods were randomly assaulted. John Ross Taylor, then a young man in his mid-twenties, was briefly associated with Arcand's organization, but he eventually joined the Canadian Union of Fascists. Ontario's dominant fascist at that time appears to have been Joseph Farr. A sergeant-major in the British Army and a member of the Orange Order, he first gained prominence as the head of the Swastika Association of Canada, and later of the Canadian Nationalist Party. The latter organization was closely associated with one bearing the same name in Western Canada, led by William Whittaker. Eventually the National Unity Party was founded, amalgamating Arcand's Parti National Social Chrétien with the Ontario and Western branches of the Canadian Nationalist Party.

A somewhat different phenomenon was the Brownshirt Party, formed in Kitchener, Ontario, and the Deutscher Bund, or German League, established in Waterloo in 1934. The first was basically the design of one Otto Becker, who had come to Canada from Germany in 1929, and the second was organized by a Nazi agent, Dr Karl Gerhardt.[25] According to Betcherman, the fascist recruiters attracted to Kitchener (formerly called Berlin) by its large German population (then 53 per cent) met with little success. Yet as Wagner points out, by 1937-38 the Deutscher Bund had grown to about 2000 followers across the country, almost 100 of them German Nazi Party members.[26]

The years following the Second World War have been justifiably described as 'the sanitary decades'.[27] Fascism had become a dirty word, and the world had had enough of racism and anti-Semitism. Nevertheless, it would be a mistake to assume that the right wing had dropped off the face of the earth. From the late 1940s through the 1950s there was a small but steady trickle of organized right-wing activity in Canada. Arcand, for example, following his 1945 release from concentration camp, attempted to reassert his political presence. Under the banner of the National Unity Party, he ran for office in the 1949 federal election, placing second with 5,590 votes.[28] Provided by Duplessis with translating and editing work after his release, Arcand died in poverty in 1967. In the late 1940s Ron Gostick established his Canadian Intelligence Publications, and quickly gained a reputation for anti-Semitism.[29] By the late 1950s John Ross Taylor had embarked on a new venture: a right-wing mail-order business called Natural Order. In Toronto at the same time was the White Canada Party, run by a self-styled genius called George Rolland who made his living as a watch-maker.[30] He preached about the biological inferiority of blacks and advocated a policy of white purity and racial segregation. Although the White Canada Party was essentially a one-man show, it would be wrong to dismiss it as totally insignificant. For example, during the 1950s Rolland ran for public office year after year; contesting a position on the Toronto Board of Control, he managed to win 4,000 votes in 1955, 5,500 in 1956, and 5,633 in 1957.

Thus a right-wing presence did exist in Canada throughout the 1950s, but it was minute, sporadic, and low-keyed. By the 1960s it was evident that something different was in the air. A more confident right wing had begun to materialize—open, aggressive, brazen, and vocal. By 1963 Gostick's Christian Action Movement, a forerunner of today's Canadian League of Rights, had been established, and a curious collection of social-credit enthusiasts, some advocating monetary reform and others more interested in reviving Hitler's political program, began to gather around Neil Carmichael, a Toronto-based coin and stamp dealer. The two most significant organizations, however, were the Canadian Nazi Party and the Edmund Burke Society. The first, explicitly fascist and racist, was led by two young Toronto residents, David Stanley and John Beattie. Stanley, a high-school student at the time, promoted the available racist literature (such as Lambert's *Key to the Mystery*) and wrote his own version, *The Red Rabbi*, which labelled the late Rabbi Abraham Feinberg a communist. Stanley's favourite tactic was to distribute leaflets carrying such messages as 'Communism Is Jewish' and 'Hitler Was Right'. This he did with great energy, stuffing them into apartment mail-boxes, scattering them around shopping malls, dropping them from the tops of buildings, and on one occasion depositing them in various cities across western Canada as he travelled by bus to Vancouver, giving the false impression of a rapidly accelerating Nazi presence in the country.

Stanley's mission brought him into contact with several other committed fascists, including John Ross Taylor, and he eventually became involved with the latter's Natural Order. By then the Canadian political establishment was becoming increasingly concerned about hate propaganda, and in 1965 both Stanley and Taylor lost their mailing privileges.[31] The younger man's future looked anything but promising at that juncture, but in a turn of events that I have not seen paralleled for any other member of the radical right in Canada, Stanley dropped out of the movement—apparently after reading a book, Hoffer's *The True Believer*, in which he saw himself portrayed. He denounced Beattie and the Nazi Party and apologized to Canadian Jews (especially Rabbi Feinberg) for his past activity. This recantation did not occur, however, until after he had coached Beattie in fascist principles. Until that point Stanley, although two years Beattie's junior, had clearly been the leader. But as Stanley's enthusiasm dwindled, Beattie's grew. Affecting Nazi mannerisms and littering his home (which served as party headquarters) with swastikas, he declared to an outraged public that only Christ had been a greater man than Hitler, and only the Bible was superior to *Mein Kampf*. Whereas Stanley had a penchant for slipping fascist literature under doors, Beattie was more attracted to the podium. His auditorium, or more precisely his arena, was Allan Gardens in Toronto, where his outdoor rallies, two in 1965 and another in 1966, set off a staggering reaction. Crowds of nearly 5,000 people, most of them there to protest against Beattie, mauled and punched him, and several organizations sprang up to confront the Canadian Nazi Party, such as the N3 Fighters Against Racial Hatred—named after Newton's third law, that for every action there is an opposite and equal reaction. Although the Canadian Nazi Party was eventually accepted by George Lincoln Rockwell (then the leader of the American Nazi Party) as an affiliated branch of the World Union of National Socialists, Beattie's days of glory were clearly numbered. By 1967 he was in prison, serving six months for conspiring to commit public mischief (he had stuck swastika emblems into the lawns of prominent Jews). By the time he was released, the Canadian Nazi Party had been transformed into the Canadian National Socialist Party, a London-based organization that has sputtered along ever since on the far-right periphery.

The other major organization to emerge in the 1960s was the Edmund Burke Society. Although it falls into the category of what I call the fringe right, it nevertheless is significant, for it became the breeding-ground for a host of organizations on both the far right and the fringe right that were to make their appearance during the next two decades.[32] Indeed, two of the Edmund Burke Society's three founders, Don Andrews and Paul Fromm, went on to become the dominant figures on the far and fringe rights respectively. Emerging at a period when opposition to the Vietnam War was at its height on university campuses, the avowedly anti-communist Edmund Burke Society—with its major strength at the University of Toronto—soon proved to be as addicted to violent street-confrontations as were the left-wing groups that it opposed.

The Nazi phase of the 1960s and the appearance of the Edmund Burke Society were simply a prelude of things to come. In the 1970s and 1980s there was a virtual explosion of right-wing activity. Indeed, fully 45 of the 60 radical right organizations that have existed (at least on paper) in Canada since the Second World War were founded during that period, including the Western Guard, the Nationalist Party, the Ku Klux Klan, the Aryan Nations, Concerned Parents of German Descent, and the Canadian Anti-Soviet Action Committee.[33]

The general characteristics of the organized radical right in Canada since 1945 are presented in Table 1. What must be stressed from the outset is that the sheer number of organizations gives an exaggerated impression of the strength of the right wing. Less than one-third of them can be considered major groups, and more than a quarter were front organizations—changes of names usually intended to cover the tracks of those involved in racist activity or to create the impression that radical-right groups were sprouting up everywhere.

TABLE 1:

GENERAL CHARACTERISTICS OF 60 EXTREME-RIGHT
ORGANIZATIONS

When founded	n	%	Focus	n	%
before 1945*	2	3	multi-issue	54	90
1945-60	1	2	single-issue	6	10
1961-70	12	20			
1971-80	30	50	Religious status		
1981 on	15	25			
			secular	44	73
Location			Christian	14	23
			anti-Christian	3	5
Canada-wide	4	7			
Ontario	43	71	Importance		
British Columbia	7	12			
Alberta	2	3	major	18	30
Other provinces or			minor	25	42
beyond Canada	4	7	front	17	28

*founded before 1945 and still in existence after the Second World War.

Christianity was the *raison d'être* for about one-quarter of these organizations; their right-wing orientations were merely a secondary product of a dominant theocratic world-view. Yet it can be said that almost all the 'secular' groups were trying to turn the tide against what they saw as a massive attack on Western Christian civilization. Even the three anti-Christian organizations were themselves religious groups, whose members believed that Christianity was either alien to white people, a spiritual form of Marxism, or simply inadequate to fight the white man's battle.[34] Unlike the fringe-right groups, which often emerged to confront a single issue, such as homosexuality or foreign aid, the majority of far-right organizations tended to focus on a whole range of issues, such as the supposed demise of the white man, anti-Semitism, communism, immigration, and homosexuality. A number of these organizations claimed a nation-wide membership. Yet the vast majority were concentrated in one or two provinces, especially Ontario.

Table 2 summarizes the basic characteristics of my data on 448 members of extreme-right organizations since the Second World War. Seventy-five per cent of them lived in Ontario, mostly in urban centres. White supremacist organizations usually claim that about one-third of their membership is female; yet my data show a figure of 13 per cent for the radical right overall. Furthermore, the extreme right is primarily a movement of men: the number of high-ranking women can be counted on the fingers of one hand. Almost all of these organizations are split between open and secret members. The former can be usefully broken down into leaders and active followers. Active followers are visible members who attend regular meetings, paint slogans on walls, and can be counted on to turn up at rallies. Secret or supporting members are those behind the scenes, people who share an organization's beliefs and goals, subscribe to its publications, and often donate funds, but are not prepared to do so openly.

TABLE 2:

GENERAL CHARACTERISTICS OF 448 MEMBERS OF RADICAL-RIGHT ORGANIZATIONS

	Ont.	B.C.	Alta.	Other*	Total	%**
Place of residence	338	72	10	28	448	100
	(75%)	(16%)	(2%)	(6%)		
Sex						
male	297	56	10	27	390	87
female	41	16	—	1	58	13
Urban/rural dimension						
urban	264	69	7	19	359	95
rural	13	2	2	2	19	5
Total	277	71	9	21	378	100
Unknown	61	1	1	7	70	—
Position in organization						
leader	22	9	2	7	40	9
active follower	131	12	7	3	153	35
supporting member	173	50	1	18	242	56
Total	326	71	10	28	435	56
Unknown	22	1	—	—	13	—

*'Other' means provinces other than Ontario, British Columbia, and Alberta, or beyond Canada.

**In this table, percentages are calculated in terms of known cases.

Most of the radical-right members were Protestants between 20 and 40 years of age; many came from broken homes and were themselves separated or divorced. In terms of ethnic origin, the vast majority were Eastern European or British. The involvement of the former stemmed from their concern about communism, and often a more or less deep-rooted anti-Semitism that they or their parents had carried with them to Canada. Those of British background lamented the dilution of Canada's British flavour brought about by Third World immigration, and saw the rampant changes in society as a threat to their position as the dominant ethnic group. The educational background of the radical right is perhaps more surprising, at least according to my limited data. Often the extreme right is dismissed as the gathering ground for the ignorant and uneducated, with the assumption that if only we could get them back to school they would see the error of their ways. Yet 62 per cent of the 93 individuals for whom I have solid data had attended university, college, or technical school.[35] Moreover, I suspect that this percentage can be generalized to all 448 radical-right members. It is probable that my 93 cases consist of the most visible members of the radical right, including leaders and active followers. The sector least represented is that of the supporting members. Often they remain anonymous because they are well-educated, economically secure, and reluctant to jeopardize their positions. Supporting members constitute the largest of the three categories, and it is possible that if all of them were included, the educational level of the radical right would be even higher than I have reported. One thing, therefore, is certain: we may question the quality and type of education that these individuals have received, but to see education *per se* as the panacea for the crippling problems brought on by racism is simplistic and superficial.[36]

Beliefs

It may be erroneous to dismiss the far right as a handful of illiterate roughnecks, but what about their mental status? Is the popular image of the white supremacist and neo-fascist as a wild-eyed maniac, totally out of tune with reality, also wrong? Consider the following beliefs, stated in the course of my interviews: the CN tower in Toronto was built as a communications satellite for Jews in Canada, in order for them to direct Jews around the globe in pursuit of world domination; the Mississauga train disaster in the 1970s never occurred—it was simply a ruse to cover up the evidence of a secret civil war then raging in Canada between Jews and Aryans, involving as well Russian, French, and British troops; Queen Elizabeth II has arranged for airplanes to fly constantly over the Toronto residence of one white supremacist, to protect this future leader of a fascist Canada; thousands of German Nazi soldiers have lived underground in Antarctica since the Second World War, and soon will emerge to fulfil Hitler's dreams; Hitler himself was actually a Jew, but a good one, for he realized that Jews were a menace to society and had to be culled out; watching TV is dangerous because of the subliminal messages meant to weaken the moral fibre of white people; white sugar causes homosexuality.

Most Canadians, I assume, would dismiss these views as ridiculous, but that would also be the reaction of many members of the radical right. As the leaders have sometimes complained, the movement attracts too many nuts and misfits, whose bizarre ideas undermine everyone's reputation. That does not mean, however, that the more conventional beliefs and goals of the far right are merely variations on the political philosophy that informs the establishment parties. Central to radical-right beliefs are blatant racism and anti-Semitism. Black people, according to the white supremacists, are genetically inferior. Often scientific studies are cited such as Jenson's work on IQ,[37] or Coon's contention that blacks evolved into *Homo sapiens* 200,000 years later than whites, which supposedly accounts for their purported incapacity for civilization.[38] Inter-racial breeding is said to be more dangerous than the atomic bomb. Race-mixing is portrayed as unnatural—literally against nature, bound to fail. Race riots, rather than being deplorable, are seen as occasions to rejoice; they are merely natural manifestations of the antagonism between different species, and may be a sign that white people are finally waking up. Similarly, if blacks are raping white women and looting shops, they are not to be blamed—they are supposedly only doing what comes naturally.

Sometimes the perspective of the white supremacist has been more sophisticated. Thus when I interviewed David Duke, a formerly prominent Klan leader in the US, who had considerable influence on the Klan's development in Canada in the early 1980s under Alexander McQuirter, he asked whether it was fair for a person to be hired because of his or her skin colour, rather than qualifications. The punchline was that in Duke's view it was white people, not blacks, who were being discriminated against—the consequence of affirmative-action programs. McQuirter, for his part, distinguished between positive and negative racism. He denied that he hated blacks, and claimed his only concern was to stand up for the rights of white people, who in his opinion were teetering on the verge of extinction. Numerous white supremacists claimed that white people had a moral responsibility to look after the 'inferior' races; racial segregation, in their view, would be as beneficial to blacks as to whites, for blacks would no longer have to compete with whites and suffer daily reminders of their inadequacies.

McQuirter sometimes stated that whites are not superior in all things. The Japanese and the Chinese, in his opinion, are more talented than whites in mathematical endeavours. But that just demonstrates, according to him, that the races are indeed different, and that white people have a peculiar genius: they don't sit around all day counting numbers—instead, they are explorers, given to creative ventures.

Whereas blacks are regarded by the neo-fascists as stupid, Jews are thought to be exceptionally intelligent. Yet in the judgement of the far right, that simply makes them more dangerous; besides, unlike the 'generous and humane' gentile, the Jew's intelligence is supposedly destructive and misanthropic—sure indications that Jews are the children of the Devil.

The right-wing members I interviewed repeatedly dismissed the Holocaust as a hoax, arguing that Jews were actually safer inside the Nazi concentration camps than outside them. Some also argued that Jews have no claim to Israel at all, as the vast majority are said to be the descendants of the Khazars, a southern Russian people who converted to Judaism in the ninth century. The media, financial institutions, and the courts (often the term 'jewdicial' system is used) are supposedly controlled by Jews, with ZOG (Zionist Occupation Government) just around the corner. Communism and capitalism are said to be in cahoots, twin programs directed by Jews en route to fulfilling their long-established international conspiracy to dominate the world. Race riots are seen as products of that conspiracy, as blacks and whites, manipulated by Jews, kill each other off. In one respect, the members of the far right often express reluctant admiration for Jews: in their view, Zionism itself is racist, and Jews are the world's most virulent and successful racial supremacists. With all this in mind, Jews and blacks can be forgiven for being skeptical of the radical right's claim that it could be either minority's best friend.

Activities

Although the Canadian radical right has been bellicose in ideology, advocating the forceful overthrow of 'the Jewish-controlled, liberal-left establishment', it has not been as violent as its counterpart below the border. A great deal of its activity has been directed internally, to holding regular meetings and preaching to the already converted; when its attention has turned to the wider society, it has usually (though not always) taken the form of dispersing racist propaganda, rather than physically attacking minorities. Of course, the definitions of 'violence' could arguably be stretched to embrace the mere message that blacks are stupid or Jews are dangerous. That message probably foments racial strain at least indirectly, increasing the chance of physical confrontation. Moreover, from the victim's perspective, racist propaganda may be regarded as only minutely less painful than a punch in the face.

The main organizations, like the Western Guard and the Nationalist Party, have produced their own regular publications. Some groups have set down explicit guidelines for manipulating public opinion, such as how to write a letter to the editor, and how to obtain media coverage. Right-wing representatives have been interviewed on radio talk shows, and have occasionally appeared on TV. Some of them—usually the most prominent members—have contested elections. Andrews, for example, the current leader of the Nationalist Party, ran for mayor of Toronto in 1972, 1974, and 1976, gaining 1,958 (1 per cent), 5,792 (4.6 per cent) and 7,129 (5.3 per cent) votes. Others have run for alderman and for positions on boards of education. There was virtually no delusion that they would be victorious in these elections; instead, the purpose was merely to take advantage of the public forum in order to put across the white-supremacist viewpoint. On dozens of occasions, leaflets denouncing communist and Jewish leaders and proclaiming white superiority have been distributed, and similar messages painted on construction hoardings, synagogues, and churches. Dollar bills with 'white power' stamped on them were at times sent to prominent minority members—a contribution towards their return fares to Africa or wherever. In the 1980s, the Klan has engaged in several cross-burnings, and this organization and others have made concerted efforts to recruit in secondary schools, aided at times by teachers who invited them to address their students.[39] Attempts have also been made, sometimes successfully, to infiltrate anti-racist organizations. Despite all this activity, the time has been found to celebrate the birthdays of Hitler and Mussolini.

In 1971 Geza Matrai, a Hungarian refugee who has since emerged as the dominating force behind the Canadian Anti-Soviet Action Committee (CASAC), gained fame in right-wing circles when he managed to leap onto the back of former Soviet Premier Kosygin on a state visit to Ottawa. A decade later the Toronto-based Klan announced its plans to establish training camps for the use of firearms and explosives. This was mostly a propaganda ploy. Indeed, when the radical right has moved beyond propaganda to outright violence, its opponents have more often than not been the left wing. The days of the Edmund Burke Society were marked by the 'counter-demonstration', as the right wing did battle on the streets with left-wing student organizations opposed to the Vietnam War. In recent years that pattern has repeated itself: the Ku Klux Klan could hold a rally in downtown Toronto and attract only a handful of blacks and Jews, but CPC-ML (Communist Party of Canada-Marxist-Leninist) forces would be there to confront it, as well as other left-wing groups.

It is common knowledge that the left wing is internally divided to a remarkable degree, often because of competing interpretations of Marxist-Leninist philosophy or dogma, but the same is true of the right wing. This is not, however, due to conflicting interpretations of right-wing ideology—for the most part, the racist world-view is straightforward and simplistic. But the right wing is often divided over strategy and tactics: whether to concentrate on building an organization of true believers or on dispersing propaganda to the wider public; whether to openly promote the goals of white supremacy or to conceal these behind a more presentable façade; whether to aim the message at all white people or to focus on the cream of the crop—the presumed 'true' Aryan, distinct from Slavs and southern Europeans, who at times are referred to as 'semi-Jews' or 'semi- niggers'. Then, too, there is the competition for top dog—the *Führer* syndrome. The effortless arrogance of the true believer—especially among the leadership—makes it unacceptable to play second fiddle, or even for organizations to meaningfully co-operate with each other, perhaps *because* the ideological dif-

ferences among them are so minute. Finally, there is the mental outlook of the committed racists. These people spend a large part of their
conscious deliberations despising the bulk of the world's population.
Consumed by massive negativity, searching for hidden conspiracies
around every corner, the members of the far right have been program-
med to think the worst about each other.

It would be wrong to conclude from the internal dissension of the
radical right in Canada that the movement in general is in disarray.
There does exist some semblance of an international right-wing network. Canadian-based organizations often exchange publications with
organizations abroad. Committed racists and anti-Semites from countries like the US and Britain occasionally visit their counterparts in
Canada, and the converse. Sometimes conferences are organized, attracting true believers from several nations. Members of the Canadian
far right have also been in contact with fascists in other countries (and
reputedly even with representatives of foreign governments), with the
purpose of obtaining financial backing. Although my information suggests that they occasionally were successful in these endeavours, most
of the finances for the far right in Canada came from membership fees,
the sales of literature, small donations, gainful employment, and various illegal schemes, such as the Ku Klux Klan's scam with counterfeit
birth certificates and passports.[40]

The wider society

How has the radical right been able to exist in Canada, a country that
has enjoyed an enviable reputation for racial tolerance? As Hughes and
Kallen have observed, racism in Canada has been as deeply rooted as in
the United States.[41] When Canada emerged from the experience of colonization, the major victims were, as in every other such case, the native peoples. Valentine has pointed out that as a result of successive
government strategies to dominate and control native peoples, today
they 'have the lowest incomes, the poorest health, and the highest rates
of unemployment of any single group in the country.'[42] They are also
over-represented in jails and under-represented in the educational system. In some cases, such as that of the now extinct Beothuk of New-
foundland in the eighteenth century, native peoples were the victims of
outright slaughter.[43] Many Canadians probably are not aware that their
country once was host to slavery. The first slaves were Indian captives
sold to traders.[44] Eventually black slaves were brought to Canada, and
in Nova Scotia there were slave sales and newspaper advertisements for
runaways.[45] Indeed, slavery lasted longer in Canada than in the northern United States, and many fugitive slaves actually escaped from
Canada to New England.[46]

In 1849 racial segregation was legalized in schools in Ontario.[47] As
late as the 1930s, in Alberta, an Indian student who had won a prize for

obtaining the highest academic standing in Grade 12 was told that she did not qualify. In the same decade a black student was refused a scholarship that she had won, on the assumption that no opportunities to use it would be offered to her.[48] In British Columbia classrooms in the 1950s and 1960s, Grade 4 students still used a workbook called *Ten Little Niggers*.[49]

It was during the 1930s that swastika clubs began to emerge in the country, and although fascists like Arcand and Taylor were interned for the duration of the Second World War, that was also the period when Canadian government officials shut the country's doors to Jewish refugees.[50] This brings us to the topic of immigration. As Kallen has stated: 'A racist immigration policy is one of the most invidious techniques utilized by those in power to guarantee their ethnic ascendancy in any society.'[51] More than 15,000 Chinese had been brought to Canada to work on the Canadian Pacific Railway, but when it was completed in 1885, a head tax, eventually reaching $500, was established to discourage further Chinese immigration.[52] Until 1953 'climatic suitability' was formally included in the Immigration Act. As Corbett[53] and Frideres[54] have concluded, Canada's immigration policy up to that point was formally and explicitly racist. Although significant changes in immigration policy have been introduced since then, a number of scholarly studies continue to demonstrate the existence of widespread racism in the country. Outstanding among these is an investigation of employment opportunities conducted by Henry and Ginzberg, who found that whites have three job prospects to every one for blacks.[55]

Many Canadians, I suspect, would be prepared to dismiss the radical right as a foreign entity—or perhaps as an American virus that temporarily has crossed the border—with virtually no implications for the wider society. Yet as this brief survey suggests, the racism embedded in the wider society has provided an environment hospitable to white-supremacist organizations. It is not my contention that the former has 'caused' the latter. Indeed, a much more interesting question, to which I now turn, is whether the two have a common source: namely, the Canadian state.

The state and the police

Let me sketch out two opposing models. From the state's perspective, racism appears to be regarded as a regrettable but atypical social problem, located, when it does occur, among the ranks of the ignorant masses. The mandate of the enlightened state is to employ its forces, including the police and the courts, to protect minority members from the vile assaults launched by deviant members of society. There are a number of variations on this model, all of which flash the reassuring message that the state is not culpable. For example, racism can be written off as the short-lived consequence of social rupture, such as a downswing in the economy or a sharp increase in Third World immigration. Racial and ethnic tension can be explained away as almost 'natural' primordial loyalties that have been given renewed meaning in a rapidly changing world. Then, too, there is the 'immigrant analogy': the notion that each new wave of immigrants must almost inevitably endure a period of more or less severe prejudice and discrimination until the next wave becomes the target. Even if it is accepted that institutional racism existed in the past—embedded, for example, in immigration policy—there is a ready answer: such practices merely reflected the discriminatory tendencies rooted in the wider society; in other words, it was the people, not the government, who were racists. Moreover, it can be argued with considerable justification that in recent decades Canada as a nation has become much more open and democratic, as evidenced by a keen concern about human rights, attempts to rid immigration policy of its most blatant bigotry, and legal restrictions on a wide range of discriminatory behaviour based on race, ethnicity, and religion. The very fact that Canada has been transformed from a closed, highly controlled society to a more open and liberal one can be used to defend the state: these changes usher in their own problems, such as the increased potential for a wide spectrum of social and political protest, including that on the far right.

The far-left perspective provides quite a different picture. Here we find the assertions that the police are fascists, that racism is intrinsic to the capitalist system, and that a degree of complicity exists between white-supremacist, neo-Nazi organizations and the state itself. Many Marxists would contend that the various organizations that constitute the radical right and the racism embedded in the institutions of the wider society are related manifestations of efforts by the wealthy to divide the poor, and in that way to sustain patterns of power and privilege.

Those of us who want to champion the liberal-democratic state may be inclined to dismiss the far-left perspective as ideological nonsense. Yet a sober analysis suggests that it is the state's model, at least as I have characterized it, that is more vulnerable to criticism. First of all, the assumption that racism in Canada has amounted to little more than a few ephemeral social dislocations and the acts of a scattered handful of deviant actors is sharply repudiated by the significant degree to which discrimination has been institutionalized.[56] As regards the tendency of members of ethnic groups to band together, undoubtedly that is a fact of the contemporary social scene. But inter-ethnic conflicts are generally animated by the underlying division of labour, reflecting the class structure of a society. Moreover, ethnic strain does not equal racism; indeed, by emphasizing ethnic strains in place of racial ones, the degree of racism in a society is often obscured. The 'immigrant analogy' is equally misleading; while successive waves of European immigrants may well have found acceptance and prosperity in due time, that has not always been the experience of dark-skinned immigrants. For them, discrimination is not merely a hurdle for the first generation—each successive generation must confront the obstacle anew. Similarly, today's more open and liberal society may well give birth to a wide range of extreme social and political behaviour. But to interpret the emergence of fascist-oriented groups advocating racial purity solely on these grounds is to ignore the long history of the phenomenon, dating back at least to the 1920s.

A review of the relevant theoretical and historical issues adds force to these critical remarks about the state. There is a line of liberal argument, represented notably by Lipset,[57] that conceives of fascist movements as extremism at the centre—a middle-class protest against both capitalism and socialism, brought about by the frustration and alienation accompanying rapid social change and the actor's relative or absolute downward status mobility. An alternative, possibly more plausible, interpretation is Horton's argument that 'right tendencies are always inherit in capitalism in crisis',[58] or Dixon's, that right- wing resurgence is a response to a world crisis in capitalist accumulation.[59] Their viewpoints echo the well-known slogan that fascism constitutes the last refuge of capitalism. As far as racism *per se* is concerned, Nikolinakos may have been overly provocative in claiming that capitalist countries that have not inherited a racial problem have created one for themselves.[60] Yet an understanding of the essential nature of racism leads us to ponder the state's position. Ethnocentrism may be as old as organized social interaction, but racism is not. Racism as an ideology took root during the era of European colonization, thus coinciding with the advent of capitalism. While there are several pre-conditions to racial ideology, including ethnocentrism, xenophobia, nationalism, and scapegoating, as well as the self-doubt and insecurity that are part of the human psyche, racism above all else is a political phenomenon. As Baker has stated: 'Race relations are essentially group power contests.'[61] In Ruth Benedict's words: 'Racism remains . . . merely another instance of the persecution of minorities for the advantage of those in power.'[62] Hughes and Kallen wrote: 'Racism, in the context of majority-minority relations, is a political tool, wielded by the dominant ethnic group to justify the status quo and rationalize the disability to which the minority group is subject.'[63] As the locus of power and authority, the state would appear to be implicated in the racial syndrome.[64]

In terms of the historical record, the first thing to make clear is the actual character of the nation's past. Conventional wisdom, even academic wisdom,[65] suggests that in comparison with that of the United States, Canada's history has been placid and harmonious. The ready explanation concerns our admirable values of tolerance, order, and respect for authority. Is this reading of Canadian history a myth? Such was the conclusion that one author arrived at almost two decades ago. McNaught argued that not only is Canada's non-violent image belied by its past, but also that violence in Canada has had a special character: to a much greater extent than in the United States, it has been linked to the state.[66] Echoing McNaught's thesis, Reg Whitaker, in his contribution to this volume, distinguishes between state repression and political repression. The latter, consisting of coercive forces in interest groups and private organizations outside the state apparatus, has not been nearly as prevalent in Canada as state repression.

Even more damning, in terms of a possible right-wing bias, has been the actual manner in which the state's repressive machinery has been employed. The consistent target of repression, at least in the past, has been the left wing. The official historian of the RCMP has confirmed that between the two world wars the RCMP's main target was the Communist Party of Canada.[67] On the verge of the Second World War, as Whitaker has reported, the head of the RCMP's security service warned the government that communism, not fascism, was the real menace. Indeed, it is difficult not to agree with Elizabeth Grace and Colin Leys in their paper that from the point of view of Canada's security forces, subversion has meant anti-capitalist ideas and activities, not anti-democratic ones. The irony is that the communist phobia appears to have been largely misplaced. Both Whittaker and Grace and Leys point out that the communists in Canada neither conspired to nor advocated the violent overthrow of the government. Moreover, in today's world, communist parties throughout the West appear to have accepted the democratic electoral process. Certainly, as Grant Amyot has shown, this is the case as regards the Italian Communist Party (PCI), and the same, it must be said, holds true for Le Pen's right-wing National Front in France (while several organizations in Canada are similar in their ideology to the National Front, none has gained even a small victory at the ballot box).

Could it be that the anti-communist phobia and repressive thrust of the state apparatus are things of the past, snuffed out by a more open, just, and mature political climate? As pointed out in the 1986-87 SIRC Report, CSIS appeared to take little interest in attempts to raise funds for the contras in Nicaragua, while perceiving opposition to the government in El Salvador (and its US supporters) as evidence of subversion.[68] As Grace and Leys suggest, an anti-left bias apparently continues to operate in CSIS.

As far as my own study of the right wing is concerned, I found a wide range of contradictory attitudes regarding the political orientation of the police. Members of visible minorities often saw policemen as representative of the enemy. One black person, a professional man with his roots dating back several generations in western Canada, told me of being stopped by a policeman on the street and ordered to produce evidence of his Canadian citizenship. Another prominent black person in Toronto was accosted by police who mistook him for a fugitive—perhaps an example of the 'they all look alike' syndrome in action. Occasionally the police have pulled over blacks driving expensive vehicles, on the assumption that the latter were stolen or obtained by other illegal means. Emmett Cardinal Carter observed in his report on tensions between the police and minorities in Toronto: 'Perhaps nothing in all my research was more universal than a sense of frustration about real or fancied injustice or harassment at the hands of police officers.'[69] As Charles Roach has pointed out, racial prejudice among policemen is a much more serious problem than among citizens at large, because the police possess the legitimate power and force to act out their prejudices on innocent victims.[70] From the viewpoint of the right wing, policemen have often been regarded as silent partners in the grand design to halt the decline of Western civilization. In the 1960s the Edmund Burke Society distributed flyers with the message 'Our Cops are Tops', and John Beattie, the Canadian Nazi Party's head man, urged Canadian citizens to teach their children that policemen are their friends. A former head of Metro Toronto's Ethnic Squad remarked in 1981 that the rigid right includes senior police officers.[71] An intelligence officer in British Columbia pointed out to me that non-reflective policemen are inclined to agree with much of the right wing's conservative platform, without questioning the implied racist message. It is well known, moreover, that policemen in the US have been disproportionately attracted to racist organizations like the Ku Klux Klan.[72]

All of this would seem to lend credibility to the left-wing claim that the police themselves have right-wing, perhaps even fascist, leanings.[73] Yet there is another side to the story. What has been remarkable about Canada is that to my knowledge so few policemen have been members of the organized right wing. This in itself does not disprove an unconscious, structured bias within the various police services in favour of the right over the left. But it is a fact, at least in recent years, that the police have played a major role in containing Canada's right wing. Members of the Edmund Burke Society soon realized that the police were not very eager to respond to the proffered partnership. Indeed, before that organization folded in 1972, it had begun to complain about the unfair treatment of the 'political police'. Over the years, undercover police agents and hired infiltrators—including such *agents provocateurs* as Robert Toope in the Western Guard—have provided constant surveillance of the principal far-right organizations. As I eventually realized while conducting my study, there probably was very little that I learned about the right wing (in terms of facts, if not analysis) that was not already known by the nation's various intelligence agencies.[74]

Any effort to understand the police's role regarding the right wing and racism must consider two important issues. First, policing by its very nature is conservative, an effort to maintain the status quo. Attempts by the police to contain and eradicate the radical right do not necessarily reflect a dedicated opposition to it. Rather, the police are opposed to all sectors of society that upset the applecart, including the extreme right as well as the extreme left. As one policeman commented, life for his colleagues would be a lot easier without the looney left and the rigid right.

The second issue has even greater implications, and applies not only to the police but also to the state in general. The ambiguity surrounding the police forces' orientation to racism, with some of the evidence condemning them and some of it applauding them, is instructive. In my judgement, there is currently a deep contradiction within the state apparatus regarding racial matters, in that official sectors of society flawed by racist inclinations and an anti-left orientation, institutionalized over the decades, should now be participating in eradicating racism and restricting the right wing, in response to the new values of openness, liberty, and justice. Conditioned as it is by the two sides of the contradiction, the Canadian state flip-flops back and forth between highly publicized (and even genuine) attacks on racism and heated denials that the country has a problem at all—which only deepen it. A great deal of the ambiguity surrounding the police forces' relationship to racism is a product of that contradiction.

The politics of opposition

From the perspective of the Canadian state and its citizens, there are several compelling reasons for opposing the radical right. The first is the deceptive issue of anti-communism. The far right, when compared to the anti-capitalist far left, may appear to be the more hospitable force, but the fact is that anti-communism is a major issue only in the ranks of the fringe right. Many members of the ultra-right do indeed start out as anti-communists, but by the time they commit themselves to the fascist cause, anti-communism has been rendered secondary, overwhelmed by the politics of racial purity and anti-Semitism. Furthermore, right-wing opposition to communism does not add up to support for the capitalist system. Not only is the far right adamantly opposed to what it labels 'speculative, financial or monopoly' capitalism, but it also is fundamentally against the democratic system. Recall the words of Arcand, who dismissed liberal democracy as an invention of the Jews, intended to to put a throttlehold on the world's finances. In short, the far right in Canada does not seek merely to defeat the forces of communism, and in that way to defend the political integrity of the country: it aspires to replace capitalism and democracy with fascism.[75]

There are other reasons for lowering the boom on the radical right. A political program that advocates privilege and power for a minority of the world's population on the basis of pigmentation and genes alone is morally offensive. Then too, there is the far right's philosophical position. Seizing on what in essence are nothing more than pan-human weaknesses—the search for scapegoats, ethnocentrism, xenophobia, and unease in the face of social change—the radical right does not attempt to surmount these flaws in the human condition but, rather, exploits them, driving the wedge in deeper. A society based on such a misanthropic philosophy can hardly be expected to be counted among the high points of history. And if these political, moral, and philosophical objections are not enough, there is always the pragmatic one. Few issues can create more havoc in contemporary society than racism and anti-Semitism. If organizations like the Klan, the Western Guard, and the Aryan Nations are left unopposed, will multicultural Canada be able to withstand the strain?

It is one thing to contend that the far right ought to be opposed, if only because it poses a threat to the quality of Canadian democracy. It is quite another matter to indicate just how that opposition can be achieved. Whenever groups like the Ku Klux Klan have barged into the public eye, there has been no lack of individuals and organizations to confront them. Anti-racists, however, soon discover that in order to lay hands on the white supremacists, they must tip-toe through a minefield. For example, should a distinction be made between prejudice (attitudes) and discrimination (action)? Should people be permitted to think and say what they wish, as long as they don't put their ideas into play and actually go out and attack someone? Does the answer depend on the setting—public or private? During my interviews in Alberta in relation to the James Keegstra case, even many of his opponents said that if the man wants to stand on the street corner and mouth his pet theories, who cares? What they were against was the articulation of racist and anti-Semitic ideas in the school system and in the town's council chambers (Keegstra had been a secondary-school teacher and the mayor of the town of Eckville).

There is also the dilemma between freedom of expression and freedom from prejudice and discrimination. Which is the more critical value? Of paramount importance here are the different perspectives of non-victims and victims. The former (like myself) can indulge in abstract discussions of the fundamental significance of freedom of speech. The latter don't have that luxury. And one thing is certain: in no society in the world is freedom of speech unlimited, nor could it be, for it inevitably runs up against other values. Even within the university community there are taboo subjects—to some extent, racism itself is one. Members of the right wing almost always attempt to convert their causes into freedom-of-expression issues, as in the Keegstra and Ernst Zundel cases. Yet what is often not realized is that the racists and anti-Semites themselves draw the line when *their* enemies, such as the left wing and the gay community, speak out against them.

The attempt to confront committed racists is sometimes described as a catch-22 situation. Should the racists be ignored or opposed? If one ignores them, is that tantamount to condoning them? If one opposes them, does that in effect promote them by expanding their profile? Over and over again, when faced with an onslaught from the government, the police, the various human-rights commissions, or anti-racist groups, members of the far right have expressed pleasure. Attacks against the Klan, remarked McQuirter, were badges of honour; they were signs that the organization was gaining ground—otherwise it would have been ignored. As often was said in right-wing circles, the liberal-left establishment (which, from the far-right perspective, includes the Tory party) will only smear those they fear. No doubt some of these reactions can be dismissed as wishful thinking or mere rationalization. Yet opposition can constitute a mutually sustaining social relationship, in which racist and anti-racist groups feed off each other.

Sometimes anti-racist activists have distinguished between what is known as the insulation or isolation technique and overt, aggressive opposition to racists and anti-Semites. The first should not be confused with the avoidance syndrome—burying one's head in the sand and hoping that the problem will fade away. The insulation technique is an active policy, and immensely more effective: it amounts to denying racist organizations a public profile. But its usefulness is over when the fortunes of racist organizations dramatically improve, as reflected in an increased constituency. Yet even the decision to openly and aggressively oppose organizations and individuals, such as the Klan and Keegstra in the 1980s, is not unambiguous. What constitutes effective, overt opposition? Should organizations like the Klan be banned? Would that simply drive them underground, leaving the problem unsolved, or perhaps encouraging fascists to conceal their spots and join fringe-right groups? If far-right organizations are banned, where does one draw the line? Would that mean banning any group opposed to the status quo?

The repeated reaction of most politicians to the far-right resurgence in the early 1980s was to express repugnance about white supremacists and anti-Semites, but to declare that nothing can be done until they break the laws of the land. Somewhat humorously, in one case involving a small Ku Klux Klan adventure in the Yukon, the politicians were shown to be very wrong. Dozens of citizens of Whitehorse, led by a 490-pound civil servant, visited the Klan leaders and suggested that it would be wise to fold up the operation. They did so promptly.

Despite what appear to be almost insurmountable obstacles to effective curtailment of the far right, it is my firm opinion that an ascending racist right must not be allowed to roam unchecked. To argue otherwise—because of a deep commitment to free speech or for any other reason—is to stand back and watch as the rights of minorities are trampled underfoot. This does not mean, however, that a special police force such as CSIS should be involved in monitoring the radical right—or the radical left, for that matter. It is true that in each of the main far-right organizations there are usually at least a couple of individuals prone to violent acts. And it is a fact that some of these organizations, through their international contacts, occasionally engage in what the state might interpret as seditious or subversive behaviour. Essentially, though, the far right's actions and beliefs are matters of legality and morality. If members of organizations like the Klan break the laws of the land, which they often do, existing police agencies are there to deal with them. If white supremacists and anti-Semites offend the morality of the nation, and do so with impunity because the legal system—despite the new anti-hate laws—is impotent, then it is perhaps time to write into the criminal code a carefully constructed but more effective system of laws addressed to racial prejudice and discrimination.

Conclusion

The peculiar nature of the far-right threat to the Canadian democratic system is that to some extent it constitutes an attack from within, generated in part by the properties of capitalism itself and therefore all the more seductive and insidious. The twin programs of fascism and racism, one might say, are for Western democracies the sociological equivalent of Freud's psychological *id*. A well-balanced individual does not permit the *id* free reign, and it is my personal conviction that the vast majority of Canadians would be equally reluctant to allow the 'dark side' of capitalist democracy—the fascist and racist elements—to dim the values of justice and liberty. Yet while Canada as a nation has moved a considerable distance from the closed, authoritative regime of the past, I fear that in the future racism is likely to become a greater rather than a lesser social problem. The only hope, left-wing enthusiasts might contend, is a socialist revolution. But that scenario is unrealistic. Canada is not about to be transformed into another Soviet satellite; moreover, it is far from proven that racism and anti-Semitism become obsolete with the triumph of socialism. In practical terms, it is not a Marxist-inspired revolution that is going to solve our problems; nor is CSIS surveillance of 'subversives' going to do the trick. Perhaps the best we can hope for is a criminal-justice system that will sustain the nation's ethical integrity in the field of race relations. Such a system will not in itself put an end to prejudice and discrimination. But it may help to defuse the potential racial powder-kegs of the future.

Notes

C.E.S. FRANKS: INTRODUCTION

[1]See the report of the commission: Commission of Inquiry Concerning Certain Activities of the Royal Canadian Mounted Police, Second Report, *Freedom and Security Under the Law* (Ottawa: Minister of Supply and Services, 1981), vol. I, part III, 'Problems in the System . . . RCMP Practices and Activities Not Authorized or Provided for by Law—Institutionalized Wrongdoing'.

[2]See C.E.S. Franks, 'The Political Control of Security Activities', *Queen's Quarterly* 91, no. 3 (Autumn 1984), pp. 565-77.

[3]Canada, *Security and Intelligence Review Committee, Annual Report, 1986-87*, p. 33.

[4]Ibid., p. 40.

[5]Ibid., p. 37.

[6]Ibid., p. 40.

[7]A useful study of CSIS is Geoffrey R. Weller, 'The Canadian Security Intelligence Service Under Stress', *Canadian Public Administration* 31, no. 2 (Summer 1988), pp. 239-302.

[8]Brian Chapman, *Police State* (London: Macmillan, 1970), pp. 82-3.

[9]Patrick Devlin, *The Enforcement of Morals* (Oxford: Oxford University Press, 1965), pp. 12-14.

JOHN D. WHYTE AND ALLAN MACDONALD: DISSENT AND NATIONAL SECURITY AND DISSENT SOME MORE

[1]Statutes of Canada 1984, c.21.

[2]Ibid., s.12.

[3]Ibid., s.12.

[4]Ibid., s.2.

[5]Ibid., s.13.

[6]Ibid., s.14.

[7]Ibid., s.15.

[8]Ibid., s.2.

[9]H. Kalven,'The Partial Sanction: A General Analysis', in J. Kalven, ed., *A Worthy Tradition: Freedom of Speech in America* (New York: Harper and Row, 1988), p. 301.

[10]Ibid., pp. 301-14.

[11]The connection between the activity of contracting and the political structure of democracy is more fully explored in M. Pickard, 'Why Joseph Borowski Has Standing', *University of Toronto Law Journal* 36 (1986), pp. 48-51.

[12]See J. Whyte, 'Legality and Legitimacy', *Queen's Law Journal* 12 (1987), p. 1.

[13]The connection between the idea of liberty and the responsibility to make change is drawn in this passage from A. Nevins and H. Commager, *A Pocket History of the United States*, 5th ed. (New York: Washington Square Press, 1967):

> What is Man born for, but to be a Reformer, a Remaker of what man has made, a renouncer of lies, a restorer of truth and good?' So asked Emerson at the

beginning of the era of reform. And when, with the Civil War, that era drew to a close and materialism took over, the great editor-reformer Horace Greeley looked back upon it and concluded that 'though the life of the Reformer may seem rugged and arduous, it were hard to say that any other was worth living at all. . . . Not to have been a Reformer is not to have truly lived (p. 174).

14For a general statement of the purpose behind the rule of law see *Roncarelli* v. *Duplessis* [1959] *Supreme Court Reports*, p. 121.

15*Dominion Law Reports* (4th), 19 (1985), pp. 22-3.

16P. Hanks, 'National Security: A Political Concept', *Monash University Law Review* 14, p. 114.

17See, e.g., M. Rankin, 'National Security: Information, Accountability, and the Canadian Security Intelligence Service', *University of Toronto Law Journal* 36 (1986) in which it is observed: 'When US President Nixon fought to remain in office . . . it was national security that was most frequently advanced as the reason for not allowing access to his records and materials' (p. 250).

18This admittedly controversial claim is based on the quality of political rhetoric in the early nineteenth century in America; see, e.g., Nevins and Commager, *Pocket History of the United States*, pp. 158-74.

19Rankin, 'National Security', p. 253.

20See, for example, J. Callwood, 'Target for abortion foes, tough carpenter is a hero to staff at clinic', *Globe and Mail*, 17 Feb. 1988, p. A2.

21D. Apter, 'Notes on the Underground: Left Violence and the National State' in S. Graubard, *The State* (New York: W.W. Norton, 1981), p. 156.

22Security Intelligence Review Committee, *Annual Report, 1986-87* (1987), p. 23.

23Ibid., p. 37.

24M.L. Friedland, 'National Security: The Legal Dimensions', (Ottawa: Commission of Inquiry Concerning Certain Activities of the Royal Canadian Mounted Police, 1979).

25Revised Statutes of Canada 1970, c. C-34, as amended.

26Ibid., c. O-3, as amended.

27Ibid., c. W-2.

28Friedland, 'National Security'; with regard to suggested changes to the section on sabotage, see p. 49.

29Cf. *R.* v. *Barron* (1918) *Canadian Criminal Cases* 30, p. 326 (Sask. C.A.) and *R.* v. *Weir* (1929), *Canadian Criminal Cases* 52, p. 111 (Ont. Co. Ct.).

30Ibid., p. 117

31[1951] *Supreme Court Reports*, p. 265.

32Ibid., p. 288.

33Why the concept of subversion fails to provide guidance has been summarized by R.J. Spjut ('Defining Subversion', *British Journal of Law and Society* 6 [1979]) as follows:

There is no concept of 'subversion' in constitutional law and the word has no generally understood meaning for political and legal theorists. In constitutional law, the abuse of liberty is proscribed only if a criminal offence is committed, and this, as a rule, must portend or actually breach public peace. Violence may be an unlawful assembly, riot or even treason; the advocacy of violence may be incitement or seditious libel. These offenses are normative concepts in that they define precisely behaviour which threatens public order or the state (p. 254).

Here Spjut cites for authority Max Lerner's definition of 'political offenders': 'conspiracy, rebellion, sedition, treason, lese majesty, assassination, military destruction and mutiny'. Nowhere does Lerner mention subversion ('Political offenders' in E. Seligman, ed., *Encyclopedia of the Social Sciences*, vol. 11 [New York: Macmillan, 1963], p. 199).

34At a certain level, anyway, such a remark would be ridiculous. The criminal law, after all—at least to the extent it is passed under section 91(27) of the Constitution Act and commensurate with the Charter—is constitutional too.

[35]Joseph Vining, *The Authoritative and the Authoritarian* (Chicago: University of Chicago Press, 1986), p. 61.

[36]About constitutional law and mirrors, Philip Bobbitt (*Constitutional Fate: Theory of the Constitution* [Oxford University Press, 1982] writes:

> The Constitutional law of the United States is not a snapshot; like the mirrored wall behind a ballet dancer's rail, it is not placed so to reflect a particular image but to enable, through patient practice, the creation of an unbroken sequence of images. Thus is the dancer make inseparable from the unceasing changes in the light. We have been taught to think that this mirror showed back only ourselves, just as we were once taught that it would yield nature's secret arrangement. Our teachers were wrong, captivated by a picture of a dancing class, ignoring the inseparable unribboning relationship between the motion that law must be and the participant-spectators whose presence makes the motion meaningful (pp. 248-9).

[37]Michel Foucault, *The History of Sexuality* vol. I, *An Introduction* (New York: Vintage, 1980), pp. 100-1.

[38]E.P. Thomson, 'Customs in Common', lecture presented at Queen's University, 3 Feb. 1988.

[39]For a detailed account of the evolution of surveillance as a mechanism of power, see Michel Foucault, *Discipline and Punish* (New York: Vintage, 1979).

[40]Jean Baudrillard in *The Ecstasy of Communication* (trans. Bernard and Caroline Schutze, ed. Slyvere Lotringer [New York: Semiotext(e), 1987], p. 22):

> We no longer partake of the drama of alienation, but are in the ecstasy of communication. And this ecstasy is obscene. Obscene is that which eliminates the gaze, the image and every representation. Obscenity is not confined to sexuality, because today there is a pornography of information and communication, a pornography of circuits and net-works. . . .
>
> It is no longer the obscenity of the hidden, the repressed, the obscure, but that of the visible, the all-too-visible, the more-visible-than-visible; it is the obscenity of that which no longer contains a secret and is entirely soluble in information and communication.

CHRISTIAN BAY: CIVIL DISOBEDIENCE: THE INNER AND OUTER LIMITS

[1]Robert Michels, *Political Parties: A Sociological Study of the Oligarchical Tendencies of Modern Democracy* (New York: Free Press, 1949).

[2]For a summary, see Lester W. Milbrath and M.L. Goel, *Political Participation*, 2nd ed. (Chicago: Rand McNally, 1977).

[3]See below, p. 49.

[4]Immanuel Kant, *Groundwork of the Metaphysic of Morals* (New York: Harper and Row, 1964).

[5]Jeremy Bentham, *An Introduction to the Principles of Morals and Legislation* (New York: Hafner, 1948).

[6]Christian Bay, 'Civil Disobedience', in *International Encyclopedia of the Social Sciences*, vol. 2 (New York: Macmillan, 1968), p. 473; also in Bay, 'Civil Disobedience: Prerequisite for Democracy in Mass Society', in David Spitz, ed., *Political Theory and Social Change* (New York: Atherton, 1967), p. 166.

[7]See Richard E. Rubenstein, *Alchemists of Revolution: Terrorism in the Modern World* (New York: Basic, 1987).

[8]Peter Rosset and John Vandermeer, eds, *Nicaragua: Unfinished Revolution. The New Nicaragua Reader* (New York: Grove, 1986); Marvin E. Gettleman *et al.*, eds, *El Salvador: Central America in the New Cold War*, rev. and updated (New York: Grove, 1986).

[9]Rubenstein, *Alchemists of Revolution*.

[10]Jean-Jacques Rousseau, *The Social Contract and Discourses* (New York: Dutton, 1973), pp. 131-2.

[11]Ibid., p. 132.

[12]Thomas McPherson, *Political Obligation* (London: Routledge and Kegan Paul, 1967), p. 4.

[13]Ronald Dworkin, *Taking Rights Seriously* (Cambridge, Mass.: Harvard University Press, 1978), pp. 171-3.

[14]Ibid., p. 172.

[15]David Braybrooke, *Meeting Needs* (Princeton: Princeton University Press, 1987), p. 147.

[16]Kant, *Groundwork*.

[17]*Plato's Gorgias* (New York: Liberal Arts Press, 1952).

[18]Braybrooke, *Meeting Needs*, p. 36.

[19]Abraham H. Maslow, *Toward a Psychology of Being* (Princeton, N.J.: Van Nostrand, 1962).

[20]Abraham H. Maslow, *Motivation and Personality* (New York: Harper, 1954).

[21]Ronald Manzer, *Canada: A Socio-Political Report* (Toronto: McGraw-Hill Ryerson, 1974).

[22]Ronald Inglehart, *The Silent Revolution: Changing Values and Political Styles Among Western Publics* (Princeton: Princeton University Press, 1977).

[23]For further amplification, see Christian Bay, *Strategies of Political Emancipation* (Notre Dame, Ind.: University of Notre Dame Press, 1981).

[24]See John Burton, *Deviance, Terrorism & War* (Oxford: Martin Robertson, 1979); Rubenstein, *Alchemists of Revolution*.

[25]Carole Pateman, *The Problem of Political Obligation* (Berkeley: University of California Press, 1979), p. 5 and 'Afterword'.

[26]John Rawls, *A Theory of Justice* (Cambridge, Mass.: Harvard University Press, 1971), p. 366.

[27]Pateman, *Political Obligation*, p. 7.

[28]Ibid.

[29]Michels, *Political Parties*.

[30]Joseph A. Schumpeter, *Capitalism, Socialism, and Democracy*, 5th ed. (London: Allen and Unwin, 1976).

[31]Lester W. Milbrath, *Political Participation* (Chicago: Rand McNally, 1965); Milbrath and Goel, *Political Participation*, 2nd ed.

[32]Cf. C. Wright Mills, *The Power Elite* (New York: Oxford University Press, 1956).

[33]Friedrich Engels, 'The Origin of the Family, Private Property, and the State', in Robert C. Tucker, ed., *The Marx-Engels Reader* (New York: Norton, 1978); Herbert Marcuse, *One-Dimensional Man* (Boston: Beacon, 1964); Jürgen Habermas, *Legitimation Crisis* (Boston: Beacon, 1975).

[34]Cf. above, p. 41.

[35]Philip Alston, 'Conjuring Up New Human Rights: A Proposal for Quality Control', *American Journal of International Law* 78, no. 3.

[36]Jonathan Schell, *The Fate of the Earth* (New York: Knopf, 1982), p. 115.

[37]Shelton H. Davis, *Victims of the Miracle: Development and the Indians of Brazil* (New York: Cambridge University Press, 1977).

[38]Dworkin, *Taking Rights Seriously*, p. 273 and *passim*.

[39]George Woodcock, *Civil Disobedience* (Toronto: Canadian Broadcasting Corporation, 1966), p. 69.

[40]Willmoore Kendall, 'The People Versus Socrates Revisited', *Modern Age*, Winter 1958/59.

[41]See Burton Zwiebach, *Civility and Disobedience* (Cambridge: Cambridge University Press, 1975), pp. 204-6.

[42]Richard E. Flatham, *Political Obligation* (New York: Atheneum, 1972), pp. 239-40; Martin Luther King, 'The Time for Freedom Has Come', in Mulford Q. Sibley, ed., *The Quiet Battle* (Garden City, N.Y.: Anchor, 1963), p. 303.

[43]Rawls, *Theory of Justice*, p. 364.

[44]Ibid., pp. 364-5.

[45]Ibid., p. 365.

[46]Ibid.

[47]Ibid., p. 366.

[48]Ibid.

[49]Ibid., pp. 368-71.

[50]Ibid., pp. 372, 373.

[51]Ibid., p. 374.

[52]See above, pp. 44-5.

[53]Ibid., p. 302.

[54]Ibid., p. 335.

[55]Cf. Norman Daniels, 'Equal Liberty and Equal Worth of Liberty', in Daniels, ed., *Reading Rawls* (New York: Basic, 1975).

[56]Dworkin, *Taking Rights Seriously*, pp. 160-3.

[57]Ibid., p. viii.

[58]Ibid., p. 205.

[59]Ibid., pp. xi, 85, 364, *passim*.

[60]Ibid., pp. xii, xv, 272-3, *passim*.

[61]Herbert C. Kelman and Lee H. Lawrence, 'Assignment of Responsibility in the Case of Lt Calley: Preliminary Report on a National Survey', *Journal of Social Issues* 1972, pp. 177-212; see also Kelman and Lee Hamilton [née Lawrence], *Crimes of Obedience* (New Haven, Conn.: Yale University Press, in press 1988).

[62]Cf. C.B. Macpherson's critiques, *The Political Theory of Passessive Individualism: Hobbes to Locke* (Oxford: Oxford University Press, 1962) and *Democratic Theory: Essays in Retrieval* (Oxford: Oxford University Press, 1973).

[63]Rousseau, 'Origin of Inequality', in *Social Contract and Discourses*, p. 66.

[64]Rousseau, 'Discourse on Political Economy', in *Social Contract and Discourses*, p. 120.

[65]Ibid., p. 121.

[66]Albert Camus, *The Rebel* (New York: Knopf, 1956).

[67]Johan Galtung, *The True Worlds: A Transnational Perspective* (New York: Free Press, 1980), pp. 67-72 and *passim*.

[68]Ruth Leger Sivard, *World Military and Social Expenditures 1987/88* (Washington: World Priorities, 1988), p. 25.

[69]For an eloquent personal testimony to this effect, see Pierre Vallières, *Choose!* (Toronto: New Press, 1972).

[70]Peter Russell, 'The First Three Years in Charterland', *Canadian Public Administration* 28, no. 3 (1985), p. 396.

[71]Ibid.

[72]David M. Beatty, *Putting the Charter to Work* (Kingston, Ont.: McGill-Queen's University Press, 1987).

[73]Ibid., pp. 180-4.

ELIZABETH GRACE AND COLIN LEYS: THE CONCEPT OF SUBVERSION AND ITS IMPLICATIONS

The authors are indebted to Jim Littleton for invaluable advice and suggestions, though he is in no way responsible for anything stated in this paper.

[1]Vasily Grossman, *Life and Fate* (London: Fontana, 1986), p. 21.

[2]Commission of Inquiry Concerning Certain Activities of the Royal Canadian Mounted Police (McDonald Commission), *Freedom and Security Under the Law* (Ottawa: Minister of Supply and Services, 1981), vol. 2, part 1 (henceforth McDonald Report 2/1), p. 447; James Littleton, *Dissent and Subversion* (Toronto: CBC IDEAS, 1983), p. 1; Proceedings of the Special Committee of the Senate on the Canadian Security Intelligence Service (the Pitfield Committee), 1983, p. 5.

[3]Indeed, one author has called the American 1940 Smith Act directed against 'communists' and 'subversives', 'the first peacetime sedition law in American history' since the 1798 Alien and Sedition Acts (Robert Justin Goldstein, *Political Repression in Modern America: 1870 to the Present* [Cambridge, Mass.: Schenkman, 1978], p. 245). In Canada the language of the Official Secrets Act's definition of 'subversive activity' was taken directly, it seems, from the sedition section of the Criminal Code (M.L. Friedland, *National Security: The Legal Dimensions*, study prepared for the McDonald Commission [Ottawa: Minister of Supply and Services, 1980], p. 84).

[4]Friedland, *National Security*, p. 8.

[5]Judith Schenck Koffler and Bennett L. Gershman, 'The New Seditious Libel', *Cornell Law Review* 69 (1984), p. 819.

[6]For example, the draconian Alien and Sedition Acts of 1798 in the USA, which made it a crime to utter any words 'with intent to defame . . . Congress, or the . . . President, or to bring them . . . into contempt or disrepute; or to excite against them . . . the hatred of the good people in the United States' were designed to eliminate the Federalists' political rivals, the Republicans, and to dampen enthusiasm for the libertarian and egalitarian ideals coming from France (Friedland, *National Security*, p. 21; Koffler and Gershman, 'Seditious Libel', p. 827).

[7]Friedland, *National Security*, p. 22.

[8]Ibid., p. 18.

[9]Interestingly, in spite of its increasingly common use since at least the 1930s, the term 'subversion' has been conspicuously absent from official state documents, appearing in the US legal literature only in 1938, and not until 1973 (in an amendment to the Official Secrets Act) in Canada. Even now the word does not feature in the CSIS Act of 1984.

[10]See Lita-Rose Betcherman, *The Little Band: The Clashes Between the Communists and the Canadian Establishment, 1928-32* (Ottawa: Deneau, 1985), ch. 16-18.

[11]John Shattuck, 'National Security a Decade After', *Democracy* 3, no. 1 (1983), p. 59.

[12]Frank J. Donner, *The Age of Surveillance: The Aims and Methods of America's Political Intelligence System* (New York: Knopf, 1980), p. 459.

[13]Goldstein, *Political Repression*, p. 242; Donner, *Age of Surveillance*, p. 16.

[14]James Littleton, *Target Nation: Canada and the Western Intelligence Network* (Toronto: Lester and Orpen Dennys, 1986), especially ch. 6.

[15]Michael Paul Rogin, 'Control, Suppression and Intimidation', in Jack P. Greene, ed., *Encyclopedia of American Political Histroy*, vol. 1 (New York: Scribner's, 1984), p. 402.

[16]Apparently, in the late nineteenth century the Pinkerton Detective Agency's force of 2,000 trained active men and 30,000 reserves was *larger* than the American army (ibid., p. 404).

[17]Goldstein, *Political Repression*, p. 176.

[18]Athan Theoharis, *Spying on Americans: Political Surveillance from Hoover to the Huston Plan* (Philadelphia: Temple University Press, 1978), ch. 3.

[19]See, for example, Nelson Blackstock, *COINTELPRO: The FBI's Secret War on Political Freedom* (New York: Vintage, 1976); Donner, *Age of Surveillance*; Goldstein, *Political Repression*; and Rogin, 'Control, Suppression and Intimidation'.

[20]Goldstein, *Political Repression*, p. 240.

[21]Ibid., p. 245.

[22]By 1953 it is estimated that 13.5 million individuals or 20% of the labour force had been subjected to the new loyalty-security requirements for government and 'sensitive' private industry employment (Donner, *Age of Surveillance*, p. 27).

[23]It is also worth noting that it was not until Carter's 1978 Executive Order that the word 'subversion' was completely dropped from the FBI's mandate. In its place, the FBI was given a counter-intelligence mandate 'to protect against espionage and other clandestine intelligence activities . . . conducted for or on behalf of foreign powers, organizations or persons' (John T. Ellif, *The Reform of FBI Intelligence Operations* [Princeton: Princeton University Press, 1979], p. 11).

[24]Littleton, *Target Nation*, p. 23.

[25]The following discussion on the origins of security intelligence in Canada draws heavily on 'The R.C.M.P. Security Service: Historical Evolution and Current Organization', McDonald Report, 2/1, pp. 54-72.

[26]Report of the Royal Commission on Security (Mackenzie Commission, 1969), p. 6.

[27]Littleton, *Target Nation*, p. 140; McDonald Report 2/1, pp. 445-511; Robert Dion, *Crimes of the Secret Police* (Montreal: Black Rose, 1982), especially ch. 1-19.

[28]Cited in R.J. Spjut, 'Defining Subversion', *British Journal of Law and Society* 6, vol. 2 (Winter 1979), p. 254.

[29]Donner, *Age of Surveillance*, p. 5.

[30]Cited in Littleton, *Dissent and Subversion*, p. 6.

[31]E.g., McDonald Report 2/1, p. 480.

[32]Security Intelligence Review Committee, *Annual Report, 1986-87* (henceforth *SIRC Report*) (Ottawa: Ministry of Supply and Services Canada, 1987), p. 38. The McDonald Commission reported that in 1977 the RCMP Security Service, about half of whose resources were then devoted to 'counter-subversion', had 800,000 files on individuals (McDonald Report 2/1, pp. 72, 518). In February 1988 the Solicitor General announced that since the McDonald Report the Service had reduced the number of individuals investigated by the former Counter-Subversion branch by 95%; but since he deemed it 'inadvisable to cite precise numbers', it is not clear what significance this has. The closed files were to be destroyed or sent to the Archives of Canada.

[33]Cited in Littleton, *Dissent and Subversion*, p. 13.

[34]Ibid., p. 14.

[35]Both terms were used, apparently interchangeably, by the McDonald Commission (see, e.g., pp. 417, 440-1). The term 'overthrow' (or 'destruction'), it may be noted, conflates the means with the end. The effect is to divert attention from the fact that it is really particular political aims, rather than particular political means, that are being outlawed.

[36]E.g., the 1985-86 *SIRC Report*, p. 43, and the 1986-87 *Report*, pp. 16, 33-40, and *passim*.

[37]McDonald Report 2/1, p. 417.

[38]John Sawatsky, in evidence to the Pitfield Committee, p. 8:14. In 1982 in the US Dr Samuel T. Francis, advocating the removal of restrictions on the FBI, argued that '[t]he FBI cannot investigate unless it suspects violence. But how can it suspect violence unless it has investigated?' (Frank J. Donner, 'Rounding Up the Usual Suspects: The New FBI Guidelines', *The Nation* 235, no. 4 [7-14 Aug. 1982], p. 111).

[39]Littleton, *Target Nation*, p. 157.

[40]*SIRC Report 1986-87*, p. 37.

[41]McDonald Report 2/1, p. 441

[42]Ibid.

[43]Ibid., p. 407.

[44]Ibid., p. 409.

[45]Ibid., p. 46.

[46]Also on p. 409.

[47]On the RCMP's role in the process leading to the drafting and enactment of the CSIS Act see Littleton, *Target Nation*, pp. 149-51. Documents produced in the House of Commons by Svend Robinson, MP, in September 1987 indicated that CSIS targets 'Marxist-Leninists' as such (*Globe and Mail* 31 Sept. 1987).

[48]Whitaker cited in Littleton, *Target Nation*, p. 29.

[49]The expression 'Cold War ideology' should really be used in a generic sense. English anti-papism in the sixteenth and seventeenth centuries, anti-(Irish) nationalist unionism in the nineteenth century, American anti-communism and Stalinist anti-capitalism in the twentieth century, etc., are all forms of Cold War ideology in the sense that they make an external threat the paramount determinant of questions of internal order.

[50]Donner, 'Rounding Up the Usual Suspects', p. 111.

[51]For example, in 1980 the right-wing Washington-based Heritage Foundation issued a report calling for increased surveillance of all 'terrorist' and 'potentially subversive' political groups, including the 'anti-defense and anti-nuclear lobbies' (cited in Kenneth O'Reilly, *Hoover and the Un-Americans: The FBI, HUAC, and the Red Menace* [Philadelphia: Temple University Press, 1983], p. 289). The report also stressed that 'clergymen, students, businessmen, entertainers, labour officials, journalists, and government workers all may engage in subversive activities without being fully aware of the extent, purpose, or control of their activities' (cited in Shattuck, 'National Security', p. 59).

[52]*SIRC Reports: 1985-86*, pp. 25-6, and *1986-87*, pp. 12-14, 23.

[53]See Grant Amyot's chapter in this volume, pp. 169-90).

[54]McDonald Report 2/1, p. 441.

[55]Theoharis, *Spying on Americans*, p. 175.

[56]Tony Bunyan, *The Political Police in Britain* (New York: St Martin's, 1976), p. 134.

[57]McDonald Report 2/1, p. 474.

[58]Chomsky cited in Blackstock, *COINTELPRO*, p. 17.

[59]They were not intended to. The Solicitor General, when explaining the intentions of the original Bill C 157, told the Pitfield Committee in 1983 that it 'should not be thought of as a creation of a new agency, but as the continuation of an existing agency under . . . improved terms and conditions' (Pitfield Committee hearings, p. 1:22).

[60]*SIRC Report 1986-87*, pp. 36-7, 39.

[61]See Reginald Whitaker, 'Witchhunt in the Civil Service: Ottawa's New Security Force Has Taken on the Role of an Orwellian-style Thought Police', *This Magazine* 20, no. 4 (Oct./Nov. 1986), pp. 24-9, on the André Henri case, and the transcript of CSIS evidence in the Robert Thompson case.

[62]McDonald Report 2/1, p. 409.

[63]The data on the FBI's use of resources are based on the files of the FBI office in Media, Pennsylvania, stolen in 1971: see Chomsky in Blackstock, *COINTELPRO*, p. 17. The GAO report is cited in Donner, *Age of Surveillance*, pp. 71, 74).

[64]Christopher Andrew, *Secret Service: The Making of the British Intelligence Community* (London: Heinemann, 1985), ch. 9-11; Peter Wright, *Spycatcher* (Toronto: Stoddart, 1987), ch. 17 and *passim*.

[65]Pitfield Committee hearings, p. 8:9.

[66]See Wright, *Spycatcher*, pp. 368-72; *New Statesman*, 20 Feb. 1981; Amyot in this volume, p. 186.

[67]Andrew, *Secret Service*, p. 308.

[68]Michael Mandel, 'Discrediting the McDonald Commission', *Canadian Forum* 61, 716 (March 1982), pp. 14-17.

[69]The claim that there had been no legislation governing the RCMP Security Service was rightly condemned as false by Michael Mandel in an article in 1985: 'In fact we have always had the Criminal Code and the Post Office Act and all the other legislation that made it criminal to do what the RCMP were doing. The [1984 CSIS] Act legalises these crimes . . . '(Mandel, 'Freedom of Expression and National Security', *University of Western Ontario Law Review* 23, no. 2 [1985], p. 206).

[70]*SIRC Report 1986-87*, p. 9.

[71]*Globe and Mail* 14 Sept. 1987. The problem cannot, moreover, be solved by the Ministry of Justice's announced intention of having its lawyers participate in such hearings to argue against the issue of a warrant, since these lawyers will not have access to the CSIS files on which the affidavits are based.

[72]Jean-Paul Brodeur, 'On Evaluating Threats to the National Security of Canada and the Civil Rights of Canadians' (paper presented at SIRC's research seminar, 'Canadian Security Intelligence in the 1980s', Meech Lake, Ottawa, 11 Oct. 1985), p. 1.

[73]See note 68 above.

[74]Cited in Mandel, 'Discrediting', p. 15. It should be noted, however, that the procedures adopted by the Chief Justice for hearing warrant applications by CSIS do prevent the 'judge-shopping' sometimes practised by the RCMP; but they are not secured by any provision of the CSIS Act.

[75]*SIRC Report 1986-87*, p. 7.

[76]Simon de Jong, NDP MP for Regina East, commented as follows on this aspect of Bill C 9, following an observation originally made in evidence to the Pitfield Committee by Prof. Peter Russell, the former Director of Research for the McDonald Commission: ' . . . even though it [the proposed Review Committee] is composed either of former members of Cabinet or members of the Privy Council, it cannot be trusted with all the documents, and Members of Parliament can be trusted even less. So much for the government's trust in the democratic system. The very reason it is setting up this so-called agency is to protect our democratic system. But it has no belief in the democratic system itself' (*House of Commons Debates* 13 Feb. 1984, p. 1330).

[77]E.g., *SIRC Report: 1985-86*, p. 44, and *1986-87*, p. 40.

[78]The 1986-87 *SIRC Report*'s treatment of the issue of the use of public servants as informers ('sources', in the euphemism of the trade) may fairly be cited as an example. A Mr Jack Gold had been removed from a senior position in the federal civil service, and his career prospects damaged, because the RCMP Security Service had complained to his superiors that he had refused to inform them of the names of other people with whom he had been associated, in his private capacity, in the campaign for nuclear disarmament. Under the heading 'Public Servants as Sources' the complete comment of the Committee was: 'Concerns have been raised about the use of federal government employees as sources because of the pressure they might feel to cooperate with CSIS in order to protect their jobs. A secret directive issued by the Solicitor General lays down general principles governing the use of federal employees as sources' (p. 16).

[79]It is important not to overestimate SIRC's value as a safeguard in cases of individual complaints against CSIS. While quasi-judicial forms are observed, SIRC hearings are not a court, its members are not judges, and complainants have no enforceable procedural rights. Above all, complainants may not see the case against them presented by CSIS, and they and their lawyers are obliged to leave the hearings whenever CSIS evidence is presented. Everything depends on the judgement of the SIRC member or members conducting the hearing, and on the degree of veracity of the CSIS witnesses, both of which are likely to vary). Finally, CSIS has no power to enforce any finding it may make.

[80]See note 83 below.

[81]In 1987 two appellants to SIRC in security-screening cases (Messrs Henri and Thompson) successfully sought to appeal their cases to the Court of Appeal under the provision in the Federal Courts Act (not the CSIS Act), which allow for appeals against decisions arising from determinations by quasi-judicial bodies. How wide an opportunity this will prove to give complainants against CSIS to take their cases to court remains to be seen. The Court of Appeal subsequently rejected Thompson's appeal for reinstatement on the grounds that it had no power to order it.

[82]The McDonald Commission had paid close attention to the special importance of declaring parliamentary politics off limits to the proposed CSIS: see McDonald Report 2/1, pp. 466, 468-9.

[83]A good starting point might be two of the amendments to Bill C 9 proposed by former Solicitor General Warren Allmand in the House of Commons on 18 June 1984: ' . . . "threats to the security of Canada" means . . . (a) foreign activities within Canada which are harmful to the vital national interests of Canada, and (b) activities within or relating

to Canada involving the threat or use of acts of serious violence against persons or property for the purpose of achieving political objectives within Canada . . .' (pp. 4704-5).

[84]For a succinct review of the CSE's activities and the scope of modern eavesdropping technology see the speech by a former Conservative Solicitor General, Allan Lawrence, in the Commons debate on Bill C 9 on 16 March 1984. Mr Lawrence concluded: 'I suspect, although I have no proof, that accountable, effective control, supervision or prohibition, as the case may be, is largely illusory in this country' (p. 2179).

[85]SIRC has expressed concern about this possibility: see the 1986-87 *Report*, pp. 27-9. See also H. Mackenzie, 'Spies under Fire', *Maclean's*, 28 Sept. 1987, p. 14.

[86]James Kelleher, 'Notes for a speech by the Honourable James Kelleher, Solicitor General of Canada, to the Conference on "Advocacy, Protest and Dissent" (news release, 25 Feb. 1988), p. 7.

[87]Ibid., emphasis added.

ATHAN THEOHARIS: THE FBI AND DISSENT IN THE UNITED STATES

[1]American Youth Congress folder, Official and Confidential Files of FBI Assistant Director Louis Nichols (henceforth cited as Nichols O&C).

[2]Memo, Ladd to Hoover, 1 Dec. 1942, Miscellaneous A-Z folder, Nichols O&C.

[3]Memo, Ladd to Hoover, 11 Sept. 1942, FBI 62-116758; Memo, Ladd to Tamm, 21 Oct. 1942, FBI 62-116758.

[4]Joseph Lash Folder, Folder # 103, Official and Confidential File of FBI Director J. Edgar Hoover (henceforth cited as Hoover O&C); Joseph Lash, *Love Eleanor: Eleanor Roosevelt and Her Friends* (Garden City: Doubleday, 1962), p. 461.

[5]Memo, Nichols to Hoover, 8 Jan. 1953, Dwight Eisenhower folder, Nichols O&C; Memo, Nichols to Hoover, 2 Feb. 1954, Joseph Lash folder, Folder # 103, Hoover O&C.

[6]FBI Report, New York Field Office, 7 June 1941; Letter, Hoover to name deleted, 2 Dec. 1940; Memo, McKee to Hoover, 12 Dec. 1941; Letter, Hoover to McKee, 24 Dec. 1941; and undated Routing Slip, Hoover to Tamm and Ladd; all in Mrs Paul Fejos, née Inga Arvad folder, Folder #7, Hoover O&C.

[7]The FBI Director did not brief Attorney General Biddle of his other decisions authorizing FBI agents to bug John Kennedy's hotel room in Charleston, South Carolina, bug Arvad's Washington apartment, or break into Arvad's Washington apartment to photocopy her correspondence.

[8]Letter, McKee to Hoover, 22 Jan. 1942; FBI Report, Washington, D.C. Field Office, 22 Jan. 1942; FBI Report, Washington, D.C. Field Office, 6 Jan. 1942; Memo, Ladd to Hoover, 17 Jan. 1942; Memo, Hoover to Riddle, 21 Jan. 1942; Personal and Confidential Letter, Hoover to McKee, 30 Jan. 1942, Memo, Mumford to Ladd, 21 Jan. 1942; Memo, Kramer to Ladd, 28 Jan. 1942; all in Fejos-Arvad folder, Folder #7, Hoover O&C.

[9]This is documented by Hoover's response to a subsequent request from Edward Ennis, the director of the Justice Department's Alien Enemy Control Unit. Ennis had asked Hoover for any information on Arvad to determine whether to order her detention as a dangerous alien. Hoover could produce none. (Memo, Ennis to Hoover, 4 Feb. 1942 and Memo, Hoover to Ennis, 20 Feb. 1942, both in Fejos-Arvad folder, Folder #7, Hoover O&C.)

[10]Memo, Burton to Ladd, 3 Feb. 1942; Personal and Confidential Letter, McKee to Hoover, 5 Feb. 1942; Wiretap Summaries, 31 Jan. 3, 5, 10, 17, 19, and 20 Feb., and 1, 2, and 7 March, 1942; Personal and Confidential Letter, McKee to Hoover, 3 Feb. 1942; Personal and Confidential Letter, McKee to Hoover, 10 Feb. 1942; Personal and Confidential Letter, Ruggles to Hoover, 9 Feb. 1942; FBI Report, Savannah (Georgia) Field Office, 9 Feb. 1942; Memo, Ladd to Tamm, 6 Feb. 1942; FBI Report, Washington, D.C. Field

Office, 12 Feb. 1942; Memo, Fitch to Ladd, 11 Feb. 1942; Letter, McKee to Hoover, 18 Feb. 1942; Memo, Ladd to Tamm, 10 Feb. 1942; Personal and Confidential Letter, Ruggles to Hoover, 11 Feb. 1942; Memo, Tamm to Hoover, 3 Feb. 1942; Personal and Confidential Letter, Ruggles to Hoover, 23 Feb. 1942; Personal and Confidential Letter, McKee to Hoover, 24 Feb. 1942; FBI Report, Washington, D.C. Field Office, 4 March 1942; Memo, Ladd to Tamm, 2 March 1942; Personal and Confidential Letter, McKee to Hoover, 5 March 1942; Memo, Ladd to Hoover, 6 Feb 1942; Personal and Confidential Letter, McKee to Hoover, 13 March 1942; FBI Report, Washington, D.C. Field Office, 8 April 1942; all in Fejos-Arvad folder, Folder # 7, Hoover O&C.

11Confidential Memo, Conroy to Hoover, 30 May 1944; Confidential Memo, Conroy to Hoover, 3 Aug. 1944; Confidential Letter, Conroy to Hoover, 12 July 1944; undated Note Card re instructions by Nichols that Ladd should handle this case in 'his absence'; Confidential Letter, Hoover to McKee, 27 April 1942; Routing Slip, Nichols to Files Section, 7 May 1942; Routing Slip, Mumford to Nichols, 16 April 1942; Routing Slip, Security Division Supervisor, 6 July 1942; all in Fejos-Arvad folder, Folder # 7, Hoover O&C. Memo, Bassett to Callahan, 13 Feb. 1975, President John F. Kennedy folder, Folder # 13, Hoover O&C.

12SAC Letter No. 512, 24 March 1952, FBI 66-04-x92. Hoover's order restricting access to this file is reiterated in Memo, Nichols to Tolson, 14 April 1953, Joseph Bryan III folder, Nichols O&C.

13Bureau Bulletin No. 37, Series 1946, 10 July 1946, FBI 66-03-759.

14Report, SAC St Louis to Hoover, 29 Jan. 1954; OBSCENE Letter, partial transcript from wiretap to Vitale, 29 Jan. 1954; Memo, Price to Rosen, 2 Feb. 1954; ten-page report on Hyde, withheld in entirety; all in Dwight Eisenhower folder, Nichols O&C.

15Memo, Hoover to Tolson, Belmont, DeLoach, and Sullivan, 29 Jan. 1965 and Memo, Hoover to Tolson, 2 April 1965, both in Personal File of FBI Associate Director Clyde Tolson, Vol. 1.

16Letter, Charles Dollar (Deputy Director, National Archives FBI Records Appraisal Project Staff) to Athan Theoharis, 11 Dec. 1981.

17This tap was installed on 25 Jan. 1943 and was discontinued on 20 Dec. 1947.

18This tap was in operation from 4 April 1947 until 27 Oct. 1950.

19This union was tapped far more intensively. One tap lasted from 20 Oct. 1948 until 9 June 1950; a second tap from 9 through 15 June 1950; a third tap from 20 June through 9 Oct. 1950; and a fourth tap was initiated on 22 March 1951 (no discontinuance date is listed).

20This union was tapped three times: from 6 Oct. 1942 until 28 May 1945, reinstituted from 22 June through 31 Oct. 1945 and again from 23 Nov. 1945 through 30 June 1945; a second tap was installed on 14 Aug. 1942 which was discontinued on 10 Oct. 1945 only to be briefly reinstalled from 12 Oct. through 5 Nov. 1945; and the third tap was operational from 19 Sept. 1946 until 17 Jan. 1948.

21This tap was operational from 17 July through 9 Oct. 1950.

22Three taps were installed: one lasting from 10 Sept. 1945 through 15 Sept. 1950; a second from 30 June through 1 Dec. 1948; and the third from 17 July through 9 Oct. 1950.

23The UAW was bugged five different times: three on 10 Sept. 1944, a fourth from 5 through 7 Jan. 1945, and the fifty on 24 Aug. 1946.

24Bugged three times—on 22 Feb. 1947, 9 April 1948, and 9-10 Dec. 1949—this union was also tapped twice (and one tap lasted from 15 Nov. 1950 until 22 Dec. 1955).

25A meeting of this union was bugged from 1 through 3 July 1944.

26This bug was installed on 20 Nov. 1944 and was discontinued on 15 Dec. 1944.

27'Black Bag' jobs folder, Folder # 36, Hoover O&C. Memo, FBI Executives Conference to Tolston, 10 March 1953, FBI 66-2095-100 and Memo, Hoover to Tolson, Ladd, Nichols, Belmont, Clegg, Glavin, Harbo, Rosen, Gearty, Holloman, and Mohr, 19 March 1953, FBI 66-2095-100. Memo, name deleted agent to SAC New York, 26 April 1954, FBI 62-117166-131 Bulky Enclosures Section 1; Memo, name deleted agent to SAC New York, 20

May 1954, FBI 62-117166-131 Bulky Enclosures Section 1; Memo, Simon, 23 Nov. 23, 1955, FBI 62-117166-unserialized; Blind Memo, Re: Highly Confidential Anonymous Sources, undated but March 1961, FBI 62-117166-unserialized; Memo, SAC Philadelphia to File, 22 March 1963, FBI 62-117166-31x.

[28]Athan Theoharis, 'In-House Cover-up: Researching FBI Files,' in Theoharis, *Beyond the Hiss Case: The FBI, Congress, and the Cold War* (Philadelphia: Temple University Press, 1982), pp. 35, 46, 51-4.

[29]Created in October 1941 on Hoover's explicit order to supplement the FBI Director's two office files, the Nichols file contains sensitive do-not-file type documents pertaining to political and investigative matters about which Hoover was directly interested. Perhaps for this reason Nichols's office file escaped Hoover's March 1953 requirement that FBI assistant directors' office files be purged every six months. Furthermore, Nichols's office file was not destroyed with his retirement from the Bureau in 1957 to accept the vice-presidency of the Schenley Corporation.

[30]American Youth Congress folder, Nichols O&C. The second copy of this photocopied correspondence was filed in the Eleanor Roosevelt folder, Nichols O&C.

[31]Department of Justice folder, Nichols O&C.

[32]Harry Bridges folder, Nichols O&C; Carol King folder, Nichols O&C; Smear Campaign folders, Nichols O&C. The document recording the break-in to Carol King's law office in an undated, blind abstract summarizing FBI Assistant Director D. Milton Ladd's memo to Hoover and is filed in the Bridges folder.

[33]Memos, name deleted agent to SAC New York, 14 May 1954 and 25 Sept. 1956, FBI 62-117166-131 Bulky Enclosure Section C.

[34]Memos, name deleted agent to SAC New York, 8 June 1954 and 23 May 1956, FBI 62-117166-131 Bulky Enclosure Section C.

[35]Memo, SAC New York to Hoover, 4 March 1963, FBI 62-117166-131 Bulky Enclosure Section M.

[36]Memo, name deleted agent to SAC New York, 28 Oct. 1958, FBI 62- 117166-131 Bulky Enclosure Section C.

[37]Memo, name deleted agent to SAC New York, 19 Nov. 1953, FBI 62- 117166-131 Bulky Enclosure Section 3.

[38]Memos, name deleted agent to SAC New York, 30 Nov. and 13 Dec. 1971, FBI 62-117166-Enclosure behind the file Section 5; and 30 Nov. and 13 Dec. 1971, FBI 62-117166-131 Bulky Enclosure Section 6.

[39]Memo, Hottel to Hoover, 23 July 1950, FBI 62-117166-5514.

[40]Memo, SAC New Haven to SAC New York, 17 Aug. 1953, FBI 62-117166- 131.

[41]Memo, name deleted agent to SAC New York, 30 Sept. 1955, FBI 62- 117166-131 Bulky Enclosure Section 3.

[42]Memo, ADIC [Assistant Director in Charge] to Kelley, 5 April 1976, FBI 62-117166-x96. Memo, name deleted agent to SAC New York, 12 June 1968, FBI 62-117166-5339; Memo, name deleted agent to SAC New York, 28 May 1968, FBI 62-117166-5343.

[43]Memo, name deleted agent to File, 31 Jan. 1956, FBI 62-117166-131 Bulky Enclosure Section 4.

[44]Memo, name deleted agent to SAC New York, 23 Dec. 1954, FBI 62- 117166-131 Bulky Enclosure Section 1. Memo, name deleted agent to SAC New York, 4 June 1956, FBI 62-117166-131 Bulky Enclosure Section 4.

[45]For a sample of these break-ins, see Teletypes, SAC New York to Director, 10 Dec. 1965 - Sept. 1966, FBI 62-117166-x24.

[46]Memo, SAC New York to Hoover, 12 April 1955 and Memo, name deleted agent to SAC New York, 5 April 1955, FBI 62-117166-131 Bulky Enclosure Section 2.

[47]Memo, name deleted agent to SAC New York, 9 May 1955, FBI 62-117166- 131 Bulky Enclosure Section 2.

[48]Memo, SAC New York to Hoover, 24 May 1955, FBI 62-117166-131 Bulky Enclosure Section 2.

[49]Airtel, Director to ADIC, 9 May 1977, FBI 62-117166-105x; Airtel, ADIC to Director, 13 May 1977, FBI 62-117166-123; Memos, name deleted agent to SAC New York, 7 June 1962, FBI 62-117166-3696 and 16 Feb. 1962, FBI 62-117166-3842.

[50]Not for File Memo, 9 July 1968, FBI 62-117166-95x.

[51]Not for File Memo, 10 Jan. 1966, FBI 62-117166-95x.

[52]Memo, Kelley to Pottinger, 18 Dec. 1975, FBI 62-117166-x65.

[53]Memo, name deleted agent to File, 18 Aug. 1955, FBI 62-117166-131 Bulky Enclosure Section 3.

[54]Memo, name deleted agent to SAC New York, 9 Sept. 1955, FBI 62- 117166-131 Bulky Enclosure Section 3.

[55]Memo, name deleted agent to SAC New York, 4 Feb. 1955 and Memo, SAC New York to Hoover, 13 Jan. 1955, FBI 62-117166-131 Bulky Enclosure Section 2; Memo, name deleted agent to File, 19 Sept. 19, 1955, FBI 62-117166-131 Bulky Enclosure Section 2.

[56]Memo, name deleted agent to SAC New York, 15 Feb. 1955, FBI 62- 117166-131 Bulky Enclosure Section 2.

[57]Memo, name deleted agent to SAC New York, 15 Oct. 1954, FBI 62- 117166-151 Bulky Enclosure Section 1; Memos, name deleted agent to SAC New York, 28 Feb. and 1 March 1955, FBI 62-117166-131 Bulky Enclosure Section 2.

[58]Memo, name deleted agent to SAC New York, 27 Dec. 1955, FBI 62- 117166-131 Bulky Enclosure Section 3.

[59]Memo, SAC New York to Hoover, 10 Feb. 1964, FBI 62-117166-4781; Memo, name deleted agent to SAC New York, 5 Feb. 1964, FBI 62- 117166-4785.

[60]Memo, Kelley to Pottinger, 1 Dec. 1975, FBI 62-117166-x58; Airtel, ADIC to Kelley, 2 March 1976, FBI 62-117166-x88; Memo, Kelley to SAC New York, 18 Feb. 1976, FBI 62-117166-x82; Memo, name deleted agent to SAC New York, 18 April 1963, FBI 62-117166-4345; Memo, name deleted agent to SAC New York, undated, FBI 62-117166-3709; Memo, name deleted agent to SAC New York, 4 May 1961, FBI 62-117166- 3340; Memo, name deleted agent to SAC New York, 12 July 1961, FBI 62- 117166-3665; Memo, name deleted agent to SAC New York, 14 Aug. 1961, FBI 62-117166-3643.

[61]Memos, name deleted agent to SAC New York, 24 Aug. 1962, FBI 62-117166-4225 and 21 May 1963, FBI 62-177166-4301.

[62]Memo, name deleted agent to SAC New York, 16 Oct. 1963, FBI 62- 117166-4173.

[63]Memo, name deleted agent to SAC New York, 4 Dec. 1959, FBI 62- 117166-2656.

[64]Memo, name deleted agent to SAC New York, 12 Aug. 1957, FBI 62- 117166-1727.

[65]Memo, name deleted agent to File, 28 March 1957, FBI 62-117166-1417.

[66]Memos, SAC New York to Hoover, 19 Oct. 1954, FBI 62-117166-131 Bulky Enclosure Section 1 and 21 June 1955, FBI 62-117166-131 Bulky Enclosure Section 3.

[67]Memo, Kelley to SAC New Orleans, 11 Sept. 1975, FBI 62-117166- x18; Teletype, SAC New Orleans to Kelley, 17 Sept. 1975, FBI 62- 117166-x22.

[68]Memo, McCabe to SAC New York, 13 Dec. 1957, FBI 62-117166-1558; Memo, name deleted agent to SAC New York, 13 Dec. 1957, FBI 62- 117166-1563.

[69]Memo, McCabe to SAC New York, 5 March 1958, FBI 62-117166-1932; Memo, name deleted agent to SAC New York, 5 March 1958, FBI 62-117166-1933; Memo, name deleted agent to SAC New York, 15 Oct. 1958, FBI 62- 117166-2146.

[70]Memos, name deleted agent to SAC New York, 9 Dec. 1963, FBI 62- 117166-4493 and 26 Nov. 1963, FBI 62-117166-4506.

[71]Memo, name deleted agent to SAC New York, 6 Feb. 1964, FBI 62- 117166-4783.

[72]Memo, Bryant to SAC New York, 31 March 1959, FBI 62-117166-2454.

[73]Memo, name deleted agent to SAC New York, 20 Dec. 1961, FBI 62- 117166-3511.

[74]Memo, name deleted agent to SAC New York, 13 June 1962, FBI 62- 117166-3691.

[75]Memo, name deleted agent to SAC New York, 29 June 1962, FBI 62- 117166-3673.

[76]Memos, name deleted agent to SAC New York, 30 April 1963, FBI 62- 117166-4330 and 22 April 1963, FBI 62-117166-4340.

[77]Memo, name deleted agent to SAC New York, 8 Jan. 1962, FBI 62- 117166-131.

[78]Memo, name deleted agent to SAC New York, 17 April 1962, FBI 62- 117166-3765.

[79]Theoharis, 'Introduction', in *Beyond the Hiss Case*, pp. 10-11; Theoharis, *Spying on Americans: Political Surveillance from Hoover to the Huston Plan* (Philadelphia: Temple University Press, 1978), p. 242.

[80]John Elliff, *The Reform of FBI Intelligence Operations* (Princeton: Princeton University Press, 1979), pp. 10-11, 101, 133; Theoharis, 'Introduction', in *Beyond the Hiss Case*, pp. 13-16; *Federal Register* 40, no. 235 (8 Dec. 1981), pp. 59949-52.

[81]Elliff, *FBI Intelligence Operations*, p. 101; Theoharis, *Spying on Americans*, pp. 63-4; *New York Times*, 18 Sept. 1987, p. 1; 'Has the FBI Really Changed?' *The Nation*, 17 Oct. 1987), pp. 399-400.

[82]Section 100, FBI Manual of Investigation, 31 Jan. 1978, pp. 525-53; see particularly pp. 526, 528, 540, 541. The text of the guidelines is also reprinted in Elliff, *FBI Intelligence Operations*, pp. 196-202.

[83]In a September 1987 interview with *Washington Times* editor Arnaud deBorchgrave, Reagan starkly articulated his broad-brush anti-Communist convictions. Claiming that 'pro-Soviet agents of influence' had successfully discouraged Congress from investigating 'communist leanings' among both congressmen and political activists by 'making it unfashionable to be anti-communist' and further that 'a great many in the media and the Press' possibly were willing agents of Soviet influence or dupes of Communist disinformation efforts, Reagan lamented the dissolution of the once-infamous House Committee on Un-American Activities. Reflecting nostalgically on that Committee's earlier role, Reagan ruefully commented: 'There was once a Congress in which they had a committee that would investigate even one of their own members if it was believed that that person had communist involvement or communist leanings. Well, they've done away with those committees. That shows the success of what the Soviets were able to do in this country with making it unfashionable to be anti- communist' (*Milwaukee Journal*, 1 Oct. 1987, p. 3A).

[84]Attorney General's Guidelines on Domestic Security/Terrorism Investigations, 7 March 1983, issued in press release, Department of Justice, 7 March 1983. The guidelines are printed in 32 *Criminal Law Report* (BNA), pp. 3087-92.

[85]*The Nation*, 14 Nov. 1987, p. 542; *Milwaukee Journal*, 6 Dec. 1987, p. 19A.

[86]*New York Times*, 28 Jan. 1988, p. 1 and 30 Jan. 1988, p. 1; *Milwaukee Journal*, 28 Jan. 1988, p. 3A and 29 Jan. 1988, p. 2A; *The Chronicle of Higher Education*, 10 Feb. 1988, p. A1; *Civil Liberties* (Winter 1988), p. 1.

[87]The testimony of FBI officials before the Senate Select Committee on Intelligence suggests that questionable techniques were employed during this investigation. One congressional source worried that 'there has been a return to the Red Squads and the use of local resources in an improper way' while Senator William Cohen queried whether there were 'too few constraints on the [FBI's] investigative activities in the field' *The Nation*, 12 March 1988, p. 332.

[88]During the Iran-Contra hearings, for example, Lt Col. Oliver North admitted that his communications with National Security Council (NSC) Advisor John Poindexter had been based on a 'do not log' procedure—to ensure that these documents were not logged in the NSC's records system. Only North's ignorance about the mechanics of the NSC's word-processing system averted the total destruction of these sensitive policy documents.

[89]This point is underscored by the way the FBI's intensive monitoring of the individuals/organizations opposed to the Reagan administration's central American policies came to be disclosed. The disclosure resulted not from an inquiry initiated by the Congress, but from the release of FBI documents in response to a Freedom of Information Act request of the Center for Constitutional Rights on behalf of CISPES. These documents, moreover, were releasable only because this FBI investigation was terminated in 1985.

AUREL BRAUN: DISSENT AND THE STATE IN EASTERN EUROPE

[1] *Toronto Star*, 7 Feb. 1988.

[2] See Ghita Ionescu, *The Breakup of the Soviet Empire in Eastern Europe* (Baltimore, Md.: Penguin Special, 1965).

[3] *Pravda* (Moscow), 3 July 1988.

[4] Ibid., 2 July 1988.

[5] *Toronto Star*, 2 July 1988.

[6] Ibid.

[7] *New York Times*, 3 July 1988.

[8] Ibid.

[9] *Globe and Mail*, 12 July 1988.

[10] *Toronto Star*, 24 July 1988.

[11] Ibid.

[12] Ibid.

[13] Josef Brodsky cited in Tony Judt *et al.*, *Debating the Nature of Dissent in Eastern Europe* (Washington, D.C.: Wilson Center, East European Program, Occasional Paper No. 9, 1987), p. 75.

[14] K. Jowitt, 'Inclusion and mobilization in European Leninist regimes', *World Politics* no. 1 (1975), p. 86.

[15] M. Shafir, 'The Socialist Republic of Romania' in B. Szajkoweki, ed., *Marxist Governments: A World Survey*, vol. 3 (London: Macmillan, 1981), pp. 602 ff.

[16] R.S. Sharlet, 'Systematic political science and communist system', in F.J. Fleron, Jr, ed., *Communist Studies and the Social Sciences: Essays on Methodology and Empirical Theory* (Chicago: Rand MacNally, 1969).

[17] Judt, *Debating the Nature of Dissent*, pp. 3-4.

[18] See Ivan Volgyes, *Politics in Eastern Europe* (Chicago: Dorsey Press, 1986), pp. 197-212.

[19] Jeremy Azrael, 'Is Coercion Withering Away?' *Problems of Communism* 11 (1962), pp. 9-17.

[20] A broad definition of dissent is required here that includes nonconformity and unconventional activity and not just programmatic opposition.

[21] See the excellent article by Donna Bahry and Brian D. Silver, 'Intimidation and the symbolic uses of terror in the U.S.S.R.,' *American Political Science Review* 81, no. 4 (Dec. 1987), pp. 1066-72.

[22] *Pravda*, 30 March 1989.

[23] Jane Leftwich Curry, 'Comments', in Judt *et al.*, *Dissent in Eastern Europe*, p. 57.

[24] *Globe and Mail*, 16 Nov. 1987; *Facts on File*, 27 Nov. 1987, p. 883.

[25] Ibid.

[26] H.G. Skilling, *Charter 77 and Human Rights in Czechoslovakia* (Winchester, Mass.: Allen and Unwin, 1981), pp. 7-9.

[27] Ibid., p. 19.

[28] Ibid., p. 211.

[29] Václav Havel, "Moc bezmornych' ['The Power of the Powerless'] excerpts in *Studie* 5 (1979), pp. 408-16, as cited by Skilling, pp. 179-80.

[30] Miroslav Kusy, 'Charta a realny socialismus' ['The Charter and real socialism'] *Svedectvi* 15, no. 59 (1979), pp. 18-21, as cited in Skilling, *Charter 77*, p. 179.

[31] Skilling, *Charter 77*, pp. 138-45.

[32] Ibid.

[33] Ibid., p. 138.

[34] Ibid.

35Zdenek Suda, 'Czechoslovakia', *Yearbook on International Communist Affairs 1987* (Stanford, Cal.: Hoover Institution Press, 1987), p. 290.

36Agence France Presse, Prague, 1 Sept. 1986.

37*New York Times*, 12 Dec. 1986.

38Sentences ranged from probation to 16 months in prison (*Facts on File*, March 1987, p. 166).

39*New York Times*, 6 July 1986.

40*Frankfurter Randschau* (Frankfurt), 11 Jan. 1986.

41*New York Times*, 29 Sept. 1987.

42Arthur R. Rachwald, 'Poland', in *Yearbook on International Communist Affairs, 1987*, p. 319.

43Radio Warsaw, PAP (Polish news service), 2 June 1986; *Foreign Broadcast Information Service* (*FBIS*), *Eastern Europe*, 3 June 1986.

44*New York Times*, 12 Sept. 1986.

45*San Francisco Examiner*, 14 Sept. 1987.

46Rachwald, 'Poland', p. 320.

47Tanjug (Yugoslav news service), Domestic Service, 16 June 1986; *FBIS*, 17 June 1986.

48Nicolaos Stavrou, 'Albania', in *Yearbook on International Communist Affairs 1987*, p. 268.

49*Rude Pravo* (Prague) 25 June 1986; *FBIS*, 26 June 1986.

50*Neues Deutschland*, 27 March 1986; *FBIS*, 28 March 1986.

51Michael Sodaro, 'The GDR', in Jane Leftwich Curry, *Dissent in Eastern Europe* (New York: Praeger, 1983), pp. 85-9.

52Ivan Szelenyi, in R.J. Tökes, ed., *Opposition in Eastern Europe* (Baltimore: Johns Hopkins University Press, 1979), p. 188.

53*Facts on File*, 21 March 1987, p. 186.

54*Globe and Mail*, 8 Jan. 1988.

55Miklos Haraszti, *The Velvet Prison: Artists Under State Socialism* (New York: Basic Books, 1987).

56*Globe and Mail*, 12 Jan. 1989.

57*Eastern Europe Newsletter* (London) vol. 3, no. 4 (22 Feb. 1989), p. 4.

58*New York Times*, 28 Aug. 1988.

59*Toronto Star*, 1 April 1989.

60Ibid.

61*Globe and Mail*, 10 March 1989.

62*Népszabadság* (Budapest), 1 Feb. 1986.

63Bennett Kovrig, 'Hungary', in *Yearbook on International Communist Affairs, 1987*, pp. 305-6.

64*New York Times*, 6 Aug. 1987.

65*Globe and Mail*, 17 Sept. 1987.

66*Newsweek*, 18 July 1988, p. 38.

67*Globe and Mail*, 9 Jan. 1989.

68*Népszobadság* (Budapest), 3 Jan. 1989.

69*Globe and Mail*, 26 Oct. 1987; *Facts on File*, 6 Oct. 1987, p. 762.

70Ibid.

71*Toronto Star*, 18 Nov. 1987.

72*Globe and Mail*, 27 Oct. 1987.

73*New York Times*, 30 Nov. 1987.

74*Toronto Star*, 1 Feb. 1988.

75*Times* (London), 15 Dec. 1986.

76J.F. Brown, 'Poland Since Martial Law', Rand Note (Santa Monica) N-2822-RC, December 1988, p. 26

77Ibid.

78*Polityka* (Warsaw) 26 July 1986; *FBIS*, 28 July 1986.

[79]Brown, 'Poland Since Martial Law', p. 32.

[80]*Globe and Mail*, 30 Oct. 1987; *Viesnik* (Belgrade) 21 Oct. 1986; Radio Free Europe *Research*, 20 Nov. 1986.

[81]Tanjug, 21 Nov. 1986; *FBIS*, 24 Nov. 1986.

[82]*Globe and Mail*, 17 March 1989.

[83]Radio Free Europe Research, *Yugoslavia*, 27 March 1986.

[84]*Facts on File*, 16 Oct. 1987, p. 765.

[85]*Times* (London), 7 Feb. 1987.

[86]*Facts on File*, 24 April 1987, p. 295.

[87]US Joint Economic Committee of Congress, *East European Economies* (Washington), 28 March 1986, p. 113.

[88]Jadwiga Staar, 'The German Democratic Republic', in *Yearbook on International Communist Affairs, 1987*, p. 298.

[89]*Globe and Mail*, 20 Nov. 1987.

[90]*Christian Science Monitor*, 4 April 1986.

[91]*Scinteia* (Bucharest), 5 Feb. 1987.

[92]*Zeri i Populit* (Tirana), 11 July 1986; *FBIS*, 14 July 1986.

[93]M.E. Fischer, 'The Politics of Inequality in Romania,' in D.N. Nelson, ed., *Communism and the Politics of Inequality* (Lexington, Mass.: Lexington Books, 1983), pp. 192-3.

[94]Trond Gilberg, 'Modernization, human rights and nationalism: the case of Romania', in G. Klein and M.J. Reban, eds, *The Politics of Ethnicity in Eastern Europe* (New York: Columbia University Press, 1981), pp. 195-6.

[95]*Globe and Mail*, 19 Feb. 1988.

[96]Kenneth Jowitt, *The Leninist Response to National Dependency* (Berkeley: Institute of International Studies, University of California, 1983), pp. 69-71, and 'Soviet neo-traditionalism: political corruption of a Leninist regime,' *Soviet Studies* no. 3 (1983).

[97]Aurel Braun, 'Structural Change and its Consequences for the Nationalities of Romania,' *Sudost-Europa* (Munich), 7/8 (1986), pp. 422-30.

[98]*Toronto Star*, 26 Feb. 1989.

[99]*New York Times*, 19 Feb. 1989.

[100]*New York Times*, 21 Feb. 1988; *Globe and Mail*, 17 Feb. 1988.

[101]*Izvestia* (Moscow), 27 May 1987.

[102]Nikolaous Stavrou, 'Yugoslavia', in *Yearbook on International Communist Affairs, 1987*, p. 387.

[103]*New York Times*, 23 May 1986.

[104]*Globe and Mail*, 29 March 1989.

[105]Ibid.

[106]Amnesty International (London), *Bulgaria: Imprisonment of Ethnic Turks*, April 1986.

[107]Ibid.

[108]Keesing's Contemporary Archives, Nov. 1987, vol. ee, p. 35517.

[109]*New York Times*, 27 Feb. 1976.

[110]*Argumenty* (Warsaw), 8 June 1986.

[111]*Times*, 31 June 1986.

[112]*Times*, 25 April 1986.

[113]Ibid.

[114]*Frankfurter Rundschau* (Frankfurt), 11 Jan. 1986.

[115]Volgyes, *Politics in Eastern Europe*, p. 210; *Le Monde* (Paris), 21 Jan. 1986.

[116]Agence France Press, 26 Nov. 1986.

[117]*New York Times*, 21 Feb. 1986.

[118]*Christian Science Monitor*, 18 Aug. 1986; *New York Times*, 4 June 1986.

[119]*Christian Science Monitor*, 18 Aug. 1986.

[120]*New York Times*, 2 Sept. 1986.

[121]Agence France Press, 20 Dec. 1986; *FBIS*, 21 Dec. 1986.

PHILIPPE FAUCHER AND KEVIN FITZGIBBONS: DISSENT AND THE STATE IN LATIN AMERICA

We wish to thank Professor C.E.S. Franks, the editor of this collection, for his thorough professional support, Catherine Legrand for her comments and friendly advice when doubts reached paralyzing heights, Jorge Nef for the courteousness of his disagreement, and the readers for their useful comments and suggestions.

[1]This is where our analytical definition of dissent differs from the descriptive definition proposed by Dogenharat and Day: '[Political dissent has been used to embrace] various kinds of expression of political opposition outside the legal structure of the state concerned, i.e. forces which constitute an actual or potential threat to the stability of the state' (Henry Dogenharat and Alan Day, eds, *Political Dissent. An International Guide to Dissident, Extra-Parliamentary, Guerrilla and Illegal Political Movements*, A Keesing's reference publication [Detroit: Gare Research Co., 1983], p. xi).

[2]On authoritarianism in Latin America see Howard J. Wiardia, 'Toward a Framework for the Study of Political Change in the Iberic-Latin Tradition: The Corporative Model'. *World Politics* 25, no. 2 (Jan. 1973), pp. 206-35; James M. Malloy, ed., *Authoritarianism and Corporatism in Latin America* (Pittsburg: University of Pittsburg Press, 1977); Guillermo O'Donnell, *Modernization and Bureaucratic-Authoritarianism: Studies in South American Politics* (Berkeley: Institute of International Studies, University of California, 1973); Guillermo O'Donnell, 'Reflections on the Patterns of Change in the Bureaucratic-Authoritarian State', *Latin American Research Review* 12, no. 1 (Winter 1978), pp. 3-38; Guillermo O'Donnell, '?Y a mi, qué me importa? Notas sobre sociabilidad y politica en Argentina y Brasil', *Working Paper no. 9*, January 1984, The Helen Kellogg Institute for International Studies, University of Notre Dame; Guillermo O'Donnell, *1966-1973, El Estado burocrático autoritario; Triunfos, derrotas y crisis* (Buenos Aires: Editorial de Belgrano, 1982); David Collier, ed., *The New Authoritarianism in Latin America* (Princeton: Princeton University Press, 1979); Simon Schwartzman, *Bases do Autoritarismo Brasileiro* (Rio de Janeiro: Editora Campus, 1982); Ernest A. Duff and John F. McCamant, *Violence and Repression in Latin America, A Quantitative and Historical Analysis* (New York: Free Press, 1976).

For the definition of 'authoritarianism', these authors generally refer to Juan Linz, 'An Authoritarian Regime: Spain', in E. Allardt and S. Rokkan, eds, *Mass Politics, Studies in Political Sociology* (New York: Free Press, 1970). It reads as follows: 'Authoritarian regimes are political systems with limited, nor responsible, political pluralism; without elaborate and guiding ideology (but with distinctive mentalities); without intensive nor extensive political mobilization (except at some points in their development); and in which a leader (or occasionally a small group) exercises power within formally ill-defined limits but actually quite precise ones'.

[3]Alain Rouquié, *L'État militaire en Amérique latine* (Paris: Seuil, 1982), pp. 45-6 (our translation).

[4]Alain Touraine, *Les sociétés dépendantes* (Paris: Duculot, 1976), ch. 3; also Alain Touraine, *La parole et le sang* (Paris: Éditions Odile Jacob, 1988), p. 76.

[5]This fundamental distinction flows directly from the analytical framework of Alain Touraine in *Production de la société* (Paris: Seuil, 1973).

[6]Touraine, *La Parole et le sang*, p. 74.

[7]The dark side of command, which flows from these unequal yet non-neutral relations, is a violence that has recently been baptized by theologians as 'structural' and is seldom seen by the observer. Only the violence of the excluded makes front-page news. The daily brutality with which we are dealing—the landless peasant, the 'settler' fallen out of favour, that of the troop that expels factory workers for simple wage demands—is not a phenomenon of the past. Violence from above is ever-present in the most seemingly regulated societies to such zones of freedom as modern wage industries with an organized and

combative proletariat, confronted with social conflict or economic tension' (Rouquié, *L'État militaire*, p. 48 [our translation]).

[8]'[. . .] the concentration of social power illegitimizes *ipso facto* all measures which do not reflect or conform with the relations of domination' (Alain Rouquié, *Amérique latine; Introduction à l'Extrême-Occident* [Paris: Seuil, 1987], p. 114 [our translation]).

[9]Ibid., p. 123 (our translation).

[10]Ibid., p. 114 (our translation).

[11]Touraine, *La parole et le sang*, p. 332.

[12]Golbery do Couto e Silva, *Conjunctura Política Nacional. O Poder Executivo & Geopolítica do Brasil* (Rio de Janeiro: Livraria José Olympio Editora, 1981), p. 431, as quoted by Maria Helena Moreira Alves, *Estado e oposicao no Brasil (1964-1984)* (Petropolis: Editora Vozes, 1984), p. 40 (our translation).

[13]At most it can be referred to as a reference framework. Anti-communism is another such ideology. Although it is pervasive in western democracies, its manifestations have been quite different from country to country as well as at different historical times.

[14]Victor Villanueva, *El CAEM y las fuersa armadas peruanas* (Lima: Institutos de Estudios Peruanos, 1972).

[15]Cynthia McClintock and Abraham F. Lowenthal, *The Peruvian Experiment Reconsidered* (Princeton: Princeton University Press, 1983).

[16]Richard J. Barnet makes a similar statement, not inspired by El Salvador or Paraguay, but referring to the prevailing situation in the United States. He writes: 'The only even quasi-official definition of 'national security' I have found is in a dictionary that was prepared for the Joint Chiefs of Staff: 'a. a military or defense advantage over any foreign nation or group of nations, or b. a favorable foreign relations position, or c. a defense posture capable of successfully resisting hostile or destructive action from within, overt or covert'. . . . Security is treated as a scarce commodity. If I have more of it, you must by definition have less of it. The inevitable result is that each player seeks more security by making his potential adversaries more insecure. This is obviously a prescription for permanent war in one form or another' ('Reflections. Rethinking National Strategy', *The New Yorker*, 21 March 1988, p. 107).

This permanent war perspective is echoed by Henry Kissinger who wrote: 'The foundation of stable order is the relative security—and therefore the relative insecurity—of its members'. (In Martin Kalb and Bernard Kalb, *Kissinger* [Boston: Little, Brown, 1974], p. 102).

[17]By 'homogeneity', we mean that the points of convergency are greater than the occasional differences.

[18]Rouquié, *Amérique latine*, pp. 121, 124.

[19]In a land screaming for justice, the newly elected President Cerezo of Guatemala has made it clearly known that his administration has no intention of initiating an agrarian reform.

[20]'The victor's fear is derived from the traumatic experience before the victory; from the perception of the created effects on the defeated; from the obscure premonition that the repressive machine put into action against the vanquished could one day transform into an uncontrollable Frankenstein; from the feeling that all victory is fleeting; and from the backlash of terror of the revenge of the defeated' (Manuel Antonio M. Garretón, 'Panorama del Miedo en los Regimenes Militares: un Esquema General' [paper prepared for the conference *La Cultura del Miedo*, Buenos Aires, May 1985, revised in September 1987; our translation], p. 2).

[21]The following part will closely follow the line of Garretón's fine essay.

[22]Such as the Indian communities in the Peruvian Province of Ayacucho, who are reported to be victims of both the armed forces, for refusing to collaborate, and the Sendero Luminoso rebels, for resisting espousal of the revolutionary cause.

[23]As described in the study of I. Santi and S. Sigal, 'Autoritarisme et légitimité dans les

discours militaires: Argentine et Chili' (Paris: Groupe de recherche sur l'Amérique latine, 1983).

[24] Amnesty International, *Chile Briefing*, Sept. 1986, p. 2.

[25] CONADEP, *Nunca Más; Informe de la Comisión nacional sobre la desaparición de personas* (Buenos Aires: Eudeba, 1986).

[26] R. Dworkin, 'Report from Hell', *New York Review of Books*, 17 July 1986, p. 11.

[27] Cynthia Brown, ed., *With Friends Like These. . . The Americas Watch Report on Human Rights & U.S. Policy in Latin America* (New York: Pantheon, 1985).

[28] Other groups targeted were university and high-school students (21%); professionals, such as lawyers and doctors (10.7%); professors (5.7%); autonomous individuals (5%); housewives (3.8%); draftees and minor police officials (2.5%); journalists (1.6%); artists and actors (1.3%), and clergy (0.3%). CONADEP, *Nunca Más*, p. 296.

[29] Latin American Regional Report, Southern Cone (4 Aug. 1989), p. 4.

[30] See the classic work of Edwin Lieuwen, 'The Changing Role of the Military in Latin America', *Journal of Inter-American Studies* 3, no. 4 (Oct. 1961), pp. 559-69.

[31] Amnesty International, *Chile Briefing*, p. 14.

[32] Inter-Church Committee on Human Rights in Latin America, *Newsletter* (Toronto), no. 1-2 (1987), p. 16.

[33] Amnesty International, *Chile Briefing*, p. 22.

[34] Ibid.

[35] Inter-Church Committee, *Newsletter*, p. 15.

[36] 'On the record of its first year in office, in its lack of commitment and its apparent incapacity to act, the new civilian government in Guatemala has failed the test. Formal changes in government structure have not resulted from or in a fundamental change of power. The rigid reactionary nature of the social project in Guatemala remains very much intact' (Inter-Church Committee, *Newsletter*, p. 29).

'The Guatemalan officers, however, have made it clear to the Cerezo government that they will not tolerate interference in their counterinsurgency programs, nor will they allow fundamental reforms in economic and social institutions' Richard R. Fagen, *Forging Peace. The Challenge of Central America* [New York: Basil Blackwell, 1987], p. 30).

[37] Amnesty International, *Guatemala: The Human Rights Record* (London: Amnesty International Publications, 1987), p. 5.

[38] Armed guerrilla insurgency is found mainly in the departments of El Quiche, Sololá, Sacatepéquez, Alta and Baja Verapaz, Huehuetenango, San Marcos, El Petén, Chimaltenango, Escuinila, Quetzaltenango, and Retaljuleu.

[39] *Landino* is a term used to distinguish rural people of mixed blood, who usually have Spanish as a mother tongue and do not wear traditional native dress, from pure-blooded Indians.

[40] Amnesty International, *Guatemala*, Appendix IV.

[41] '[Decree law 08-86] rules out any possibility of prosecuting the perpetrators of such crimes or their accomplices. Prosecution of anyone who concealed these crimes is also ruled out. According to the local and foreign press this and other decree laws passed in the final days of the Mejia Victores administration, appear to have been drafted in agreement with the incoming civilian government of President Vinicio Cerezo Arévalo. During his presidential campaign he had made it clear that he would not sanction the prosecution of members of the military and security forces for past human rights violations' (Amnesty International, *Guatemala.*, p. 5).

[42] One of the extremely rare and unsuccessful attempts to restore control over police forces occurred only two weeks after the new Cerezo government took office. 'On February 4th the police force's Special Operations Reaction Battalion (BROE) surrounded the installations of the Department of Technical Investigations (DIT). All 600 members of the DIT were taken to the National Police's Second Precinct where most were held for more than 24 hours. The following day President Cerezo, citing constant denunciations of human rights abuses, announced that the department was being dissolved, about one hun-

dred of its personnel fired for abuses and the rest re-assigned to uniformed units. Only one of these fired for abuses was charged (with the murder of a fellow officer). Half of the five hundred slated for re-assignment subsequently quit the force. Some, it is feared, may be continuing their former activities on a fee-for-service basis' (Inter-Church Committee, *Newsletter*, 1987, p. 30).

[43]Many studies have shown how unions have been integrated in the vertical system of domination. Even popular mobilization was used/manipulated by governments in the power struggle that opposed conflicting élites; they are called populist regimes. See Luciano Martins, *Pouvoir et développement économique: formation et évolution des structures politiques au Brésil* (Paris: Anthropos, 1976), ch. 3.

[44]This is what the Brazilian Partido des Trabalhadores (PT) is trying to achieve with great difficulty, having to fight constantly both internally and externally against offers of co-optation.

[45]Rouquié, *L'État militaire*, p. 49 (our translation).

[46]Thomas Bruneau and Philippe Faucher, 'Back to Politics: The Freed Path to Regime Change in Latin America and Southern Europe', Paper presented to the conference: 'Démocraties en Amérique latine', Université de Montréal, March 1987.

G. GRANT AMYOT: VIA ITALIANA AL SOCIALISMO: THE ITALIAN COMMUNIST PARTY AND DEMOCRACY

[1]Joseph LaPalombara, *Democracy, Italian Style* (New Haven: Yale, 1987), pp. 237-8 (emphasis added).

[2]For instance, Luigi Granelli, Christian Democratic Minister for Scientific Research, said recently: 'The PCI has now conformed to the models of the great social-democratic parties and it is therefore impossible to discriminate against it' (*L'Espresso*, 16 Aug. 1987, p. 13). The same article contains similar statements by other DC leaders. Cf. LaPalombara, *Democracy*, pp. 131-2, for a similar statement by Ciriaco De Mita, Secretary of the DC.

[3]See ibid., pp. 235-9.

[4]Ibid., p. 238.

[5]For a fuller account of the evolution of the PCI's strategy, see Grant Amyot, *The Italian Communist Party: The Crisis of the Popular Front Strategy* (London: Croom Helm, 1981), ch. 2.

[6]In his famous 1895 introduction to Marx's *The Class Struggles in France*, Engels had suggested the socialist parties would soon come to power by electoral means without an economic crisis, but this was not the dominant interpretation at the time, and the introduction was altered by the editors of the German Social-Democratic journal where it appeared.

[7]Lenin's *Imperialism, the Highest Stage of Capitalism* (1917), based in large part on Rudolf Hilferding's *Finance Capital* (1910), traced the war back to the growth of large monopoly firms and the linking of banks and industry typical of advanced capitalism.

[8]See Joan Barth Urban, *Moscow and the Italian Communist Party* (Ithaca: Cornell, 1986), ch. 4.

[9]'La politica di unità nazionale dei comunisti' (1944), in Palmiro Togliatti, *La politica di Salerno* (Rome: Editori Riuniti, 1969), p. 13 (my trans.). Available in English translation in Palmiro Togliatti, *On Gramsci and Other Writings*, ed. and intro. Donald Sassoon (London: Lawrence and Wishart, 1979), pp. 37-8.

[10]See Urban, *Moscow*, chs. 1-4, and Togliatti, 'Sulle particolarità della rivoluzione spagnuola' in Palmiro Togliatti, *Sul movimento operaio internazionale*, ed. Franco Ferri (Rome: Editori Riuniti, 1972).

[11]Leo Valiani, 'La Resistenza italiana', *Rivista storica italiana*, 85, 1 (1973).

268 Dissent and the State

[12]Grant Amyot, 'The Italian Left in the Reconstruction Period (1944-47): Neither Revolution nor Structural Reform', *Europa* 5, no. 2 (1982).

[13]See Fernando Claudin, *The Communist Movement: From Comintern to Cominform*, Part II (New York: Monthly Review, 1975), pp. 379-81.

[14]On the basic principles of the Constitution, see Costantino Mortati, *Istituzioni di diritto pubblico*, I (Padua: CEDAM, 1969), pp. 140-9 and Giangiulio Ambrosini, Introduction to *Costituzione italiana* (Turin: Einaudi, 1975), pp. xxiv-l.

[15]*Costituzione italiana*, p. 3 (my trans.). Available in English translation in Norman Kogan, *The Government of Italy* (New York: Crowell, 1962), pp. 188-9.

[16]'Elementi per una Dichiarazione programmatica', approved by the 8th Congress of the PCI, in Alberto Cecchi, ed., *Storia del P.C.I. attraverso i congressi* (Rome: Newton Compton, 1977), pp. 179-80.

[17]The earlier thesis that the US role was central has been subject to much debate. See, for instance, Antonio Gambino, *Storia del dopoguerra*, 2nd ed, 2 vols (Bari: Laterza, 1978), ch. 8-10 and Pietro Scoppola, *Gli anni della Costituente fra politica e storia* (Bologna: Mulino, 1980).

[18]See Amyot, *Italian Communist Party*, pp. 46-9.

[19]Secchia's organization section, comprising the most active cadres, did maintain a skeletal structure ready to return to clandestinity, but it existed largely on paper and disappeared after 1956. I obtained this information from conversations with former members of the section.

[20]See Togliatti's speech at an April 1954 Central Committee meeting, 'Per un accordo tra comunisti e cattolici per salvare la civiltà umana', in P. Togliatti, *Comunisti, socialisti, cattolici* (Rome: Editori Riuniti, 1974).

[21]See, e.g., Giorgio Amendola, *Il rinnovamento del PCI* (Rome: Editori Riuniti, 1978), pp. 42-5.

[22]Cf. Donald Sassoon, *Togliatti e la via italiana al socialismo* (Turin: Einaudi, 1980), pp. 208 ff. See also the shorter English version, *The Strategy of the Italian Communist Party: From the Resistance to the Historic Compromise* (New York: St. Martin's, 1981), ch. 7.

[23]Sassoon, *Togliatti*, pp. 209-11, presents some of the major documents.

[24]'Elementi per una Dichiarazione programmatica', pp. 180-1.

[25]Ibid., p. 177.

[26]Amyot, *Italian Communist Party*, pp. 25-8.

[27]See Anon., *La strage di Stato* (Rome: La nuova sinistra/Samonà e Savelli, 1970).

[28]'Riflessioni dopo i fatti del Cile', three articles originally published in *Rinascita*, 28 Sept. and 5 and 12 Oct. 1973, reprinted in Rodolfo Mechini, ed., *I comunisti italiani e il Cile* (Rome: Editori Riuniti, 1973).

[29]Ibid., pp. 31, 36.

[30]Ibid., p. 36.

[31]Ibid., p. 20.

[32]See Giuseppe Di Palma, *Surviving without Governing: the Italian Parties in Parliament* (Berkeley: University of California Press, 1977).

[33]Urban, *Moscow*, pp. 343-4.

[34]Giorgio Galli, *L'Italia sotterranea: Storia, politica e scandali* (Bari: Laterza, 1983), p. 92.

[35]In Pietro Valenza, ed., *I paesi socialisti nell'analisi dei comunisti italiani* (Rome: Newton Compton, 1978), p. 9 (my trans.). Available in English translation in Togliatti, *On Gramsci*, p. 122.

[36]Interview, pp. 15-18 (pp. 128-35 in Togliatti, *On Gramsci*).

[37]See Sassoon, *Togliatti*, ch. 6.

[38]See, e.g., Pietro Ingrao, 'L'origine degli errori', *Rinascita* 18, no. 12 (Dec. 1961).

[39]See Sassoon, *Togliatti*, pp. 178-80.

[40]Amyot, *Italian Communist Party*, pp. 178-9, 190-1.

[41]Urban, *Moscow*, pp. 17, 343.

[42]*Corriere della Sera*, 15 June 1976.

[43]*L'Unità*, 16 Dec. 1981, p. 1.

[44]Urban, *Moscow*, p. 332.

[45]Joan Barth Urban, 'The PCI's 17th Congress: a triumph of the "new internationalism"' in Raffaella Nanetti, et al., eds, *Italian Politics: A Review*, vol. 2 (London: Pinter, 1988), pp. 48-50 and *L'Espresso*, 15 Jan. 1989, p. 26.

[46]*La Repubblica*, 21/22 Dec. 1986, and Antonio Gambino, 'I nuovi russi', *L'Espresso*, 11 Jan. 1987.

[47]See Angelo Bolaffi et al., eds., *Per una analisi del neofascismo*, Quaderni di Democrazia e Diritto, 1 (Rome: Editori Riuniti, 1976), pp. 175-6.

[48]Bolaffi (ibid., pp. 175-218) contains extracts from the request of the Rome prosecutor's office for permission to proceed against the MSI's leaders on the charge of reconstitution of the Fascist party, which support this contention.

[49]The PCI called for the dissolution of the MSI at the time of the riots in protest against the latter's 1960 Genoa congress (*L'Unità*, 4 July 1960). By 1976, however, its attitude had changed strikingly, and the Communist protests against the shooting of a young Communist by a campaigning MSI deputy significantly did not include a demand for the party's dissolution. (See e.g., ibid., 3 June 1976).

[50]E.g., Giorgio Amendola, 'I comunisti e il movimento studentesco: necessità della lotta su due fronti', *Rinascita*, 12 April 1968.

[51]*L'Unità*, 23 Feb. 1978, quoted in Robin Wagner-Pacifici, *The Moro Morality Play* (Chicago: University of Chicago Press, 1986), p. 85.

[52]Ibid., p. 132.

[53]See LaPalombara, *Democracy*, pp. 183-4.

[54]Galli, *L'Italia sotterranea*, pp. 227-38. Ten years after the Moro kidnapping, new revelations are still being made, though the entire truth may never be known.

[55]Bolaffi, *Per una analisi del neofascismo*, p. 137.

[56] See Giorgio Bocca, *Il caso 7 aprile: Toni Negri e la grande inquisizione* (Milan: Feltrinelli, 1980) and Giovanni Palombarini, *7 aprile: il processo e la storia* (Venice: Arsenale Cooperativa, 1982).

[57]See *L'Unità*, 29 Nov. 1987 and *La Repubblica*, 27 Nov. 1987.

[58]Berlinguer in Mechini, *I comunisti italiani*, p. 24.

[59]Cf. Palmiro Togliatti, *Lectures on Fascism* (London: Lawrence and Wishart, 1976 [1935]).

[60]Gramsci, *Selections from the Prison Notebooks*, ed. and trans. Q. Hoare and G. Nowell Smith (London: Lawrence and Wishart, 1971), pp. 235-8.

[61]Galli, *L'Italia sotteranea*, pp. 90-8.

[62]See G. Hodgson, 'The US Response', in Paolo Filo della Torre et al., eds, *Eurocommunism: Myth or Reality?* (Harmondsworth: Penguin, 1979), pp. 288-9.

[63]See Filo della Torre, *passim*, especially ch. 4 and 5.

[64]See *L'Espresso*, 5 July 1987, on the vote against the new Vice-Secretary-General by the *miglioristi*, eleven of the thirty-eight members of the PCI Executive. Among the contributions of the *miglioristi* to the debate on the nature of the PCI, see Napoleone Colajanni, *Comunisti al bivio* (Milan: Mondadori, 1987) and Leonardo Paggi, *I comunisti italiani e il riformismo: un confronto con le socialdemocrazie europee* (Turin: Einaudi, 1986).

[65]See Grant Amyot, 'Via italiana al riformismo: the PCI and Occhetto's "New Course"' in *Italian Politics: A Review* vol. 4, ed. Raffaella Nanetti and R. Catanzaro (forthcoming).

[66]Amyot, *Italian Communist Party*, p. 209.

[67]Grant Amyot, 'Italy: the Long Twilight of the DC Regime', in Steven Wolinetz, ed., *Parties and Party Systems in Liberal Democracies* (London: Routledge, 1988). According to Paggi, the PCI has not even been as reformist as the Northern European social democracies because it has attempted to accommodate the interests of too many strata instead of straightforwardly representing its principal constituency, the working class (*I comunisti italiani e il riformismo*). While Paggi is right on many counts, I would emphasize that the Italian context forces us to place a different interpretation on the party's behaviour.

270 | Dissent and the State

⁶⁸See Adam Przeworski and John Sprague, *Paper Stones: A History of Electoral Socialism* (Chicago: University of Chicago Press, 1986), and 'Party Strategy, Class Organization, and Individual Voting', ch. 3 in Adam Przeworski, *Capitalism and Social Democracy* (Cambridge: Cambridge University Press, 1985).
⁶⁹Amyot, *Italian Communist Party*, p. 24.

REG WHITAKER: LEFT-WING DISSENT AND THE STATE: CANADA IN THE COLD WAR ERA

¹At its founding, the Canadian party took on a dual form, with a 'secret' or 'illegal' organization paralleling the visible form. But this conspiratorial pretence of secrecy was dropped officially in 1924. In the early wartime period of enforced illegality during the Nazi-Soviet Pact (1939-41), the Communists did distribute underground pamphlets, which exhorted Canadians to take up arms and transform the war into a 'civil war against the bourgeoisie' (Norman Penner, *Canadian Communism: the Stalin Years and Beyond* [Toronto: Methuen, 1988] pp. 167-8. This was, however, an isolated example of rhetorical excess and there is of course no evidence that anyone, including the Communist rank-and-file, heeded this absurd and politically suicidal line.
²S.W. Horall, 'Canada's security service: a brief history', RCMP *Quarterly* 50, no. 3 (Summer 1985), p. 45.
³The RCMP branch devoted to counter-subversion and counter-espionage underwent many name changes over the years (Intelligence Section, Special Branch, Security Service, etc.). For simplicity, I will refer here simply to the 'security service' regardless of its formal designation.
⁴Public Archives of Canada (PAC), Norman Robertson Papers, v. 12, f. 147, Rivett-Carnac to Robertson, 24 Jan. 1939.
⁵See Reg Whitaker, 'Official repression of Communism during World War II', *Labour/le Travail* 17 (Spring 1986), pp. 133-68.
⁶*The Report of the Royal Commission Appointed under Order in Council PC 411 of February 5, 1946 To Investigate the Facts . . .* etc. (Ottawa, 1946); the Commission documents and exhibits, with associated internal papers, etc. were requested by me under the Access to Information Act in 1983. After an extraordinarily long delay, the Privy Council Office complied in the fall of 1984. The documents, less some material exempted under various clauses of the Act, are now in the Public Archives of Canada.
⁷Reg Whitaker, 'Fighting the Cold War on the Home Front: America, Britain, Australia and Canada', *Socialist Register 1984: The Uses of Anti-Communism* (London: Merlin Press, 1984), p. 24.
⁸This appears to be the argument of Lawrence Aronsen in a highly misleading and inadequately documented article, '"Peace, order and good government during the Cold War"', *Intelligence and National Security* 1, no. 3 (Sept. 1986), pp. 357-80.
⁹*Report*, p. 689.
¹⁰Reg Whitaker, 'Origins of the Canadian Government's internal security system, 1946-1952', *Canadian Historical Review* 65, no. 2 (June 1984); Public Archives, Immigration Branch Records, accession 83-84/347, Peter Dwyer to Security Panel, 10 Jan. 1957; Commission of Inquiry Concerning Certain Activities of the RCMP, Second Report, *Freedom and Security under the Law*, vol. 2 (Ottawa: Minister of Supply and Services, 1981) p. 788. Aronsen, in 'Peace, order and good government', makes the ridiculous claim that no more than 'few thousand' civil servants were ever screened.
¹¹'Security investigation of government employees', 24 Sept. 1952, quoted in Whitaker, 'Origins', p. 182.
¹²Royal Commission on Security, *Report* (Abridged) (Ottawa, 1969), 6; *Freedom and*

Security, vol. 2, p. 793. Treasury Board Circular No. 1986-26, 'Government Security Policy', 18 June 1986.

[13]Confidential interviews. In two recent cases that have become public, those of Jack Gold and André Henri, the former before the Federal Court and the latter before SIRC, charges of blackmailing for co-operation have been aired; see Reg Whitaker, 'Witchhunt in the civil service', *This Magazine* 20, no. 4 (Oct./Nov. 1986), pp. 24-30.

[14]*Jack Gold* v. *the Queen*, Federal Court of Canada, 1987.

[15]The information on immigration is drawn from my *Double Standard: The Secret History of Canadian Immigration* (Toronto: Lester and Orpen Dennys, 1987).

[16]Commission of Inquiry on War Criminals, *Report*, Part 1: Public (Ottawa 1986); David Matas with Susan Charendoff, *Justice Delayed: Nazi War Criminals in Canada* (Toronto: Summerhill, 1987); Sol Littman, *The Rauca Case: War Criminal on Trial* (Toronto: Lester and Orpen Dennys, 1983).

[17]*Double Standard*, 211.

[18]Early in 1988 the story was revealed of a Polish airline hijacker convicted to prison in Western Europe and later run past Canadian immigration controls by the security service so that he could work for CSIS within the Polish Canadian community (Rick Gibbons, 'Polish hijacker says RCMP recruited him in Europe to be spy', *Globe and Mail*, 22 Jan. 1988, and 'Polish spy network alleged in Canada', 23 Jan. 1988).

Despite intrusive surveillance of Communist-front ethnic organizations over the years, it would be a great exaggeration to assert that the security service has been responsible for their decline. Especially among Eastern European groups, revulsion against the example of Soviet Communism has been genuine and widespread and probably owes little or nothing to the activities of the security service.

[19]'Fighting the Cold War on the Home Front', pp. 43-51.

[20]The ideas in the preceding paragraphs are elaborated and documented in more detail in Whitaker, 'The Cold War and the myth of liberal-internationalism: Canadian foreign policy reconsidered, 1945-1953', Paper presented to a joint session of the annual meetings of the Canadian Historical Association and the Canadian Political Science Association, Winnipeg, 8 June 1986.

[21]James Barros, *No Sense of Evil* (Toronto: Deneau, 1986). I have responded critically to Barros's case in 'Return to the crucible: the persecution of Herbert Norman', *Canadian Forum*, Nov. 1986, pp. 11-28. See also the sympathetic and in my view, much more reliable, *Innocence Is Not Enough: the Life and Death of Herbert Norman* (Vancouver: Douglas and McIntyre, 1986) by Roger Bowen, along with the earlier collection edited by Bowen, *E.H. Norman, His Life and Scholarship* (Toronto: University of Toronto Press, 1984).

[22]C.W. Harvison to L.H. Nicholson, 26 July 1955, CSIS files (obtained under Access to Information).

[23]*Freedom and Security under the Law*, vols. 1 and 2; Sawatsky, *Men in the Shadows: the RCMP Security Service* (Toronto: Doubleday, 1980).

[24]*People and Process in Transition*, Report to the Solicitor General by the independent advisory team on the Canadian Security Intelligence Service (October 1987); Solicitor General of Canada, 'Kelleher sets mid-course correction for CSIS', news release (30 Nov. 1987).

[25]One must always qualify judgements on the effectiveness of counter-espionage operations with the proviso that they are based on public evidence: real successes in counter-espionage may of course have remained secret. But see John Sawatsky, *For Services Rendered: Leslie James Bennett and the RCMP Security Service* (Toronto: Doubleday, 1982) for the contrary opinion: 'Like the coyote flubbing his attacks ᴖn the defiant roadrunner, whatever the Security Service did failed to defeat, much less faze, the Soviets' (p. 188).

[26]Keith Walden, *Visions of Order: the Canadian Mounties in Symbol and Myth* (Toronto: Butterworths, 1982), especially pp. 117-36.

[27]C.E. Rivett-Carnac to the Director of Criminal Investigation, 'Re: Reorganization—Special Branch, headquarters and divisions', 6 Jan. 1947. CSIS files, copy obtained under Access to Information.

[28]These bulletins, circulated internally under varying names, have been released for the period from the early 1920s through the mid-1950s by Access requests made by myself or by Professor Greg Kealey of Memorial University. CSIS has agreed to waive copyright to allow publication of these bulletins as source books in Canadian history. The Committee on Labour Studies plans to publish successive volumes under the joint editorship of Professor Kealey and myself.

[29]The revelation that Marc Boivin, CSN strike organizer convicted of conspiracy to plant a bomb in a hotel, had been for some fifteen years a security service 'source' (or possibly more) was particularly unsettling, raising, as it inevitably does, questions about *agent provocateur* tactics.

[30]Security Intelligence Review Committee, 'Section 54 report to the Solicitor General of Canada on CSIS' use of its investigative powers with respect to the labour movement', 25 March 1988.

[31]Irving Abella, *Nationalism, Communism and Canadian Labour* (Toronto: University of Toronto, 1973) offers the most detailed account of the anti-Communist purges within the CCL. The TLC purges will be treated extensively in a forthcoming book by Reg Whitaker and Gary Marcuse, *Cold War Canada*. On the waterfront struggle, William Kaplan's *Everything That Floats: Pat Sullivan, Hal Banks and the Seamen's Union of Canada* (Toronto: University of Toronto Press, 1987) is a very well-documented account which accepts the basic premise that Communism is an illegitimate participant in trade-union activities (while in no way apologizing for the conduct of the SIU).

[32]Two standard social-democratic sources on the CCF-NDP and the union movement apply this precise double standard to the Communists apparently without question: Walter Young, *The Anatomy of a Party: the National CCF, 1932-1961* (Toronto: University of Toronto Press, 1969) pp. 254-85; Gad Horowitz, *Canadian Labour in Politics* (Toronto: University of Toronto Press, 1968) pp. 85-131.

[33]National Archives, Privy Council Office Records, series 18, vol. 103, files S-100-M & S-100-I (1) (1949-50); vol. 188, file S-100-D; vol. 189, file S-100-I (1) (1951). The UE in fact signed a contract with Canadian General Electric that denied an employee the right to grieve against the effect of government instructions in matters of national security in defence-related work. The Security Panel looked to this 'interesting development' as a model for other, less left-wing, unions.

[34]A former civilian analyst in the RCMP security service, Mark McClung, recalled in an interview that he had once proposed a full-scale study of the objectives of Communist activity in the union movement, but his suggestion was rejected on the grounds that no purpose could be served by such a study.

[35]Whitaker, *Double Standard*, pp. 154-64.

[36]On American Cold War liberalism, see, *inter alia*, Mary Sperling McAuliffe, *Crisis on the Left: Cold War Politics and American Liberals 1947-1954* (Amherst, Mass.: University of Massachusetts Press, 1978); Richard Freeland, *The Truman Doctrine and the Origins of McCarthyism* (N.Y.: New York University Press, 2nd ed. 1985); and Athan Theoharis, *Seeds of Repression: Harry S Truman and the Origins of McCarthyism* (Chicago: Quadrangle Books, 1971).

[37]Sawatsky reports that Coldwell 'became the conservative anchor on the commission and often argued against some of the more liberal proposals of his two fellow commissioners' (*Men In the Shadows*, p. 194). Coldwell told me in 1965 that his proudest achievement of all his years in politics was helping to bring Canada into NATO.

[38]In retrospect, Lewis freely admitted that with the expulsion of the left-nationalist Waffle movement in the early 1970s, 'the best brains in the party were swept out'. He nevertheless felt that the kind of radical socialism that the Waffle represented could not be ab-

sorbed or tolerated by a social democratic party (interviews with the author, Ottawa, 1979).

[39]There have been unconfirmed reports that the CIA carried out surveillance of the Barrett NDP government in BC from 1972 to 1975. The activities of so-called 'friendly' intelligence agencies on Canadian soil raise a host of interesting issues, but go beyond the scope of the present essay.

[40]Commission of Inquiry Concerning Certain Activities of the RCMP, Third Report (Ottawa: Minister of Supply and Services, 1981).

[41]Gouvernement du Québec, Ministère de la justice, *Rapport de la Commission d'enquête sur des opérations policières en térritoire québecois* (Québec, 1981); McDonald Commission, as cited. I have written an analysis of some of the major issues involved in 'Canada: the RCMP scandals' in A. Markovits and M. Silverstein, eds., *The Politics of Scandal: Power and Process in Liberal Democracies* (N.Y.: Holmes and Meier, 1988).

[42]Among the visible public manifestations have been the Boivin affair and the evidence of trade-union penetration; infiltration of peace campaigns; the surveillance of a left-wing magazine; the falsified wiretap application that led to the resignation of CSIS Director Ted Finn; the unexplained erasure of surveillance tapes of suspects in the Air India disaster; and a number of public-service and citizenship security cases in which CSIS evidence has been rejected by the civilian review committee.

[43]I have documented this change in the area of immigration security policy in *Double Standard*, especially pp. 233-7 and ff.

[44]James Littleton, *Target Nation: Canada and the Western Intelligence Network* (Toronto: Lester and Orpen Dennys, 1986) p. 152.

[45]Joseph F. Fletcher, 'Mass and elite attitudes about wiretapping in Canada: implications for democratic theory and practice', Unpublished research paper (December 1987). Professor Fletcher's study of mass and élite opinion samples does indicate that on general questions of freedom of expression, élites tend to be somewhat more liberal. However, on the specific issue of the authorization of wiretaps on groups or persons apparently representing threats to security as defined in the CSIS Act (spies, foreign agents, terrorists, and subversives), in each case the mass sample was less supportive than the élite samples. Interestingly, wiretaps on terrorists received the highest level of approval (66 per cent of the mass sample; 81 per cent of the élite samples), while wiretaps on subversives received the lowest level of approval from the mass sample: indeed, the mass sample was almost two to one against (34.4 per cent 'yes' to 63.7 per cent 'no'), while élite opinion was narrowly in favour (51.2 per cent 'yes' to 47.3 per cent 'no').

[46]In a speech to the participants in the 'Domestic Security: Issues for Democracy' conference at Osgoode Hall Law School, York University, 8 May 1987, Finn insisted that Soviet-sponsored subversion represented the greatest single threat to the security of Canada.

[47]Canada. Parliament. Senate. Special Committee on Terrorism and the Public Safety, *Terrorism: The Report of the Senate Special Committee on Terrorism and the Public Safety* (Ottawa, 1987) pp. 9-10.

[48]There is the case of the Litton bombers responsible for attacks on property. Despite their extraordinary tough sentencing, these activists had eschewed attacks on people and so in a sense fall outside of the European-style definition of left-wing terrorists.

[49]See the mainly reasonable proposals made in *Terrorism*.

JANINE KRIEBER: PROTEST AND FRINGE GROUPS IN QUÉBEC

[1]Nathalie Petrowsky, 'Que sont-ils devenus?', *Le Devoir*, 2 Dec. 1979.

[2]Jean-Marc Piotte, *La communauté perdue: Petite histoire des militantismes* (Montreal: vlb éditeur, 1987).

[3]These three films were the result of a study of former militants now in their forties: *Notes de arrière-saison* (20 min.); *Les temps des cigales* (30 min.); and *Charade chinoise* (91 min.), produced by the National Film Board of Canada.

[4]Léon Dion, *Québec 1945-2000*, vol. I, *A la recherche du Québec* (Québec: Les Presses de l'Université Laval, 1989).

[5]By 'discursive strategy' I mean the use of certain properties of language, most often its connotative properties, to build a narration that, through its effects, becomes an instrument of political action. On the effect of legends on the writing of history, see Jean-Pierre Faye, *Théorie du récit: Introduction aux langages totalitaires* (Paris: Hermann, 1972).

[6]By ideological cores, we mean something very close to the idea of the 'empty structure', which, to have meaning, must be part of a 'package', but nevertheless has the ability to determine the meaning of the whole (Roland Barthes, 'Introduction à l'analyse structurale du récit', in *L'analyse structurale des récits* [Paris: Seuil, 1981], pp. 7-33; re-issue of an article published in *Communication 8* [1966]). Faye (*Théorie du récit*) notes the attractive force of these signs, which become magnetic elements in ideological discourses.

[7]G. Bergeron, *Le gouverne politique* (Paris, Québec: Mouton, 1977), p. 33.

[8]It is no coincidence that the first modern insurrectionist terrorist group chose the name of Narodnaya Volya.

[9]Bergeron, *La gouverne politique*, p. 33 (trans.)

[10]Serge Moscovici, *Psychosociologie des minorités actives* (Paris: PUF, 1979).

[11]'. . . the only variable with explanatory power, . . . which is entirely independent of the majority, the minority and authority, in its determination of influence (Ibid., p. 111) (trans.).

[12]Moscovici, *Psychosociologie des minorités*, p. 164. For a general theoretical discussion, refer to Jean Piaget, *L'épistémologie génétique* (Paris: Presses universitaires de France, 1970).

[13]Lewis A. Coser, *The Function of Social Conflict* (Glencoe: Free Press, 1956).

[14]Gilles Lebel, *Horizon 1980. Une étude sur l'évolution de l'économie du Québec de 1946 à 1968 et sur ses perspectives d'avenir* (Gouvernement du Québec, 1970).

[15]Québec, Bureau de la Statistique, *Démographie québécoise: Passé, présent et avenir* (Quebec: Éditeur officiel, 1983).

[16]The reform of the public service, suffrage for women, mandatory school attendance, the creation of Hydro-Québec, and the Labour Code. See Paul-André Linteau et al., *Histoire du Québec contemporaine: Le Québec depuis 1930* (Montreal: Boréal Express, 1986), pp. 141-3. Analyses of relative deprivation could be applied to this historical process (separation—withdrawal into self-protest) (Ted Robert Gurr, *Why Men Rebel* [Princeton: Princeton University Press, 1970]).

[17]Fernand Dumont, Jean Hamelin, Jean-Paul Montminy, *Idéologies au Canada français: 1940-1976, vol. 1, La presse—la litterature* (Québec: Presses del'Université Laval, 1981), pp. 43-4.

[18]Borduas, in Daniel Latouche and Diane Poliquin-Bourassa, *Le manuel de la parole: Manifestes québécois*, vol. 2, *1900 à 1959* (Montréal: Boréal Express, 1978), p. 279 (trans.)

[19]Ibid., p. 280.

[20] Ibid., p. 281.

[21]The spearhead of this movement was certainly the man who became the prestigious editor-in-chief of *Le Devoir*, André Laurendeau.

[22]Linteau et al., *Histoire du Québec contemporain*, p. 395.

[23]In Latouche and Poliquin-Bourassa, *Le manuel de la parole*, vol. 3, *1960 à 1976* (Montréal: Boréal Express, 1979), p. 37.

[24]Léon Dion has already identified and analyzed the breaking up of Québec nationalism into various socio-political programs: 'Four means of expressing Québec nationalism can

be identified: a conservative nationalism that, in most of its forms, is defined by lukewarm acceptance of the Canadian political community and by reference to a pre-industrial type of society strongly tainting the sought-after political regime with corporatism; a liberal nationalism . . . that, to the contrary, commits itself fully to the Welfare State and unreservedly supports the idea of a modern, urban and industrial society; a social-democratic nationalism that, because of its ideology, preaches separatism . . . ; a socialist nationalism that, in the end, . . . in its Marxist-Leninist form, aims at radical revolution' (Dion, *Nationalismes et politique au Québec* [Montréal: Hurtubise HMH, 1975], p. 132 [trans.]).

[25] Raoul Roy is considered by many to be the true 'father' of the FLQ.

[26] In Latouche and Poliquin-Bourassa, *Le manuel de la parole*, vol. 2, p. 338 (trans.).

[27] For instance, the theme of the repressive colonial state applied to the Canadian federal state, or the extraordinary success of the expression 'white niggers', which automatically associates Québecers with 'the wretched of the earth'. Pierre Vallières' book *White Niggers of America* (Montréal: Parti-Pris, 1974) is built entirely on this process of association between the case of Québec and the protest ideology of the 1960s.

[28] Two editors of *Parti pris* re-published articles with a major about-face in their positions following the breakup of the RIN and the creation of the PQ (Gilles Bourque and Gilles Dostaler, *Socialisme et indépendance* [Montréal: Boréal Express, 1980]).

[29] In Latouche and Poliquin-Bourassa, *Le manuel de la parole*, vol. 3, p. 52 (trans.).

[30] Ibid., p. 55.

[31] If one is particularly interested in the history of the FLQ, see Louis Fournier, *FLQ. Histoire d'un mouvement clandestin* (Montréal: Québec/Amérique, 1982).

[32] A record of those days was published by Jean Tainturier, *De Gaulle à Quebec: Le dossier des quatre journées* (Montréal: Éditions du Jour, 1967).

[33] In Latouche and Poliquin-Bourassa, *Le Manuel de la parole*, vol. 3, p. 33 (trans.)

[34] For a first-hand account by two militants of this first generation, see Michèle Tremblay, *De Cuba, le FLQ parle* (Montréal: Éditions Intel, 1975), to be read with a critical eye.

[35] I refer here to Rudi Dutschke. In Québec no leader officially took this position, but many simply accepted what the 'system' offered them: teachers, public servants, journalists, editors, and others.

[36] In Latouche and Poliquin-Bourassa, *Le manuel de la parole*, vol. 3, p. 113 (trans.)

[37] Ibid.

[38] In this case, examples abound. As an illustration, we need only the little book published by the Centre de formation populaire, which does not deal with the issue of nationhood until page 134, and summarizes the tactical problems of unionism as follows: 'Until now, it is the Parti Québécois that has been the political springboard for the struggle for independence. Without wishing or being able to decide what the PQ is (its class base, its political strategy, its program . . .) no one can dispute either that the PQ does not have its roots in the struggles of the working class or that it is not the political instrument of that movement, even though in the current situation it is the party least removed from the interests of workers' (Louis Favreau, *Les travailleurs face au pouvoir* [Montréal: Centre de formation populaire/Québec Presse, 1972], pp. 134-5 [trans.]). For an illustration of the debate among Marxists, see the article by Samuel Walsh, 'Quelques questions tactiques soulevées par la victoire du Parti québécois' in Guy Desautels et al., *Pour l'autodétermination du Québec* (Montréal: Éditions Nouvelles Frontières, 1980.

[39] (Editor's note) In 1982 Lévesque diminished the salaries of all government employees, including civil servants, teachers, professors, etc., by a significant amount. This was done by decree (the equivalent of an Order-In-Council) rather than by legislation, and alienated his government from the intellectual and administrative élite.

[40] Piotte, *La communauté perdue*, p. 125.

[41] See the journal *Possibles 10* 2 (1986), 'Du côté des intellectuel-le-s'.

STANLEY BARRETT: THE FAR RIGHT IN CANADA

This paper is taken from my larger study, *Is God a Racist? The Right Wing in Canada* (Toronto, Buffalo and London: University of Toronto Press, 1987).

[1] *White Racism in the 1980s*, a report from the pages of *The Tennessean*, n.d., p. 6.

[2] A. Forster and B. Epstein, *Report on the Ku Klux Klan* (Anti-Defamation League of B'nai B'rith, 1965), p. 13.

[3] S. Lipset and E. Raab, *The Politics of Unreason: Right Wing Extremism in America, 1790-1970* (New York, Evanston, and London: Harper and Row, 1970), p. 21.

[4] Ibid., p. 124.

[5] W. King, 'The Violent Rebirth of the Klan', *New York Times Magazine*, December 1980.

[6] R. Winks, *The Blacks in Canada* (New Haven: Yale University Press, 1971), p. 320.

[7] T. Henson, 'Ku Klux Klan in Western Canada', *Alberta History* 25, no. 4 (1977), pp. 1-8.

[8] W. Calderwood, 'Religious Reactions to the Ku Klux Klan in Saskatchewan', *Saskatchewan History* 26, no. 3 (1973), pp. 103-14.

[9] J. Sher, *White Hoods: Canada's Ku Klux Klan* (Vancouver: New Star, 1983), p. 27.

[10] Ibid.

[11] Winks, *Blacks in Canada*, p. 286.

[12] C. Kilian, *Go Do Some Great Thing* (Vancouver: Douglas and McIntyre, 1978), p. 161.

[13] P. Kyba, 'Ballots and Burning Crosses—The Election of 1929', in Norman Ward and Duff Spafford, eds, *Politics in Saskatchewan* (Toronto: Longmans, 1968), pp. 105-23.

[14] P. Kyba, 'The Saskatchewan General Election of 1929', MA Thesis, Dept. of Economics and Political Science, University of Saskatchewan, 1964, p. 27.

[15] Sher, *White Hoods*, pp. 53-6.

[16] 'The Ku Klux Klan in Saskatchewan' *Queen's Quarterly* 35 (1928), p. 600.

[17] W. Calderwood, 'Pulpit, Press, and Political Reactions to the Ku Klux Klan in Saskatchewan', in S. Clark, J. Grayson, and L. Grayson, eds, *Prophecy and Protest* (Toronto: Gage, 1975), p. 164.

[18] L. Betcherman, *The Swastika and the the Maple Leaf: Fascist Movements in Canada in the Thirties* (Toronto: Fitzhenry and Whiteside, 1975), p. 4.

[19] Ibid., p. 89.

[20] M. Weinfeld, 'La question juive au Québec', *Midstream* 23, p. 24.

[21] Betcherman, *Swastika and the Maple Leaf*, p. 12.

[22] Ibid., pp. 34-6.

[23] Ibid., p. 45.

[24] C. Levitt and W. Shaffir, *The Riots at Christie Pits* (Toronto: Lester and Orpen Dennys, 1987).

[25] Betcherman, *Swastika and the Maple Leaf*, p. 55.

[26] J. Wagner, *Brothers Beyond the Sea: National Socialism in Canada* (Waterloo, Ont.: Wilfrid Laurier University Press, 1981), p. 68.

[27] E. Raab, 'Anti-Semitism in the 1980s', *Midstream* 32 (Feb. 1983), p. 14.

[28] *Globe and Mail*, 15 Nov. 1965.

[29] B. Epstein and A. Forster, *The Radical Right Report on the John Birch Society and Its Allies* (New York: Random House, 1967), p. 136.

[30] *Toronto Telegram*, 23 Nov. 1960.

[31] An advisory committee chaired by Maxwell Cohen, an ex-dean of the McGill Law School, had been established by the minister of justice, to examine hate propaganda in Canada; former prime minister Pierre Trudeau was a member of the committee. See *Report of the Special Committee of Hate Propaganda in Canada* (Ottawa: Queen's Printer, 1966).

[32] The radical right is anti-black, anti-Semitic, anti-communist, anti-egalitarian, anti-homosexual, anti-feminism, anti-abortion, anti-Third World immigration, anti-peace

movement, and anti-world government; it also advocates violence. The fringe right shares many of these elements, but it denies that it is racist, anti-Semitic or fascist, and it eschews violence. This paper is restricted to the description and analysis of the radical right. For data on the fringe right, see Part Three in Barrett, *Is God a Racist?*

[33] A comparable sharp increase in fringe-right groups also took place at that time. Included were the Edmund Burke Society, Campus Alternative, Alternative Forum, Citizens for Foreign Aid Reform (C-FAR), Catholics Against Terrorism, and YAF (Young Americans for Freedom).

[34] The most potent of these religious alternatives is a movement known as Identity, traced back to the British Israel movement in the late 1800s. Identity promotes the view that Jesus Christ was born in Britain and that the true Israel people of the Bible are Anglo-Saxons, Scandinavians, and Germans. Identity provides spiritual support for the radical-right movement. See 'The 'Identity Churches': A Theology of Hate', *ADL Facts* 28, no. 1 (Spring 1983).

[35] Almost 60 per cent of the committed racists (based on my data for 141 cases) had professional or white-collar occupations.

[36] The popular image of the far-right members as ignorant thugs isn't entirely wrong. Hanging around most of these organizations are a handful of 'heavies', often young, poorly educated people who find it easier to fight than to think. Yet to overlook the more numerous well-educated members, which the media and politicians often do, is to obfuscate the far-right phenomenon and therefore entrench it. Even the academic literature more often than not promotes the line that the higher the level of education, the more tolerant the individual. Obviously, the definitive study of the relationship between racism and education has yet to be done.

[37] A Jenson, 'How Much Can we Boost IQ and Scholastic Achievement?', *Harvard Education Review* 39, pp. 1-123.

[38] C. Coon, *The Origins of Race* (New York: Knopf, 1962).

[39] As a result of the public uproar, the Klan's access to schools was abruptly terminated by vigilant school officials.

[40] See Barrett, *Is God a Racist?*, ch. 6.

[41] D. Hughes and E. Kallen, *The Anatomy of Racism* (Montreal: Harvest House, 1974), p. 214.

[42] V. Valentine, 'Native Peoples and Canadian Society: A Profile of Issues and Trends', in R.J. Reitz and V. Valentine, eds, *Cultural Boundaries and the Cohesion of Canada* (Montreal: Institute for Research on Public Policy, 1980), p. 47.

[43] D. Hill. *Human Rights in Canada: A Focus on Racism* (Canadian Labour Congress, 1977), p. 7.

[44] I. Greaves, *The Negro in Canada* (Montreal: McGill University Economic Studies, 1930), p. 9.

[45] B. Jones, 'Nova Scotia Blacks: A Quest for a Place in the Canadian Ethnic Mosaic', in V. D'Oyley, ed., *Black Presence in Multi-Ethnic Canada* (Vancouver: Faculty of Education, University of British Columbia; and Toronto: Ontario Institute for Studies in Education, 1978), p. 82.

[46] R. Winks, 'The Canadian Negro: A Historical Assessment—Part I', *Journal of Negro History* 53, no. 4 (1968), p. 288.

[47] W. Head, *The Black Presence in the Canadian Mosaic* (Ontario Human Rights Commission, 1975), p. 12.

[48] P. Tunteng, 'Racism and the Montreal Computer Incident of 1969', *Race* 14 (1973), p. 231.

[49] Kilian, *Some Great Thing*, p. 164.

[50] I. Abella and H. Troper, *None Is Too Many* (Toronto: Lester and Orpen Dennys, 1982).

[51] E. Kallen, *Ethnicity and Human Rights in Canada* (Toronto: Gage, 1982), p. 140.

[52] B. Bolaria and P. Li, *Racial Oppression in Canada* (Toronto: Garamond, 1985), p. 86.

[53]D. Corbett, *Canada's Immigration Policy* (Toronto: University of Toronto Press, 1957).

[54]J. Frideres, 'Racism in Canada: Alive and Well', *Western Canadian Journal of Anthropology* 6, no. 4 (1976), pp. 124-45.

[55]F. Henry and E. Ginzberg, *Who Gets the Work: A Test of Racial Discrimination in Employment* (Toronto: Urban Alliance on Race Relations and the Social Planning Council of Metropolitan Toronto, 1985).

[56]See Barrett, *Is God a Racist?*, ch. 11.

[57]S. Lipset, 'Fascism as the Extremism of the Centre', in G. Allardyce, ed., *The Place of Fascism in European History* (Englewood Cliffs, N.J.: Prentice-Hall, 1971), p. 113.

[58]J. Horton, 'The Rise of the Right: A Global View', *Crime and Social Justice*, Summer 1981, p. 9.

[59]M. Dixon, 'World Capitalist Crisis and the Rise of the Right', *Contemporary Marxism* no. 4 (1981-82), p. 2.

[60]M. Nikolinakos, 'Notes on an Economic Theory of Racism', *Race* 14 (1973), pp. 365-81.

[61]D. Baker, 'Race and Power: Comparative Approaches to the Analysis of Race Relations', *Ethnic and Racial Studies* 1, no. 3 (1978), p. 316.

[62]R. Benedict, *Race: Science and Politics* (New York: Viking, 1960), p. 148.

[63]Hughes and Kallen, *Anatomy of Racism*, p. 105.

[64]While there is considerable overlap between racism and anti-Semitism, the latter cannot be understood apart from the Christ-killer theme in Christianity.

[65]S.D. Clark, 'The Frontier and Democractic Theory', *Transactions of the Royal Society of Canada* 48, sec. 11, pp. 65-75.

[66]K. McNaught, 'Violence in Canadian History', in J. Moir, ed., *Character and Circumstance* (Toronto: Macmillan, 1970), pp. 66-84.

[67]S. Horrall, 'Canada's Security Service: A Brief History', RCMP *Quarterly* 50, no. 3 (1985), p. 45.

[68]Security Intelligence Review Committee, *Annual Report, 1968-87* (Ottawa: Minister of Supply and Services Canada, 1987), p. 37.

[69]Carter, Emmett Cardinal, 'Report to the Civic Authorities of Metropolitan Toronto and Its Citizens' (mimeo., 1979), p. 16.

[70]C. Roach, 'Minorities and Police Racism', *Prometheus* no. 2 (Winter 1980), p. 27.

[71]*Toronto Star*, 17 July 1981.

[72]C. Alexander, *The Ku Klux Klan in the Southwest* (Lexington: University of Kentucky Press, 1965).

[73]Part of the problem in drawing such a conclusion concerns the concept of fascism itself. Even as employed by academic specialists, the term is not very clear. S. Payne (*Fascism* [Madison: University of Wisconsin Press, 1980]) has gone so far as to assert that fascism is the vaguest of contemporary political terms. As C. Dandeker and B. Troyna ('Fascism: Slogan or Concept', *Patterns of Prejudice* 17, no. 4, pp. 19-30) have remarked, to a large extent fascism has merely become a slogan to hurl at one's enemies. While far-right organizations always are labelled fascist by the left wing (and justifiably so—even the white supremacists accept that label for themselves), sometimes the far right declares that it is the left wing that is fascist. During the course of my study, I ran across terms like 'liberal fascism' used to describe school-bus regulations in the US, and 'sexual fascism' in regard to laws guaranteeing homosexual rights.

[74]From the point of view of right-wing members, there was a major difference between 'the cop on the beat' and those in intelligence work or in the RCMP. Only the former were consistently regarded as 'natural' supporters of the right-wing cause.

[75]Although fascist political parties theoretically are anti-capitalist (fascism has been regarded by its advocates as an alternative to communism among anti-capitalist forces), we know from the case of Nazi Germany that that is only characteristic of their first phase. At a more advanced stage, fascist and capitalist forces tend to join together.

Selected Readings

I DISSENT AND POLITICAL THEORY

Bay, Christian. *Strategies of Political Emancipation*. Notre Dame, Indiana: University of Notre Dame Press, 1981.

_____. 'Civil Disobedience: Prerequisite for Democracy in Mass Society'. In *Political Theory and Social Change*, edited by David Spitz. New York: Atherton, 1967.

Bedau, H.A., ed. *Civil Disobedience: Theory and Practice*. New York: Macmillan, 1969.

Carter, April. *Direct Action and Liberal Democracy*. London: Routledge and Kegan Paul, 1973.

Dogenharat, Henry, and Alan Day, eds. *Political Dissent: An International Guide to Dissident, Extra-Parliamentary, Guerrilla and Illegal Political Movements*. Detroit: Gare Research Co., 1983.

Dworkin, R. 'Taking Rights Seriously'. In *Taking Rights Seriously*. London: Duckworth, 1977.

Dworkin, R. 'Civil Disobedience and Nuclear Protest'. In *Matter of Principle*. Cambridge, Mass.: Harvard University Press, 1985.

Emerson, Thomas. *The System of Freedom of Expression*. New York: Random House, 1970.

Fanon, Franz. *The Wretched of the Earth*. New York: Grove Press, 1965.

King, Martin Luther, Jr. *Stride Toward Freedom: The Montgomery Story*. New York: Harper, 1958.

Kircheimer, Otto. *Political Justice: The Use of Legal Procedures for Political Ends*. Princeton: Princeton University Press, 1961.

Mucchielli, Roger. *La Subversion*. Paris: C.L.C., 1976.

Ramsay, William M. *Four Modern Prophets: Walter Raschenbusch, Martin Luther King Jr., Gustavo Gutierrez, Rosemary Radford Ruether*. Atlanta: John Knox Press, 1986.

Rawls, John. 'A Theory of Civil Disobedience'. In *The Philosophy of Law*. edited by R. Dworkin. Oxford: Oxford University Press, 1977.

Spjut, R.J. 'Defining Subversion'. *British Journal of Law and Society* 6, no. 2 (Winter 1979): 254-61.

Thoreau, Henry David. 'Civil Disobedience'. In *Walden and Civil Disobedience*. New York: W.W. Norton, 1966.

Walzer, Michael. *Obligations: Essays on Disobedience, War and Citizenship*. Cambridge, Mass.: Harvard University Press, 1970.

Woodcock, George. *Civil Disobedience*. Toronto: Canadian Broadcasting Corporation, 1966.

II DISSENT IN CANADA

Berger, Thomas. *Fragile Freedoms: Human Rights and Dissent in Canada*. Toronto: Clarke, Irwin, 1981.

Canada. Commission of Inquiry Concerning Certain Activities of the Royal Canadian Mounted Police (the McDonald Commission). *Freedom and Security Under the Law, Second Report*. Ottawa: Minister of Supply and Services, 1981.

Canada. Ministère de la Justice. *Rapport de la commission d'enquête sur des operations policières en territoire Québécois*, 1981.

Clift, Dominique. *Le Déclin du nationalisme au Québec*. Montréal: Éditions Libre Expression, 1981.

_____. *Quebec Nationalism in Crisis*. Kingston, Ont.: McGill-Queen's University Press, 1982.

Coleman, William D. *The Independence Movement in Quebec, 1945-1980*. Toronto: University of Toronto Press, 1984.

Fournier, Louis. FLQ: *Histoire d'un mouvement clandestin*. Montréal: Quebec/Amérique, 1982. Published in English as *F.L.Q.: The Anatomy of an Underground Movement*, trans. by Edward Baxter. Toronto: NC Press, 1984.

Franks, C.E.S. *Parliament and Security Matters*. Study prepared for the Commission of Inquiry Concerning Certain Activities of the Royal Canadian Mounted Police. Ottawa: Minister of Supply and Services, 1980.

_____. 'The Political Control of Security Activities'. *Queen's Quarterly* 91, no. 3 (Autumn 1984): 565-77.

Friedland, M.L. *National Security: The Legal Dimensions*. Study prepared for the Commission of Inquiry Concerning Certain Activities of the Royal Canadian Mounted Police. Ottawa: Minister of Supply and Services, 1980.

Haggart, Ron, and Aubrey E. Golden, *Rumours of War*. Toronto: New Press, 1971.

Kelly, William, and Nora Kelly. *Policing in Canada*. Toronto: Macmillan, 1976.

Littleton, James. *Target Nation: Canada and the Western Intelligence Network*. Toronto: Lester and Orpen Dennys, 1986.

Mann, Edward, and John Alan Lee. *RCMP vs the People: Inside Canada's Security Service*. Don Mills, Ont.: General Publishing, 1979.

McNaught, K. 'Political Trials and the Canadian Political Tradition'. In *Courts and Trials: A Multidisciplinary Approach*. edited by M.L. Friedland. Toronto: University of Toronto Press, 1975.

_____, and D. Bercuson. *The Winnipeg Strike: 1919*. Don Mills, Ont.: Longman, 1974.

Pelletier, Gérard. *Le Crise d'octobre*. Montréal: Éditions du Jour, 1971.

Québec. Ministère de la Justice. *Rapport sur la crise d'octobre 1970*, 1981.

Sawatsky, John. *Gouzenko: The Untold Story*. Toronto: Macmillan, 1984.

_____. *Men In the Shadows: The RCMP Security Service*. Toronto: Doubleday, 1980.

Security Intelligence Review Committee. *Annual Report, 1984-85*. Ottawa, Minister of Supply and Services, 1985.

_____. *Annual Report, 1985-86*. Ottawa: Minister of Supply and Services, 1986.

_____. *Annual Report, 1986-87*. Ottawa: Minister of Supply and Services, 1987.

_____. *Annual Report, 1987-88*. Ottawa: Minister of Supply and Services, 1988.

Smith, Denis. *Bleeding Hearts . . . Bleeding Country, Canada and the Quebec Crisis*. Edmonton: Hurtig, 1971.

Vallières, Pierre. *Nègres blancs d'Amérique; Autobiographie précoce d'un 'terroriste' québécois*. Montréal: Éditions Parti Pris, 1969. Published in English as *White Niggers of America: The Precocious Autobiography of a Quebec 'Terrorist'*, trans. by Joan Pinkham. New York: Monthly Review Press, 1971.

III DISSENT IN AMERICA

Bell, Daniel, ed. *The Radical Right*. Garden City, N.Y.: Doubleday, 1963.

Blackstock, Nelson. *COINTELPRO: The FBI's Secret War on Political Freedom*. New York: Vintage Books, 1976.

Donner, Frank J. *The Age of Surveillance: The Aims and Methods of America's Political Intelligence System*. New York: Alfred A. Knopf, 1980.

Ellif, John T. *The Reform of FBI Intelligence Operations*. Princeton: Princeton University Press, 1979.

Goldstein, Robert Justin. *Political Repression in Modern America: 1870 to the Present*. Cambridge, Mass.: Schenkman, 1978.

Grodzins, Morton. *The Loyal and the Disloyal: Social Boundaries of Patriotism and Treason*. Chicago: University of Chicago Press, 1956.

Kalven, H. *A Worthy Tradition: Freedom of Speech in America*, edited by J. Kalven. New York: Harper and Row, 1988.

Morgan, Richard. *Domestic Intelligence: Monitoring Dissent in America*. Austin: University of Texas Press, 1980.

Navasky, Victor. *Naming Names*. New York: Viking Press, 1980.

O'Reilly, Kenneth. *Hoover and the Un-Americans: The FBI, HUAC, and the Red Manace*. Philadelphia: Temple University Press, 1983.

Theoharis, Athan. *Beyond the Hiss Case: the FBI, Congress and the Cold War*. Philadelphia: Temple University Press, 1982.

_____. *Spying on Americans: Political Surveillance from Hoover to the Huston Plan*. Philadelphia: Temple University Press, 1978.

United States Senate Select Committee to Study Governmental Operations with Respect to Intelligence Operations. *Final Report*. 94th Congress, 2nd session, 1975.

IV DISSENT IN THE EAST BLOC

Connor, Walter D. 'Dissent in a Complex Society: The Soviet Case'. *Problems of Communism* 22, no. 2 (March-April 1973): 40-52.

Curry, Jane Leftwich. *Dissent in Eastern Europe*. New York: Praeger, 1983.

Haraszti, Miklos. *The Velvet Prison: Artists Under State Socialism*. New York: Basic Books, 1987.

Judt, Tony, et al. *Debating the Nature of Dissent in Eastern Europe*. Washington, D.C.: Wilson Center, 1987.

Parchomenko, Walter. *Soviet Images of Dissidents and Nonconformists*. New York: Praeger, 1986.

Reddaway, Peter. 'Policy towards Dissent since Khrushchev' In *Authority, Power and Policy in the USSR*. 2nd edn, edited by T.H. Rigby, Archie Brown, and Peter Reddaway. London: Macmillan, 1983.

Singer, Daniel. *The Road to Gdansk: Poland and the USSR*. New York: Monthly Review Press, 1981.

Tökés, R.J., ed. *Opposition in Eastern Europe*. Baltimore: Johns Hopkins University Press, 1979.

_____. *Dissent in the USSR: Politics, Ideology and People*. Baltimore: Johns Hopkins University Press, 1975.

V   DISSENT IN WESTERN EUROPE

Amyot, Grant. *The Italian Communist Party: the Crisis of the Popular Front Strategy*. London: Croom Helm, 1981.

Andrew, Christopher. *Secret Service: The Making of the British Intelligence Community*. London: Heinemann, 1985.

Berki, R.N. *Security and Society: Reflections on Law, Order and Politics*. London: J.M. Dent, 1986.

Bunyan, Tony. *The Political Police in Britain*. New York: St Martin's Press, 1976.

Coogan, Tim Pat. *The I.R.A.* Glasgow: Fontana/Collins, 1987.

Institute for the Study of Conflict. *Political Violence and Civil Disobedience in Western Europe, 1982. Conflict Studies*, no. 145.

Janke, Peter. *Spanish Separtism: Eta's Threat to Basque Democracy. Conflict Studies*, no. 123 (Oct. 1980).

LaPalombara, Joseph. *Democracy, Italian Style*. New Haven: Yale University Press, 1977.

Thompson, E.P. *Writing by Candlelight*. London: Merlin Press, 1980.

Wright, Peter. *Spycatcher*. Toronto: Stoddart, 1987.

VI   DISSENT IN LATIN AMERICA

Eckstein, Susan, ed. *Power and Popular Protest: Latin American Social Movements*. Berkeley: University of California Press, 1988.

Gott, Richard. *Guerilla Movements in Latin America*. London: Nelson, 1970.

Horowitz, Irving Louis, *et al.*, eds. *Latin American Radicalism: A Doc-*

umentary Report on Left and Nationalist Movements. New York: Random House, 1969.

O'Donnell, Guillermo, and Philippe C. Schmitter. *Transitions from Authoritarian Rule: Tentative Conclusions about Uncertain Democracies*. Baltimore: Johns Hopkins University Press, 1986.

Stepan, Alfred. *Rethinking Military Politics*. Princeton: Princeton University Press, 1987.

VII   DISSENT IN AFRICA

Frankel, Philip H. 'South Africa: The Politics of Police Control'. *Comparative Politics* 12, no. 4: 481-99.

Gibson, Richard. *African Liberation Movements: Contemporary Struggles against White Minority Rule*. London: Oxford University Press for the Institute of Race Relations, 1972.

Hachten, William A., and C. Anthony Gifford. *The Press and Apartheid: Repression and Propoganda in South Africa*. Madison, Wis.: University of Wisconsin Press, 1984.

Mathews, Anthony S. *Law, Order and Liberty in South Africa*. Capetown: Juta and Co. Ltd., 1971.

Omond, Roger. *The Apartheid Handbook: A Guide to South Africa's Everyday Racial Politics*. 2nd edn. Harmondsworth: Penguin, 1986.

Paton, Alan. *The Long View*. New York: Praeger, 1968.

Index

Albania: economic dissent, 131, ethnic dissent, 134; religion, 135, 136
Aliens Registration (Smith) Act (US, 1940): 67
Alfonsín, Raúl: 151, 154-5
Allmand, Warren: 83
Amnesty International: 44
Anti-communism: 62, 65; in Canada, 13-14, 192, 194; in US, 67, 68; *see also* Cold War ideology; Subversion
Anti-Semitism, *see* Right-wing organizations
Aquino, Corazon: 57
Argentina: 139, 140, 149; amnesty law, 154; 'disappearances', 151, 153, 154; and National Security Doctrine, 155; opposition and dissent, 152-3; prosecutions for human-rights violations, 151, 154, 165; repressive framework, 151-2; Sábato Commission, 153, 154; security forces, 152; social tensions, 151
Armenia: 112
Arvad, Inga: 90-2
Australia: 201; Australian Security and Intelligence Organization, 72, 73

Ball, Desmond: 72-3
Baltic republics: 118
Bergeron, Gérard: 212
Berlinger, Enrico: 176-8, 180, 182
Bill C9: 80-1, 83; 'safeguards', 81
Bill C157: 73, 80
Bolivia: 139
Borduas, Paul-Emile, see Québec: *Refus global*
Bulgaria: ethnic tensions, 134

Camus, Albert: 57, 223
Capitalism: 13; and far right, 243, 246
Central America: US policy in, 13, 42
Charter of Rights and Freedoms: 30, 31, 38, 44, 59, 208
Chile: 140, 149; clandestine right-wing groups, 159; coup (1973), 155, 177; death squads, 157; elections (1989), 156, 160; and National Security Doctrine, 145; opposition and dissent, 158-9; plebiscite (1988), 156; repressive framework, 156-8; repressive strategies, 159-160; as terrorist state, 165-6
CIA: 29, 66, 68; and Italian right wing, 187
Cité libre: 218
Citizenship: 44-5; 'Hobbesian', 43, 55; in Latin America, 140; 'Lockean', 43, 55; 'Rousseauian', 44, 55, 56; 'rational-humanist', 40, 41, 44, 55, 56-9
Cold War ideology: 8, 9, 11, 15, 19, 62, 65, 76-8; in Canada, 191, 194, 195, 206, 207-8, 209, 210; and National Security Doctrine, 144-6
Coldwell, M.J.: 205-6
Coleridge, Lord Justice: 33
Communism: in Eastern Europe, 111-37 *passim*; 'Eurocommunism', 172, 180, 188;

'Popular Front' strategy, 171-3, 176, 189; and far right, 8, 244; theory, 170-1, 176; as threat, 10-11; Togliatti on, 179-80; *see also* Anti-communism; PCI
Communist Party: Australia, 188; Canada, 8, 65, 192-4; France, 188; Great Britain, 188; Greece, 174, 188; Italy, *see* PCI; Japan, 188; Philippines, 57; Spain, 179, 188; Sweden, 188; USSR, 111-12; US, 7, 105
Constitutionalism: 26-7
Counter-subversion: liberal democracy and, 84; *see also* CSIS; Subversion
Criminal Code, 31, 32, 64, 65
CSIS: accountability, 2, 81; counter-subversion, 2, 4, 11, 29, 72, 78-9, 85; creation of, 2, 71; and far right, 225; mandate, 2, 21-2, 81, 147; structure, 2; US influence on, 3, 29, 75, 77; *see also* CSIS Act; SIRC
CSIS Act: 2, 21-3, 26, 37; and Criminal Code, 31; definition of 'threats to security', 2, 21-2, 73-5; and political dissent, 23; reform, 84-5
Czechoslovakia: Charter 77 group, 119-21; leadership change (1987), 111; legitimacy of regime, 114-15; religion, 136; Soviet invasion (1968), 111, 180; and youth, 123

Democracy: and Cold War ideology, 77; and capitalism, 13; and dissent, 6-7, 12, 15, 23-6, 62; and law, 12; and human rights, 18-19, 40-61; in Latin America, 167-8; and national security, 25; and PCI, 169-90; and political obligation, 48-9, 55-8; and 'subversion', 83-4; and values, 23-5, 26-7, 38
Disobedience, civil: 10, 40-61; in Canada, 57-8; definitions, 42, 52-3; 'inner limits', 43, 51-5; 'outer limits', 56-9; as a right, 42; 'uncivil', 41-2, 43
Dissent: acceptable and unacceptable, 6-13, 19; and Canadian law, 21-39; definitions, 139; and democracy, 15; and freedom, 25; legality/legitimacy, 6-13; limits to, 224; and repression (Latin America), 140; state responses to, 13-19; *see also* Protest
Dominion Police Force: 69, 70
Donner, Frank: 72
Drew, George: 200, 201
Duplessis, Maurice: 200, 215, 216, 227
Dworkin, Ronald: 44-5, 46, 53-4

Eastern Europe: anti-Russianism/Sovietism, 134-5; cultural diversity, 114; definitions, 113-14; economic dissent, 126-31; ethnic tensions, 132; intelligentsia, 123; legitimacy of regimes, 114-15; Leninism in, 118; nationalist dissent, 131-5; 'party mentality', 116; political dissent, 118-26; political reform, 124-6; religious dissent, 135-6; 'repressive tolerance' strategy, 123-4; 'rights activism', 115, 116; *see also* individual countries
Endicott, Dr James, 200, 206